BLACKSTONE
GRIDDLE COOKBOOK

Table of Contents

Breakfast Hash

This Blackstone Breakfast Hash Recipe is incredibly simple to prepare! This is one of those large breakfast meals that may also be served as a dinner dish!

cooking time: 40 minutes

Servings: 10

Ingredients

- 2 O'Brien Frozen Potato Bags
- 1 Sausage Rope
- 8 Slices Thick Cut Bacon
- 12 Eggs
- 1/2 Red Onion
- Green Onion

Instruction

1. Start your Blackstone and lubricate it. If you're new to Blackstone Griddles,
2. Turn the heat all the way down once your griddle is preheated and oiled. Make sure you have two spatulas and a scraper on hand to prepare this dinner.
3. Spread the frozen potatoes out onto your griddle first, so they can begin to thaw and brown.
4. In a large mixing basin, whisk together the scrambled eggs. To make the eggs fluffier, I add roughly 1/2 cup of water to them.
5. Cut up your sausage, onion, and bacon while the potatoes are cooking.
6. Push the potatoes to the other side of the griddle, and at this point, add your onions to the potatoes on the griddle
7. Place the bacon on the griddle's other side and increase the heat on that burner so it cooks faster. Place the sausage in the center of the pan on low heat; it will cook quickly enough at this temperature.
8. Allow these to cook until the bacon has reached the desired crispiness.
9. Pour the egg mixture on the other side of the griddle after moving the meat into the potato mixture.
10. The eggs will scramble quickly, move them about with one of the spatulas to ensure that they do.
11. Start mixing your eggs into your potatoes and meat combination when they're almost done.
12. When they're thoroughly combined, sprinkle with cheese and turn the griddle off.
13. While the cheese was melting, I dashed in and made toast.
14. Serve and have fun!!

French Toast On Blackstone Griddle

French Toast on a Blackstone Griddle is a great way to have a big breakfast at home or while camping! Plus, there are all the extras like bacon and eggs!

cooking time: 15 minutes

Servings: 10

Ingredients

- Texas Toast Bread
- Eggs
- Cinnamon
- Milk

Instructions

1. Start by heating your griddle to a low-medium setting and preparing your French Toast Egg mixture.
2. Crack your eggs in a large mixing basin, add a splash of milk, and a dash of vanilla extract.
3. Whisk the egg mixture until it is well combined.
4. Add the cinnamon and stir once more.
5. After your Blackstone has warmed up, sprinkle a little amount of vegetable oil over with a paper towel. I do this to ensure that the french toast does not stick to the surface.
6. Make sure both sides of your bread are coated in the egg mixture!
7. Place the bread on the griddle and continue to do so until the griddle is completely packed; I was able to fit an entire loaf of Texas Toast bread on my 36-inch griddle.
8. Check to see whether the egg mixture is done after a few minutes and flip to the other side when ready. Flipping French toast will be much simpler with a long spatula from the Blackstone Accessory package!
9. Remove the French Toast from the oven after the second side is done and serve!!
10. Use the Blackstone Scrapper to remove any food debris and reoil a bit more if you're preparing additional French Toast (we baked a second loaf of bread to have leftovers).
11. Rep until you've used up all of your bread.
12. Turn off the griddle, clean it, and reoil it so that it can be covered and stored after it has cooled.

Perfect Camping Griddle Breakfast Skillet

French Toast on a Blackstone Griddle is a great way to have a big breakfast at home or while camping! Plus, there are all the extras like bacon and eggs!

cooking time: 35 minutes

Servings: 5

Ingredients

- Eggs
- 4 lbs Gold Potatoes
- 1 lb Bacon
- 5 Polish sausages
- Cheese
- Minced Garlic
- Salt
- Pepper

Instructions

1. Your potatoes should be washed and dried.
2. All of the vegetables should be sliced and diced, and the sausages should be polished.
3. When you heat up your griddle, brush it with a little oil or bacon fat to aid in nonsticking and sauteing the food.
4. Combine the potatoes, onion, and polish sausage on your griddle.
5. Add salt and pepper to taste.
6. Cook until potatoes are fork tender.
7. Remove the potatoes from the oven and place them in a dish or another plate to keep warm.
8. Fry your bacon till it's done to your liking and then fry your eggs at the same time (or scrambled eggs)
9. Serve everything together and enjoy!! We topped ours with shredded cheese and you could mix in sour cream as well!

Italian Breakfast Lavash

cooking time: 15 minutes

Servings: 4

Ingredients

- 2 Lavash Flat Breads
- ½ lb Prosciutto, deli sliced
- ½ lb Capicola, deli sliced
- ½ lb Genoa Salami, deli sliced thin
- ½ lb Mortadella, deli sliced
- ½ lb Mozzarella, deli sliced
- ½ lb Provolone cheese, deli sliced thin
- 4 Eggs
- Balsamic Glaze
- Cento, hot pepper spread
- 2 c Arugula
- 1 tbsp Extra Virgin Olive Oil
- Salt & Pepper, to taste
- Spray extra light tasting olive oil

Instructions

1. Preheat the griddle to a low temperature.
2. Toss the arugula with the extra virgin olive oil and season with salt and pepper.
3. Spray one side of the lavash bread lightly with oil and lay it on the griddle.
4. On the griddle, cook 2 eggs per lavash to desired doneness while adding provolone cheese, Italian meats, and provolone cheese on top. Place the cheese against the lavash to act as a glue to keep the sandwich together.Spread some spicy pepper spread on top.
5. Remove the cooked eggs from the griddle and place them evenly on one side of the lavash.
6. To each sandwich, add about a cup of arugula. Drizzle balsamic glaze over the top. To make a sandwich, fold the lavash in half. Enjoy by cutting it in half or thirds.

Chorizo Breakfast Burrito

This is the best Chorizo Breakfast Burrito. This breakfast burrito will impress your family and friends with soft scrambled eggs, delectable chorizo, jack cheese, pico de gallo, Mexican crema, and crispy hash browns.

cooking time: 35 minutes

Servings: 6

Ingredients

- 6 flour tortillas (burrito sized)
- 1 pound Mexican chorizo
- 6 ounces Monterey Jack cheese (shredded)
- 4 Tablespoons Mexican crema
- 4 Tablespoons butter

CRISPY HASH BROWNS

- 3 medium russet potatoes
- 4 Tablespoons beef tallow
- Sait (to taste)
- Pepper (to taste)

SOFT SCRAMBLED EGGS

- 6 large eggs
- 1/2 cup heavy whipping cream
- 1/2 teaspoon salt

PICO DE GALLO

- 1 pint cherry tomatoes (cut in half)
- 1/4 cup cilantro
- 2 Tablespoons red onion (finely minced)
- 1/2 jalapeno (seeded and finely minced)
- juice of 1 lime
- salt (to taste)
- pepper (to taste)

Instructions

1. Preheat the griddle (or stovetop) to medium-high.
2. Your three potatoes should be washed and grated before being placed on double-layered paper towels. With the paper towels, press out as much moisture as possible.
3. Crack 6 eggs into a large mixing basin or pourable measuring cup to start. Lightly whisk in the heavy whipping cream and 1/2 teaspoon of salt with a fork.
4. Get your pico de gallo ready. In a mixing dish, add all of the ingredients and whisk to incorporate.
5. Make your way to the griddle. Allow half of the beef tallow to melt on the griddle. Season the shredded potatoes with salt and pepper on top of the melted beef tallow. Arrange them in a neat, equal layer.then wait until they're golden brown before flipping them.
6. Toss the hash browns over the top with the remaining beef tallow, allowing it to melt into the potatoes. This will aid in crisping the opposite side.

7. Cook the chorizo on the stovetop. With the end of your spatula, break it apart. Add your eggs to your griddle when your chorizo is almost done and your potatoes have been turned.

8. 2 Tablespoons butter, melted on the coldest section of the griddle top (turn off a burner if need be). Cook, stirring regularly with a spatula, your egg mixture on top of the melted butter. Cook for a total of 2-3 minutes.

9. To begin assembling your burritos, place your eggs, chorizo, and hash browns on a platter.

10. Assemble the ingredients for your burritos. Add a tablespoon of eggs, a dollop of chorizo, crispy hash browns, and grated cheese to each tortilla shell. Tightly roll them up.

11. 2 tblsp. butter, melted on the griddle Place the wrapped burritos on the griddle seam side down and cook for 1-2 minutes, or until crispy on the outside.

12. Serve with pico de gallo and Mexican crema on the side

Blackstone Sausage-Stuffed Hash Browns

On a gas griddle, Blackstone Packed Hash Browns are stuffed with sausage and cheese, then topped with bacon, cheese, and a fried egg.

cooking time: 50 minutes

Servings: 6

Ingredients

- 3 cups dehydrated hash browns
- 3 cups hot water
- 1/4 cup finely diced onions
- 1/4 cup butter
- 10 pieces thick-sliced bacon
- 1/2 pound breakfast sausage
- 1/4 - 1/3 cup oil
- Salt, pepper, and garlic
- 2 cups shredded cheddar cheese

Instructions

1. Cook the onions for 3-4 minutes with roughly a tablespoon of butter.
2. Place the hash browns on the griddle and drizzle a tablespoon or two of oil over them.
3. Cook for several minutes, or until a golden-brown crust forms on the bottom. With a big spatula,
4. Flip the pancakes and sprinkle with extra oil. Half of the hash browns should be covered in cheese and sausage. Flip the half that isn't covered with sausage and cheese over the top when the bottom side has browned, sandwiching in the sausage and egg.
5. Turn the griddle down to low heat and top with bacon pieces and more cheese. Cook, stirring occasionally, until the cheese has melted.

The Griddle Omelet

This omelet comes together quickly and is extremely thin and packed with contents. It's just like what you'd find in a diner!

cooking time: 15 minutes

Servings: 1

Ingredients

- 2 or 3 large eggs, beaten very well with a pinch of salt
- 1 Tablespoon butter
- 1/2 cup assorted vegetables
- 1-2 ounces cheese
- Salt and pepper
- Parsley for garnish (optional)

Instruction

1. Fillings should be sautéed for about a minute to soften them somewhat. You can do this in a separate skillet or on the griddle.
2. Preheat the griddle. A drop of water should splatter all over it.
3. Add the butter to the griddle and quickly stir it around with the spatula to coat everything.
4. Add the eggs once the butter has stopped sizzling. Scoop all of the eggs into a rough rectangle using a spatula.
5. Place the cheese on top, along with any other fillings you have.
6. Fold the paper in half. Fold the top half over the fillings, followed by the bottom half.
7. You now have two choices: Remove the omelet from the heat. It's finished! Some people prefer their omelets with a little runny egg around the edges. OR, using the spatula, delicately flip (or roll) the omelet over so the seam of the fold is down on the griddle.
8. If you continue to cook it like this for another 30 seconds or so, the egg will be fully cooked. By this time, the cheese should be completely melted.

Crunchwrap

Learn the best method on how to prepare breakfast crunchwrap at home and how to fold a crunchwrap for a perfectly golden-brown seal.

cooking time: 20 minutes

Servings: 4

Ingredients

- Large flour tortillas Crispy
- corn tortillas
- 5 Scrambled eggs
- 3 Hashbrowns
- 6 Slices of American cheese
- ½ Cup of sharp cheddar cheese
- Hot Italian sausage links, decased
- Everything Bagel Seasoning

Instruction

1. Cook the decased sausage links to a ground beef consistency on your Blackstone Griddle over medium-high heat.
2. Cook the hashbrowns in a lot of butter, turning them on both sides.
3. Make the eggs scrambled to your satisfaction.
4. Warm the flour tortillas on the griddle for a few seconds and then set them aside.
5. Top eggs with Everything Bagel Seasoning and cheese on a tortilla. Place a crispy corn tortilla on top of the cheese, then add another layer of cheese and sausage on top of that. Fold the flour tortilla gently around the stack of toppings after adding the hashbrowns.
6. Start with the bottom of the flour tortilla and fold the edge up over the center to make the crunch wrap. Fold the flour tortilla over the center fillings as you work your way around.
7. 14 cup cheddar cheese on the griddle Then, with the folded side down, lay the crunch wrap on top of the cheese to create a crunchy cheddar seal. Turn the crunch wrap toast over to the other side. To serve, remove the pancakes from the griddle and cut them in half.

Goober

Goober can be made in no time for your family with only a few ingredients. For breakfast, they're delicious with maple syrup, and for dessert, they're delicious with chocolate syrup.

cooking time: 10 minutes

Servings: 4

Ingredients

- 1 loaf of Texas Toast
- Grape Jelly
- Creamy Peanut Butter
- 1 tsp Vanilla
- 1 cup Brown Sugar
- ¾ cup Half and Half
- 1 Tbsp Butter

Instructions

1. Make a typical PB&J sandwich with the desired jelly-to-peanut-butter ratio.
2. Combine two eggs, 1 teaspoon vanilla, 1 cup brown sugar, and 34 cups Half & Half in a medium mixing basin.
3. 1 tbsp butter, melted on the griddle (set to medium-high heat).
4. Cook for 3-5 minutes on the griddle after dipping and coating the PB&J in the mixture. Cook for another 3-5 minutes on the other side.
5. Place on a plate and enjoy!

Southwest Chile and Cheddar Omelette CJ's

cooking time: 10 minutes

Servings: 4

Ingredients

- 4 eggs
- Breakfast Sausage
- Shredded cheese
- Yellow onion
- Bell pepper
- Jalapeño
- Avocado
- Cilantro
- Black beans (rinsed)
- Canned Hatch chopped Green Chile
- Cholula hot sauce
- Crispy tortilla strips (dressing isle)
- Salt
- Pepper
- BS Hatch Chile and cheddar seasoning
- BS Taco Fajita Seasoning
- Blackstone Large Omelette Egg Ring

Instructions

1. Pre-heat one side of your griddle top to medium and the other to high. Place a small sauce pan with about one cup of olive oil on the side set to high to heat up. When

your medium side is hot, add the sausage patties to the griddle and cook for 15 seconds before flipping and smashing. This allows one side to gently sear, making it easier to crush with your spatula without it sticking to your spatula. You could use parchment paper instead, but this is a simple fix.

2. Slice 2-3 corn tortilla strips into thin strips while your sausage is cooking; this will be a crunchy garnish at the end. You can add your tortilla strips to cook in the oil once it has reached 350 degrees.

3. Now that you've got a few minutes on your hands, dice your green bell pepper, red bell pepper, and yellow onion. You can also slice your jalapeo into pinwheels or chop it up (round slices). Finally, cut an avocado in half, remove the core, scoop out one side, and slice thinly for garnish.

4. When the vegetables are done, crack four eggs into a mixing dish, season with salt and pepper, and whisk them together. Your sausage should be cooked through at this point. Place your big Blackstone omelette ring on the griddle and pour 2 eggs, half of your egg mixture, onto the ring. Slide the sausage to a cool zone or remove from the griddle. There should be enough to go around the entire ring. Don't add too much egg mixture; trust me, if you add all four eggs, it'll be a train wreck to fold properly. Because this is a rapid process, grab a tiny handful of the chopped ingredients and stir them into the egg mixture. Add a spoonful or two of rinsed black beans, then cut the sausage patties in half (they should look like half moons) and place three halves on one side of the egg ring. Finally, toss in a handful of grated cheese. I like to season the items lightly with the Blackstone Hatch Chile and Cheddar spice and heat until the bottoms of the eggs are cooked. You can now remove the egg ring, grab a spatula, and confidently fold one half of the omelette over the other (creating another half moon). Also, make sure to turn the side without the sausage.) Allow for another minute of cooking before flipping and cooking for another minute. While that is cooking, you can prepare another omelette by repeating the process.

5. Your tortilla strips should be done by now. Remove the strips to a paper towel to drain and rapidly season with Blackstone Taco Fajita Seasoning. 6. To plate and serve, place one omelette on a plate, top with a healthy spoonful of chopped hatch green Chile, 2-3 slices of avocado, a few strips of crispy tortilla strips, tear some fresh cilantro and sprinkle on top, lightly dust with Chile and cheddar seasoning, and drizzle with desired amount of Cholula hot sauce.

Johnny Cakes with Bourbon Salted Caramel Sauce

cooking time: 25 minutes

Servings: 4

Ingredients

- 1 cup All-purpose Glour
- 1 cup coarse Cornmeal
- 1 tablespoon Baking Powder
- 2 tablespoons Sugar
- 3 large Eggs
- ¼ cup liquid Bacon fat
- 1 cup Buttermilk

Bourbon Salted Caramel Sauce:

- ½ cup Bourbon
- ¼ cup Water
- 1 cup granulated Sugar
- 3 tablespoon Unsalted Butter
- 1 cup Heavy Cream
- 1 teaspoon Vanilla Extract
- 2 teaspoons kosher Salt

Instructions

1. Combine the bourbon, water, and sugar in a large sauté pan. Bring to a low simmer over medium-high heat, stirring occasionally, until the bubbles become huge and the color turns a faint amber. Add the butter and continue to mix until it is completely melted and integrated. Combine the heavy cream, vanilla extract, and salt in a mixing bowl. Stir to combine, then remove from heat to cool.
2. Combine the flour, cornmeal, and baking powder in a large mixing bowl.
3. Add the eggs and bacon fat to a separate mixing dish and whisk well.
4. In the flour and cornmeal basin, crack the eggs and add the bacon fat. 12 cup buttermilk, mixed evenly with a spatula To achieve the desired consistency, add more buttermilk.

Apple Stuffed French Toast with Bourbon Caramel Sauce

cooking time: 25 minutes

Servings: 4

Ingredients

- 8 thick slices of French Bread
- 3 cups Bourbon
- 2/3 cup White Sugar
- 2 large Green Apples, small dice

- ½ Green Apple Brunoise (finely diced)
- 8 oz. softened Cream Cheese
- 2 tablespoon Cinnamon Sugar
- ¼ cup Whole Milk

EGG MIX:

- 4 Eggs
- 1 tablespoon Cinnamon Sugar
- ¼ cup Milk

Instructions

1. Add the apples, bourbon, and sugar to a large sauté pan over medium-high heat. Bring to a boil, then reduce until the consistency is similar to maple syrup. Remove from the fire.
2. Combine the cream cheese, cinnamon sugar, finely diced apples, and milk in a large mixing bowl. Mix well to ensure that everything is uniformly distributed.
3. Add the egg mixture components to a casserole dish and stir to combine evenly.
4. Make a sandwich with a second piece of bread and some of the cream cheese mixture on one side. Rep with the rest of the bread.
5. Coat both sides of the sandwiches in the egg mixture. Cook the French toast sandwiches on a griddle with a little oil or non-stick spray over medium heat. Cook each side for 3-4 minutes.
6. When the french toast is done, cut it in half and place it on a serving plate. Drizzle some of the cooked

apples on top of the caramel sauce. Serve garnished with fresh mint or powdered sugar.

Breakfast Sausage & Egg Baskets

cooking time: 15 minutes

Servings: 4

Ingredients

- 6 Eggs
- 1 ½ cups All-Purpose Flour
- 2 tablespoons White Sugar
- 1 teaspoon Ground Cinnamon
- 1 teaspoon Ground Chipotle
- 1/3 cup Whole Milk
- 4 Breakfast Sausage Patties
- ½ cup shredded Cheddar Cheese
- Maple Syrup
- Powdered Sugar

Instructions

1. Cook the sausage patties until they are thoroughly cooked over medium heat. Remove the item and set it aside for later.
2. Combine the flour, sugar, 1 egg, cinnamon, chipotle, and milk in a large mixing basin. To ensure that all of the ingredients are evenly

distributed, whisk them together. If your batter is too thick, add a little more milk.

3. Fill a squeeze bottle with the mixture and a narrow nozzle. Make a criss-cross design with the batter on the griddle. Cook for 2-3 minutes before flipping. Repeat.

4. Break the yolk of 1 egg into the center of the pancake basket and spread it out to the edges. 1 sausage patty, a sprinkling of salt and pepper, and a smidgeon of cheese Fold the side of the basket into the middle with two spatulas to make a square. Cook for an extra minute and flip

5. Cut away any overhanging pancake batter from the sides to level out the shape for presentation. Serve with maple syrup and powdered sugar on the side.

6. Enjoy!

Griddle Girl Breakfast Pancake Tacos

cooking time: 15 minutes

Servings: 4

Ingredients

- 1 cup pancake mix
- 2/3 cup water
- ½ cup strawberries
- ½ cup blackberries
- ½ cup blueberries
- A few sprigs fresh mint
- 8 oz softened cream cheese
- 2 tbsp heavy whipping cream
- ½ cup powdered sugar
- 1 tbsp butter
- maple syrup

Instructions

1. Pour the pancake mix and water into a mixing basin, swirl to incorporate, and set aside.

2. Mint is roughly chopped and berries are cut into bite-size bits.

3. Cream together cream cheese, heavy cream, and powdered sugar in a mixing bowl. Combine all ingredients in a mixing bowl and set aside.

4. Preheat the griddle to medium heat. Cook pancakes with 1 tbsp butter.

5. Take the pancakes out of the pan and place them in a taco tray.

6. Fill each pancake taco with 1-2 tablespoons cream cheese, fruit, and syrup drizzle.

7. Enjoy!

Ricotta Lemon Griddle Cakes

cooking time: 20 minutes

Servings: 4

Ingredients

DRY INGREDIENTS:

- 1 cup all purpose flour
- 1 tbsp baking powder
- 1 tbsp baking soda
- 2 tbsp sugar
- ¼ tsp salt

WET INGREDIENTS:

- 1 ¼ cup whole milk ricotta
- 2 eggs
- ⅔ cup milk
- Juice from one large lemon
- 1 ½ tsp pure vanilla extract
- Butter for cooking
- Zest from one large lemon

Instructions

1. Combine the wet ingredients in one mixing bowl and the dry ingredients in the other. Combine the wet ingredients in a mixing bowl.
2. To blend the dry and wet ingredients, add them slowly to the wet mixing bowl. Allow to sit for 10 minutes or until the Blackstone reaches medium heat.

3. Using a 14 cup measuring cup per pancake, swirl butter to melt where the pancakes will be cooked.
4. Cook for 2 minutes per side, flipping once, or until bubbles emerge.

Croque Madame

cooking time: 25 minutes

Servings: 6

Ingredients

- 1 loaf crusty sour dough bread
- 1 wedge gruyere cheese, grated
- 1 lb ham, tavern, black forest, or your favorite
- 1/4 lb baby swiss cheese
- 1/4 lb muenster cheese
- Dijon mustard
- butter
- 6 eggs

BÉCHAMEL SAUCE:

- 2 tbsp butter
- 2 tbsp flour
- 1 cup milk
- 1 tsp nutmeg
- black pepper

Instructions

1. Layer muenster cheese, ham, gruyere cheese, ham, and baby swiss cheese on the inside of each

piece of bread and begin building sandwiches by spreading Dijon mustard on the inside of each slice of bread and layering muenster cheese, ham, gruyere cheese, ham, and baby swiss cheese. The cheese should be on the outside of the bread as well as in the center, as it is the glue that holds our sandwich together. Remove from the equation.

2. Using low heat, heat a small pot directly on the Blackstone surface or on the Blackstone side burner. Allow the butter to gradually melt before whisking in the flour. Continue whisking until golden brown and aromatic, then add the milk a quarter cup at a time, whisking constantly. As the sauce simmer, it will thicken. Nutmeg and black pepper to taste.

3. Spread butter on the Blackstone surface on moderate to medium low heat and add sandwiches to toast till golden brown on both sides. It's crucial to cook the cheeses slowly and steadily so that they heat up and melt completely.

4. Just before the sandwiches are done, make sunny side up eggs.

5. Assemble sandwiches by laying them down on a plate. Béchamel sauce, shredded gruyere cheese, and a sunny side up egg go on top of each sandwich.

6. With a fork and knife, dig in!

Ultimate Breakfast Platter

cooking time: 20 minutes

Servings: 6

Ingredients

GRIDDLED ITEMS:

- Bacon
- Sausage Links
- Pancakes

AIR FRYER ITEMS:

- Eggs

ADDITIONAL ITEMS:

Fruit:

- Strawberries
- Raspberries
- Blackberries
- Oranges
- Juice

LOX AND BAGELS:

- Mini Bagels (toast on griddle top for a couple minutes)
- Salmon
- Cream Cheese
- Cucumbers
- Red Onions
- Sesame Seeds

YOGURT PARFAIT:

- Strawberry Yogurt
- Granola
- Fresh Raspberries

Instructions

1. Begin by browning your bacon and sausage in a skillet. Then cook your pancakes with your preferred pancake mix.
2. Place eggs on the tray of your Air Fryer and turn it to low. Set a timer for 15 minutes and prepare a large dish of ice water in advance.
3. Remove the eggs from the oven when the timer goes off and place them in the ice bath to cool.
4. Begin to arrange all of your components on a large platter in a pleasing manner. Your guests will be enthralled by its splendor and eager to dive in!

Blackstone Brats with Peppers and Onions Recipe

cooking time: 25 minutes

Servings: 5

Ingredients

- 1 Package of Bratwurst, I used Beer Brats, Johnsonville)
- 1 green bell pepper, sliced into strips
- 1 red bell pepper, sliced into strips
- orange bell pepper, sliced into strips
- 1 yellow onion, sliced into strips
- 5 hoagie rolls
- 2-3 tablespoons oil
- Salt and Pepper

Instructions

1. To begin, wash and slice your peppers and onions. I cut the peppers and onions into long strips, like you would for a fajita mix.
2. Then, without cutting all the way through your bratwurst, slice it lengthwise. This allows you to open up the brat and make a butterfly cut.
3. Turn your Blackstone Grill on high and pour some oil on top. Place your brats on the grill cut side down.
4. Then, on the other side of the flat top grill, add extra oil, followed by your peppers and onions.
5. Season with salt & pepper and a splash of water.
6. You'll cook your brats for around 5 minutes before flipping them over until they're golden brown. Cook until the brats are thoroughly cooked on the opposite side. The interior temperature should be 160 degrees.

7. Saute the vegetables until they are softened and blackened in areas.
8. When the brats are almost done, brush a small area of the grill with oil and arrange your cut hoagie buns. On one side, toast them till golden brown.
9. To make the bratwurst, lay a brat on a bun and top with onion and peppers. Serve with your favorite sides to go with these brats with peppers and onions!

Funfetti Pancakes

cooking time: 15 minutes

Servings: 4

Ingredients

PANCAKES-

- 1 Cup Funfetti Cake Mix
- 1 Cup Pancake Mix
- 1 Cup Milk
- 2 Eggs
- 2 tbsp Sprinkles
- 1 tsp Vanilla

ICING:

- 1 Cup Powdered Sugar
- 2 tbsp Cream
- 1 tsp Vanilla
- TOPPINGS:

- Whipped Cream
- Cherries
- Sprinkles

Instructions

1. To make the pancake batter, whisk together all of the ingredients in a mixing basin.
2. Preheat the griddle to medium heat.
3. Pour 1/4 cup of batter onto the griddle top to make pancakes. Flip the pancakes once bubbles appear and cook for another 2-3 minutes.
4. 5-6 pancakes stacked on a platter, drizzled with frosting, topped with whipped cream, cherry, and additional sprinkles
5. Enjoy!

Blackstone Tex Mex Chicken and Lime Cauliflower Rice

cooking time: 55 minutes

Servings: 4-6

Ingredients

MEXICAN CHICKEN MARINADE

- 3-4 chicken breasts, trimmed and sliced thin
- 1 limes
- 1 teaspoon chili powder
- 1/2 teaspoon garlic powder
- 1/2 teaspoon onion powder
- 2 tablespoons Worcestershire sauce
- 3 tablespoons oil
- Cauliflower Rice
- 24 ounces cauliflower rice, fresh or frozen
- 1/2 lime, squeezed
- 1/4 teaspoon garlic salt with parsley

Instructions

1. Start by finely slicing the raw chicken in a Ziploc bag or container. If any fat has to be removed from the meat, trim it.
2. After that, add 1 lime that you juiced, discarding the lime after juicing. Combine the oil, chili powder, garlic powder, and onion powder in a large mixing bowl.
3. Seal the bag and massage the chicken to evenly cover it with the Mexican chicken marinade. Refrigerate for at least 30 minutes, but preferably overnight.
4. When you're ready to cook on the Blackstone, preheat your grill to medium high heat for at least 10 minutes.
5. Using a squirt of oil, coat the griddle with your chicken. Allow it to cook for 3-5 minutes on each side, or until done. Remove the chicken off the griddle once it is done.

6. Take your cauliflower rice and set it on the opposite side of the griddle while the chicken cooks. To help steam the cauliflower, pour a little water over the riced cauliflower.
7. Season with garlic salt, parsley, and the juice of half a lime. Cook until it starts to burn somewhat.
8. When the chicken is done, remove it from the pan and replace it with the cauliflower rice in the same spot. Squirt some water over the surface to help take the sticky marinade off the griddle and flavor your rice.
9. Remove the rice from the griddle once it has been seasoned.
10. In a bowl, combine the lime cauliflower rice, chicken, and desired toppings (sour cream, salsa, etc.).
11. For a quick meal, serve this Tex Mex chicken over lime cauliflower rice.

Pancake Kabobs

cooking time: 20 minutes

Servings: 4

Ingredients

- 1 Cup Pancake Mix
- 3/4 Cup Water
- 1 tsp Vanilla
- 5 Large Strawberries cut in 1/2' slices
- 3 tbsp Nutella
- 1 Medium Banana

- 3 tbsp Peanut Butter
- Syrup
- Butter
- Kabob Sticks cut into 4" pieces

Instructions

1. To make the pancake batter, whisk together the pancake mix, water, and vanilla extract in a mixing dish. Placed on the side.
2. Preheat the griddle to medium heat. Several teaspoons of butter should be melted.
3. On the griddle, pour 1 teaspoon of pancake batter. Continue making small pancakes until you have about 20. Flip them after they start to bubble and cook for another minute or two.
4. Remove the pancakes from the griddle and place them on a plate to cool while you prepare the fruit.
5. Begin with the kabobs of strawberries and Nutella. Spread Nutella on one pancake, then top with a strawberry slice and another pancake. Continue until you have a total of four layers.

Grilled Buffalo Chicken Flatbread Pizza Recipe

cooking time: 20 minutes

Servings: 4

Ingredients

- 1 8 oz. Bag of Diced Chicken Breast, Pre-Cooked
- 2 7.5 oz. Packages of Naan Flatbread
- 1/2 Cup of Ranch Dressing
- 1/3 Cup of Buffalo Sauce
- 1 16 oz. Bag of Shredded Mozzarella Cheese
- 1 Bunch of Green Onions, Chopped

Instructions

1. Preheat your grill to 350-375 degrees Fahrenheit.
2. Combine the Buffalo Sauce and Ranch Dressing in a mixing dish.
3. Top your Flatbread with the Buffalo Sauce Mixture, Chicken Breast Pieces, Mozzarella, and Green Onions.
4. Grill for 5-10 minutes, or until the cheese is melted and bubbling.
5. Remove from the grill and serve right away.

Sausage Gravy Breakfast Totchos

cooking time: 30 minutes

Servings: 6

Ingredients

- 1 lb ground sausage, (any flavor works)
- 4 tbsp butter, unsalted
- 4 tbsp all purpose flour
- 1 cup milk
- 1 cup half and half
- 1/4 tsp black pepper
- 1/4 tsp salt
- 1/4 tsp garlic powder
- 1/4 tsp onion powder
- 1/4 tsp sage
- 1/4 paprika
- 1 package frozen tater tots
- eggs
- 1 block of cheddar cheese, shredded

Instructions

1. Using your Blackstone scraper, cook ground sausage. Save all of the sausage fat by chopping the sausage into small bits.
2. Melt the butter in a deep skillet over high heat, then stir in the flour until golden brown and aromatic, about 1-2 minutes.
3. Continue to whisk in the milk and half-and-half until it thickens.
4. Combine the sausage, leftover sausage grease, and all of the dry ingredients in a large mixing bowl. If you're using a flavored or spicy sausage, dry seasonings aren't necessary.
5. Cook frozen tots on griddle starting on low heat to thaw, then increase to medium and sprinkle with a little coating of vegetable oil, sliding your spatula under the tots to help them roll without breaking, until crispy on both sides.
6. Cook as many eggs as you want while the tots are finishing up. Arrange tots, cheese, sausage gravy, and eggs on a serving plate. Enjoy!

Bacon Pancakes with Strawberry Whiskey Syrup and Whipped Cream

cooking time: 20 minutes

Servings: 2

Ingredients

- Pancake Mix
- 1 lb Bacon

- 1 Cup Milk
- 2 Eggs
- Fresh Strawberries
- Honey
- Whiskey
- Heavy Whipping Cream
- Powdered Sugar

Instructions

1. Heat the 17" Blackstone range top combo griddle to medium high before using. Cook for 4 strips of bacon. Remove the bacon from the pan and drain on paper towels. Remove the majority of the bacon fat from the griddle, but not all of it. (This is what you'll use to cook your pancakes in.)
2. 2 cups whiskey, 2-3 table spoons honey, stirred and reduced in a medium sized skillet When the bubbles in the skillet are huge, add the fresh cut strawberries and reduce the heat. Stir once in a while. If the syrup is too thick, add more whiskey.
3. 2 cups pancake mix, 2 eggs, and 1 cup milk are combined in a mixing basin. Stir until thoroughly combined, then pour into the Blackstone pancake batter dispenser.
4. Cut the bacon in half and place four pieces on a griddle set to medium-high heat. When the bacon is golden brown, cover it with pancake batter and turn it. When all sides of the pancakes are cooked, remove them from the griddle.
5. 1 cup heavy whipping cream 1 cup heavy whipping cream 1 cup heavy whipping cream 1 cup heavy whipping cream 1 cup heavy whipping cream 1 cup heavy Beat in a teaspoon of powdered sugar. When the whipped cream begins to thicken, add additional powdered sugar as needed. When you see huge peaks on the tip of your whisk, you know it's done.
6. Plate your bacon pancakes, then top with strawberry whiskey syrup and fresh whipped cream.

Boston Cream Pie Pancakes

cooking time: 20 minutes

Servings: 4

Ingredients

PANCAKES-

- 1 cup yellow cake mix
- 1 cup pancake mix
- 1 cup milk
- 1 tsp vanilla
- 2 eggs

CUSTARD FILLING-

- 1 package instant vanilla pudding mix
- 3 cups cold milk

CHOCOLATE GANACHE-

- 1 1/2 cups chocolate chips
- 1 tbs butter
- 3 tbs milk

Instructions

Custard Filling:

1. Pour the pudding mix and milk into a mixing bowl. Whisk until the sauce has thickened slightly.
2. Refrigerate while you finish the pancakes.

Ganache:

1. Microwave butter, milk, and chocolate for 30 seconds.
2. Mix everything together until it's smooth.

Pancakes:

1. Preheat the griddle to medium-low temperature.
2. Combine all of the pancake ingredients in a mixing bowl.
3. Melt some butter on the griddle's surface. Pour 1/4 cup pancake batter into griddle and cook for 3-4 minutes, or until bubbles appear. Cook for another 2-3 minutes on the other side.
4. Remove the custard from the fridge and get the ganache once you've finished cooking all of the pancakes.
5. Alternate pancakes with custard filling on a dish to create layers. Pour the ganache on top.

Blackstone Griddle Juicy Smash Burger Recipe

cooking time: 17 minutes

Servings: 6

Ingredients

- 1 - 2 pounds Ground Beef (depending on how many you are making)
- Seasonings of your choice, I used salt and pepper only
- Butter
- Cheese Slices
- Toppings: Lettuce, tomatoes, onions, pickles, or anything else you like

Instructions

1. Set the Blackstone Griddle to medium-high heat.
2. Fill a 1/4 or 1/3 measuring cup halfway with ground beef. Don't push down on it. (You may make them bigger or smaller if you wish, but those are the sizes we favor.) It should be packed loosely. Form them into a ball with your hands, taking care not to overwork them. Don't overdo it, and don't overpack them.

3. Butter the griddle with a stick of butter. (Alternatively, use your preferred oil)
4. Place the burger balls on the preheated griddle. Allow 3-4 minutes for them to sizzle. Press the burgers flat using a fairly big spatula.

Blackstone Mexican Street Corn Recipe

Blackstone Mexican Street Corn is an easy recipe to create having a squeeze bottle with oil when making this can be recommended because it helps the eggs not to stick when making that part

cooking time: 17 minutes

Servings: 10

Ingredients

- 4 Cans Whole Kernel Corn
- Vegetable Oil
- 4 Tbsp Mayonnaise
- 4 Tbsp Sour Cream
- 1 Tbsp Lime Juice
- 1 Tsp Chili Powder
- Dash Of Cayenne Pepper
- Salt
- Pepper
- Crumbled Queso Fresco

- Chopped Fresh Cilantro

Instructions

1. Open your corn cans and strain them; I let mine rest for about 10 minutes in an over-the-sink strainer to make sure they were well strained. •
2. Coat your Blackstone Griddle in oil and give it a good swirl.
3. Spread your corn out on your griddle once it's hot and ready.
4. Move the corn about on the griddle to ensure that it cooks evenly.
5. Take your corn out of the pan and set it aside.
6. Combine the soured cream, mayonnaise, lime juice, flavorer, and cayenne pepper in a basin large enough to hold the corn.
7. Toss with shredded queso fresco and cilantro, to taste, and serve.

Fried Rice Leftover Smoked Turkey Recipe

The Leftover Smoked Turkey dish Recipe could be a good way to assign leftover smoked turkey while also putting your Blackstone griddle to good use! to form this, shred leftover smoked turkey from a vacation feast. Sriracha sauce, chili paste, or maybe ginger may be wont to boost the Chinese fried rice.

cooking time: 30 minutes

Servings: 12

Ingredients

- shredded smoked turkey
- 1 dozen of eggs
- 3 cups polished rice
- peas
- carrots
- salt
- pepper
- condiment
- oil
- minced garlic

Instructions

1. Begin by preparing the polished rice. For this, i take advantage of a rice cooker to cook my rice.
2. Spread out your rice on a cooking utensil to permit to dry out some after it's done cooking, I let mine dry out for about an hour or two.
3. Start prepping out your other ingredients shredding leftover smoked turkey, veggies, and the rest you choose to add.
4. Whisk your eggs during a bowl and add just a splash of water, the water helps them to be a touch fluffier. Add a small amount of salt and pepper to your egg mixture.
5. After your rice is done cooking, spread it out on a cooking utensil to allow it to dry out a little.
6. Begin preparing the remainder of your ingredients by shredding leftover smoked turkey, vegetables, and whatever else you choose to add.
7. In a mixing bowl, whisk your eggs and add a dash of water to make them a little fluffier. sprinkle the egg mixture with a bit of salt and pepper.
8. Re-oil your Blackstone griddle and fire it up.
9. Arrange the turkey and rice on the freshly greased grill.
10. Add the minced garlic and a couple soy sauces, and simmer while stirring with spatulas.
11. If it appears to be sticking, add a tiny bit of more oil.*
12. After that, pour the eggs on the other side of the griddle and combine the turkey and rice with the vegetables.
13. Once the eggs have begun to cook, combine everything.
14. Toss everything together at once, sprinkle with extra soy if desired, and heat until the eggs are thoroughly cooked.
15. Serve and have fun!!

Brisket Grilled Cheese On The Blackstone

GRIDDLE Brisket Grilled Cheese On The Blackstone Griddle is a delicious way to use up leftover brisket! Grilled cheese with smoked brisket has an incredible taste! To prepare these, either use shredded brisket or brisket slices. You may add various cheeses, such as Monterey Jack or Pepper Jack, to mix up the flavor

cooking time: 10 minutes

Servings: 2

Ingredients

- Slices Texas Toast Butter
- Shredded Cheddar Cheese
- Shredded Or Sliced Smoked Brisket

Instructions

1. Using a new amount of oil, prepare your Blackstone Griddle. You'll need two slices of Texas Toast for this sandwich, so butter one side.
2. On your texas toast, spread the crumbled cheese. Using shredded leftover smoked brisket or pieces of brisket, top the shredded cheese. If your brisket was in the fridge, reheat it up in a skillet or microwave it for 30 seconds to ensure it will be warm enough in your sandwich.
3. Place the brisket on top of the shredded cheese, then additional shredded cheese on top of that.
4. Place another piece of Texas Toast on top of the cheese, buttering the side that is on top.
5. Preheat your Blackstone griddle or a pan on the stovetop to low-medium heat.
6. Place the constructed sandwich on the griddle, or in the pan, after the griddle is hot.
7. Allow to cook until the bottom slice begins to brown, then turn the entire sandwich.
8. Remove and serve!

Fried Rice Recipe Leftover Shredded Pork On The Blackstone

The Blackstone's Leftover Shredded Pork Fried Rice Recipe is a delicious fried rice recipe! The taste of leftover smoked pulled pork in the Hibachi fried rice was incredible!

cooking time: 31 minutes

Servings: 20

Ingredients

- Leftover Smoked Pulled Pork Shoulder
- Egg • Cooked White Rice
- Peas
- Carrots
- Salt
- Pepper
- Soy Sauce
- Minced Garlic

Instructions

1. Cook your white rice the night before or a few hours before you're ready to prepare your fried rice.

2. After your rice is done cooking, spread it out on a baking sheet to dry out a little. I usually let mine dry out for an hour or two depending on what else is going on before supper.

3. Take your leftover smoked pulled pork out of the fridge and shred it if necessary.

4. In a mixing dish, whisk your eggs with a dash of water to make them a little fluffier. Season the egg mixture with salt and pepper. Re-oil your Blackstone griddle if necessary after it has been fired up.

5. All I have to do is switch it on and re-oil it because I have mine ready to go at all times. Spread the pork and rice out to warm up; I drizzled it with soy sauce and added some chopped garlic as well.

6. After that, I add my vegetables to the meat and let them simmer alongside it. Then combine everything on one side of the griddle, including the rice, meat, and vegetables.

7. Pour your eggs onto the opposite side of the griddle and cook until done;

8. if the griddle appears to be dry, pour on a little extra vegetable oil. In your rice, these will be diced up like scrambled eggs. When your eggs are done, combine them with everything else on the griddle

9. . Drizzle with soy sauce and cook for a few minutes more on the griddle. Serve and have fun!!

Steak Fried Rice On The Blackstone Griddle

On The Blackstone, Teriyaki Steak Fried Rice is the ideal midweek meal! It's simple to make, and the marinade gives the steak a fantastic taste! To keep the kitchen clean and easy to clean, cook on the Blackstone! With a rice cooker and frozen carrots and peas, you can make a simple meal that the whole family will enjoy! Cook this hibachi-style dish outside and you'll appear like an expert chef!

cooking time: 45 minutes

Servings: 12

Ingredients

- Egg
- Cooked White Rice
- Peas • Carrots
- Salt • Pepper
- Soy Sauce
- Minced Garlic
- 3 Lbs Trimmed Petite Sirloin
- Montreal Steak Seasoning
- Yoshida Teriyaki
- Teriyaki Marinade

Instructions

1. Combine the Sesame Seeds, Yoshida Teriyaki, Teriyaki Marinade, and Worcestershire Sauce in a container.
2. Remove some of the extra fat from your steak by dicing it into little pieces.
3. Place your steaks in the marinade container and let overnight if possible, or at least for a couple of hours.
4. Cook your white rice a few hours before you're ready to prepare your fried rice. Cooking your white rice the night before is also an option. My white rice is cooked in a rice cooker.
5. After the rice has finished cooking, put it out on a baking sheet to allow it to dry out a little. Allow for an hour or two of drying time before creating the fried rice. Remove the steak from the fridge and lay it out to come to room temperature while you finish the rest of the preparations.
6. In a mixing bowl, whisk your eggs with a dash of water to make them a little fluffier. Season the egg mixture with salt and pepper.
7. Re-oil your Blackstone griddle if necessary after it has been fired up. I keep mine charged and ready to use at all times; all I have to do is switch it on and re-oil it.
8. When the griddle reaches cooking temperature, remove the steak from the sauce mixture with a slotted spoon.

9. As soon as the steak starts to brown, lay the rice in the center of the griddle and top with the frozen veggies and minced garlic.
10. Allow both to fry on the griddle, stirring/moving around occasionally with a spatula.
11. Pour your eggs onto the opposite side of the griddle to fry; if the griddle appears to be dry, pour a little extra vegetable oil on it. During cooking, the eggs will be split up like scrambled eggs.
12. Drizzle some soy sauce over the rice and let it aside to simmer while the eggs and chicken finish cooking.
13. Combine the eggs, rice, and veggies when they are half cooked but still runny.
14. Combine the meat and rice and simmer for a few minutes longer Serve and have fun!!

Shrimp Fried Rice On Blackstone Griddle

On Blackstone, Shrimp Fried Rice The griddle is ideal for a fast midweek supper! To keep the kitchen clean and easy to clean, cook on Blackstone!

cooking time: 35minutes

Servings: 16

Ingredients

- Thawed Shrimp Egg
- Cooked White Rice
- Peas Carrots
- Salt
- Pepper
- Soy Sauce
- Minced Garlic

Instructions

1. with cold water until it has frozen. If the shrimp's shells need to be removed, do so, and de-vine them as well.
2. Remove the chicken from the fridge and lay it out to come to room temperature while you finish the rest of the preparations.
3. Whisk your eggs with a splash of water in a large mixing basin. A dash of water, I've discovered, makes for fluffier eggs.
4. Season your egg mixture with salt and pepper. Re-oil your Blackstone griddle if necessary after it has been fired up. I keep mine charged and ready to use at all times; all I have to do is switch it on and re-oil it.
5. Pour a little additional vegetable oil into a small bowl, then put your shrimp in after the oil has warmed up. This was done to aid in the cooking of Cook your white rice a few hours before you're ready to prepare your fried rice.
6. Cooking your white rice the night before is also an option. My white rice is cooked in a rice cooker.

7. After the rice has finished cooking, put it out on a baking sheet to allow it to dry out a little. Allow for an hour or two of drying time before creating the fried rice.

8. If your shrimp are frozen, place them in a dish of cold water and submerge them. I frequently replace my water the shrimp while also ensuring that it did not stick.

9. Sprinkle some minced garlic and soy sauce over the rice and spread it out on the griddle. The peas and carrots should be spread out next to the rice and allowed to cook if frozen; if thawed, they should warm up quickly.

10. Pour your eggs onto the opposite side of the griddle to fry; if the griddle appears to be dry, pour a little extra vegetable oil on it.

11. The eggs will seem scrambled while they cook, and they will be cut up similarly like scrambled eggs.

12. Combine the eggs, rice, peas, and carrots in a mixing bowl. I prefer to stir them into the rice while they are still runny.

13. When the shrimp is done cooking, combine it with the remaining rice. Remove from the oven and serve!

Eggroll In A Bowl On The Blackstone Griddle

On the Blackstone Griddle, create this Eggroll In A Bowl for a quick and simple midweek supper! It's a child favorite that's also keto!

cooking time: 25minutes

Servings: 8

Ingredients

- Oil 3 Tbsp rice vinegar
- Soy Sauce
- Salt
- 3 Lbs
- Ground Pork Sausage
- 3 Bags Ready-Mix
- Dry Coleslaw
- Chopped Onion Minced
- Garlic
- 2 Tsp Sesame
- Pepper

Instructions

1. Make sure your Blackstone griddle is ready to use by cleaning it, filling the propane tank, putting cooking utensils on it, and oiling it.
2. Collect all of your ingredients.

3. Warm up your Blackstone Griddle once you're ready. Start cooking your ground pork and season it with salt and pepper to taste.

4. You may use a meat chopper or the spatial and scraper that included with the Blackstone Accessory package.

5. Set the pork to one side and reoil the opposite side of the griddle after it's partly done.

6. Open the coleslaw bags on the empty side of the griddle and scatter them out on that side. On the cabbage side, add your onion and minced garlic.

7. Use one of the long (or two) to mix the cabbage up and keep chopping'/cooking the pork on the other side of the grill. Add the Seasame Oil, Rice Vinegar, and a splash of Soy Sauce to the top of the cabbage after it begins to wilt and soften. You may also add a dash of soy sauce to the pork for added flavor.

8. Continue to stir the cabbage mixture with your long spatula to spread the liquids.

9. Start mixing the pork with the cabbage once the cabbage is more cooked; this is a lot of fun if you use both long Spatulas.

10. Remove the griddle from the heat and serve!! I always go back out with a cup of water after taking the meal in. The scraper is then used to scrape food bits from the griddle.

11. I pour the water on, which causes it to steam a little, so I can scrape some more and then wash it down dry.

12. When I'm done eating, I return to the kitchen and re-oil the griddle so it's ready to use the following time.

13. Also, be sure to remove the filthy drain container and give the entire area a good clean down. If you're storing yours outside, make sure to cover the griddle after it's completely cold.

Pizza Grilled Cheese On The Blackstone Griddle

The Blackstone Griddle Pizza Grilled Cheese is a quick and easy meal or appetizer! Change it up whatever you like, and it's a kid-pleaser as well!

cooking time: 40 minutes

Servings: 30

Ingredients

- Frozen Garlic
- Bread Pizza
- Sauce Mozzarella
- Cheese Bacon
- Crumbles
- Canadian Bacon
- Diced Up

Instructions

1. Start by heating up your Blackstone Griddle; if you're not sure how to care for your Blackstone Griddle, check out my post here; my griddle was ready to use. If you need to clean and re-oil your griddle, do so. Because mine was clean, I used a smidgeon of oil to re-grease it. Gather your ingredients while your griddle heats up.

2. Once your griddle is hot, place your bread on it; I used frozen garlic bread. Allow one side of the bread to toast to a golden brown toastiness.

3. Turn the bread pieces over and start putting pizza toppings on half of them. Instead of a grilled cheese sandwich with two slices of bread, you may make all open-faced sandwiches.

4. You may begin stacking your sandwiches after the opposite side of the bread has been toasted.

5. The cheese melted thanks to the heat from the bread's bottom. Serve and have fun!! These may also be dipped in extra pizza sauce, garlic butter, or alfredo sauce.

Hibachi Fried Rice on a Blackstone Griddle

On a Blackstone Griddle, make a Japanese steakhouse.Hibachi Fried Rice. This is simple to make with any meat and vegetables of your choosing and tastes just like

cooking time: 55minutes

Servings: 12

Ingredients

- Chopped Up Bacon
- Egg
- Cooked White Rice
- Peas
- Carrots
- Green Onions
- Salt
- Pepper
- Soy Sauce
- Minced Garlic

Instructions

1. In a large mixing bowl, combine the minced garlic and the meat mixture.
2. Begin to combine the rice, meat, and vegetables.
3. Pour your eggs onto one side of the griddle and cook for a few minutes. In your rice, these will be diced
4. up like scrambled eggs.
5. Mix everything together, sprinkle with soy sauce, and fry for a few more minutes on the griddle. Begin by preparing your white rice. My white rice is cooked in a rice cooker. Making huge quantities of rice at once is considerably easier with a rice cooker.
6. After your rice is done cooking, spread it out on a baking sheet to dry out a little. I usually let mine dry out for an hour or two, depending on what's going on.
7. Begin preparing the rest of your ingredients by cutting your meat, vegetables, and anything else you want to include.
8. In a mixing dish, whisk your eggs with a dash of water to make them a little fluffier. Season your egg mixture with salt and pepper.
9. Re-oil your Blackstone griddle and fire it up. All I have to do is switch it on and re-oil it because I have mine ready to go at all times.
10. On one side of the griddle, spread out the bacon or pork, and on the other side, spread out the rice.
11. Cook for a few minutes, stirring periodically.
12. The beautiful thing about this recipe is that you can customize it to your liking.
13. Next, I add my fresh or frozen vegetables to the bacon and let them to cook in the bacon fat with the bacon
14. Serve and have fun!!

French Toast On Blackstone Griddle

French Toast on a Blackstone Griddle is a great way to have a big breakfast at home or while camping! Plus, there are all the extras like bacon and eggs!

cooking time: 15minutes

Servings: 10

Ingredients

- 4 lbs Gold Potatoes
- 1 lb Bacon
- 5 Polish sausages
- Cheese
- Minced Garlic
- Salt
- Pepper

Instructions

1. Serve everything together and enjoy!! We topped ours with shredded cheese and you could mix in sour cream as well! Your potatoes should be washed and dried.
2. All of the vegetables should be sliced and diced, and the sausages should be polished.
3. When you heat up your griddle, brush it with a little oil or bacon fat to aid in nonsticking and sauteing the food.
4. Combine the potatoes, onion, and polish sausage on your griddle.
5. Add salt and pepper to taste.
6. Cook until potatoes are fork tender.
7. Remove the potatoes from the oven and place them in a dish or another plate to keep warm.
8. Fry your bacon till it's done to your liking and then fry your eggs at the same time (or scrambled eggs)

double-layered paper towels. With the paper towels, press out as much moisture as possible.

1. Crack 6 eggs into a large mixing basin or pourable measuring cup to start. Lightly whisk in the heavy whipping cream and 1/2 teaspoon of salt with a fork.
2. Get your pico de gallo ready. In a mixing dish, add all of the ingredients and whisk to incorporate.
3. Make your way to the griddle. Allow half of the beef tallow to melt on the griddle. Season the shredded potatoes with salt and pepper on top of the melted beef tallow. Arrange them in a neat, equal layer.then wait until they're golden brown before flipping them.
4. Toss the hash browns over the top with the remaining beef tallow, allowing it to melt into the potatoes. This will aid in crisping the opposite side.
5. Cook the chorizo on the stovetop. With the end of your spatula, break it apart. Add your eggs to your griddle when your chorizo is almost done and your potatoes have been turned.
6. 2 Tablespoons butter, melted on the coldest section of the griddle top (turn off a burner if need be). Cook, stirring regularly with a spatula, your egg mixture on top of the melted butter. Cook for a total of 2-3 minutes.
7. To begin assembling your burritos, place your eggs, chorizo, and hash browns on a platter.
8. Assemble the ingredients for your burritos. Add a tablespoon of eggs, a dollop of chorizo, crispy hash

browns, and grated cheese to each tortilla shell. Tightly roll them up.

9. 2 tblsp. butter, melted on the griddle Place the wrapped burritos on the griddle seam side down and cook for 1-2 minutes, or until crispy on the outside.

10. Serve with pico de gallo and Mexican crema on the side.

Griddle Corn Cakes with Honey Butter

Cooking them on a griddle or in a skillet takes a little longer than baking them, but it's definitely worth it in my view. It will also go much faster if you have a large electric griddle.

cooking time: 30 minutes

Servings: 1

Ingredients

- 2/3 cup sugar
- 1/4 cup honey
- 1/2 cup melted butter
- 2 large eggs, beaten
- 1/2 teaspoon baking soda
- 1 cup buttermilk
- 1/4 cup 2% or whole milk
- 1/2 teaspoon salt
- 1 cup cornmeal
- 1 cup flour
- Butter for pan

Honey Butter

- 1 stick salted butter, room temp
- 1/4 cup honey

Instructions

1. Combine all of the corn cake ingredients in a large mixing bowl until most of the lumps are gone.
2. Don't overdo it with the mixing! Melt a little amount of butter in a pan over medium heat.
3. Place approximately 1/4 cup of batter in the pan and smoosh it down into a flat circle if necessary.
4. Cook for 2 minutes until browned, then turn and finish cooking. Continue with the remainder of the batter until it's all done.
5. Combine honey and 1/2 cup butter in a mixing bowl and stir until smooth. Serve alongside the warm corn cakes.
6. Turn the griddle down to low heat and top with bacon pieces and more cheese. Cook, stirring occasionally, until the cheese has melted.

Blackstone Seared Chicken Breasts

Seared chicken breasts are delicious, juicy, and tender, and they're perfect for topping salads, putting into spaghetti, or serving with homemade risotto!

cooking time: 17 minutes

Servings: 4

Ingredients

- 2 chicken breasts
- salt and pepper
- 2 tablespoons olive oil
- 2 tablespoons white wine

Instructions

1. Don't be afraid to season your chicken breasts! To properly stand out, chicken requires a lot of taste.
2. Preheat your griddle on low heat with a surface temperature of roughly 350°. This is when an infrared pistol comes in handy.
3. Grease the griddle. Canola, vegetable, olive, and avocado oils all work well in this recipe. We used olive oil particularly, but don't let that stop you if you don't have any!
4. Cover the seasoned chicken and place it on the griddle. Allow for 3-4 minutes of cooking time. Once golden brown, flip and re-cover.
5. Lift the cover slightly after 3-4 minutes and squirt 1-2 teaspoons of your choice cooking liquid beneath the lid.
6. Use an instant-read thermometer to check the temperature.
7. When the chicken breasts reach 160°, remove them from the oven and tent them with foil for about 5 minutes to allow them to reach the magic 165° safe temperature for chicken.
8. Slice, serve, and savor!

Blackstone English Muffins

Make your own English Muffins in the convenience of your own home! For the greatest results, use a Blackstone, but if you don't have one, a cast iron pan would suffice!

cooking time: 1hour 40 minutes

Servings: 18

Ingredients

- 1 3/4 cups whole milk, lukewarm
- 4 tablespoons salted butter, room temperature
- 1 1/2 teaspoons salt
- 2 1/2 tablespoons sugar
- 1 large egg, lightly beaten
- 4 1/2 cups (539g) Unbleached Bread Flour
- 2 teaspoons instant yeast
- cornmeal for sprinkling

Instructions

1. In a mixer, combine the milk, yeast, butter, egg, sugar, salt, and flour.
2. Blend on low until all of the ingredients are combined, then

increase to medium and mix for about 5 minutes. The dough will be very smooth and elastic when you pull it out.

3. In a well-oiled basin, flip the kneaded dough to coat it.

4. Allow the dough to rise until it is nearly doubled in size, covered. It took me approximately an hour to make mine, but I was cooking it on a heated burner. The more taste emerges as it climbs slowly.

5. After that, you'll gradually deflate the dough. Make smooth balls out of the dough.

6. Cornmeal should be sprinkled into cold pots or over the surface of a cool Blackstone.If your pans aren't non-stick, spray them with cooking spray before using them, or gently oil your Blackstone if it isn't well-seasoned.

7. Take the dough balls and flatten them into discs approximately 3/4 inch thick and 2-3 inches wide once your griddle or pans are ready.

8. Place them on a chilly griddle or pan and reduce the heat to medium-low. On the tops of the muffins, sprinkle some more corn meal.

9. Cook for 10 minutes on each side. However, check them after 5 minutes to ensure they are not over-browning.

10. Getting the heat just right takes some practice.

11. If your muffins are browning too quickly on the exterior but not entirely cooked on the inside, place them on a baking pan and bake for 15 minutes at 350 degrees.

12. Allow to cool for 10-15 minutes before splitting with a fork, toasting if desired.

13. If your muffins are browning too quickly on the exterior but not entirely cooked on the inside, place them on a baking pan and bake for 15 minutes at 350 degrees.

Blackstone Salmon Sandwich

Fresh salmon filets grilled on the Blackstone griddle are used in this delicious salmon sandwich!

cooking time: 25 minutes

Servings: 4

Ingredients

SALMON SANDWICHES

- 4 salmon filets, sandwich-sized
- 1 tablespoon olive oil
- Midnight Toker Rub*
- 1 teaspoon salt
- 4 toasted buns
- baby arugala

DILL AIOLI

- 1/2 cup mayonnaise
- 1/2 teaspoon lemon zest
- 2 teaspoons lemon juice
- 1/4 teaspoon salt

- 1/2 teaspoon minced fresh dill

Instructions

1. Combine all of the dill mayo ingredients in a mixing bowl and chill. Preheat the Blackstone griddle to medium.
2. After brushing each salmon filet with olive oil, generously sprinkle with Midnight Toker and salt.
3. Cook the fillets on the griddle until the internal temperature reaches 130°-135°, or until the desired temperature is reached.
4. The buns should be toasted.
5. Allow the filets to cool for 5 minutes after removing them from the griddle.
6. Spread some aioli on the toasted buns, then top with the salmon filet, lettuce, and the other bread.
7. Serve immediately!

Blackstone Crispy French Fries

A few of fresh Russet potatoes are coated in avocado oil, sprinkled with robust spices, then fried directly in your air fryer to make these wonderful homemade fries!

cooking time: 25 minutes

Servings: 6

Ingredients

- 2 large Russet potatoes
- 3 tablespoons avocado oil
- 1/2 teaspoon salt
- 2 tablespoons Spiceology Moss

Instructions

1. Wash your potatoes thoroughly before slicing them into sticks.
2. Toss with the oil in a basin after drying with a clean dish towel or paper towels.
3. Toss in the seasonings to make sure they're properly distributed.
4. Place the seasoned, greased potatoes in the basket. Don't overpack! They don't have to be in a single layer, but there has to be enough exposed surface area on each for the air to strike them and crisp them up.
5. Preheat your air fryer to 425 degrees (or as high as it will go) and add the potatoes.
6. Fry for 5-6 minutes, then shake the basket to throw the fries about and cook for an additional 5-6 minutes.
7. Cook and shake your fries until they are golden brown and as Crispy as you want them to be.

Blackstone Blackened Fish Sandwich

Try this quick griddle elote that's conveniently off the cob if you're looking for a great side dish to go with your next supper! We used frozen corn in this recipe, but you could simply use fresh corn and remove the kernels by hand.

cooking time: 20 minutes

Servings: 6

Ingredients

- 4 slices of bacon (save the fat)
- 3 cups frozen corn
- 1/2 teaspoon fresh cracked pepper
- 1 teaspoon chile margarita seasoning
- 2 ounces cream cheese
- 1/4 cup whole milk
- 3 tablespoons green onions
- 1/2 cup cotija cheese
- 2 tablespoons chopped cilantro

Instructions

1. Season both sides of the filets with the blackening seasoning and put aside.
2. Preheat your blackstone for 10-15 minutes on medium-low heat.
3. Apply a small layer of oil to the griddle and set the fish on it.

4. Cook each side for 4-5 minutes.
5. Remove the pancakes from the griddle and set them aside.
6. Toast the buns and top with the fish, baby arugula, and, if wanted, tartar sauce or mayonnaise.

Blackstone Mexican Street Corn Off the Cob

After being seasoned with Cajun Blackening flavor, fresh white fish is swiftly fried on the Blackstone griddle. Delicious and simple dish

cooking time: 20 minutes

Servings: 6

Ingredients

- 6 white fish filets, skinless
- 2 tablespoons blackening seasoning
- 2 tablespoons olive oil
- 6 brioche buns
- Baby arugula
- Tartar sauce or mayo

Instructions

1. Preheat your gas griddle on a low heat setting. crisp the bacon in a skillet.

2. Remove the bacon and dice it, leaving the fat on the griddle.

3. Microwave frozen corn for 1-3 minutes, or just long enough to keep it from becoming completely frozen. using a heated griddle to cook huge amounts of frozen items may distort your griddle.

4. Cook the corn for a few minutes on the griddle, turning constantly with a big spatula. season with salt, pepper, and chile margarita spice if desired.

5. Place the cream cheese and milk in a circle in the center of the corn mound. allow it to boil for a few minutes, stirring occasionally to keep it from sticking together.

6. Return the chopped bacon, green onions, and cotija cheese to the pan. stir until everything is well blended. if you have one, cover with a dome for the last minute of cooking.

7. Remove the griddle from the heat and sprinkle with cilantro. serve immediately.

Blackstone Filet MIgnon with Lobster

Treat yourself and/or someone you care about to a fine restaurant-quality meal in the comfort of your own home! tender filet mignon with a meaty flavor. on top, a buttery lobster tail. your special someone will be blown away.

cooking time: 20 minutes

Servings: 6

Ingredients

- 1 6-ounce filet mignon
- 1 4-ounce lobster tail
- 1/4 teaspoon salt
- 1/8 teaspoon pepper
- 1/8 teaspoon garlic powder
- 1 tablespoon butter
- 1/2 teaspoon old bay seasoning

Instructions

1. Preheat your griddle to medium-high heat, as directed by the manufacturer.the flesh from the lobster tail should be removed.

2. Season both sides of the steak and lobster tail with a mixture of salt, pepper, and garlic powder. season both sides of the lobster tail with old bay seasoning.

3. Place your steak on top of 1/2 of the butter on the griddle top. allow your steak to cook for 3 minutes before fliping it.

4. Check the temperature after another three minutes of cooking. when the internal temperature of the steak reaches 125 degrees, remove it from the grill and set it aside to rest for five minutes.

5. While the steak is resting, brush the grill top with the remaining butter

and place the lobster tail on top.
after two minutes, flip the lobster
and cook for another two minutes. if
you have one, place it on top of the
dome.

6. Remove the lobster from the grill
   and serve it on top of the steak.

Blackstone Steak Fajitas

Before being fried on a hot gas griddle, fresh, delicate steak was rapidly marinated. serve with a smattering of sauteed bell peppers and onions, as well as as many tortillas as you can manage.

cooking time: 45 minutes

Servings: 1

Ingredients

- 6 pounds steak*
- 2 teaspoons salt
- 1/2 teaspoon pepper
- 2 tablespoons the spice guy fajita seasoning**, divided
- 1 small can el pato jalapeno salsa
- 3 bell peppers, multi-colored
- 1 large onion
- 3 tablespoons avocado oil
- tortillas, of your choice

Instructions

1. Against the grain, slice the meat into small pieces. add salt, pepper, and 1 1/2 teaspoons of fajita spice to taste.
2. Put it in a plastic baggie or a container. allow 30 minutes for the el pato jalapeno salsa to soak in.
3. Slice your veggies and season with the remaining fajita spice while the steak sits.
4. Preheat your blackstone griddle for 10-15 minutes on high heat. place your oil on the griddle and spread it out evenly before placing your meat on one side and vegetables on the other.
5. Cook the steak, tossing it occasionally, until it is done to your liking. when the veggies are still tender-crisp, remove them from the griddle.
6. Before serving, heat your tortillas briefly on the griddle with all of your favorite fajita ingredients.

Blackstone Italian Dunkers

this old-school cafeteria lunch has been reimagined and has become a new family favorite! a dippable lunch or dinner including cheesy garlic bread dipped in heart meat sauce.

cooking time: 20 minutes

Servings: 6

Ingredients

- 1 loaf italian (or french) bread
- 1 stick salted butter
- 2 tablespoons johnny's garlic bread seasoning
- 1 cup shredded parmesan cheese
- 2 cups shredded mozzarella cheese (optional, and not included in photos)
- 1 pound ground beef

- 1 teaspoon salt, pepper, garlic blend (or approximately 1/3 teaspoon of each to add up to 1 teaspoon if you don't have a blend.)
- 1 - 48 ounce jar marinara

Instructions

1. Make circles out of the bread. spread the butter and garlic bread spice on both the front and back sides of the slices.
2. Preheat the blackstone on the stovetop over moderate heat. for the greatest results, set the temperature to roughly 325°f.
3. Over medium heat, brown the ground meat. spg (salt, pepper, and paprika) toss the cooked ground beef with the marinara sauce in a skillet.
4. While toasting the garlic bread, place the pan on the griddle to heat.
5. Toast the garlic bread on both sides until golden brown.
6. Top with cheese(s) if preferred, then cover or broil for a minute until melted and bubbling.
7. Serve the beefy marinade with toasted garlic bread for dipping!

Blackstone Griddle Steak Street Tacos

These tasty street tacos are swiftly cooked on the blackstone griddle and served with the usual onion, cilantro, and spicy sauce for a true street taco right in your own garden!

cooking time: 20 minutes

Servings: 8

Ingredients

- 4 pounds beef skirt steak
- 2 limes, juiced
- 1 teaspoon salt
- 1/2 teaspoon pepper
- 1/2 teaspoon garlic powder
- 1 tablespoon chile lime rub from spiceology
- corn tortillas
- 1 small white onion, finely diced
- 1 bunch cilantro, chopped
- Hot sauce of your choosing

Instructions

1. Sprinkle all of the salt, pepper, garlic powder, and chile-lime rub evenly over the steak. allow it to sit in the fridge for approximately an hour, uncovered and seasoned. (if you're short on time, you may skip this step.)

2. Prepare all of your vegetables while the steak is cooking.
3. Preheat your blackstone gas griddle for 10-15 minutes on medium heat.
4. Place a small coating of oil on the griddle and warm all of your tortillas on both sides. wrap them securely in foil to keep them warm.
5. Cut the steak into thin strips against the grain, then divide the uncooked meat into bite-sized pieces by cutting across all of the strips.
6. Add a little more oil to the pan and place the steak in a thin layer on the heated griddle.
7. Allow the steak to sizzle and cook for a few minutes, or until a light crust forms on the bottom.with a big spatula, flip the steak to the other side and mix it up a little.
8. Squeeze the lime juice over the steak and swirl it around, then take it from the grill as soon as possible

Blackstone Frozen French Fries

It's never been easier to griddle frozen fries! fire up the blackstone and grab a bag of your favorite frozen fries

cooking time: 17 minutes

Servings: 12

Ingredients

- 1 bag frozen fries
- 1/2 cup oil (canola, avocado, or similar)
- 1 teaspoon seasoning salt

Instructions

1. Preheat your griddle for 15-20 minutes on medium-low heat.
2. Apply a thick coating of oil to the griddle. don't cut corners! by collecting handfuls of fries and distributing them over the griddle in a single layer, the fries will be equally distributed. if you pour the entire frozen bag on the griddle, the griddle may get deformed.
3. Use your cover if you have one. it's quite ok if you don't the key to excellent griddle fries is to avoid overworking them. that is, set the spatula down and wait until they are golden before flipping them.
4. Continue until all sides are crispy to your liking

Blackstone Bacon Cheeseburger

Ground american wagyu beef, kurobuta bacon, and sharp melted cheddar cheese go into this burger. please, no more bacon, and no veggies!

cooking time: 25 minutes

Servings: 6

Ingredients

- 3 pounds ground waygu beef
- salt and pepper
- 12 pieces kurobuta bacon
- 6 slices aged sharp cheddar
- 6 brioche buns
- Toppings of your choosing

Instructions

1. Preheat your griddle over medium heat for 10-15 minutes.form your burger into 6 patties that are slightly bigger than your buns and have a depression in the centre while the griddle heats up.
2. Season the patties on both sides with salt and pepper.toast your buns while the bacon cooks. if your griddle is large enough, you may begin cooking the burgers once the bacon is approximately halfway done.
3. Cook the burgers for 4-5 minutes on each side, or until they reach a temperature of 145° for medium-rare and 160° for medium. (if you're using a high-quality burger, you can cook it to this temperature, but if you're worried about food poisoning, proceed with caution.)
4. Top the burgers with cheese pieces and a big dome to melt during the last 3 minutes of cooking.
5. Assemble the dish, then top with your favorite condiments and serve!

Blackstone Griddle Bacon Blue Cheese Burger

Ground american wagyu beef, kurobuta bacon, and crumbled melty blue cheese make up this blackstone burger. All of this is sandwiched between two toasted brioche buns for a burger that may possibly be the ideal blue cheese burger.

cooking time: 25 minutes

Servings: 6

Ingredients

- 3 pounds ground waygu beef
- salt and pepper
- 12 pieces kurobuta bacon
- 1 1/2 cups crumbled blue cheese
- 6 brioche buns
- toppings of your choosing

Instructions

1. Preheat your griddle over medium heat for 10-15 minutes.
2. Form your burger into 6 patties that are slightly bigger than your buns and have a depression in the centre while the griddle heats up.
3. Season the patties on both sides with salt and pepper. toast your buns while the bacon cooks. if your griddle is large enough, you may begin cooking the burgers once the bacon is approximately halfway done.
4. Cook the burgers for 4-5 minutes on each side, or until they reach a temperature of 145° for medium-rare and 160° for medium. (if you're using a high-quality burger, you can cook it to this temperature, but if you're worried about food poisoning, proceed with caution.)
5. Top the burgers with blue cheese crumbles and a big dome to melt during the last 3 minutes of cooking.
6. Assemble the dish, then top with your favorite condiments and serve!

Blackstone Smashed Potatoes

These soft baby potatoes are salt boiled before being crushed and fried on the blackstone griddle until the skin is a crisy, delectable crust. These soft baby potatoes are salt boiled before being crushed and fried on the blackstone griddle until the skin is a crisy, delectable crust.

cooking time: 40 minutes

Servings: 6

Ingredients

- 1 pound baby potatoes
- kosher salt
- rosemary
- 4 tablespoons oil
- 4 tablespoons butter

Instructions

1. Pre-cook your young potatoes until fork-tender in well-salted water.drain the potatoes and dry them for 60 minutes on a baking sheet coated with paper towels.
2. If you want to speed up the drying process or add a little smoke to the mix, set your oven or pellet grill to 180-200 degrees. using this way, cook them for around 20-30 minutes.
3. Preheat your griddle to medium to medium-low heat after the potatoes are dry. place the potatoes on the frying surface with some oil and butter, allowing about 2 inches between each potato.
4. Squish the potatoes down with a hefty spatula or griddle press so that more of the surface touches the griddle.

5. Season with salt and pepper and fry for a few minutes, or until the bottoms are golden brown.
6. Drizzle a little oil over the top of the potatoes, and if required, add more butter to the griddle, before flipping the potatoes to fry and crisp up the other side.
7. Remove to a platter and top with a sprinkling of chopped rosemary before serving.

Blackstone Chicken with Mushroom Gravy

The blackstone is used to make this buttery sautéed chicken, which is then drowned in mushroom gravy

cooking time: 35 minutes

Servings: 8

Ingredients

- 2 large boneless skinless chicken breasts
- 1 teaspoon avocado oil
- 1/4 teaspoon salt
- 1/4 teaspoon onion powder
- 1/4 teaspoon garlic powder
- 1/4 teaspoon black pepper

Instructions

1. Preheat your flat top griddle on medium-low heat after turning it on.
2. Preheat a medium-sized cast iron pan on the griddle surface at the same time.while you're waiting for the griddle to heat up, brush your chicken breasts with oil and season them with the dry seasonings.
3. After the griddle has heated up, place your chicken breasts on it and cook for six minutes on each side.
4. After chicken breasts have attained an internal temperature of at least 165 degrees fahrenheit, they are safe to consume.
5. While the breasts are cooking, sauté the mushrooms in the cast iron pan with 1/4 teaspoon of salt and 1 tablespoon of butter.
6. While the mushrooms are cooking,
7. Keep stirring them.
8. Cook until all of the juices have evaporated.
9. When the mushrooms are done, add the remaining butter and flour to the pan and simmer for three minutes to reduce the liquid

Blackstone Blackened Shrimp Caesar Wrap

Our blackened shrimp caesar wrap mixes blackened shrimp with fresh caesar dressing and a wrap to create a tasty and quick lunch!

cooking time: 20 minutes

Servings: 4

Ingredients

- 1 pound peeled and deveined shrimp
- 1 tablespoon cajun blackening season
- 1/2 teaspoon salt
- 1/4 teaspoon cayenne pepper
- 1 tablespoon olive oil
- 1 small cucumber
- 1 medium tomato
- 1/2 cup creamy caesar dressing
- 1 head romaine lettuce
- 4 large tortilla shells
- 1 tablespoon shredded parmesan

Instructions

1. To begin, cut the tomato and cucumber into 1/2" pieces and leave them. set aside your romaine lettuce, which should be chopped into 1-1 1/2" pieces.
2. Clean your shrimp by rinsing them and patting them dry with a paper towel before placing them in a medium-sized mixing dish.
3. Toss the shrimp in the basin with the cajun spice, salt, and cayenne pepper until they are uniformly covered.
4. Preheat your griddle over medium heat, then pour in the olive oil and distribute it evenly across the top.
5. Place all of the shrimp on the griddle with the olive oil and cook for 1 1/2 to 2 minutes.
6. Cook for another 1 1/2 to 2 minutes on the other side after flipping the shrimp.
7. Remove the shrimp from the griddle and set aside for 10 minutes to cool. while the shrimp is cooling, soften the tortillas on the griddle.it's time to start assembling your wraps after the shrimp have cooled.
8. In a large mixing dish, combine the lettuce, cucumber, and tomato, as well as the shrimp. toss in the caesar dressing until well combined.
9. One of the tortillas should be placed on a level surface. top the tortilla with a portion of the salad and a sprinkle of parmesan cheese. wrap everything up carefully, being sure to retain all of the contents within the tortilla.
10. Enjoy your wrap by cutting it in half at a 45-degree angle.

Blackstone Stromboli or Calzone

If you use pre-made pizza dough, this easy blackstone calzone or stromboli recipe will have supper on the table in 30 minutes, and you can fill them with a limitless variety of kid-friendly fillings

cooking time: 35 minutes

Servings: 4

Ingredients

- 1 ball pizza dough
- 1 batch pizza sauce
- 2 tablespoons oil

PIZZA TOPPINGS SUCH AS:

- pepperoni
- ham
- pineapple
- onion
- mushroom
- green peppers
- black olives
- ground beef

Instructions

1. Preheat your blackstone to a low heat setting. for stromboli, roll out the pizza dough into a huge rectangle, or two large circles for calzones.
2. Cover the dough with a thin coating of sauce, leaving the edges free of sauce so they can seal properly.
3. Put your favorite toppings and cheese inside. for a stromboli, roll it up, or fold it over for a calzone. wet the edges and fully seal them.
4. Place on a cutting board lined with parchment paper and set aside.
5. Place the oil on the griddle and spread it out so that your entire stromboli or calzone fits on the greased surface.
6. Roll the stromboli using the parchment paper as a sling, or cover the dough (seam-side-down for stromboli).
7. Allow them fry for a few minutes, until gently browned, before flipping.return the stromboli to the pan and continue to flip until both sides are golden brown.
8. Place the calzone or stromboli on a wire rack after both sides are browned, then cover with a lid and continue to cook until the internal temperature reaches 200° and the dough is cooked within.
9. Remove from the oven and serve with the remaining sauce for dipping!

Blackstone Crab Scampi Recipe

While cooking on a gas griddle, steamed crab is covered with garlic, butter, and white wine. the sauce seeps into the crab's nooks and crevices, infusing it with flavor

cooking time: 6 minutes

Servings: 6

Ingredients

- 6 pounds pre-cooked crab
- 1 cup melted salted butter
- 2 teaspoons kosher salt
- 1 tablespoon old bay seasoning blend
- 2 tablespoons minced garlic
- 1 cup dry white wine

Instructions

1. Preheat the griddle to medium-high heat.season the crab with salt and old bay and toss it on the griddle to coat. the garlic should be spooned on first, followed by the butter.
2. Cook for a minute, moving the crabs and garlic butter about on the griddle with the tons.
3. Cover and steam for 2-3 minutes after pouring the wine over the crab.
4. Continue scraping and spooning the wine/garlic/butter sauce over the top of the crabs with a bench scraper.
5. Remove from the oven and serve immediately!

Blackstone Monte Cristo

This tasty monte cristo is prepared right on your blackstone griddle! this famous diner sandwich is made comprised of ham, cheese, and (essentially) french toast. don't forget about the raspberry preserves!

cooking time: 25 minutes

Servings: 6

ingredients

- 4 eggs
- 1/3 cup half and half
- 12 pieces of white bread
- 2 tablespoons mayo
- 2 tablespoons mustard
- 18 thin slices swiss or gruyere cheese
- 2 pounds deli thin-sliced ham
- Powdered sugar
- Raspberry jam

Instructions

1. Preheat your griddle on a low heat setting. in a large shallow bowl, whisk together the eggs and half

and half until well blended. one side of your bread should be drenched in egg wax.

2. Place in a single layer on a parchment-lined baking sheet, eggy side down. 1 teaspoon mayo and 1 teaspoon mustard on each sandwich bread pair, mayo on one and mustard on the other.

3. On each slice of bread, place one piece of cheese. distribute the ham evenly across the 12 slices of bread.

4. Place one half of each sandwich bread pair with the remaining 6 pieces of cheese. (each sandwich should include three slices of cheese.) to construct whole sandwiches, join the sandwich pieces together.

5. Butter the griddle well and arrange the sandwiches on it. cover with a big spatula and gently press down.

6. Cook until the bread is toasted and the egg mixture is set, then turn it and cook until browned on the other side.

7. Remove from the oven, sprinkle with powdered sugar, and serve with raspberry jam on the side.

Blackstone Sausage and Egg Loaded Hash Browns

Sausage and egg loaded hash browns are loaded with scrambled eggs and sautéed sausage, tons of cheese, and then sandwiched with additional crispy hash browns on your gas griddle!

cooking time: 25 minutes

Servings: 6

ingredients

- 3 cups dehydrated hash browns
- 3 cups hot water
- 1/4 cup finely diced onions (optional)
- 1/4 cup butter
- 1/2 pound breakfast sausage links, sliced
- 6 eggs, whisked
- 1/4 cup whole milk
- 1/4 - 1/3 cup oil
- Salt, pepper, and garlic
- 2 cups shredded cheddar cheese

Instructions

1. In a dish, combine the hash browns and the boiling water, and soak for

15 minutes. remove any surplus water.

2. Preheat your gas griddle over medium-low heat while the hash browns soak. cook the onions for 3-4 minutes with roughly a tablespoon of butter.

3. Place the hash browns on the griddle and drizzle a tablespoon or two of oil over them.

4. Set aside some additional butter to brown the sliced sausages and scramble the eggs while the hashbrowns are cooking.

5. If you want to, you can do it jointly.

6. Cook the hash browns for several minutes, or until a golden-brown crust forms on the bottom.

7. If you flip or check too often, the browning process will be interfered with. with a big spatula, flip the pancakes and sprinkle with extra oil.

8. Top half of them with the eggs, sausage, and cheese after the bottom side is done.

9. Lightly press down to somewhat flatten it. half of the hashbrowns should be on top. if desired, top with more cheese and melt on a low heat setting on the griddle.

10. Cook, stirring occasionally, until the cheese has melted. serve immediately!

Blackstone Griddle Eggs in a Basket

Breakfast does not have to be difficult. in virtually little time, you can make something that the whole family will love

cooking time: 15 minutes

Servings: 6

ingredients

- 6 slices bread
- 6 tablespoons butter
- 6 fresh eggs
- salt and pepper
- canola oil, for the griddle

Instructions

1. Preheat your blackstone griddle at a low heat setting.while the griddle heats up, butter both sides of your bread and use a serrated knife to delicately cut off the centre of each slice. you'll be toasting these pieces on the griddle, so keep them safe! bring your eggs and bread to the griddle and set the bread on it.

2. Allow the first side of the bread to toast before flipping it over. both sides of the cut-out pieces should be toasted.

3. Fill each hole with an egg, season with salt and pepper, and cover with a big lid or melting dome (s).
4. Cook until the whites are firm but the yolks are still runny, about 5 minutes. only flip if you're extremely daring, as there's a good risk the yolk may break.

Blackstone Teriyaki Steak Yakisoba

This tasty beef teri-yakisoba is made with a ton of onions, bell peppers, pea pods, and fresh yakisoba noodles in a stir fry. dinner alternative that is really quick and simple!

cooking time: 25 minutes

Servings: 8

ingredients

- 16 ounces fresh steak
- 1 bottle iron chef sesame garlic sauce
- 4 tablespoons oil
- 1/2 cup sliced onions
- 1 cup asparagus, cut into 1" pieces
- 1 sliced bell pepper
- 1 cup sugar snap pea pods
- 1 cup sliced mushrooms
- 17 ounces fresh yakisoba noodles

Instructions

1. Cut your steaks against the grain and toss with half of your sauce. refrigerate for 4 hours before serving.
2. Cut the onions, peppers, and mushrooms into thin slices. prepare all of your vegetables ahead of time.
3. Preheat your griddle to medium-high heat, add 1 tablespoon of oil and a splash of sesame oil to the griddle, and immediately stir-fry the veggies until they are crisp-tender (about 3-4 minutes).
4. Remove the griddle from the heat, cover, and put aside.
5. On the griddle, heat another tablespoon of oil and toss in the noodles. stir fried the meat on the other side of the grill.
6. Cook for another 1-2 minutes before combining and tossing with the veggies.
7. Turn off the griddle and pour the remaining sauce on top.toss the noodles, pork, and veggies together in a mixing bowl.

Blackstone Marinated Portabella Mushrooms

Before being flash grilled on the flat top griddle, portabella mushrooms are marinated in a shoyu and red wine vinegar marinade with fresh herbs.

cooking time: 45 minutes

Servings: 8

Ingredients

- 2 large portobello mushrooms
- 2 tablespoons olive oil
- 1 tablespoon red wine vinegar
- 1 tablespoon cherry blossom shoyu
- 1/4 teaspoon salt
- 1/4 teaspoon pepper
- 1 tablespoon butter

Instructions

1. Remove the stems from the mushrooms and scrape away all of the gills from beneath the cap.
2. Drizzle olive oil over the top and bottom of the mushroom cap, then arrange top-down and season with salt, pepper, vinegar, and shoyu.
3. Cover and marinate for 30 minutes in the refrigerator.
4. Carefully set the mushrooms on the prepared medium-high griddle, being careful not to spill the marinade.
5. Place the butter in the middle of the caps and close them. allow for four minutes of cooking time.
6. Remove the lid and continue to cook for another minute.
7. Using a knife or a bench scraper, cut the caps into slices. the marinade will overflow onto the griddle, creating a large sauce.
8. Cook for another minute, then remove from the griddle and, if desired, scrape off any remaining sauce eat!

Blackstone Sirloin Cap Steak Recipe

Our blackstone top sirloin cap steak is tender, flavorful, and incredibly simple to prepare! break out the butter and a little s&p and fire up that griddle!

cooking time: 15 minutes

Servings: 6

Ingredients

- Salt
- Pepper
- Butter

- Top sirloin cap steak

Instructions

1. Direct sear method preheat the blackstone to a medium setting. season your steak with salt and pepper before grilling it.
2. Allow it to sit for a few minutes! you'll need some time for the crust to form. during the cooking process, though, dollop some butter around it.
3. Turn the steak over and heat until a crust forms on the second side as well more butter, flipping, and sizzling until the steak reaches the temperature you wish.
4. For the greatest results, use a meat thermometer until you develop a feel for things. for a medium-rare steak when sliced, the temperature should be around 125° when you pull it.
5. Sear in the backwards direction season your meat and smoke it at 180°-200° on a smoker.
6. Allow the steak to reverse sear for approximately an hour, or until it reaches an internal temperature of 120 degrees.
7. Remove the meat from the pellet grill or smoker and place it on a prepared flat top griddle set to medium to high heat.
8. Allow for a crust to form by searing for 2-3 minutes per side.

Blackstone Steak Bites

Tender steak chunks are marinated in a soy, pineapple, and garlic sauce that also serves as the dish's sauce!

cooking time: 35 minutes

Servings: 6

Ingredients

- 1 1/2 pounds steak, cut into 1" cubes
- 1 tablespoon oil
- SAUCE
- 1 cup soy sauce
- 1/3 cup vegetable oil
- 1/2 cup pineapple juice
- 2 tablespoons honey
- 1 1/2 teaspoons sriracha sauce, or a little more if you like it spicier!
- 1 1/2 teaspoons minced garlic
- 1 tablespoon corn starch
- 1/2 Cup of cold water Top sirloin cap steak

Instructions

1. Direct sear method preheat the blackstone to a medium setting. season your steak with salt and pepper before grilling it.
2. Allow it to sit for a few minutes! you'll need some time for the crust to form. during the cooking process,

though, dollop some butter around it.

3. Turn the steak over and heat until a crust forms on the second side as well more butter, flipping, and sizzling until the steak reaches the temperature you wish.

4. For the greatest results, use a meat thermometer until you develop a feel for things. for a medium-rare steak when sliced, the temperature should be around 125° when you pull it.

5. Sear in the backwards direction season your meat and smoke it at 180°-200° on a smoker.

6. Allow the steak to reverse sear for approximately an hour, or until it reaches an internal temperature of 120 degrees.

7. Remove the meat from the pellet grill or smoker and place it on a prepared flat top griddle set to medium to high heat.

8. Allow for a crust to form by searing for 2-3 minutes per side.

Betty's Italian Meatballs

cooking time: 15 minutes

Servings: 6

Ingredients

- 1 lb ground meat, meatball mixture of beef, pork & veal
- 1/2 c bread crumb, fresh cubed stale bread crust removed or panko
- 1/4 c milk
- 1 egg
- 2 garlic cloves, grated
- 1/2 c fresh grated pecorino romano or parmesan cheese
- 2 tbs flat leaf Italian parsley, chopped
- 1 tsp extra virgin olive oil
- salt and pepper to taste

Instructions

1. In a large mixing bowl, combine bread crumbs and milk. Allow the milk to absorb into the bread.Combine the ground meat mixture and the remaining ingredients in a mixing bowl.

2. Mix all of the ingredients together with your hands, being careful not to overmix.

3. Meatballs should be rolled into desired size.

4. Preheat the Blackstone to 325 degrees or medium-medium low heat. Drizzle olive oil on the griddle and place meatballs in it.

5. Cook meatballs until browned on all sides, flipping once. Cook for about 8-10 minutes, depending on the size of the meatballs.

6. Serve meatballs when fully cooked, or brown them on each side and

finish cooking them in your favorite pasta sauce, as seen in the video.

Betty's Burger Fry & Vegetable Sauce

cooking time: 5 minutes

Servings: 6

Ingredients

- 1 c Dukes mayonnaise
- ½ c Ketchup
- ½ c Mustard
- ⅓ c Pickle juice
- 2 tbsp Worcestershire sauce
- 2-4 fresh Garlic cloves, grated
- ½ c White Onion grated
- 2 tsp Paprika
- Salt & Pepper to taste
- 1/2 c Pickles, finely chopped (optional see video)

Instructions

1. Mix all ingredients and enjoy!

NOTE: Keep refrigerated for up to 3 weeks! Burgers, chicken, sandwiches, fries, and grilled vegetables are all delicious!

White BBQ Sauce Chicken Party Platter

cooking time: 240 minutes

Servings: 5

Ingredients

- 3 lb chicken breast
- 1/4 c oil, avocado or extra light tasting olive oil
- 1 tbsp dried parsley
- White BBQ Sauce:
- 2 cups Mayo, Dukes preferred
- 4 fresh Garlic cloves, finely grated
- 3 tbsp fresh squeezed Lemon Juice (or one small lemon)
- 1 tbsp Black Pepper
- 1 tsp Salt
- 1 tsp Sugar
- 1 /3 cup White Wine Vinegar

Instructions

2. Combine all of the ingredients for the White BBQ Sauce and chill for at least 30 minutes before using.
3. Cut chicken into bite-size pieces and marinate in 1/2 cup white bbq sauce, 1/4 cup oil, and dried parsley for 30 minutes to 4 hours. (Or just enough to coat gently)
4. On medium high heat, cook the chicken until it is fully cooked.

5. Serve the chicken with a dipping sauce made from white barbecue sauce.
6. Note: For dipping, serve the chicken with White BBQ Sauce.

Italian Family Style Fish

cooking time: 15 minutes

Servings: 3

Ingredients

- 2 6-8oz fillets of white fish (Mahi Mahi, grouper, halibut)
- 2 pints grape tomatoes
- 4 fresh garlic cloves
- 1 small onion, white or yellow
- 1 green bell pepper
- flat leaf parsley
- fresh basil
- ½ cup extra virgin olive oil
- ¼ c Blackstone loaded Italian sear and serve (optional)
- Salt and pepper to taste
- Crusty Italian Bread

Instructions

1. Tomatoes should be cut in half or quarters. Cut onions and peppers into dice, using as much or as little of each onion and pepper as you like. Garlic should be smashed and severely chopped.
2. Preheat a cast iron skillet or a disposable aluminum pan to medium heat, large enough to hold the fish (around 350-375). Drizzle in the oil and simmer for 3 minutes with the onions and peppers before adding the garlic, tomatoes, and torn parsley and basil. Season with salt and pepper and toss in the oil to coat. Allow to cook, covered with a lid or dome, for a few minutes, checking and stirring.
3. In the meantime, blot the fish dry with paper towels, sprinkle with olive oil, and season with salt and freshly cracked black pepper. Sear the presentation side for 1-2 minutes, then turn and sear for another 1-2 minutes before placing the fish in the center of the tomatoes, covering and allowing the fish to cook through while the tomatoes cook down.
4. Serve with Italian bread for scooping and garnished with basil.

Party Peppers

cooking time: 25 minutes

Servings: 8

Ingredients

- 1 lb Bag Sweet Mini Peppers, or Jalapeño
- 1 lb Sweet Italian Sausage
- 1 block Cream Cheese, softened

- 1 cup Parmesan Romano Cheese
- 1 cup Sharp Cheddar Cheese, grated
- 1 cup Mexican Blend Cheese, grated
- 2 Garlic Cloves, grated
- Salt and Pepper

Instructions

1. 1 pound sweet Italian sausage, cooked and crumbled on your Blackstone Griddle, drained and placed in a large mixing dish. Combine the cheeses, garlic, and cooked sausage in a mixing bowl and season with salt and pepper to taste.
2. Slice peppers in half, removing any membrane and seeds but leaving the stems on for display and as a handle.
3. Fill peppers with sausage mixture. Refrigerate the peppers until ready to use!
4. Cook for 10 minutes in a Blackstone airfryer at 375°F, or until heated through and bubbling, and peppers are tender to your taste, checking every few minutes. Serve immediately, garnished with parsley.
5. Hot Italian sausage is a good choice for spicy peppers. This is a terrific make-ahead snack that can be kept in the fridge until ready to cook for a quick and easy appetizer!

Sesame Green Beans

cooking time: 15 minutes

Servings: 6

Ingredients

- 2lb Green Beans, fresh
- Seasoned Wok Oil
- Blackstone All Purpose Seasoning
- 4-6 fresh Garlic Cloves, minced or grated
- Sesame Oil
- Sesame Seeds
- Salt and Pepper

Instructions

1. Toss fresh green beans lightly and evenly in seasoned wok oil.
2. Add the green beans to a preheated Blackstone griddle over medium heat. Every few minutes, tossing. Season to taste with salt and pepper, as well as a thin dusting of Blackstone's All Purpose Seasoning.
3. When the green beans are nearly done, mix in the fresh garlic and continue to cook until the green beans are done to your preference. Mine has a small crunch to it, which I like.
4. Serve green beans with a small drizzle of sesame oil and a scattering of sesame seeds on top.

5. If you have Kewpie Mayonnaise on hand, pour it across the top or along the side for dipping!

Quick Pickled Red Onions

cooking time: 10 minutes

Servings: 1

Ingredients

- 1-2 red onions, sliced or chopped
- 1 c water boiling
- ½ c white distilled vinegar
- ¾ c apple cider vinegar
- 6 sprigs of dill, torn of fresh (2 tbsp dried)
- 3 tsp salt
- 2 tsp peppercorns
- 2 tbsp sugar
- 3 whole garlic cloves
- 4 bay leaves
- 32 oz glass jar

Instructions

1. To fill the jar, cut enough red onions. Whether sliced or chopped, the choice is yours.
2. Bring the vinegar and water to a boil. Salt and sugar can be added to dissolve in the boiling fluid or added in layers as the jar is filled.
3. Layer and stuff everything down tight. 13 onions and 13 seasonings, including garlic, bay leaves, and dill
4. Fill the jar with boiling liquid and rapidly seal and close it tightly. Shake the jar gently. Allow 30 minutes to cook on the counter.
5. Enjoy your meal once it's finished cooking!
6. Notes: Keep refrigerated for up to two weeks. Tacos, nachos, sandwiches, pizzas, eggs, and more can all benefit from the addition of onions.
7. If desired, add hot peppers or dried pepper flakes to spice up the onions.
8. Depending on how vinegary you like them, you can adjust the water to vinegar ratio.

Cheeseburger Filled Homemade Eggrolls

cooking time: 1Hr 10 minutes

Servings: 2

Ingredients

- 1 lb beef (ground, shaped into balls or burger patties)
- ½ to 1 lb cheese, American preferred
- 1 Onion, chopped

- Blackstone Whiskey Burger Seasoning
- 1 tbsp Butter, unsalted
- 1 tbsp Olive Oil
- Oil for frying
- Wrappers
- 2 cups all purpose Flour, sifted
- 1 large Egg
- ¼-½ c Water
- ¾ tsp Salt
- Cornstarch
- Betty's Burger Sauce
- 1 c Dukes Mayonnaise
- ½ c Ketchup
- ½ c Mustard
- ⅓ c Pickle Juice
- 2 tbsp Worcestershire Sauce
- 2-4 fresh Garlic cloves, grated
- ½ c White Onion grated
- 2 tsp Paprika
- 1 tsp Salt, or to taste
- 1 tsp Pepper, or to taste

Instructions

1. Set aside soft flour in a large mixing bowl.
2. In a separate bowl, whisk together the egg, salt, and water, then add to the sifted flour. Begin incorporating ingredients with a rubber spatula. See the video for more information.
3. Using cornstarch, lightly dust a clean counter or work surface. Knead in the egg roll mixture for 10-15 minutes. Place dough in a bowl, cover with a moist towel, and let aside for 40 minutes on the kitchen counter.

4. Preheat the Blackstone to medium-high heat and melt the butter with the olive oil before adding the chopped onions. Cook for 3 minutes, tossing the onions in the butter and oil to coat them, seasoning with your favorite Blackstone seasoning.
5. Add the beef to the onions and smash with the Blackstone burger press if using patties or balls. Season with Blackstone seasoning to taste. Flip the meat and top with the desired amount of cheese. Then break apart the meat with a scraper or spatula and mix in the onions. Remove the pan from the heat and set it aside to cool.
6. After the 40 minutes have passed and the meat has cooled, cut a piece of egg roll dough the size of a golf ball and roll it thin on a cornstarch dusted surface. The dough can be rolled out to any size you want, from micro to huge.
7. To learn how to make egg rolls, watch the video below. Place the meat on top, along with any more cheese if wanted, and roll it up.
8. Using a mixture of water and cornstarch, caulk the edges. Rep until all of the meat has been used.
9. Preheat the Blackstone to medium-low to low heat, then drizzle just enough oil into each egg roll. Allow eggrolls to cook low and slow, flipping tongs to crisp each side to a golden brown color. Egg rolls can also be made in the Blackstone airfryer. Lightly coat each side with

oil and cook on medium for about 5 minutes, or until golden brown.

10. Enjoy your eggrolls with burger sauce!

11. Burger sauce can be stored in the refrigerator for up to three weeks. If desired, garnish with sliced pickles. Try it with fries, vegetables, crab cakes, and other dishes.

Pineapple Sriracha Chicken Nachos

cooking time: 25 minutes

Servings: 4

Ingredients

- ½ lb Chicken, chopped
- ½ lb Shrimp, wild caught, chopped
- BLACKSTONE Pineapple Sriracha Seasoning
- 2 tbsp Olive oil, divided
- 1 bag Tortilla chips
- 1 C White Cheddar, hand grated
- 1 C Sharp Cheddar, hand grated
- 1 Jalapeños, sliced
- 1 cup crushed Pineapple
- ¾ c BBQ Sauce
- ¼ c Sriracha
- 1 tbsp Honey
- 1 c Guacamole
- 1 bunch Cilantro, chopped
- ¼ c Red Onions, chopped

Instructions

1. Chop the chicken into small pieces and combine with 1 tablespoon of oil and seasoning in a mixing bowl. Refrigerate for 20 minutes after covering. Rep with the shrimp. If the shrimp are little, they can be left whole.

2. Combine bbq sauce, sriracha, and honey in a mixing bowl.

3. Cook the chicken and shrimp separately on the BLACKSTONE over medium heat. Turn the chicken using spatulas to sear each side. Total time is about 4-5 minutes. Shrimp will take about 2-3 minutes to cook in total.

4. 1 minute per side on the griddle, remove and set aside jalapeo slices

5. To crisp and warm tortilla chips, place them in air fryer drawers prepared to high heat for 2-3 minutes. Remove the chips from the griddle and immediately cover with half of the shredded cheeses in an aluminum tray over low heat.

6. Drizzle the barbeque sauce all over the nachos.

7. Place the chicken and shrimp on top of the chips that have been laid out. Season with salt and pepper. Toss in the remaining cheese.

8. Crushed pineapple, onions, cilantro, and jalapeos are strewn out on top of the nachos. In the center, place guacamole and sour cream. Enjoy!

Smashed Potatoes on the Blackstone

cooking time: 20 minutes

Servings: 4

Ingredients

- 1.5 lb bag of your favorite baby Potatoes
- 2 tbsp extra virgin Olive Oil
- 2 tbsp Butter, melted
- 2 tbsp Pecorino Romano or Parmesan cheese
- 1 tbsp Blackstone Steakhouse Seasoning
- 1 tbsp flat leaf Parsley, chopped
- Drizzle of olive oil for potatoes
- Butter for griddle

Instructions

1. After washing the potatoes, pierce them twice with a fork and set them in a microwave-safe dish. Microwave potatoes until cooked through on the baked potato option, or until a toothpick inserted into the center comes out clean. *Potatoes can also be boiled till tender.
2. To keep the potatoes warm, brush them with a little oil and wrap them in plastic wrap until ready to crush on the griddle.

3. Combine the olive oil, butter, cheese, spice, and parsley in a small mixing bowl.

Cheesesteak & Eggs

cooking time: 25 minutes

Servings: 3

Ingredients

- 1-1.5 lb boneless Ribeye steak
- 4-6 eggs
- 3 tbsp Half and Half
- deli thin sliced American cheese, Boar's head
- deli thin sliced Provolone cheese, Boar's head
- 1 small Sweet Onion, diced
- 1 tbsp oil
- Salt and Pepper to taste
- Italian Roll, bagel or bread of choice
- Sriracha Ketchup, optional
- ¼ c Ketchup
- ¼ c Sriracha

Instructions

1. Place the ribeye in the freezer for 15 minutes, then take it and shave or slice it into strips as thinly as possible. The less fat you have, the better.

2. In a bowl, whisk together the eggs and milk and leave aside.
3. oil over medium-high heat and add onion. Cook for 3 minutes or until onions are transparent, then set aside to keep warm, leaving the oil behind.
4. Increase the heat to high and add the shaved ribeye. Tear apart meat into tiny pieces with two spatulas or a scraper, moving it around constantly for a rapid cook while enabling the meat to brown. Approximately 3-5 minutes.
5. Reduce the heat to low and stir in the onions. Salt & pepper to taste. Spread the steak out in a broad circle on the griddle, then add the eggs, turn off the heat, and gently scramble the eggs and meat together. Adding the necessary amount of cheese and allowing it to melt completely.
6. Serve in an Italian hoagie roll or make a panini-style sourdough sandwich on a griddle. Drizzle sriracha ketchup across toasted and buttered bread for scooping, and enjoy!

Feta Pasta with Shrimp

cooking time: 20 minutes

Servings: 3

Ingredients

- 1 lb shrimp (substitute protein of choice)
- 8 oz pasta cooked, drained reserve ¾ c pasta water
- 8 oz feta cheese, block
- 2 pints cherry tomatoes
- ½ c extra virgin olive oil
- 4 garlic cloves, smashed and chopped
- Handful each fresh Italian parsley and basil
- Italian blend seasoning
- 1 tsp fennel seed
- 1 tsp minced garlic
- 1 ½ tsp minced onion
- 1 tsp basil
- 1 tsp oregano
- 1 tsp parsley flakes
- 1 ½ crushed red pepper flakes
- ½ tsp salt
- ¼ tsp sugar
- ½ tsp pepper
- ½ tsp celery seed

Instructions

1. To produce an Italian blend, combine the dry ingredients. To store, place in an airtight container.

2. Cook pasta until al dente, then drain and set aside, reserving 12 cup pasta water.
3. Leave the tails on when peeling and butterflying shrimp. Place shrimp on skewers (if desired), drizzle with olive oil, and season with Italian seasoning.
4. Toss tomatoes with a drizzle of olive oil and season with Italian blend in a small roasting pan (or create a roasting boat out of tinfoil to fit in the Blackstone airfryer drawer). Place the feta block in the center of the tomatoes, drizzle with the remaining oil, and season the top of the cheese.
5. In a preheated air fryer drawer set to high heat, combine tomatoes and cheese. Allow for 10 minutes of cooking time.
6. Meanwhile, fry the shrimp for 2-3 minutes per side on medium high heat.
7. Examine the tomatoes and the cheese. The tomatoes should burst or split apart, and the cheese should melt. Cooking time may need to be increased by up to 10 minutes, so check every five minutes.
8. Remove the tomatoes and cheese, add the fresh garlic, and combine the cheese and tomatoes to make your pasta sauce. Pour sauce over cooked pasta and add as much or as little pasta water as needed.

Blackstone Steak Bites

Tender steak chunks are marinated in a soy, pineapple, and garlic sauce that also serves as the dish's sauce

cooking time: 35 minutes

Servings: 6

Ingredients

- 1 1/2 Pounds Steak, Cut Into 1" Cubes
- 1 Tablespoon Oil

SAUCE

- 1 cup soy sauce
- 1/3 cup vegetable oil
- 1/2 cup pineapple juice
- 2 tablespoons honey
- 1 1/2 teaspoons sriracha sauce, or a little more if you like it spicier!
- 1 1/2 teaspoons minced garlic
- 1 tablespoon corn starch
- 1/2 cup cold water

Instructions

1. In a 1-gallon ziplock bag, combine all ingredients and marinate the steak for 36-48 hours in the refrigerator. when you're ready to cook, take the steak out of the marinade and place it in a bowl to set aside.

2. Pour the marinade into a medium saucepan and bring to a simmer over medium heat.
3. Cook for another 5 minutes, then remove from the heat. combine 1/2 cup cold water and 1 tablespoon corn starch in a mixing bowl and stir until no lumps remain.
4. Stir the slurry into the boiling sauce and cook until it has thickened slightly.
5. Remove the pan from the heat and set it aside.
6. Preheat your flat-top griddle to medium. place a small amount of oil on the pan and cook the steak for no more than 4-5 minutes.
7. Make sure you don't overcook it! remove the griddle from the heat and serve over rice.
8. Drizzle the sauce on top of the chicken.

Griddle Cloud Eggs

Griddle cloud eggs contain a runny egg yolk and fluffy egg whites. Egg whites have been beaten to a stiff peak, seasoned to perfection, dusted with parmesan cheese, cooked somewhat, then the yolk has been added to the middle and cooked a bit Longer.

cooking time: 5 minutes

Servings: 4

Ingredients

- Egg, large 1 each
- Parmesan cheese 1/2 teaspoon

Instructions

1. Reduce the heat to the lowest setting on the griddle. There are no wind guards to be used.
2. Separate the egg whites from the yolks in separate basins. whip the egg whites for about 90 seconds with a hand mixer until firm peaks form. please don't overmix place a sheet of parchment paper on the flat top of a warm griddle.
3. Scoop the fluffy egg white into a mound on the parchment paper. To construct a nest shape, cut a small hole in the center of the whites.
4. On top of the white, sprinkle the parmesan cheese and seasonings.
5. Cook for 2 minutes with a dome on top. Uncover the egg yolk and lay it in the center of the fluffy egg white.
6. Replace the lid and cook for a further 2 minutes, or until the whites are golden brown and the yolk is set transfer the cloud egg to a serving plate using a spatula.

Blackstone Fish Tacos

Seasoned fresh fish is placed on the gas flat top griddle for one of the greatest fish tacos you'll ever have. the peach salsa is the cherry on top. Bright, fresh, and bursting with flavor. try them out right now!

cooking time: 25 minutes

Servings: 6

Ingredients

- 1 1/2 pound white fish (we used cobia)
- 4 tablespoons butter
- 1 tablespoon olive oil
- 1 teaspoon salt
- 1/2 teaspoon pepper
- 1/2 teaspoon granulated garlic
- 1/2 teaspoon onion powder
- 1 tablespoon sugar
- 2 ounces triple sec orange liqueur
- 2 ounces orange juice

GARNISH

- Shredded cabbage
- Hot sauce
- Cilantro (if desired)

Instructions

1. Clean your fish by rinsing it in cold water and patting it dry with paper towels. Prepare the fish by chopping it into 3/4" pieces.
2. Season with salt, pepper, garlic powder, and onion powder, and toss thoroughly.
3. Toss the seasoned fish cubes with the olive oil in a mixing basin until uniformly covered.
4. Preheat your flat top griddle over medium to medium-high heat and place a pat of butter in the center.
5. Spread your fish out over the butter once it starts to bubble allow the butter to brown the bottom of the fish for about 1 1/2 minutes before flipping. After flipping the fish, immediately sprinkle the sugar on top and cook for another 1 1/2 minutes before turning.
6. Pour the orange liqueur and juice over the fish, cover with a melting dome, and heat for an additional minute.
7. Remove the steaks from the grill and stuff them into tortillas. top with shredded cabbage, spicy sauce of your choice, and a generous helping of the peach salsa

Quick Blackstone Runza Recipe

Fill runza with seasoned ground meat, cabbage, onions, and cheese before wrapping them in crescent roll dough and cooking them on your gas griddle.

cooking time: 25 minutes

Servings: 6

Ingredients

- 2 tablespoons butter
- 6 cups shredded cabbage
- 1 large onion, sliced
- 1/2 teaspoon seasoning salt (like lawry's or johnny's)
- 1 pound ground beef (80/20 blend)
- 1/2 teaspoon salt
- 1/2 teaspoon pepper
- 1/2 teaspoon garlic powder
- 1/2 teaspoon onion powder
- 6 slices american cheese (or cheddar if you aren't into american)
- 1 tube crescent roll dough sheet

Instructions

1. Preheat the blackstone to medium-high heat. Place some butter on half of the griddle and fry the onions once they are tender and gently browned, remove them from the griddle.
2. Cook the cabbage on the opposite half of the pan with extra butter. When the onion is softened and cooked, transfer it to the onion dish.
3. Season the ground beef with salt and pepper, then brown it on the blackstone. Place the crescent roll sheet on the griddle after removing it from the fridge.
4. Fill half of it with the filling, leaving space on the sides open.
5. Fold over the second half of the dough sheet and cover with cheese. If you have the talents, flip once. if you don't, cover the runza and turn off the heat.
6. Serve by slicing into pieces.

Blackstone Blackened Shrimp Tacos

Before being folded in a warm tortilla and drizzled in strawberry salsa, quick shrimp tacos are blackened and grilled on the blackstone.

cooking time: 25 minutes

Servings: 6

Ingredients

- Shrimp tacos
- 1 pound peeled and deveined shrimp
- 1 tablespoon cajun blackening seasoning
- 1/2 teaspoon salt
- 1/4 teaspoon cayenne pepper
- 1 cup shredded green cabbage
- 1-2 tablespoons avocado oil
- 8 medium-sized flour tortillas

Instructions

1. Preheat your blackstone over a medium heat setting.
2. Use the blackening seasoning, salt, and cayenne to season your shrimp cook the shrimp for 3-4 minutes, or until they have become pink and are no longer transparent.
3. Remove the tortillas from the griddle and put them on top to

warm them up a bit before stuffing them with shrimp, cabbage, strawberry salsa, and whatever spicy sauce you're bold enough to add on top

Blackstone Philly Cheesesteaks

When you have a blackstone, making delicious handmade philly cheesesteaks is not only doable, but also simple! Gas griddles are one of the most important cooking equipment for achieving restaurant-quality results at home.

cooking time: 15 minutes

Servings: 6

Ingredients

- 3 Pounds Thinly Sliced Ribeye
- 1 Tablespoon OIL
- Salt
- Pepper
- Provolone or cheese whiz
- Buns
- Butter
- Peppers and onions (optional)

Instructions

1. Preheat your gas griddle over medium heat until it reaches the desired temperature.

2. Butter your buns and toast them briefly put some butter on one half of the griddle, along with the onions and peppers if you're going that route, and some oil on the other.
3. Allow it to warm, but not to the point of smoking, before adding the meat season the meat to taste with salt and pepper, and move it about with big metal spatulas as needed.
4. Turn off the griddle after adding the cheese and covering it with a dome. The cheese will be melted by the remaining heat.
5. Fill your buns with cheese-covered ribeye, then top with whichever peppers and onions you desire.

Blackstone Mini Oreo Cheesecakes

A mini oreo cheesecake is a delicious bite-sized treat. This small cheesecake recipe will be the focus of your family gathering if you serve it on a blackstone griddle. Mini cheesecakes can be prepared in advance and stored in the refrigerator until ready to serve. Finish with a swirl of fruit topping or a dollop of whipped cream.

cooking time: 45 minutes

Servings: 4

Ingredients

- Cream Cheese, Softened 8 Oz (226 G)
- Sugar, Granulated 1/4 Cup (1.8 Oz) (51 G)
- Egg, Large 1 Each (1.7 Oz) (48 G)
- Vanilla 1 teaspoon (0.2 oz) (5 g)
- Oreo, golden 9 each (3.8 oz) (109 g)
- Fruit topping 1/3 cup (3.25 oz) (92 g)

Instructions

1. Reduce the heat to low and preheat the griddle to create the cheesecake, gather all of the ingredients.
2. Add the cream cheese to a mixing bowl equipped with a flat paddle and beat on low to break up the cream cheese.
3. Scrape down the sides of the basin and continue mixing for another minute after that, add the sugar, egg, and vanilla extract.
4. Mix on low speed for 5 minutes, or until smooth. Make careful to scrape the bowl's sides as required.
5. If the mixture remains lumpy, increase the speed to medium high (6) and beat until smooth. In a cupcake pan, place 9 paper cupcake liners. toss the golden oreos into the paper liners' bottoms.
6. Add the cheesecake batter to the top of the oreo with a #20 scooper. Preheat the griddle and place the cupcake pan on it.
7. Place a lid on top. Use a big roasting pan, a large foil pan, or a huge dome.

8. Preheat oven to 350°f and bake for 30 minutes. to see how they're doing, check in every 10 minutes.

Blackstone Shrimp Fajitas

Simple shrimp fajitas are cooked in minutes on the blackstone griddle for a quick supper with a lot of flavor.

cooking time: 20 minutes

Servings: 6

Ingredients

- Avocado oil
- 1 green pepper
- 1 yellow pepper
- 1 red pepper
- 1 medium yellow onion
- 3 pounds large raw shrimp (washed, peeled, and deveined)

Pre-made seasoning

- 2 tablespoons spiceology chile margarita

Or use this homemade seasoning

- 1 teaspoon chili powder
- 1/2 teaspoon garlic powder
- 1/2 teaspoon onion powder
- 1/2 teaspoon salt
- 1/4 teaspoon cumin

Instructions

1. Combine the spice ingredients and evenly sprinkle over the shrimp and veggies.
2. Preheat your griddle to medium-high heat and spread some avocado oil on it.
3. Pour the shrimp and veggies onto the griddle and cook for 1-2 minutes, stirring occasionally.
4. Cook until the shrimp is pink and the veggies are crisp-tender, flipping everything over using large spatulas.
5. Serve with warm tortillas with your favorite toppings.

Blackstone Griddle Quesadillas

A flat top griddle is ideal for quesadillas! My blackstone steak quesadillas transform leftover steak into something delicious. Dinner idea that is simple, filling, and kid-friendly

cooking time: 15 minutes

Servings: 6

Ingredients

- 12 Flour Tortillas

- 3 cups cooked steak (approximately. you can use more or less if you'd like!)
- 1 tablespoon chili lime seasoning (or your favorite
- 3 cups shredded mexican-blend cheese
- oil for greasing the griddle

Instructions

1. Preheat the griddle to medium-to-medium-high.
2. Apply a thin layer of oil to the griddle, then set the remaining steak on top and season with the chili lime spice.
3. Cook for 1-2 minutes, just long enough to bring it to room temperature add a little more oil to the pan, then top with a tortilla, cheese, meat, more cheese, and another tortilla.
4. Cook for 2-3 minutes with a melted lid on the quesadilla cook for a further 2-3 minutes on the other side, and then continue until all of the quesadillas are done.

Blackstone Vegetable Yakisoba

Broccoli, zucchini, green beans, peppers, and onions abound in this delightful vegetable yakisoba. Keep it vegetarian or add your favorite protein to it!

cooking time: 25 minutes

Servings: 8

Ingredients

Sauce

- 2 tablespoons soy sauce
- 4 tablespoons water
- 2 tablespoons mirin
- 1 teaspoon sesame oil
- 2 teaspoons minced garlic
- 2 teaspoons chili garlic sauce
- 1 teaspoon sriracha
- 2 tablespoons brown sugar
- 1/2 teaspoon ground ginger
- 1 tablespoon cornstarch
- 1 teaspoon canola oil
- Stir-fry
- 3-4 tablespoons oil
- 1/2 cup sliced onions
- 1 sliced bell pepper
- 1 cup chopped broccoli
- 1 cup sliced zucchini
- 1/2 cup matchstick carrots
- 1 handful baby spinach (optional)
- 17 ounces fresh yakisoba noodles

Instructions

1. To make the sauce, add all of the ingredients in a mixing bowl and whisk to incorporate.
2. Remove from the equation.
3. Preheat your griddle to medium-high heat, add 1 tablespoon of oil

and a splash of sesame oil to the griddle, and immediately stir-fry the veggies until they are crisp-tender (about 3-4 minutes).

4. Remove the griddle from the heat, cover, and put aside preheat the griddle with the remaining tablespoon of oil and toss in the noodles, veggies, and shrimp.

5. After a minute of stirring, pour in the sauce stir until the sauce has thickened, keeping as much of it with the noodles as possible (and not running into the oil bucket), and serve right away

6.

Blackstone Griddle Cakes

In just 12 minutes, blackstone griddle cakes are cooked to perfection. Griddle cakes are fast and easy to create for that special occasion when you don't have an oven. Chef sherry's buttercream frosting goes perfectly with this griddle cake recipe.

cooking time: 17 minutes

Servings: 4

Ingredients

- Yellow cake mix 15.25 oz
- Vegetable oil 1/3 cup
- Eggs, large 3 each
- Water 1 cup

Instructions

1. Gather all the ingredients to pre-heat the flat-top, turn the griddle to the lowest setting. In a mixing dish, combine the eggs, oil, cake mix, and water, being careful to follow the guidelines on the package. it's preferable to use a kitchenaid mixer.

2. To help level out the lumps in the batter, mix for 2 minutes coat the insides of your 4 inch round pans with pan oil measure 3 level scoops each pan using a #20 scoop.

3. Using a blackstone griddle to bake place the pan on the griddle, which has been preheated on low, and use a basting cover to thoroughly cover the cake pan. this acts as an oven by trapping heat under the cover, allowing the cake to bake after around 10 minutes, open the lid partially to check on the cake's progress.

4. Check for doneness with a toothpick if it appears to be entirely done. if the cake isn't done, bake it for a few more minutes is the bottom of your cake burning or getting darker than you want it to be? crumple two pieces of foil into a long log each. set the foil pieces in an x on the griddle and place the pan on top of the foil pieces when you're ready to bake your cake.

5. Check to see if your cake pan is level. bake according to the package directions.

6. After the cakes have cooled, take the tops off to ensure that they are all level.

chef sherry's buttercream icing is simple to make and perfect for decorating any cake. get the recipe for buttercream frosting here! this frosting may be made ahead of time and kept in an airtight container. Use a piping bag and a #2d wilton star tip to add the frosting to the cake for a professional finish. To make the cake even more spectacular, sprinkle it with your favorite sprinkles

Blackstone Steak Tacos

These blackstone steak tacos are a tasty, quick, and easy way to make street tacos at home!

cooking time: 5 minutes

Servings: 6

Ingredients

- 2 pounds flank steak
- 1 lime
- 1 teaspoon cumin
- 1 teaspoon salt
- 1 teaspoon pepper
- 1/2 teaspoon cayenne pepper
- 2 tablespoons oil

Instructions

1. In a small dish, combine the dry ingredients and leave aside.
2. Make half-inch slices out of your flank steak.
3. Always cut in the opposite direction of the grain place the meat in a bowl and sprinkle the dry ingredients over the steak strips, mixing well until all of the meat is coated.
4. Wrap your meat in plastic wrap and place it in the fridge for 1 hour preheat your flat top over a high heat source.
5. Place both limes face down on the flat top after cutting them in half pour your oil over the flat top as soon as it reaches temperature, followed by the steak.
6. Spread the meat equally on the frying surface and cook for two minutes before flipping it while the meat is still cooking, remove the lime halves from the grill and squeeze the juice from one of them onto the steak.
7. Allow the meat to finish cooking for another 2-3 minutes before removing it from the pan.
8. Heat up some tortillas by laying them down on the flat top.
9. After around twenty seconds, flip them and after another twenty seconds, pull them.
10. Allow them to linger no longer than that or they will start to burn.
11. Layer some meat slices onto your tortillas, along with whichever taco toppings you choose, and consume

Blackstone Grill Steak

blackstone griddle steak is a quick and easy main entrée that anybody can master in under 15 minutes.

cooking time: 15 minutes

Servings: 1

Ingredients

- 1 steak
- Salt
- Pepper

Instructions

1. Method of searing directly preheat the blackstone to a medium-high temperature.
2. Season your steak with salt and pepper before grilling it.
3. Allow it to build a crust by not touching it for many minutes.
4. Cook, flipping once, until the opposite side acquires a crust and the steak reaches the desired temperature if your steak is unusually thick, like this one is, you'll also want to brown the sides. If the steak is very thick and connected to the bone, such as a tomahawk or cowboy ribeye, decrease the heat to medium-low and cook it with a dome or cover to ensure equal cooking.
5. Sear in the backwards direction season your meat and smoke it at 180°-200° on a smoker.
6. Allow the steak to reverse sear for approximately an Hour, or until it reaches an internal temperature of 120 degrees.
7. Remove the meat from the pellet grill or smoker and place it on a prepared flat top griddle set to medium to high heat.
8. Allow for a crust to form by searing for 2-3 minutes per side

Stuffed Breakfast Croissant with Steak

These simple breakfast sandwiches are tasty and easy to make for a crowd.

cooking time: 20 minutes

Servings: 4

Ingredients

- 4 croissants
- 6 ounces ribeye steak, cooked
- 2 tablespoons butter
- 8 large eggs
- 1/4 cup whole milk
- 1/4 teaspoon black pepper
- 1/4 teaspoon garlic salt
- 4 ounces shredded cheddar cheese

Instructions

1. Place the croissants in the oven and set the temperature to low or warm.
2. Set aside your cooked steak in cubes.
3. In a medium nonstick skillet or on your blackstone griddle, melt the butter over low to medium-low heat.
4. Whisk together your eggs, milk, and salt & pepper while the butter is melting.
5. place the steak in the heated butter and allow it to sizzle for a minute or so.
6. Turn it over.
7. Pour the eggs over the melted butter, and scramble them slowly using a rubber spatula.
8. Toss in the crumbled cheese after flipping once.
9. Cook over low heat, covered, until the cheese has melted and the eggs have set.Take the croissants out of the oven and cut them in half. Inside, stuff the scrambled eggs. Serve immediately

Pulled Pork Grilled Cheese

Ooey gooey grilled cheese sandwiches and amazingly delicious pulled pork!! The greatest grilled cheese is made with sweet and tender pulled pork and deli style cheddar cheese sandwiched between two slices of grilled ciabatta bread.

cooking time: 10 minutes

Servings: 1

Ingredients

- Bread, sliced 2 each
- Cheddar cheese, slice 1 each
- Pulled pork 2 oz
- Butter 1 tablespoon
- Bbq sauce 1 tablespoon

Instruction

1. To make the ideal grilled cheese sandwich, gather all of your components.
2. Begin by buttering one side of each bread slice one of the slices of bread should be turned over so that the butter side is on the bottom and the unbuttered side is facing up.
3. On top of the bread, spread a layer of cheddar cheese after that, top the cheese with a layer of shredded pulled pork.
4. Add a squirt of your favorite bbq sauce to the pulled pork.
5. Finally, lay the buttered side of the second piece of bread on top of the bbq pulled pork.
6. Cook for 2 minutes on each side in a griddle pan over medium-low heat until browned on both sides. If a griddle weight is available, use it.

Bacon Onion Smash Burgers

These simple flat top grilled smash burgers will be the talk of the town at your next dinner party. Make restaurant-quality burgers at home instead of going to the drive-through.

cooking time: 25 minutes

Servings: 8

Ingredients

BACON-WRAPPED ONIONS

- 8 Slices Onions
- 16 Slices thin bacon

Instruction

1. Thinly slice your onion into 1/2" - 3/4" thick pieces make 8 equal-sized balls out of the burgers. season with salt and pepper on the tops. Preheat a griddle, flat top, or cast iron skillet over medium to high heat. Place the burger balls on the grill and break them down with a burger smasher, bacon press, or heavy-duty spatula as soon as possible cook for a few minutes, until a dark brown crust forms, then season the uncooked side of the burger before flipping. Cover with a melted lid (if required) and heat for another couple of minutes, or until the bottom has

created a crust as well remove the pan from the flat top and serve immediately

Kimchi Gyoza Recipe

Homemade kimchi gyoza will take your breath away! It's also a lot easier to construct than you may think, and the folds are simple to master after a few tries

cooking time: 45 minutes

Servings: 4

Ingredients

- 1 package round gyoza wrappers
- 1 pound ground pork
- 1 cup kimchi, chopped
- 1 bunch green onions or scallions (greens only), chopped
- 1 tablespoon minced garlic
- 2 teaspoons sesame oil
- 3 tablespoons soy sauce
- 1 tablespoon mirin
- 1/2 teaspoon gochujang (optional)

Instructions

2. In a large mixing bowl, mix together the ground pork, kimchi, green onions, garlic, sesame oil, soy sauce, mirin, and gochujang (if using). mix everything together with your hands

until everything is uniformly distributed.

3. Remove a wrapper from the packaging with care and dampen the edges. fold a half-circle with a heaping scoop of filling within.
4. Make little pleats in the gyoza's edges and repeat until all of the stuffing is gone. remove from the equation.
5. Preheat your blackstone griddle for 10-15 minutes on low heat. apply a liberal amount of oil to the griddle and set the gyoza seam-side up.
6. Allow to fry for 3-4 minutes, or until golden brown on the bottom prepare a big domed cover and spritz some water over the griddle in the middle of the dumplings.
7. Cover fast to steam.
8. Check the dumplings and listen for the water to evaporate. the interior temperature must be at least 160 degrees fahrenheit. if it isn't, add a little more steam you may brown the other side of the gyoza if you like, but it's not required.
9. Remove from the oven and serve with the dipping sauce.

Smoked Beef Pancit Recipe

On the blackstone griddle, this smoked beef pancit dish stir-fries a delectable and tender smoked beef roast with carrots, cabbage, and green onion before tossing it with rice vermicelli noodles

cooking time: 5 hours 20 minutes

Servings: 6

Ingredients

- 2 pounds whole beef sirloin roast
- 1 tablespoon (or your favorite beef rub)
- 16 ounces rice vermicelli noodles

VEGETABLES

- 8 ounces green cabbage
- 2 whole carrots
- 2 green onions

SAUCE

- 1/4 cup soy sauce
- 1 cup beef stock
- 1 tablespoon sugar
- 1/2 teaspoon black pepper

Instructions

1. Preheat your grill to 225 degrees fahrenheit.
2. Place the steak on the grill after rubbing it. cook for 3-4 hours, or until the roast is probe-tender and the internal temperature reaches 198-202°f.
3. If the roast begins to stall, wrap it and continue cooking to expedite the process. Soak the noodles in water. usually, 10 minutes in hot water is plenty. on the griddle, they'll finish cooking.

4. Slice the green onions (greens and white portions), cabbage, and carrots as the noodles soak. remove from the equation. set aside a mixture of soy sauce, beef stock, sugar, and black pepper.

5. Preheat your griddle to medium-high heat and double-check that you've completed all of your prep work and have everything you'll need.you can't leave a stir fry on the blackstone alone while it's cooking. don't forget the serving tray for when the food is ready.

6. With a few teaspoons of oil, place the carrots and cabbage on the griddle. cook for 2 minutes, turning often, after seasoning with salt and pepper transfer the veggies to a cool portion of the griddle, add a little more oil, and then the drained vermicelli noodles.

7. Pour the sauce over the noodles in little amounts at a time, adding more as needed as the previous amount absorbs into the noodles. add the green onions, sliced stir fry the smoked beef momentarily on another side of the griddle until it is heated through, then combine the veggies and meat place everything on a serving platter and serve.

Duck Fried Rice

Duck fried rice is similar to take-out, except it's done on your gas griddle at home! The blackstone will provide you with your favorite teppanyaki-style fried rice without requiring you to leave your home.

cooking time: 40 minutes

Servings: 6

Ingredients

- 4 Tablespoons canola oil, divided
- 1 small onion, diced
- 1 teaspoon minced garlic
- 2 Duck breasts, diced
- 1 cup frozen peas and carrots
- 3 cups cooked jasmine rice, chilled
- 2 eggs, lightly beaten
- 1/8 cup soy sauce
- 1 teaspoon sesame oil
- Salt and pepper

Instructions

1. Preheat your griddle to medium-high or high heat (you don't want to burn the oil), and pour roughly a tablespoon of oil onto it.
2. Stir in the onions, frozen peas, and carrots until everything is cooked through and the edges are crispy.
3. Cook for 2-3 minutes after adding the duck breast transfer the duck breast and veggies to the side of the griddle that isn't heated (if your griddle has multiple heat zones, turn one down).
4. Remove it off the griddle and place it in a pan if necessary. It should ideally stay warm but not continue to cook.

5. Add extra oil to the griddle and let it to heat up. Add the chilled rice to the pan and break it up with a spatula.

6. Continue to move it across the griddle, covering it evenly with oil and allowing it to brown. During the last minute of cooking, add the garlic. (if necessary, add extra oil at any point during the procedure.)

7. Stir and mix the duck breast, veggies, and rice together until everything is uniformly incorporated.

8. Drizzle the soy sauce and sesame oil on top, stirring and cooking until evenly dispersed.

9. Make a hole in the rice and fill it with a bit extra oil. Inside, crack the eggs, whisk with a spatula, then toss with the rice to incorporate.

Strawberries and Cream Pancakes

cooking time: 45 minutes

Servings: 6

Ingredients:

Pancakes:

- 2/3 cup all purpose flour
- Tsp baking powde
- 1 tbsp suga
- A pinch of salt

- 2 tsp lemon zest
- 5 strawberries chopped into bits
- 1 egg, separated
- 1/2 cup milk
- 1/3 cup ricotta cheese
- 2 tbsp melted butter
- 1tsp pure vanilla extract
- Whipped cream (for finishing)
- Cream Cheese Filling:
- 12 oz cream cheese, room temperature
- 1/4 cup sugar
- 1 cup whipping cream
- 2 tbs lemon juice
- Strawberry Syrup:
- 1 pint of Strawberries cut into to chunks
- 1/4 cup sugar
- 2 tbs lemon Juice

Instructions:

1. Combine all dry ingredients in a mixing basin.

2. In a separate dish, whisk together the egg yolks, milk, ricotta, butter, and vanilla extract.

3. Slowly add the dry ingredients and mix on low until they are thoroughly blended.

4. Whisk the egg whites until firm peaks form, then fold them into the pancake batter carefully. Then fold in the strawberry chunks lightly.

5. Set aside while you make the filling and the syrup.

6. Cream together cream cheese, sugar, and lemon juice in a stand mixer. Reduce the speed to low and fold in the whipped cream.

Refrigerate until your syrup is finished.

7. In a sauce pan, combine the chopped strawberries, sugar, and lemon juice and cook until the liquids have thickened somewhat. It takes around 20-25 minutes.
8. Preheat the griddle to medium.
9. On a griddle, melt a tablespoon of butter.
10. Pour 1/4 cup pancake mix into griddle and heat until bubbles appear and edges begin to brown slightly.
11. Approximately 3–4 minutes Cook for another 3 minutes on the other side.

Grab a platter and begin piling your pancakes once they've all been cooked. Start with a pancake, then put some cream cheese filling on top and sprinkle some strawberry pieces on top. Steps should be repeated until you get a decent stack. Finish with a dollop of whipped cream and the leftover strawberry syrup.

Bacon, Egg, And Cheese Pancake Slider

cooking time: minutes

Servings: 4

Ingredients:

- Pancake mix (follow package directions)
- 6 strips of bacon
- 6 eggs
- 6 slices of cheddar cheese
- 2 TBS butter
- Syrup

Instructions:

1. To create 12 small pancakes, follow the directions on the container of pancake mix.
2. Fry bacon on one side of the griddle top. Cook 12 tiny pancakes on the opposite side.
3. Remove the bacon and set it aside on a paper towel once it has reached the desired crispness.
4. Remove the pancakes from the pan and put them aside.1 at a time, scramble eggs and place onto griddle.
5. When the egg is done, sprinkle it with cheese and cover it with a pot lid or dome to let it melt.
6. Place 6 pancakes on a dish to make sliders.
7. Add an egg and bacon to the top, then another pancake on top. If desired, drizzle with syrup.

S'mores Pancakes

cooking time: 20 minutes

Ingredients:

- Graham crackers
- Brown Sugar
- Cinnamon
- Mini or small marshmallows
- Semi-sweet or dark chocolate chips
- Chocolate Syrup
- Caramel Syrup

Instructions:

1. Heat the griddle to medium or medium-low. The number of burners on your griddle and the size of your griddle will determine the heat settings. TIP:Pancakes cook best on a griddle surface that has been preheated to over 375 degrees Fahrenheit.
2. Follow the manufacturer's directions to make the required amount of pancake batter. Toss in the marshmallows, chocolate chips, cinnamon, brown sugar, and graham cracker crumbs until well combined.
3. Add enough ingredients to ensure a s'mores surprise in every mouthful, but keep the batter flowing.
4. Using your preferred nonstick cooking spray, spray the griddle top.
5. Drop batter onto hot griddle top with a ladle.
6. Check the bottom side of the pancake with a thin spatula.
7. Flip pancake when bottom side is golden brown.
8. Cook the second side of the pancake until golden brown.
9. Place a cooking/cookie sheet on the griddle's empty side.
10. While you're creating additional pancakes, remove them from the griddle and set them on the raised cooking/cookie sheet.
11. If the pancakes are thick, I recommend leaving them on the baking/cookie sheet for a few minutes to ensure that the insides are fully cooked and not runny.
12. Remove the cooked pancakes from the pan.
13. Serve with marshmallows, chocolate chips, chocolate syrup, caramel syrup, graham crackers, and a sprinkle of cinnamon on top.
14. Take pleasure in your delicious S'mores Pancakes!

Nate's Favorite Breakfast

cooking time: 10 minutes

Servings: 4

Ingredients:

- 4 pieces of bacon
- 4 maple sausage patties

- 1/3 cup mayonnaise
- 1 tablespoon prepared horseradish
- 2 teaspoons Worcestershire sauce
- 4 eggs
- Blackstone Breakfast Blend Seasoning
- 4 slices American cheese
- 4 potato rolls, sliced

Directions:

1. Cook your bacon and sausage patties on your Blackstone over medium-high heat.
2. Cook your eggs sunny side up in a little of the bacon grease that has been moved over. Add some Blackstone Breakfast Seasoning to the mix.
3. Combine the mayonnaise, horseradish, and Worcestershire sauce in a small mixing basin. Mix equally with a whisk and set aside for later.
4. When the sausage and bacon are done, layer the bacon on top of the sausage and top with a slice of American cheese to melt.
5. Toast your potato rolls and spread part of the sauce on the bottom piece of bread before layering the sausage, bacon, and cheese on top.
6. Place your eggs on top of the sandwich and top with the top bread once they're cooked to your liking.

Mini Ham And Cheddar Quiche Cups

cooking time: 45 minutes

Servings: 4

Ingredients:

- Eggs
- 4 tablespoons cream cheese, softened
- 2 tablespoons half and half or milk
- ½ cup shredded cheddar cheese
- 1 tablespoon butter
- 3/4 cup diced ham

Instructions:

1. Melt the butter on a preheated medium griddle.
2. Sauté the ham for 5 minutes, or until it begins to color slightly.
3. Remove from the equation.
4. Whisk together the eggs, cream cheese, and half-and-half until completely smooth. If preferred, season with a touch of salt and pepper.
5. Preheat the AirFryer to 375 degrees Fahrenheit for 10 minutes.
6. In a mixing bowl, combine the ham and cheddar cheese.
7. Grease four medium ramekins with nonstick cooking spray or butter. Pour the egg mixture evenly into the

four ramekins and cook for 15-20 minutes in the AirFryer, or until the egg mixture has set and is fully cooked.

Hibachi-Style Griddle Pork Fried Rice

cooking time: 40 minutes

Servings: 8

Ingredients:

- 4 tablespoons canola oil, divided
- 1 small onion, diced
- 1 cup diced Chinese BBQ Pork
- 1 cup frozen peas and carrots
- 3 cups cooked Jasmine rice, chilled
- 2 eggs, lightly beaten
- 1/8 cup soy sauce
- 1 teaspoon sesame oil
- salt and pepper

Instructions:

1. Preheat your griddle to medium-high or high heat (you don't want to burn the oil), and pour roughly a tablespoon of oil onto it.
2. Add the onions and barbecue pork to the pan and stir fry for 2 minutes.
3. Stir in the frozen peas and carrots and cook until cooked through and crunchy around the edges.
4. Transfer the pork and veggies to the side of the griddle that isn't heated (if your griddle has multiple heat zones, turn one down).
5. Add extra oil to the griddle and let it to heat up. Add the chilled rice to the pan and break it up with a spatula. Continue to move it across the griddle, covering it evenly with oil and allowing it to brown. As required, add extra oil.
6. Stir and mix the meat, veggies, and rice together until they are uniformly incorporated. Drizzle the soy sauce and sesame oil on top, stirring and cooking until evenly dispersed.
7. Make a hole in the rice and fill it with a bit extra oil. Inside, crack the eggs, whisk with a spatula, then toss with the rice to incorporate.

Garlic Naan Bread

cooking time_2 HOURS 25 minutes

Servings: 8

Ingredients:

- Flour, All Purpose 3 lb
- Salt, Iodized 1 tablespoon
- Sugar, Granulated 1 tablespoon

- Egg - Room Temperature 1 each
- Milk - Room Temperature 1/2 cup
- Yogurt, Plain - Room Temp. 1/2 cup
- Olive Oil 1/4 cup
- Yeast, Active Dry 1 1/2 teaspoon
- Water 1 1/2 lbs
- Oil, For cooking bread 1/4 cup
- Butter 1/4 cup
- Garlic, Minced 1/2 teaspoon
- Parsley, Fresh 1 teaspoon

Instructions:

1. To create your flatbread, gather all of the ingredients.
2. In a mixing dish, combine the flour, salt, sugar, eggs, milk, yogurt, olive oil, and active dry yeast. A flat paddle or a dough hook can be used.
3. To form a smooth dough, add the water and mix for about 2 minutes.
4. Grease a big mixing bowl. Cover the dough with plastic wrap or a cloth and set aside.
5. Allow the dough to ferment/rise in a warm location for 2 hours. The dough should have nearly doubled in volume.
6. Divide the dough into 4 oz parts using a scale.
7. Form the dough into tennis-ball-sized balls ahead of time. Place the balls on a lightly floured board and brush them with a little oil. Cover for at least 30 minutes with a towel.
8. Start with the first dough ball and flatten it like a pancake with both hands by tossing, slapping, and gently stretching it. They should be around 6-7 inches in diameter.
9. Continue shaping the remaining dough balls until they are all done.
10. How to Make Naan There are a few different ways to make naan.
11. Place dough rounds directly on the oven floor in a deck oven. Cook till golden brown and done. Using a wooden peel paddle, remove the peel.
12. Place the dough on a sheet pan in a single layer and bake until the bread is golden in a conventional oven. Preheat the oven to 350°F and bake for 10 to 12 minutes. You may open the oven door for the last 2 minutes to assist release any extra steam that may have built up in the oven, preventing a soggy crust.

With a little grease, I baked my handmade naan in a big nonstick sauté pan on medium low heat. Cook until both sides are golden brown. On each side, it took roughly 12 to 2 minutes. Cook until all of the dough circles are golden brown.

Elevated Avocado Toast

Ingredients

- Whole Grain Bread
- Ripe Avacado
- Eggs
- Tajin Seasoning

- Cotija Cheese
- Grape Tomatoes, cut in halves
- Green Tabasco (optional)
1. Instructions
2. Heat the Blackstone to a low temperature and place the bread on top to begin toasting.
3. If desired, a small amount of butter or oil can be used to cook the eggs.
4. Crack one egg per bread and season with salt & pepper.
5. Cut the avocado in half and finely slice it. Season with salt, pepper, and Tajin seasoning and spread over bread.
6. Toss in the grape tomato halves.
7. On top of the avocado, place an over easy egg.
8. Cotija cheese and more Tajin spice on top.
9. Top with green Tabasco sauce if desired.

Corn & Jalapeno Griddle Cakes

10 Serv.

Ingredients

- Griddle Cakes
- 2 Cups of Fresh or Frozen and Defrosted Yellow Corn (about 3 ears of corn)
- 1 Jalapeno, finely chopped
- 2/3 Cup of Thinly Sliced Green Onions (about 5)

- 4 Eggs
- 1/2 Cup of Shredded Cheddar Cheese
- 2 Tablespoons of Olive Oil, plus extra for cooking
- 1/2 Cup of Flour
- 1/2 Cup of Yellow Cornmeal
- 1/2 Teaspoon of Kosher Salt
- 1/2 Teaspoon of Ground Black Pepper For Serving
- Sour Cream
- Salsa Verde
- Green Onions

Instructions

1. In a food processor, pulse 1 cup of corn kernels for a few seconds until coarsely chopped.
2. Combine the remaining corn kernels, jalapeño, green onions, eggs, cheddar, and olive oil in a large mixing bowl.
3. To blend, stir everything together.
4. Combine the dry ingredients in a separate bowl.
5. Stir gently to incorporate into the corn mixture
6. Preheat the griddle to medium-high.
7. Coat with a tiny bit of olive oil. 1/4 cup at a time, spoon the corn batter onto the griddle. It should be thick, but not so thick that it has to be flattened or spread. Cook for 2

minutes on each side, or until golden brown.

8. Serve with more green onions, Greek yogurt or sour cream, and salsa verde.

Fluffy Protein Pancakes

4 Serv. 10 Min.

Ingredients

- 1 Cup of Rolled Oats
- 1 Ripe Banana
- 2 Eggs
- 1/2 Cup of Egg Whites
- 4 Teaspoons of Baking Powder
- Pinch of Salt
- Pinch of Cinnamon
- 1-2 Scoops Protein Powder (Vanilla tastes best with this recipe)

Instructions

1. In a blender, combine all of the ingredients and mix until smooth.
2. Coat griddle with a thin layer of cooking oil or butter and heat to medium high.
3. On a heated griddle, pour roughly 1/4 cup of batter.
4. Cook for 1-2 minutes (until bubbles appear) before flipping the pancake.

5. Cook for another 1-2 minutes on the other side before plating and serving.
6. Serve with a topping of your choice of fruit, nut butter, or syrup (alters nutrition content below). Depending on whatever protein powder you choose, the nutritional information will differ significantly.

Amaretto Brioche French Toast With Chocolate Syrup

4 serv. 15 min.

Ingredients

- Toast
- 4-6 Slices of Brioche French Bread
- 3 Eggs
- 1/2 Cup of Coffee Creamer (Amaretto Flavored)
- 2 Teaspoons of Sugar
- 3 Tablespoons of Salted Butter
- Chocolate Jimmies (sprinkles)
- Almonds, Slivered or Sliced
- Chocolate Syrup
- 1/2 Cup of Sugar
- 1 Tablespoon of Special Dark Cocoa Powder
- Pinch of Sea Salt

- 3 Tablespoons of Water
- 1 Tablespoon of Salted Butter

Instructions

1. To make the chocolate syrup, mix together the sugar, cocoa, and salt with the water in the Blackstone Sauce Saucepan or a small pot on the Blackstone Griddle's lowest heat setting until smooth.
2. Whisk in the butter, a few minutes at a time, until the sauce comes together. While you're making your french toast, set aside the sauce, which will thicken as it cools.
3. Combine the eggs and sugar in a mixing bowl, then add the creamer and stir thoroughly. To a medium-low/low heated Blackstone, spread around one spoonful of butter.
4. Place one piece of bread in the butter after quickly dipping it into the egg mixture and covering both sides. Allow toast to cook for about 4-5 minutes over low heat until golden brown, then flip.
5. Add a sprinkling of jimmies and almonds to each piece of bread while the other side cooks for another 4-5 minutes.
6. Remove off the griddle, place on a platter, and drizzle with warm chocolate syrup.

Spinach Omelette

1 serv. 10 min.

Ingredients

- 3/4 Cup of Whisked Eggs
- 1.5 Cup of Fresh Spinach
- 1 Tomato, Diced
- 1/2 Purple Onion, Diced
- 1/2 Avocado, Sliced
- Shredded Cheese
- Salt and Pepper
- Sour Cream (optional)
- Hot Sauce (optional)

Instructions

1. Preheat the griddle to medium heat and add a little amount of oil or butter.
2. Season with salt and pepper and add the onions. Cook until the fresh spinach has wilted somewhat.
3. Set aside the spinach and onions. Spread a little extra oil or butter on the griddle and add the eggs one at a time.
4. Shape the eggs into a circular omelette using a spatula and season with salt and pepper.
5. To steam the top of the omelette, pour a little water over it and cover with a basting dome.
6. Toss in the spinach and onions that have been sautéed. Then top the omelette with 1/2 of your chopped

tomatoes and all of your shredded cheese.

7. Melt the cheese with the basting cover once more. Remove the cover off the omelette and fold it in half.

8. Place the omelette on a plate. Add sliced avocado, chopped tomatoes, sour cream, and spicy sauce over the top.

How To Make Crepes

4 serv. 10 min.

Ingredients

- 1 1/4 Cups of All Purpose Flour
- 3/4 Cup of Whole Milk
- 1/2 Cup of Water
- 2 Eggs
- 3 Tablespoons of Unsalted Butter, Melted
- 1 Teaspoon of Vanilla Extract
- 2 1/2 Tablespoons of Sugar

Instructions

1. Combine all of the ingredients in a large mixing basin and whisk to combine evenly. Make sure the batter is smooth and well-combined. Cover and set aside for

one hour (this allows the bubbles to subside and flour to fully hydrate.)

2. Add a small coating of butter to your Blackstone Griddle and heat it to medium heat. Approximately 14 cup of batter should be added. Form your crepe with the Crepe Spreading Tool and cook for 1-2 minutes. Flip using your Crepe Spatula. Cook for a further minute.

3. Continue with the remaining batter.

Huckleberry Pancakes

Ingredients

- 1 1/4 Cups of All-Purpose Flour
- 1/2 Teaspoon of Salt
- 1 Tablespoon of Baking Powder
- 1 1/4 Teaspoons of Sugar
- 1 Egg
- 1 Cup of Milk
- 1 Tablespoon of Butter (melted)
- 1/2 Teaspoon of Vanilla Extract
- 1/2 Cup of Huckleberries

Instructions

1. Using a whisk or fork, combine flour, salt, baking powder, and sugar in a mixing dish.

2. Separately, whisk together the egg, milk, melted butter, and vanilla extract in a separate dish. Huckleberries should be gently added to the mixture and softly

whisked in to integrate the huckleberries.

3. Mix the dry and wet ingredients together in separate bowls using a whisk.

4. Preheat your griddle to medium or low heat. Once the griddle top has achieved the correct temperature, spray it with nonstick cooking spray.

5. Pour about 1/4 cup of batter onto the griddle's surface. Repeat with properly spaced pancakes until all of the batter is utilized.

6. When the edges have bubbled and the bottom is golden brown, carefully fip the pancakes.

7. Cook the second side of the pancake until golden brown.

8. Remove the pancakes from the pan and top with butter, fresh huckleberries, huckleberry syrup, or any desired toppings.

9. Enjoy!

Mexican Breakfast Molletes

4 Serv. 35 Min.

Ingredients

- 4 Bolillos (Mexican Bread)
- 16 Oz. of Refried Beans
- 12 Oz. of Chorizo (Mexican Sausage)
- Tomatoes (Medium-Sized, Finely Chopped)
- 1/2 White Onion (Finely Chopped)
- Cilantro (Bunch, Finely Chopped)
- 1 Lime
- 1 Avocado (Finely Chopped)
- 1 Serrano Pepper (Deveined and Finely Chopped)
- 4 Eggs
- 2 Teaspoons of Vegetable Oil
- Salt (to Taste)

Instructions

1. Toss the tomatoes, onion, serrano peppers, avocado, and cilantro in a large mixing basin. Mix in the lime juice and season with salt to taste.

2. Fold the bolillos lengthwise in half.

3. Preheat the griddle to 350°F. Set the center and side burners to medium and low, respectively.

4. Spread two tablespoons of veggie on the griddle's middle. Place the chorizo on the plate. Break it up into little pieces while it cooks, being careful not to let any grease escape.

5. Smear some oil on all of the bolillo halves after the chorizo is half cooked. Place them face down on the griddle to toast. Make careful to turn the bolillos every now and then.

6. Heat the refried beans in the chorizo fat on the griddle once more. Remove the items from the flat top as soon as the bolillos are toasted and the beans are heated. Set aside the bread with the beans, chorizo, and pico de gallo on top.

7. Cook the four eggs in the leftover chorizo oil. Cook eggs sunny-side up and serve over molletes. You'll have four molletes with eggs and four without at the end.

Scrapple And Eggs Breakfast Flatbread

4 Serv. 25 Min.

Ingredients

- 4 Scrapple Slices
- Salt and Black Pepper (to Taste)
- 1 Cup of Red, Yellow, and Green Pepper (Diced)
- 2 Vidalia Onions (Diced)
- 2 Tablespoons of Butter
- 8 Eggs
- Pizza Dough (Unit)
- 1 Cup of Cheddar Cheese (Shredded)
- 2 Tablespoons of Scallions (for Garnish)

Instructions

1. Preheat the griddle to medium/high heat and lightly oil it.
2. Cook on griddle until peppers and onions are cooked but still have a tiny crunch.
3. Brown scrapple slices without rotating for 5 minutes. When one side of the slices has browned, flip them over and begin breaking them into pieces with a Blackstone spatula.
4. Cook for an additional 5 minutes after adding black pepper to taste. Remove from the equation.
5. Whisk the eggs with the salt in a mixing basin. Scramble eggs on a clean griddle over medium heat until they are done through.
6. Spread out pizza dough in a very thin rectangle with a dash of flour (can make 2 out of one unit of dough). Scramble the eggs in an equal layer on top of the crust, then top with peppers, onions, and scrapple.
7. Place on griddle over medium heat until crust is golden brown, then top with Cheddar Cheese. To melt the cheese, steam the pizza with a basting dome or a tin buffet pan. scallions on top

Whole Wheat Breakfast Burrito

10 serv.   22 min.

Ingredients

- 1 Green Pepper, Diced
- 1 Red Pepper, Diced
- 1 Yellow Pepper, Diced
- 1/2 Red Onion, Diced
- 16 Oz. of Turkey Sausage
- 12 Egg Whites

- 1/2 Cup of Shredded Cheese (Cheddar or Colby Jack)
- 10 Whole Wheat Tortillas, 10-inch Size

Instructions

1. Preheat your griddle to high and evenly coat the surface with olive oil.
2. Combine chopped peppers and onion on half of your griddle and heat.
3. To the remaining half, add the turkey sausage and crush it.
4. Combine sausage and peppers/onions after about 10 minutes (when sausage begins to brown) and put to one side of the griddle on low heat.
5. Reduce the heat to medium on the open side of your griddle.
6. Slowly pour egg whites and cheese onto the open side of your griddle.
7. To ensure that the eggs cook evenly, stir them occasionally.
8. When the eggs are almost done, add them on the griddle with the sausage and pepper/onion mixture and stir to incorporate.
9. Cook for a further 1-2 minutes, or until the eggs are done to your liking.
10. Half a cup of the egg/sausage/vegetable mixture should be folded up in 10-inch whole wheat tortillas.

Lemon Blueberry Pancakes

4 serv.   20 min.

Ingredients

1. Cup of All-purpose Flour
2. 1 Teaspoon of Salt
3. 1 Tablespoon of Baking Powder
4. 3 Tablespoons of Sugar
5. 1 Cup of Evaporated Milk
6. 3-4 Tablespoons of Lemon Juice (Juice of 1 whole Lemon)
7. 1 Egg
8. 1 Tablespoon of Vanilla
9. 2 Tablespoons of Butter
10. 1 Cup of Blueberry
11. Zest from 1 Lemon

Instructions

1. Preheat the Blackstone Griddle at low heat.
2. Combine flour, salt, baking powder, and sugar in a large mixing basin.
3. In a separate dish, squeeze the lemon juice. If desired, add lemon zest and evaporated milk. Allow 2 minutes for the mixture to rest before adding the egg, vanilla, and melted butter. Whisk gently until the batter is wet and lumps are tiny to medium.
4. Combine the wet and dry ingredients. Stir in the blueberries gradually.

5. Sprinkle a few droplets of water on the griddle's surface to see whether it's ready. Droplets of water should disperse and sizzle.
6. Using melted butter, brush the top of the griddle.
7. 14 cup batter should be poured onto the griddle.
8. Cook until little bubbles appear on the surface of the pancake. Continue to heat until the opposite side of the pancake has browned.
9. Warm it up and serve it with your preferred toppings.

Buttermilk Syrup

1 serv.   10 min.

Ingredients

- Cups of White Sugar
- 1 Cup of Buttermilk
- 1 Cup of Butter
- 1/4 Cup of Corn Syrup
- 2 Teaspoons of Baking Soda
- 4 Teaspoons of Vanilla Extract

Instructions

1. Combine all ingredients in a big saucepan and whisk to combine.
2. Bring to a boil, then reduce to a low heat and simmer for 3 minutes, stirring constantly.

3. Turn off the heat. Serve with Buttermilk Pancakes, French Toast, or Waffles while they're still warm.

Buttermilk Pancakes

1 Serv. 10 Min.

Ingredients

- Dry Ingredients
- 3 Cups of All-Purpose Flour
- 3 Tablespoons of Sugar
- 3 Teaspoons of Baking Powder
- 1 1/2 Teaspoons of Baking Soda
- 3/4 Teaspoon of Salt
- Wet Ingredients
- 3 Eggs
- 1/3 Cup of Melted Butter
- 3 Cups of Buttermilk
- 1/2 Cup of Milk

Instructions

1. Combine the dry ingredients in a large mixing basin.
2. Whisk the eggs and melted butter together in a separate basin. Combine the buttermilk and milk in a mixing bowl. Separate the two mixes until you're ready to cook.
3. Blend the wet and dry mixtures together with a wooden spoon or rubber spatula. Stir until everything

is well combined. Don't overmix the ingredients.

4. Allow 5 minutes for the batter to rest. This will allow the batter to activate and generate the essential bubbles for fluffier pancakes.

5. Turn the griddle to medium-high heat while the batter rests. Water should sizzle and dance over the griddle when splattered on it.

6. Using frying spray, coat the griddle (or use butter). Pour roughly 1/2 cup of batter each pancake onto the griddle. Check the bottoms of the pancakes from time to time and adjust the heat as needed.

New Mexico Breakfast Quesadillas

1 serv.   10 min.

Ingredients

- Eggs
- 2 Cups of Diced Russet Potatoes
- 1 Lb. of Thick Sliced Bacon
- 6 Cups of Shredded Fiesta Blend Cheese (Monterey Jack, Cheddar, Queso Quesadillas & Asadero), Divided
- 1 Fresh Minced Garlic Clove
- 1/2 Cup of Diced Red Onion
- Salt & Pepper to Taste
- Freshly Chopped Cilantro

- 505 Southwestern Hatch Valley Flame Roasted Green Chile
- 8 Large 10"-12" Flour Tortillas

Instructions

1. Preheat the Blackstone griddle to its highest setting.

2. On a griddle, cook bacon. There's no need to use any oil. Bacon produces its own grease, which may be used throughout the dish. If you want your bacon to stay flat, use the Blackstone Bacon Press (included in the Blackstone Breakfast Kit).

3. 2 cups russet potatoes, peeled and diced On the griddle top, there should be enough bacon fat to fry your potatoes by now. 1 tablespoon fresh minced garlic and 1/2 cup diced red onion should be dropped into the bacon oil. Flip the onions and garlic with a spatula. Toss in all of the diced Russet Potatoes with the onions and garlic.

4. In the meantime, your bacon should be almost done. Turn off the far right burner if using the 36" griddle. Transfer the cooked bacon to the griddle's far end. Allow the bacon to sit and keep heated in the turned-off zone. Otherwise, take cooked bacon off griddle and keep it warm by wrapping it in aluminum foil.

5. Continue to toss and stir the potatoes, onions, and garlic as they cook, integrating the flavors.

6. Eggs should be whisked together. Pour the egg mixture onto a hot, greased griddle. Season with salt and pepper to taste. On the griddle,

scrambled eggs cook quickly. As the eggs cook, use a spatula to turn them and break them up. Move them to the end of the griddle with the fried bacon after they're done frying. If using a smaller griddle, keep the eggs and fried bacon separate until the potatoes are done.

7. Cook potatoes until they have developed a small crust. Bacon should be diced. Using spatulas, combine the bacon, potatoes, and eggs.

8. Place four tortillas on top of the griddle. 3/4 cup Shredded Fiesta Blend Cheese, 1/4 cup potatoes, 1/4 cup bacon, 2 tablespoons hatch green chile (more or less to personal taste), and 1 tablespoon cilantro are evenly distributed on each tortilla. 3/4 cup cheese on top Place the top tortilla on top.

9. As the cheese melts and the contents mingle within the tortillas, flatten the quesadilla with the Blackstone Bacon Press or a spatula if required. Use a spatula to check underneath the tortilla often to ensure it gets golden brown. Turn each quesadilla carefully and continue the cooking procedure on the other side. Quesadillas are done when both sides are golden brown and the cheese within the tortillas has completely melted.

10. Using a chef's knife, slice quesadillas in the same way you would a pizza. Depending on the chosen serving size, each quesadilla creates 4 or 8 individual pieces.

Pulled Pork Breakfast Tacos

1 serv.   10 min.

Ingredients

- 1 Lb. of Wood Smoked Pulled Pork (without seasoning)
- 12 Large Eggs
- 1 Lb. of Hash Brown Potatoes
- 1 Lb. of Shredded Cheddar Cheese
- Salt to Taste
- Pork Rub or Rib Seasoning of Your Choice
- Hickory Barbecue Sauce of Your Choice
- 12 Small Taco-Sized Flour Tortillas (Approximately 5" in Diameter)

Instructions

1. Preheat the griddle to medium heat on the Blackstone. Coat the griddle top with mild olive oil after it's hot.

2. Cooking steps 3-5 at the same time is recommended.

3. On the griddle top, heat 1 pound of previously smoked (cooked) pulled pork. Season with Pork Rub or Rib Seasoning to taste. As the meat browned, flip it with a spatula.

4. 12 big eggs, sunny side up, cracked and cooked Season with salt to taste. When the yolk is still runny, remove it from the griddle top.

5. Cook a pound of shredded Hash browns on the griddle top, turning until the bottom sides are cooked.
6. When the hash browns are almost done, sprinkle with grated Cheddar cheese to taste.
7. Warm 12 small flour tortillas for tacos on the skillet until lightly toasted.
8. Serve it up: On each Tortilla, evenly distribute Hash Browns/Cheese, Eggs, and Pulled Pork. Barbecue sauce with a hickory taste.

Fall Harvest French Toast

1 Serv.   10 Min.

Ingredients

- Eggs
- 1/4 Teaspoons of Salt
- 1 Tablespoon of Brown Sugar
- 2-3 Teaspoons of Ground Cinnamon
- 1/2-1 Teaspoon of Ground Nutmeg
- 1/4 Cup of Pecans
- 1 Can Pumpkin (15oz.)
- 1 1/4 Cup of Heavy Whipping Cream
- Additional Toppings of your Choice

Instructions

1. Bread should be sliced to the proper thickness.

2. In a large mixing bowl, crack your 6 eggs and whisk them together.
3. Combine the salt, brown sugar, ground cinnamon, ground nutmeg, pecans, pumpkin can, and heavy whipping cream in a mixing bowl.
4. In a mixing dish, combine all of the ingredients.
5. Apply a little layer of cooking oil on your Blackstone griddle and heat it to a low temperature.
6. Toss the bread pieces in the batter in the mixing dish, then set them on the griddle carefully.
7. Wait until one side is done before flipping, taking care not to burn it.
8. Serve on a plate with selected toppings.

Stuffed French Toast

4 Serv.   20 Min.

Ingredients

- Oz. of Cream Cheese, Softened
- 2/3 Cup of Powdered Sugar
- 2 Teaspoons of Almond Extract
- 2 Tablespoons of Milk
- 2 Cups of Raspberries
- 1/4 Cup of Slivered Almonds
- 12-16 Slices Stale French Bread
- 4 Eggs
- 1 Cup of Half and Half

Instructions

Combine the cream cheese, powdered sugar, almond extract, and milk in a large mixing bowl. To get the correct consistency, add a spoonful of milk at a time.

Place bread slices in pairs and equally distribute the mixture on all of them. Put raspberries and almonds on one side of each pair.

To make a sandwich, fold the bread pieces together.

In a separate dish, combine the eggs, half-and-half, and a pinch of salt.

Preheat the griddle to medium-high temperature.

Set aside to rest after soaking both sides of each sandwich in the egg mixture.

Place each filled French toast on the griddle with melted butter and cook until each side is browned and cooked through.

Remove from heat, sprinkle with powdered sugar, and serve with maple syrup and any remaining raspberries and almonds.

Burgers/sandwiches.

GOOBER

3-4 Serv.   10 Min.

Ingredients:

- 1 loaf of Texas Toast
- Grape Jelly
- Creamy Peanut Butter
- 1 tsp Vanilla
- 1 cup Brown Sugar
- ¾ cup Half and Half
- 1 Tbsp Butter

Directions:

1. Make a typical PB&J sandwich with the specified jelly-to-peanut-butter ratio.
2. Combine two eggs, 1 teaspoon vanilla, 1 cup brown sugar, and 34 cups Half & Half in a medium mixing basin.
3. 1 tbsp butter, melted on the griddle (set to medium-high heat).
4. Cook for 3-5 minutes on the griddle after dipping and coating the PB&J in the mixture. Cook for another 3-5 minutes on the other side.
5. Place on a plate and enjoy!

Loaded Italian Fat Stack Pesto Chicken Sandwich

3 serv.   15-20 min.

Ingredients:

- Chicken cutlets
- Bagged and Diced Pancetta
- Sliced tomato
- Fresh basil
- Pesto (Jared)
- Fresh grated mozzarella
- Fresh grated pecorino Romano
- Jared Banana peppers
- Martin's potato rolls
- Olive oil
- Butter (for toasted bread)
- Egg rings
- Salt
- Pepper
- Blackstone Parmesan Ranch seasoning

Directions:

1. Preheat one of your Blackstone's zones to medium high heat. When your griddle is hot, drizzle a little olive oil over it and fry your diced pancetta. While the pancetta cooks, season the chicken cutlets on both sides with a light coating of olive oil, kosher salt, and coarse black pepper.

2. When the chicken is done, transfer the pancetta over to the same heat zone and fry the chicken cutlets in the pancetta grease and olive oil. Flipping your pancetta every now and again to ensure equal cooking on both sides is also a good idea. When all sides of the pancetta are golden brown, you know it's done.

3. You may toast both sides of your Martins potato Rolls on the griddle top while your protein cooks. Don't move away because this will be a rapid procedure. When the bread is a light golden brown, remove it from the griddle. You may also slice 1 tomato into thin slices and set aside at this time, as well as cut your fresh basil leaves into short ribbons.

4. To finish cooking the chicken, dab a light drizzle of your Blackstone Loaded Italian Sear & Serve sauce over it when it's 80 percent done. As the sauce boils down with the chicken, you'll see it diminishing. When the chicken is fully cooked, take it from the pan and chop it into medium-sized bits. Approximately 1/2 inch thick. At this point, you may take your pancetta and drain it on paper towels.

5. Now it's time to put the sandwich together. Reduce the heat to low and arrange four egg rings on the griddle. Add enough grated mozzarella to fill the griddle within the egg rings, then the chicken bits, a few slices of tomato, a little part of pancetta, banana peppers, a small

amount of the mixed Italian cheese blend, and more shredded mozzarella on top. Because everything is already cooked, the plan now is to just melt the cheese. Spray water around your egg rings and cover with your XL basting dome to do this.

6. Add a tiny dollop of pesto to the top of your toasted bread while the cheese is melting. When the cheese in the egg rings has melted, retain the contents in the ring and slide your spatula under the ring, keeping the ingredients within. Transfer the ring on the spatula to the heal and slide the ring over the bread. You should have a lovely melting pile of food ready to top with a little extra pesto, a few ribbons of fresh basil, a sprinkle of Blackstone Parmesan Ranch Seasoning, and the bread on top. I also like to lightly coat the top of the bun with Parmesan Ranch Seasoning. It tastes great and looks fantastic! Place on a plate and enjoy!

Cj's Frito Bandito Chopped Cheese

3 Serv.   15 Min.

Ingredients:

- 1lb 90/10 Ground beef
- 1 Yellow onion chopped
- Hoagie Sandwich buns
- Chopped Lettuce
- Sliced Tomato
- Shredded Cheese
- Chili Cheese Fritos
- BS Whiskey Burger Seasoning
- BBQ Sauce

Directions:

1. One zone of your Blackstone should be preheated on medium high, while the other should be preheated on low.
2. When your Blackstone is hot, add 1 pound of 90/10 ground beef and brown it on medium high. While it's cooking, drizzle a little olive oil over the steak and saute the yellow onions. Season with kosher salt and black pepper and toss periodically. Check on your meat and toss it regularly to ensure that it cooks evenly.
3. Season your beef with Blackstone Whiskey Burger Seasoning and a good quantity of shredded cheddar once it's done cooking. Toss all of your ingredients together with

around 1-1 1/2 cups grated cheese. You may now switch off the one-zone heat, leaving only your low-heat zone on. Allow the cheese to melt after thoroughly incorporating it.

4. Add a little olive oil to the low heat zone and toast your hoagie buns while your cheese melts. It's time to assemble once the bread has been gently toasted.

5. Add a small sprinkle of barbecue sauce to both sides of your sandwich before assembling it. Place your sliced tomato, shredded lettuce, and beef cheese and onion on one side. Now it's time to add your chili cheese to the meat. Enjoy with a side of Fritos, a drizzle of barbeque sauce, and a thin sprinkling of Whiskey Burger spice.

Italian Breakfast Lavash

2-4 serv.   15 min.

Ingredients

- Lavash Flat Breads
- ½ lb Prosciutto, deli sliced
- ½ lb Capicola, deli sliced
- ½ lb Genoa Salami, deli sliced thin
- ½ lb Mortadella, deli sliced
- ½ lb Mozzarella, deli sliced
- ½ lb Provolone cheese, deli sliced thin

- 4 Eggs
- Balsamic Glaze
- Cento, hot pepper spread
- 2 c Arugula
- 1 tbsp Extra Virgin Olive Oil
- Salt & Pepper, to taste
- Spray extra light tasting olive oil

Directions

1. Preheat the griddle to a low temperature.
2. Toss the arugula with the extra virgin olive oil and season with salt and pepper.
3. Spray one side of the lavash bread lightly with oil and lay it on the griddle.
4. On the griddle, cook 2 eggs per lavash to desired doneness while adding provolone cheese, Italian meats, and provolone cheese on top. Place the cheese against the lavash to act as a glue to keep the sandwich together.
5. Spread some spicy pepper spread on top.
6. Remove the cooked eggs from the griddle and place them equally on one side of the lavash.
7. To each sandwich, add roughly a cup of arugula. Drizzle balsamic glaze over the top. To make a sandwich, fold the lavash in half. Enjoy by cutting it in half or thirds.

CJ's Bacon and Chicken Caesar Pita Pockets

4-6 serv.   20 min.

Ingredients

- Chicken Cutlets
- Thick Cut Bacon
- Romaine Lettuce or Iceberg
- Cherry Tomatoes
- Banana Peppers
- Parmesan Cheese
- Pita Pocket Bread
- Caesar Dressing
- Blackstone Italian Sear & Serve Sauce

Directions

1. Preheat the griddle to medium-high heat. Add 4 slices of bacon to the pan after it's warmed up.
2. After that, add some olive oil to the griddle and fry two chicken cutlets in it. Make sure to keep an eye on your bacon and flip it as necessary, as well as your chicken cutlets. It should take around 5 minutes to cook the bacon, and 8-10 minutes to cook the chicken. Depending on how big your cutlets are.
3. You can chop your romaine lettuce and cherry tomatoes while your chicken and bacon are cooking.I prefer to remove the top inch or two of romaine lettuce. It doesn't have much texture, but that's a personal preference. Chop the lettuce into small pieces that will go into the pita pocket easily, and place it in a large mixing basin. Chop your cherry tomatoes anyway you like, but I normally half or quarter them before putting them in the bowl.
4. You can shred your fresh parmesan cheese while the chicken and bacon are cooking. Shred enough to fill your dish halfway and save some for a garnish at the end. Take your pita bread and cut it in half as well. Pita bread is circular and may be found at the store. To form the "pocket," just split the pita bread in half and gently open it up.When your chicken is done, take it from the griddle, along with your bacon, and drain it on paper towels. While your bacon drains and cools, cut up your chicken into tiny chunks, season with two pinches or so of salt and pepper, and a liberal dusting of Blackstone Parmesan Ranch Seasoning, and whisk to combine the ingredients before adding it to the bowl. After the bacon has been drained, slice it into tiny pieces. This may be added to your dish, but I prefer to use it as a finishing touch. It's just a fun way to display something.Add a desired quantity of Caesar dressing and roughly half as much Loaded Italian Sear and Serve sauce to the bowl with all of the ingredients and stir until all of the items are coated with the dressings.

5. Fill each pita pocket with the combined ingredients from your dish, add to the taco rack, top with bacon pieces, additional fresh grated parmesan, and a final "Post Dusting" of your Blackstone Parmesan Ranch Seasoning.

6. Finally, I like to drizzle a little of the Loaded Italian Sear over the top and serve in a small dish for more dipping sauce. Enjoy!

CJ's Hawaiian Roll Frito Bandito Chili Cheese Dog

2 Serv.   20 Min.

Ingredients:

- Hawaiian Rolls
- Hot Dogs (ball park length)
- Hormel Chili (can)
- Colby Jack Shredded Cheese
- Yellow Onion
- 2 Jalapeños
- Chili Cheese Fritos
- TD's Brew & BBQ Sauce
- Unsalted Butter
- Salt
- Pepper
- Beer

Directions:

1. Pre-heat your Blackstone Griddle top to medium high in one zone and medium in the other. Place the canned chili in a small sauce pan in the corner of your medium high zone. At this point, all we're doing is warming. Reduce the heat to low and let it to simmer after it begins to boil. The following step is now optional. To thin down the chili, I like to add a splash of beer. If you add too much, it will become overly watered down. Just enough to make things a little more manageable. Make care to examine and stir the mixture from time to time. This will prevent anything from scorching to the bottom of your sauce pan. Add your hotdogs to the medium-heat zone. The length of time you cook your dogs is entirely up to you. If you want them to have a lot of color, cook them for a little longer, but be sure to roll them every now and then so they cook evenly on all sides.

2. You may chop up your yellow onion while your hot dogs are cooking. I prefer to julienne my into a medium size. I enjoy onions a lot, so I'll chop up one full onion to feed four people. Add a little olive oil and your onions to the pan with your hotdogs to cook. Toss occasionally with a sprinkle of kosher salt and coarse black pepper to fry and caramelize. Cooking and finishing this dish should take around 5 minutes total. Let's prepare our Hawaiian roll

buns to be our hotdog buns while your dogs and onions are cooking. Break out three buns from the box while keeping them linked. This will be the bun for your hotdog. To keep them linked, it's critical that you do this softly. You'll delicately slice along one side of all three buns with a bread knife or serrated edge knife. The side of the buns, not the top, should be sliced. This is also part of the magic that allows this hotdog bun construction to function properly. If you cut too far down, your buns will split in half. Add 2 tbsp unsalted butter to the medium heat zone of your griddle once your buns are sliced. For this, you'll need to work around your dogs and onions. Butter both the split and unspilt sides of your hotdog bun. You'll want to spread butter on both sides and toast them until they're a light golden brown.

3. You may chop two jalapeos while your buns and other ingredients finish cooking on the griddle. I enjoy the spiciness of the seeds, so I keep them in. You can remove the pith and seeds if you don't want the heat. Set aside your diced jalapeos for garnish. Let's get started putting things together. After your buns have been lightly browned, take them from the griddle. Open the bun gently and place a little amount of shredded Colby jack cheese on top for the hotdog to sit on. On top of the cheese, place one hotdog. Your cheese will begin to melt because to the heat from the bun

and dog. After that, a sprinkle of TD's Original BBQ Sauce, caramelized onions, and a chosen amount of heated chili will be added. Now, you'll need Chili Cheese Fritos to truly make this childog shine; after all, it's named the Frito Bandito. Crush a handful of Fritos and sprinkle them on top of the cheese. Don't be shy with the fritos. The crunch texture and flavor are fantastic! After that, top it with extra shredded cheese and chopped jalapeos, and you're ready to eat!

Chimichurri Skirt Steak Quesadillas with Pineapple Pickled Jalapeno Peppers

2 serv.   25 min.

Ingredients

- 1, 10 oz skirt steak
- ½ bunch Flatleaf Parsley
- ½ bunch Cilantro
- 2 Limes
- 2 teaspoons minced Garlic
- 1 tablespoon Blackstone Carne Asada Seasoning

- 4 large Flour Tortillas
- 2 cups shredded Cheese
- Pickled Jalapeno:
- 1 Jalapeno, thinly sliced
- 1 Red Chile, thinly sliced
- ¼ cup Pineapple juice
- 1 tablespoon Lime juice
- 1 teaspoon Blackstone Carne Asada Seasoning
- 1 tablespoon Olive Oil

Directions

Combine the skirt steak, the juice of one lime, a little olive oil, and half of the Blackstone Carne Asada spice in a sealable plastic bag. To uniformly cover the skirt steak, seal it and toss it. Refrigerate for 15-30 minutes before serving.

In a large mixing basin, roughly chop the parsley and cilantro.

4-5 tablespoons olive oil, the remaining lime juice, minced garlic, and the remaining Blackstone Carne Asada seasoning To include all of the ingredients, mix them together evenly.

Combine all of the pickled jalapeño ingredients in a small mixing dish and stir to combine evenly.

Heat your griddle to a high setting. Remove the skirt steak from the marinade and cook on each side for 2-3 minutes.Remove the steak from the griddle after it has reached the correct doneness and set it aside to rest for 5 minutes. Slice into bite-sized pieces when they've rested.

Reduce the griddle's heat to medium. Place the tortillas on the griddle and top with cheese to make your quesadillas. Half of the tortilla should be filled with sliced steak, chimichurri, and a couple jalapeño peppers.

Fold the cheese side of the tortilla over the meat side to make the quesadilla as it begins to melt. Cook for 2-3 minutes per side, or until brown and crisp on both sides.

Slice and serve immediately.

Cheeseburger Filled Homemade Eggrolls

1 serv.   1 hour 10 minutes min.

Ingredients

- 1 lb beef (ground, shaped into balls or burger patties)
- ½ to 1 lb cheese, American preferred
- 1 Onion, chopped
- Blackstone Whiskey Burger Seasoning
- 1 tbsp Butter, unsalted
- 1 tbsp Olive Oil
- Oil for frying
- Wrappers
- 2 cups all purpose Flour, sifted
- 1 large Egg
- ¼-½ c Water

- ¾ tsp Salt
- Cornstarch
- Betty's Burger Sauce
- 1 c Dukes Mayonnaise
- ½ c Ketchup
- ½ c Mustard
- ⅓ c Pickle Juice
- 2 tbsp Worcestershire Sauce
- 2-4 fresh Garlic cloves, grated
- ½ c White Onion grated
- 2 tsp Paprika
- 1 tsp Salt, or to taste
- 1 tsp Pepper, or to taste

Directions

Set aside soft flour in a large mixing basin.

In a separate bowl, whisk together the egg, salt, and water, then add to the sifted flour. Begin incorporating ingredients with a rubber spatula. See the video for more information.

Using cornstarch, lightly dust a clean counter or work surface. Knead in the egg roll mixture for 10-15 minutes. Place dough in a bowl, cover with a moist cloth, and let aside for 40 minutes on the kitchen counter.

Preheat the Blackstone to medium-high heat and melt the butter with the olive oil before adding the chopped onions. Cook for 3 minutes, tossing the onions in the butter and oil to coat them, sprinkling with your favorite Blackstone flavor.Add the beef to the onions and smash with the Blackstone burger press if using patties or balls. Season with Blackstone seasoning to taste. Flip the meat and top with the

appropriate quantity of cheese. Then break up the meat with a scraper or spatula and mix in the onions. Remove the pan from the heat and set it aside to cool.

After the 40 minutes have passed and the meat has cooled, cut a piece of egg roll dough the size of a golf ball and roll it thin on a cornstarch dusted surface. The dough may be rolled out to any size you choose, from micro to huge.

To learn how to make egg rolls, watch the video below. Roll up the meat and any excess cheese if wanted, sealing the edges with a water-cornstarch mixture. Rep until all of the meat has been used.Preheat the Blackstone to medium-low to low heat, then sprinkle just enough oil into each egg roll. Allow eggrolls to cook low and slow, flipping tongs to crisp each side to a golden brown hue. Egg rolls may also be made in the Blackstone airfryer. Lightly coat each side with oil and cook on medium for about 5 minutes, or until golden brown.

Enjoy your eggrolls with burger sauce!

CJ's Buffalo Blue Ciabatta Chicken Sandwich

4 serv.   20 min.

Ingredients:

- Chicken Cutlets
- Ciabatta Rolls
- Precut broccoli slaw (bag)

- Red wine vinegar
- Swamp honey
- Frank's Hot sauce
- Ranch dressing
- Dukes Mayo (for toasting bread)
- Dill pickle
- Sliced Swiss cheese
- Butter (unsalted obviously)
- Blackstone Buffalo Blue seasoning
- Salt & Pepper

Directions:

On your Blackstone griddle, pre-heat one zone to Medium High/High. While that's going on, gently cover the chicken cutlets with olive oil, kosher salt, and coarse black pepper. Once your griddle is hot, pour a little olive oil on it and arrange your cutlets on top. Because the cutlets are so thin, they will cook quickly, so keep an eye on them and flip them as needed.We're going to prepare a fast hack broccoli slaw while your chicken is cooking. Add one bag of store-bought broccoli slaw, 1/4 cup red wine vinegar, 2-3 tablespoons pickle juice, 2 tablespoons honey, a sprinkle of coarse black pepper, and 1-2 tablespoons Blackstone Buffalo Blue Seasoning to a large mixing bowl, toss, and set aside. You'll get a lot brighter broccoli slaw if you do this overnight. Add 1/4 cup Franks Hot Sauce and desired amount of Ranch Dressing to a small bowl. I'd say 2 tbsp Ranch, stirred in and kept away for later.At this time, the chicken should be done, and you've probably flipped them once or twice. At this point, it's practically finished. We're going to use Franks spicy sauce to glaze our cutlets. Allow a small quantity of sauce to cover each cutlet and reduce to glaze the chicken. This will most likely take 30 seconds. Add a piece of mozzarella to each cutlet, then grab your basting dome, spritz some water around the chicken, and cover. This will allow the chicken to continue cooking and the cheese to melt.Spread a tiny quantity of dukes mayo on each side of your ciabatta bread and toast on your griddle top while the cheese melts. Duke's mayo is an excellent method to toast your buns. On the griddle, this won't take long; no more than two minutes and they'll be done. Pull off the griddle top when the bread is done and has a nice golden brown texture. On the bottom bun, spread a small amount of your special buffalo ranch sauce, a bed of your fresh broccoli slaw, one chicken cutlet, a dusting of buffalo blue Blackstone seasoning, 3-4 pickles, and a little more buffalo ranch sauce. To plate, I put a side of buffalo ranch sauce and a couple additional pickles on top of the sandwich.

Cheesesteak & Eggs

2-3 serv.   25 min.

Ingredients

- 1-1.5 lb boneless Ribeye steak
- 4-6 eggs
- 3 tbsp Half and Half
- Deli thin sliced American cheese, Boar's head

- Deli thin sliced Provolone cheese, Boar's head
- 1 small Sweet Onion, diced
- 1 tbsp oil
- Salt and Pepper to taste
- Italian Roll, bagel or bread of choice
- Sriracha Ketchup, optional
- ¼ c Ketchup
- ¼ c Sriracha

Directions:

Place the ribeye in the freezer for 15 minutes, then take it and shave or slice it into strips as thinly as possible. The less fat you have, the better.

In a dish, whisk together the eggs and milk and leave aside.

Drizzle oil over medium-high heat and add onion. Cook for 3 minutes or until onions are transparent, then set aside to keep warm, leaving the oil behind.

Increase the heat to high and add the shaved ribeye. Tear apart meat into tiny pieces using two spatulas or a scraper, moving it around repeatedly for a rapid cook while enabling the meat to brown. Approximately 3-5 minutes.

Reduce the heat to low and stir in the onions. Salt & pepper to taste. Spread the steak out in a broad circle on the griddle, then add the eggs, turn off the heat, and gently scramble the eggs and meat together. Adding the necessary amount of cheese and allowing it to melt completely.

Serve in an Italian hoagie roll or make a panini-style sourdough sandwich on a griddle. Drizzle sriracha ketchup across toasted and buttered bread for scooping, and enjoy!

Croque Monsieur

4 Serv. 20 Min.

Ingredients:

- ½ stick Unsalted Butter
- 2 tablespoons Bacon fat
- ¼ cup All-purpose Flour
- 1 ½ cup Whole Milk
- 2 cups shredded Gruyere
- 8 slices crusty White Bread
- 16 thin slices sweet Ham
- ¼ cup spicy brown Mustard
- 2 tablespoons chopped flat leaf Parsley
- Olive oil
- Salt and pepper

Directions:

Melt the butter and bacon grease together in a small sauce saucepan over medium heat. Stir in the flour until everything is well combined. After 3-4 minutes, add 1/3 of the milk and cook for another 3-4 minutes. Whisk to blend, then add the rest of the milk and whisk to combine. Over low heat, cook for a further 5-7 minutes. Season with salt and pepper to taste, then mix in 1/3 of the shredded gruyere to evenly melt.

With a little olive oil, toast the bread on both sides.

Spread a small layer of mustard on each slice of bread, then sprinkle shredded gruyere over the tops of four of them. Over the cheese, place two slices of ham and a dollop of the creamy sauce. Add two additional slices of ham and a sprinkling of shredded gruyere on top. To assemble the sandwich, lay the top piece of bread on the griddle over low heat to melt the cheese.

Slice and serve hot, garnished with chopped parsley (if wanted, burn the cheese for a touch of color), slice and serve.

Hot Italian Sausage Rigatoni in Red Sauce

4 Serv.   25 Min.

Ingredients:

- 4-6 Johnsonville Hot Italian Sausages
- ¾ cup diced Sweet Onion
- 2 tablespoons minced Garlic
- 1, 24 oz jar of Rao's Bolognese Sauce
- 2 tablespoons fresh Oregano leaves, rough chop
- 1 tablespoon fresh Basil, rough chop
- 1 cup diced Tomato
- 1 box of Rigatoni Noodles, cooked to al dente (mostly cooked)
- 1 cup fresh Spinach Leaves
- 1 cup shredded Mozzarella Cheese
- 1/3 cup fresh shredded Parmesan
- 1 large aluminum pan
- Salt and pepper
- Olive oil

Directions:

Add a little olive oil to your griddle and heat it to medium-high. Cook for 4-6 minutes, rotating frequently.

Over medium heat, place the aluminum pan on the griddle. Add the onions and a little olive oil. Cook for another 3 minutes before adding the garlic. Cook for a further 2 minutes, stirring often.

Bring the Rao's tomato sauce to a simmer over the onions and garlic. Then, with a pinch of salt and pepper, add the sausage, oregano, and basil. Cook the sausage for 5 minutes, flipping it frequently.

Remove the sausage from the sauce, slice it into bite-sized pieces, and return it to the sauce pan. Then toss in the spinach and noodles until everything is well combined.

Cover with a dome for another 5 minutes after adding the mozzarella cheese.

Serve immediately with grated parmesan and fresh basil on top. Enjoy!

Bettys Buffalo Chicken Cheesesteaks

2 serv.   20 min.

Ingredients:

- large Chicken Breast
- 1/2 c Wing Sauce, Sweet Baby Rays Mild preferred
- 1/4 cup Ranch Dressing
- 1 tsp Garlic Powder
- 1 tsp Dried Parsley
- Salt and Pepper to taste
- 1 tbsp Oil
- 1/4 lb good quality deli thin sliced American Cheese, Cooper sharp preferred
- 2 foot long Italian Hoagie rolls

Directions:

Prepare raw chicken by chopping it into tiny pieces. This may be prepared ahead of time and kept refrigerated until ready to use.

Preheat the Blackstone griddle to a medium-high temperature. Drizzle some oil on top. Cook for 3-4 minutes, or until chicken is cooked through, tossing occasionally.

Reduce the heat to medium. Add salt, pepper, garlic, and parsley to taste.

Stir in the spicy sauce and toss to evenly coat, adding more if necessary.

In a mixing bowl, combine the ranch and blue cheese dressings.

About 6 pieces of cheese should be added, and the cheese should be melted throughout the chicken.

Reduce the heat to a medium low setting. Divide the chicken into two heaps, add a few more pieces of cheese to each pile, and bake the rolls for 30-60 seconds on top of the cheese.

Place one hand on top of the roll and use the other to turn the sandwich with a long Blackstone spatula.

Place on a plate and enjoy!

Loaded Italian Pork Sandwiches

2 Serv.   15 Min.

Ingredients:

- Pork Cutlets
- ¾ cup Blackstone Loaded Italian Sear and Serve
- ½ cup Mayonnaise
- 3 tablespoons Lemon Juice
- 8 slices Salami
- 4 slices Coppa
- 8 slices Provolone

- ½ a large Red Onion, thinly sliced
- 2 cups shredded Romaine Lettuce
- 4 Potato Rolls
- Salt & Pepper
- Olive Oil

Directions:

Preheat the griddle to medium-high temperature.

Season the pork cutlets on one side with salt and pepper. Cook the pork for 3-4 minutes on the griddle with a few teaspoons of olive oil.

Combine the mayonnaise, lemon juice, a sprinkle of salt and pepper, and 2 tablespoons of the Loaded Italian Sear in a small mixing bowl. Toss everything together until it's equally distributed.

Serve the pork cutlets over the top with the leftover Loaded Italian Sear.

Top the cutlets with 2 slices of salami and 1 slice of coppa, then 1 or 2 slices of provolone. To melt, cover with a basting dome.

Toast the buns lightly.

To assemble, spread some of the sauce on the bottom bun, then top with lettuce and red onion. Serve with 1 or 2 pork cutlets on top. Add additional sauce to the top bun if preferred, and serve immediately.

Enjoy!

Cheese Chicken Sandwiches

2 Serv.   15 Min.

Ingredients:

- Chicken Cutlets
- 1 Sweet Yellow Onion, Julienn
- ½ Red Bell Pepper, Julienne
- ½ Green Bell Pepper, Julienne
- 1 cup Sliced Mushrooms
- 1/3 cup Ranch Dressing
- ¼ cup Buffalo Sauce
- 8 slices Pepper Jack Cheese
- Blackstone Cheesesteak Seasoning
- 4 Hoagie Rolls
- Salt and Pepper
- Olive Oil

Directions:

Preheat the griddle to medium-high temperature.

On both sides, season the chicken cutlets with salt, pepper, and a generous amount of Blackstone Cheesesteak Seasoning.

Cook the chicken for 3 minutes per side on a hot griddle with 2 tablespoons olive oil.

Next to the chicken, drizzle in a little more olive oil and toss in the onions, bell peppers, and mushrooms, along with a pinch of Blackstone Cheesesteak Seasoning. Cook for 3-5 minutes after tossing to evenly coat.Cut the chicken into bite-sized pieces using your spatulas or a knife after the chicken is nearly done. Make four even stacks of chicken and top each with some of the vegetables. Cover each stack with a couple slices of pepper jack cheese to melt.Combine the ranch and buffalo sauce in a small dish and spread equally on the bottom of each hoagie roll. Fill the hoagie buns with the chicken stacks, slice, and serve immediately.Enjoy!

Thanksgiving Leftovers Grilled Cheese Sandwich

1 Serv. 10 Min.

Ingredients

- Slices French Bread (Sourdough or Other Artisan Bread)
- 4 Slices Provolone Cheese
- 4 (Heaping) Cranberry Sauce
- Leftover Stuffing
- Leftover Turkey
- 4 Butter (Room Temperature)
- 1 Dried Sage

Instructions

Preheat your griddle to Medium Low (This is a thick sandwich so you want the ingredients in it to heat up before the outside burns).

Combine the butter and sage in a small dish.

Arrange the bread pieces on the table.

Place a piece of provolone cheese on one side of the bread, then a layer of stuffing, turkey, and cranberry sauce on the other.

Place the other slice of bread on top and spread the sage butter on the exterior.

Cook the sandwich on both sides until golden brown and cooked through.

BBQ Chicken Cheesesteaks

1 Serv. 20 Min.

Ingredients:

- 2- 12 inch Italian Rolls
- 1.5 lbs chicken breast
- 6 strips bacon, thick cut
- 1 tbsp Blackstone All Purpose Seasoning
- 1 cup monterary jack, shredded (sub american or cheddar)
- 1/2 cup BBQ Sauce, Duke's
- 2 tbsp red onion, diced
- 1/2 tsp parsely, garnish optional

Directions:

Set aside diced chicken breast, as tiny or large as you'd like.

Set aside the bacon, which has been cut into small pieces.

Turn the Blackstone on to medium heat, add the bacon, and fry slowly while preventing the bacon oil from pouring away; this will be the pan in which the chicken will be cooked.

Add the chicken to the bacon and bacon fat when the bacon is approximately 3/4 done. Allow the chicken to simmer for 3-5 minutes after adding the Blackstone All Purpose Seasoning and mixing it in fully. Add a sprinkle of barbeque sauce to the chicken and bacon mixture and stir well.

Reduce the heat to low and divide the meat mixture into two piles, then add the cheese and stir to melt.

Form two meat piles the same size as each roll, pour each with BBQ sauce, and set rolls on top of the meat for one minute.

With one hand holding the roll, slip a spatula beneath the meat and flip. Serve with fresh chopped red onions and parsley on the side.

CheeseChicken Sandwiches

4 serv. 10 Min.

Ingredients:

- Chicken cutlets
- 1 sweet yellow onion, julienne
- ½ red bell pepper, julienne
- ½ green bell pepper, Julienne
- 1 cup sliced mushrooms
- 1/3 cup ranch dressing
- ¼ cup buffalo sauce
- Slices pepper jack cheese
- Blackstone Cheesesteak Seasoning
- Hoagie rolls
- Salt and pepper
- Olive oil

Directions:

Preheat the griddle to medium-high temperature.

On both sides, season the chicken cutlets with salt, pepper, and a generous amount of Blackstone Cheesesteak Seasoning.

Cook the chicken for 3 minutes per side on a hot griddle with 2 tablespoons of olive oil.

Next to the chicken, drizzle in a little more olive oil and toss in the onions, bell peppers, and mushrooms, along with a pinch of Blackstone Cheesesteak Seasoning. Cook for 3-5 minutes after tossing to evenly coat.

Cut the chicken into bite-sized pieces using your spatulas or a knife after the chicken is nearly done. Make four even stacks of chicken and top each with some of the vegetables. Cover each stack with a couple of slices of pepper jack cheese to melt.

Combine the ranch and buffalo sauce in a small dish and spread equally on the bottom of each hoagie roll. Fill the hoagie buns with the chicken stacks, slice, and serve immediately.

Pickle Chic Sandwiches

8 Serv.

Ingredients:

- Boneless skinless chicken breast
- 1 cup pickle juice
- 1 tbsp All Purpose Blackstone Products Seasoning
- ¼ cup mayonnaise, Dukes preferred
- 1 8-pack brioche buns
- Slices muenster cheese
- Slices sharp cheddar cheese
- 1 box FarmRich crispy dill pickles

Horsey Sauce

- ½ c mayonnaise
- ¼ c prepared horseradish
- Dash each salt pepper and paprika

Red Cabbage Slaw

- Cups red cabbage, shredded
- ¼ cup green onions, chopped
- Tbsp extra virgin olive oil
- Tbsp red wine vinegar
- Salt and pepper to taste

Directions:

Pound the chicken breasts with a meat tenderizer until they are 12 inch thick and evenly distributed all over. Cut each breast into two halves, since one breast should produce two sandwiches. Remove the air from the bag, close it, and marinate the chicken overnight in pickle juice.

Slaw can be made by shredding or finely slicing cabbage. In a mixing dish, combine the cabbage with the green onion, oil, vinegar, salt, and pepper to evenly cover it. Remove from the equation.

Set aside the ingredients for the horsey sauce.

Drain and blot dry the chicken, then combine it with mayonnaise and Blackstone All Purpose Seasoning to evenly cover it.

Heat the Blackstone Griddle on medium and the Blackstone Airfryer on high.

Arrange the chicken on the Blackstone. Cook for 3-4 minutes each side on each side.

Cook for 4-5 minutes, or until crisp and cooked through, in a hot airfryer with Farmrich pickles.

Before removing the chicken, add one slice of each cheese to the last minute of cooking. Allow the chicken to rest while you toast the buns in the leftover chicken fat.

Layer the chicken, cheese, slaw, pickles, and horsey sauce on the sandwiches. Enjoy!

Chicken Parmesan Ranch Sandwich

4 serv. 20 min.

Ingredients:

- Chicken Cutlets
- Olive Oil
- Salt
- Pepper
- Blackstone Parmesan Ranch Seasoning
- Shredded Mozarella
- Pepperoni
- Martins Rolls Sandwich Buns
- Marinara
- Fresh Basil

Directions:

Preheat the Blackstone griddle to medium-high temperature.

Add 3 chicken cutlets to a platter and gently coat each side with olive oil, salt, pepper, and Blackstone Parmesan Ranch Seasoning.

Add a small quantity of olive oil to your griddle top and cook for 3-4 minutes on each side, or until thoroughly done. Remove the griddle from the heat and reduce it to a low setting.

Cut your chicken into rings that will fit in your egg rings.

Place Egg Rings on Griddle and stuff with enough shredded mozzarella (not too much, but enough for a lovely bed of cheese), chicken, pepperoni, and mozzarella to taste.

Cover with a basting dome and cook until the cheese is melted, spraying water over the egg rings before covering.

Place your Martins rolls on the griddle to lightly brown while the cheese melts.

When the cheese is melted, remove the dome, arrange the rolls on a tray, slide a spatula under the egg rings and toppings, and top with toasted buns. Add as much marinara as you like, as well as freshly cut basil.

Finish with a bun crown and have fun!

Chopped Cheese with Special Sauce

4-6 serv.   15 min.

Ingredients:

- 1 ½ lb 90/10 ground beef
- 2 cups diced yellow onions
- 3 tablespoons Blackstone Whiskey Burger Seasoning
- 1 ½ cups shredded cheddar
- 4-6 Hoagie rolls

- Olive oil
- Shredded lettuce (optional)
- Sliced tomato (optional)

Sauce Ingredients:

- ¼ cup mayonnaise
- ¼ cup ketchup
- ¼ cup spicy mustard
- 2 tablespoons Worcestershire sauce
- 2 teaspoons Blackstone Whiskey Burger Seasoning

Directions:

Add a little olive oil to your griddle and heat it to medium-high. Add the ground beef and cut it up into tiny pieces. Sprinkle the Blackstone Whiskey Burger Seasoning evenly over the top and toss to combine.

Next to the steak, drizzle in a little extra olive oil and toss in the onions. Cook for 3-4 minutes before combining the meat and onions. Cook for another 4-5 minutes, tossing to thoroughly distribute the ingredients.

When the steak is done, sprinkle the cheese on top and stir to properly distribute it.

Combine all of the sauce ingredients in a small mixing dish and stir to combine evenly.

Cut side down, lightly toast the Hoagie rolls.

To assemble the sandwich, spread some of the sauce on the cut side of the hoagie buns, then top with lettuce and tomato.

Serve immediately with a big dollop of the cheesy beef on top.

Frito Bandito

3 serv. 15 min.

Ingredients:

- 1 pound 80/20 ground beef
- 1 cup diced sweet yellow onion
- Blackstone Steakhouse Seasoning
- slices American Cheese
- 1 1/2 cup Chili Cheese Fritos
- Wonder Bread Honey Bun burger buns
- BBQ Sauce
- Olive oil

Directions:

Preheat your griddle to medium-high heat before you begin. A spoonful of olive oil should be added to Blackstone. To caramelize for 4-5 minutes, add sliced sweet yellow onion to one of your Blackstone's heat zones and stir with oil.

Make 4 ounce meat balls out of the ground beef. Smash the meatballs on the griddle until they are very thin. Season each burger with Blackstone Steakhouse Seasoning and grill for 1-2 minutes on each side.

Add caramelized onions, Chili Cheese Fritos, BBQ Sauce, and a piece of American cheese to the burgers before flipping them.

Melt the cheese by covering it with a dome. Place the patties on a Wonder Bread Honey Hamburger bun and serve after the cheese has melted.

Bacon Cheese Burger With Coriander Pickled Red Onions & Smoky Mayo

4 serv.   15 min.

Ingredients:

- 1 ½ pounds 80/20 ground beef
- pieces thick cut applewood smoked bacon
- 1 large red onion, thinly sliced
- 1/3 cup red wine vinegar
- 1 tablespoon ground coriander
- ¼ cup mayonnaise
- ¼ cup sour cream
- 1 tablespoon smoked paprika
- 1 teaspoon ground chipotle
- The juice of 1 lime
- 1 cup shredded lettuce
- slices cheddar cheese
- seeded hamburger buns
- Salt and pepper
- Olive oil

Directions:

Combine the onions, red wine vinegar, a drizzle of olive oil, crushed coriander, and a sprinkle of salt and pepper in a small mixing bowl. Mix well and put aside to marinate.

Preheat your griddle to medium heat and cook the bacon until it is crisp and well done. Drain on a paper towel after it's completed.

Season the ground beef on both sides with salt and pepper before forming 4 equal patties. Cook for 3-4 minutes per side in the bacon fate, or until desired doneness is reached.

Combine the mayonnaise and sour cream in a small mixing bowl with the smoked paprika, chipotle, lime juice, and a touch of salt and pepper. Mix well to ensure that everything is uniformly distributed.

To fit the bacon on top of the burger, slice it thinly. When the burgers are done, top them with a couple slices of bacon and a slice of cheese. To melt, cover with a dome.

Toast the buns lightly and spread part of the sauce on the bottom bun.

Place lettuce on the bottom bread, then the burger, then some pickled onions on top, and finally the top bun. Serve immediately.

Crunchy Crab Melts

8 serv. 20 min.

Ingredients:

- Artisan loaves, sliced roasted garlic bread
- 1 lb lump crab meat
- 1 - 8 oz block muenster cheese, shredded
- 1 - 8 oz block cheddar cheese, shredded
- Old Bay seasoning
- Dukes mayo
- Parsley

Directions:

Set aside after shredding both blocks of cheese and mixing them together. On the outside of each slice of bread, spread mayonnaise.

Place the bread, mayo side down, on a preheated Blackstone on low to medium heat.

Combine the cheeses and spread them over each slices. On one side, place the crabmeat. Old bay and parsley are used as seasonings.

Sandwich the two pieces together once the cheese has melted and the exterior of the bread has been toasted to perfection.

Serve as entire sandwiches or cut into quarters or half for bite-size appetizers!

Betty Burgers

4 serv.   15 min.

Ingredients:

- 1 pound 80/20 ground beef
- 1 cup diced tomato
- ¼ cup minced red onion
- 1 tablespoon minced garlic
- tablespoons chiffonade basil
- Blackstone Whiskey Burger Seasoning
- slices mozzarella
- ½ cup mayonnaise
- 1 tablespoon sun dried tomato puree
- small burger buns
- Olive oil
- Salt and pepper

Directions:

Combine the tomatoes, onions, garlic, and basil in a mixing bowl. Drizzle with olive oil and season with salt and pepper. Stir to blend evenly, then set aside for 10-15 minutes to marinate.

Preheat the griddle to medium-high temperature. Make 4 ounce meat balls out of the ground beef. Smash the meatballs on the griddle until they are very thin. Cook for

1-2 minutes after adding some Blackstone Whiskey Burger Seasoning to each burger.

After flipping the burgers, top with a few tablespoons of the tomato mixture and a piece of mozzarella.

Combine the mayonnaise and sun dried tomato puree in a small mixing dish.

After lightly toasting the buns, spread some sun dried tomato mayonnaise on top. Add the burger on the bottom bread once the cheese has melted, and serve immediately.

Onion Mushroom BBQ Swiss Burger

4 serv.   15 min.

Ingredients:

- Cups julienned yellow onion
- 2 cups sliced mushrooms
- 1-2 pounds 80/20 ground beef (more or less depending on how big you like your burgers)
- Blackstone Whiskey Burger Seasoning\
- BBQ Sauce
- 8 slices swiss cheese
- 4 jumbo hamburger buns
- Salt and pepper
- Olive oil

Directions:

Preheat the griddle to medium. After a few drops of olive oil, add the onions and mushrooms. Cook for 10 minutes, stirring often, with a touch of salt and pepper. Move the onions and mushrooms to the cooler side of the griddle after they have caramelized somewhat.

Make 4 equal hamburger patties out of the ground meat. On both sides, season equally with Blackstone Whiskey Burger Seasoning. Cook for 3 minutes each side on each side. Add some of the onions and mushrooms on the tops of each burger once it's cooked to your liking.

Over the vegetables, drizzle some BBQ sauce and top with two pieces of Swiss cheese. Cover to let the butter to melt.

Lightly toast the buns on both sides, then spread the bottom buns with BBQ Sauce. Place the burger on top and serve immediately.

Pickle Brined Chicken Sandwich

4 serv.

Ingredients:

- Boneless skinless chicken thighs

- 1 cup pickle juice
- Egg
- 2 tablespoons oil
- 2 cups panko breadcrumbs
- 8 pickle slices
- 1 can Jumbo biscuits
- Mayonnaise (optional)

Instructions

Remove any excess fat from the chicken thighs and throw it away. If necessary, lightly pound the chicken thighs to remove any high areas and level out the thickness of the cutlet.

12 to 48 hours before serving, marinate chicken thighs in pickle juice. When the marinade is finished, discard the pickle liquid.

Preheat the air fryer for 10 minutes on medium high.

Cook giant biscuits in the air fryer according to the manufacturer's instructions. NOTE: Because the air fryer cooks faster than a conventional oven, check the biscuits after half the time recommended by the manufacturer. Because the air fryer cooks 25 percent faster than a conventional oven, plan ahead and keep an eye on the biscuits.

Remove the biscuits from the oven and set them aside to cool.

Combine the egg and the oil in a mixing bowl.

Using a paper towel, pat dry the chicken thighs. Dredge each piece of chicken in the egg mixture and then in the panko breadcrumbs to properly coat it.

Cook the breaded chicken in the air fryer for 20-25 minutes, or until the internal temperature reaches 165°F and the outside is golden brown.

Place a fresh biscuit on top of a chicken thigh cutlet. Top with pickles and mayonnaise (if desired).

Grilled Chicken And Roasted Red Pepper Sandwiches With Fontina Cheese

4 Serv.

Ingredients

- 1 Lb. of Skinless, Boneless Chicken Breast halves or tenderloins
- 1 Tablespoon of Fresh Lemon Juice
- 1 Tablespoon of Dijon Mustard
- 2 Teaspoon of Extra Virgin Olive Oil
- 1/4 Teaspoon of Dried Marjoram
- 1/4 Teaspoon of Dried Thyme\
- 7 Oz. of Bottle Roasted Red Bell Peppers, drained and sliced
- 1 Tablespoon of Red Wine Vinegar
- 1/8 Teaspoons of Freshly Ground Black Pepper
- 1 Cup of Vertically Sliced Onion

- Teaspoon of Sugar
- 3/4 Teaspoon of Fennel Seeds, Crushed
- 1/4 Teaspoon of Crushed Red Pepper
- 1/2 Teaspoon of Salt
- 5 Garlic Cloves
- 3 Oz. of Fontina Cheese, Sliced
- 12 Oz. of Loaf Rosemary Focaccia, Cut in Half Horizontally
- 4 Teaspoon of Low-Fat Mayonnaise
- Avocado Oil

Instructions

Use tenderloins or pound chicken to a 34-inch thickness.

In a large zip-lock plastic bag, combine the lemon juice, mustard, oil, marjoram, thyme, 1 garlic clove, and chicken. Seal the bag and marinate for 2 hours or longer in the refrigerator, rotating occasionally.

Warm Blackstone over medium-high heat, then reduce to medium after it has reached room temperature.

Pour avocado oil onto the blackstone and begin sautéing the chicken on one half and the red pepper and onion mixture on the other.

Start by putting the raw chicken on the griddle.Place the onions on the griddle's other half. Add the other ingredients (4 garlic cloves, onion, sugar, fennel, crushed red pepper, and salt) and saute for 1 minute, or until the onions are starting to get soft. Cook, turning often, until the onions are soft. Cook for another five minutes after adding the red bell peppers. Add the vinegar and black pepper and mix well.

After the chicken has finished cooking, allow it to cool somewhat before slicing it.To toast the bread, make a space on the griddle. Place the cut bread on the Blackstone cut side down for a minute to warm up the interior of the bread. Mayonnaise should be uniformly spread on both sliced sides of the bread. Place the cheese on the bottom half of the bread. Place the chicken and pepper mixture on top of the cheese. Place the top half of the bread on top and softly press it down. (If desired, a griddle press can be used.)

3 minutes per side on the griddle, or until cheese melts Quarter the potatoes This recipe serves 4 people (serving size: 1 sandwich quarter)

Pesto Ranch Chicken Sandwich

1 Serv. 15 min

Ingredients

- 4-6 Chicken Cutlets
- 4 Tablespoons of Blackstone Chicken & Herb Seasoning
- 1/4 Cup of Pesto
- 1/4 Cup of Ranch Dressing
- 1/4 Cup of Mayonnaise

- 2 Tablespoons of Sun-Dried Tomato Puree/Spread
- The Juice of 1 Lemon
- 12 Large Fresh Basil Leaves
- 8 Slices Provolone Cheese
- 4 Hoagie or Sub Rolls Cut in Half
- Olive Oil

Instructions

Combine the mayonnaise, sun-dried tomato puree, and lemon juice in a small mixing dish. Combine equally and set aside for later.

Preheat the Blackstone Griddle to medium-high temperature.

On both sides, season the chicken cutlets with a little olive oil and Blackstone Chicken & Herb Seasoning. Cook for 3-4 minutes per side, or until done.

Each hoagie or sub roll should be toasted on the cut side.

Add some pesto to the bottom side of each roll, followed by some ranch dressing. Half the chicken cutlets and place them on top. Add a few basil leaves, followed by two slices of provolone cheese. Add some sun-dried tomato mayonnaise on the top buns and place on top of the sandwich.

Place the sandwiches on the Blackstone Griddle over low heat. Cook for 5 minutes, or until the cheese is melted, covered. Slice and serve immediately.

Muffuletta Panini

4 serv.   15 min.

Ingredients

- 3/4 Cup of Giardiniera
- 1/4 Cup of Chopped Kalamata Olives
- 4 Cup of Chopped Capers
- 1/4 Cup of Chopped Roasted Red Pepper
- 3/4 Lb. of Sliced Mortadella
- 3/4 Lb. of Capicola
- 3/4 Lb. of Salami
- 12 Slices Provolone
- 1/3 Cup of Sweet Pepper Relish4 Round Sandwich Rolls
- Olive Oil

Instructions

In a large mixing bowl, combine the Giardiniera, kalamata olives, capers, and red pepper. Combine equally and set aside for later.

Add a little olive oil to your Blackstone Griddle and heat it to medium heat. The sliced side of the sandwich buns should be toasted.

Fill the bottom bun of each roll with a couple of teaspoons of the giardiniera mixture. 2 slices provolone, followed by a few slices of each of the sliced meats Place a tablespoon or so of the pepper relish on top, followed by two additional pieces of cheese.

Place the top bun on top of the Blackstone. Press the sandwiches with an XL Griddle Press or a bacon weight and cook for 2-3 minutes. Flip it over and hit the button. Cook for an additional 3-4 minutes.

Slice and serve immediately.

Pork Cutlets

Ingredients

- 1 Lb. of Prime Pork Cutlets, sliced thin (about 6-7)
- 1 Cup of Italian Seasoned Bread Crumbs
- 1/2 Cup of Pecorino Romano Cheese
- 1 Teaspoon of Thyme
- Eggs
- 1/4 Cup of Milk
- 1 Teaspoon of Garlic Powder
- Salt and Pepper to taste
- Oil for Shallow Frying (Extra Virgin, Safflower, or Vegetable work great)

Instructions

Combine bread crumbs, cheese, and thyme in one of two separate containers or shallow bowls. In a separate bowl, whisk together eggs, milk, garlic powder, and salt and pepper.

Coat one cutlet at a time in egg wash, then breadcrumbs, and set aside on a tray until all of the cutlets are uniformly coated.

Preheat the Blackstone Griddle to 350 degrees Fahrenheit, medium low heat.

Drizzle oil into a space the size of your cutlet with a spray bottle, then set cutlet in oil. Rep with each cutlet. Cook for approximately 2-3 minutes, or until golden brown (cooking time depends on thickness of pork, if thicker start with lower heat and cook longer).

Drizzle oil over the cutlet before turning and cooking for another 2-3 minutes, or until golden brown. Lift the cutlet with tongs or a spatula and spray a little additional oil below.

Sprinkle with coarse sea salt and pecorino cheese and place on cooling rack.

Blue Cheese Burgers

6 serv. 12 min.

Ingredients

- Lb. of Ground Beef
- 1 Cup of Blue Cheese
- Salt & Pepper to Taste
- 1/2 Cup of Melted Butter
- 1 Large Red Onion, sliced
- Lettuce
- Tomato Slices

Instructions

Heat the Blackstone Griddle to medium-high.

1/2 of the blue cheese should be mixed into the meat.

Preheat the oven to 350°F. Make six 1/3-pound burger patties. Season with salt and pepper on both sides.

Brush a layer of butter on the Blackstone griddle. Cook the onions in the butter until they are softened.

Cook for 3-4 minutes per side on heated butter patties.

Toast the buns on the griddle till golden brown when the burgers are almost done.

Remove the patties from the griddle and arrange them on the toasted buns with a bed of lettuce. Then add the onions, extra crumbled blue cheese, and tomatoes to the burger.

Juicy Lucy Bacon Burger

4 serv.   12 min.

Ingredients

- Lb. of 80/20 Ground Beef
- 4 Pieces of Bacon

- 4 Slices of Cheddar Cheese
- Lettuce
- Tomato
- 4 Hamburger Buns
- Salt and Pepper
- Special Sauce
- 1/4 Cup of Ketchup
- 1/4 Cup of Mustard
- 1/4 Cup of Mayonnaise
- 1 Tablespoon of Dill Relish

Instructions

To obtain the ideal sear and crust on your meat, you'll need a blazing hot surface to make burger magic. To produce the greatest crust, pre-heat your Blackstone Griddle to medium-high before cooking!

4 slices bacon, cooked Remove the griddle from the heat and drain on a paper towel.

Form 8-10 oz. of beef into two thin patties on a separate platter. Place a broken up slice of cheddar cheese and a split up slice of bacon on the first burger. Seal the two patties together with the second thinly made patty. Season both sides with salt and pepper.

Cook the burger for 3-4 minutes after removing most of the bacon grease. Cover with a basting dome after flipping the burger and adding water. Cook until desired doneness is reached.

Buns should be toasted. On a cutting board, chop the lettuce and tomato pieces.

Remove the buns from the griddle after flipping them. Add special sauce, lettuce,

burger, tomato slices, and additional sauce to the dish. It's best to eat it when it's still hot.

Sweet Onion Dogs

4 Serv.   10 Min.

Ingredients

- 1 Large Vidalia Onion, sliced
- 4 Hot Dogs, scored
- 4 Hot Dog Buns
- 1 Tablespoon of Vegetable Oil
- Salt and Pepper
- Ketchup and Mustard (optional)

Instructions

Add a drizzle of vegetable oil to your Blackstone and set it to medium heat. Cook for 5-7 minutes with the onions and a touch of salt and pepper.

Add the hot dogs and heat for 4 minutes, stirring often, until the onions are slightly caramelized and transparent.

To dish, spread your favorite condiments on the buns, then place a hot dog on top, garnish with some sweet onions, and serve immediately.

Bacon Cheese Burger Dogs

4 Serv.   10 Min.

Ingredients

- 3/4 Lb. of 80/20 Ground Beef
- 4 Pieces of Bacon
- 4 Pieces of American Cheese
- 1/3 Cup of Yellow Onion, Diced
- 4 Hot Dog Buns
- Salt and Pepper
- Ketchup and Mustard (optional)

Instructions

Preheat your Blackstone to medium heat and fry the bacon for 5-6 minutes, or until well done. Remove the bacon from the griddle and drain on a paper towel after it is done.

Place 1/4 of the ground beef in the center of a sheet of plastic wrap on your cutting board. Flatten the ground beef into a rectangle slightly longer than the hot dog buns using your fingertips. Season with salt and pepper, then place one slice of bacon in the center. Half the cheese and place it on top of the bacon. Add a little amount of chopped onion.

Roll the ground beef around the bacon and cheese in plastic wrap to make a "link." It should resemble a hot dog or a sausage. For a tight burger dog, squeeze the edges and close the gaps. Add a little of salt and pepper to taste.

Cook the burger dogs for 2-3 minutes per side in the bacon fat, or until done to your liking.

To serve, place the burger dogs on the buns and top with any desired condiments.

Pastrami Cheese Burger With Smack Sauce

1 serv.   10 min.

Ingredients

- Lb. of 80/20 Ground Beef, formed into 4 burger patties
- 1 Tablespoon of Finely Chopped Jalapeno Pepper
- 1 Tablespoon of Finely Chopped Red Onion
- 2 Teaspoons of Blackstone Crazy Cajun Seasoning
- 1 Tablespoon of Lemon Juice
- 1/3 Cup of Thousand Island Dressing
- 1/4 Cup of Mayonnaise
- 1 Tablespoon of Unsalted Butter
- 1/2 Lb. of Thinly Sliced Pastrami
- 4 Slices Colby Jack Cheese
- 2 Cups of Shredded Romaine Lettuce
- Salt and Pepper

- Olive Oil

Instructions

Combine the jalapeño, red onion, Blackstone Crazy Cajun Seasoning, lemon juice, thousand island dressing, and mayonnaise in a small mixing basin. This is where the smack sauce comes in. Combine equally and set aside for later.

Pour a little olive oil into your Blackstone, which is set to medium-high heat. Season both sides of the burger patties with salt and pepper, and fry for 3-4 minutes each side in the olive oil.

Place the butter and pastrami on the other side of the griddle. Cook, stirring often, for 3-4 minutes.

Place some cooked pastrami on top of each burger patty, followed by a piece of cheese. To melt the cheese, cover with a basting dome.

After toasting the buns, spread some smack sauce on the bottoms of each. Add some shredded lettuce and a burger, then top with the top buns and serve immediately.

Oklahoma Fried Onion Burgers

4 serv.   5 min.

Ingredients

- 1/2 Lb. of 80/20 Ground Beef
- 1 Vidalia Onion (sliced paper thin)
- 4 Slices American Cheese
- 1/4 Cup of Dill Pickle Chips
- Salt

Instructions

Heat your Blackstone to a high temperature.

With the ground beef, form 2 oz. loosely packed meatballs and lay on a heated griddle. Add a sprinkle of salt to each and pound them extremely thin with your flat spatula.

Over each burger, place 2-3 ounces of finely sliced onion.

Cook for 60-90 seconds before flipping the patties so that the onions are below it. Place 1 slice of American cheese on top of each patty, then the top bun on top of that, then the bottom bun on top of that. Cook for 60 seconds more.

To plate, separate the bottom and top buns, raise the burger with the top bread and place it on the bottom bun with your spatula.

Serve with a few dill pickle chips on the side.

Gouda Ale Sliders

4 Serv.   15 Min.

Ingredients

- 1 Lb. of Smoked Gouda (shredded)
- 1 Cup of Parmesan Cheese (shredded)
- 1.5 Lb. of Roast Beef (sliced)
- 12 Oz. of Ale
- Salt & Pepper to Taste
- Granulated Garlic to Taste
- Hoagie Slider Rolls
- Potato Sticks

Instructions

On the griddle or a side burner, place a cast iron skillet or sauce pan. Set your side burner to low heat if you're using one. You can regulate the heat if you place it directly on the griddle top. In a pan, combine the shredded gouda, parmesan, and ale. Stir the mixture constantly. Maintain a low heat.

Set your griddle, or griddle zone, to high in the meanwhile. Apply a thin layer of olive oil to the surface. Place 1.5 pounds of sliced roast beef on top of a heated griddle. To cut the steak into smaller pieces, use a griddle scraper or a spatula.

Season the roast meat with black pepper, garlic granules, and salt to taste.

The roast meat is ready to eat and has already been prepared. Cook the beef until it has caramelized on the exterior and is hot to the touch.

Remove the meat from the griddle top after it has caramelized and blend it with the gouda ale mixture.

Allow to boil for a few minutes after stirring.

Place the hoagie slider rolls on top of the griddle and flip them until they are warm to the touch.

Slice hoagie buns and stuff them with roast meat and cheese.

The Better Mac

1 serv.   15 min.

Ingredients

- 1/2 Lb. of 80/20 ground beef
- 2 Slices American Cheese
- 3 Tablespoons of Minced Onion
- 2 Tablespoons of Dill Pickle Relish
- 2 Tablespoons of Thousand Island Dressing
- Shredded Iceberg Lettuce, to Taste
- Two Burger Bun Heels and 1 Sesame Bun Brown
- Salt, Pepper, and Granulated Garlic to Taste
- Butter
- Recommended: Blackstone Press & Sear Burger Tool, Wax Paper, Olive Oil

Instructions

Blackstone Preheat the griddle to high heat. Apply a thin layer of olive oil on the griddle's surface.

2 14 lb ground beef meatballs, weighed and rolled

Place meatballs on a hot griddle top, cover with wax paper, and crush with the Press & Sear Burger Tool. To get a good sear on the patty, apply pressure to the Press & Sear Burger Tool for a few seconds.

Season patties with salt and pepper to taste. We like to use a combination of salt, pepper, and garlic granules.

When the bottoms of the patties have caramelized, flip them. It will take about 4-5 minutes to complete this task (should have black and brown accents).

Top each burger with a piece of American cheese.

Apply oil to a section of the griddle top that isn't being used. Pour onions, minced, into the oil. As the onions caramelize, stir them with a spatula.

Butter the insides of two burger heels and one burger crown in the meantime. Place the buns on the heated griddle top, butter side down.

To make the unique sauce, follow these steps: Combine Dill Pickle Relish and Thousand Island Dressing in a mixing bowl.

Remove the buns when they are perfectly browned (golden brown).

You may start plating your Better Mac once the cheese has completely melted.

Begin with only one heel. It should be covered in the special sauce. To taste, top the sauce with shredded iceberg lettuce. On top of the patties, place a slice of cheese. On top of the bottom patty, place the second bun heel. Apply Special Sauce to the second bun heel. Place the second patty with cheese on top of the second bun heel. To taste, top with sauteed onions. Finish with a crown.

Have fun with your Better MAC!

Buffalo-Sriracha Ranch Chicken Sandwich

4 serv.   10 min.

Ingredients

- 4-6 Thick Cut Bacon Slices
- 4 Chicken Cutlets
- 1 Tablespoon of Unsalted Butter
- 1 Tablespoon of Hot Sauce
- 1 Tablespoon of Sriracha
- 1/3 Cup of Ranch Dressing
- 1 Cup of Shredded Lettuce
- 4 Tomato Slices
- 4 Potato Buns

- Salt & Pepper

Instructions

Cook the bacon on your Blackstone over medium heat. Drain on a paper towel after cooking.

Cook the chicken cutlets in the bacon oil over medium heat, seasoning them with salt and pepper. Cook for another 2-3 minutes before flipping. Cook for a further 2-3 minutes, or until the chicken is thoroughly done.

Place the butter, spicy sauce, and sriracha in a small sauce saucepan on the griddle. Stir until the butter has melted and the ingredients have been uniformly distributed.

Combine the ranch dressing and buffalo-sriracha sauce in a small mixing bowl. To incorporate everything, give it a good stir.

On the griddle top, toast the buns till golden.

To assemble, place some shredded lettuce on the bottom bread and top with sauce. After that, add the bacon, tomato, and chicken cutlet. Place another layer of sauce on top, followed by the top bun. Serve immediately.

Bbq Reuben Pork Sandwich

2 serv.   60 min.

Ingredients

- Pork
- 8-10 Oz. of Pork Loin Chops
- Kosher Salt to Taste
- Pepper to Taste (Freshly Ground)
- BBQ Pork Seasoning to Taste
- Swiss Chees
- Sriracha mayonnaise
- 1 Garlic Clove
- 1 Cup of Mayonnaise
- 3 Tablespoons of Sriracha
- 4 Tablespoons of Lemon Juice (Freshly Squeezed)
- 4 Rosemary Olive Loaf Bread Slices apple and fennel slaw
- 3 Tart Apples
- 2 Fennel Heads (Small)
- 1 Red Onion (Small, Thinly Sliced)
- 1/4 Cup of Olive Oil
- Salt, Pepper, and Parsley (To Taste)
- 2 Tablespoons of Lemon Juice

Instructions

In a small bowl, combine the garlic, mayonnaise, sriracha, and lemon juice to make the sriracha mayonnaise. Season to taste with salt, then cover and refrigerate the bowl.

Pour the lemon juice into a large mixing bowl to make the apple and fennel slaw.

Toss one apple in the lemon juice after cutting it in half, cored, and julienned. In a mixing dish, combine the remaining ingredients and marinate for 20 minutes.

On the Blackstone Griddle, turn it on. Set one portion to a high heat setting and the other to a low setting. The chops will be cooked on high heat, while the other ingredients will be cooked on low heat.

Season chops equally with olive oil and seasonings.

Cook the pork chops for 4 minutes on each side. Use a thermometer to check the interior temperature; it should be 145 degrees.

Remove the pork chops from the griddle and set aside for 15 minutes to rest. After that, slice.

Place sliced pork from 1 loin on the griddle's low side in a mound. Chop and cook for 1 minute in a cheesesteak style.

Cover with a basting cover to melt 2 pieces of Swiss cheese on top of the pork.

Spread sriracha mayonnaise on pieces of rosemary olive bread. Place on the griddle's low-heat zone.

Place 2 bread pieces on top of the pork loin chop with melted cheese.

Place the pork loin and cheese on top of the apple and fennel slaw.

To taste, add extra sriracha mayonnaise, and then top each sandwich with the remaining slices of bread.

Turkey Party Pita Pockets

8 Serv. 25 Min.

Ingredients

- Lb. of Ground Turkey
- 1 Cup of Cheddar Cheese, Shredded
- 1 Teaspoon of Onion Powder
- 1 Teaspoon of Paprika
- 1 Teaspoon of Cumin
- 1 Tablespoon of Chili Powder
- 1/2 Teaspoon of Pink Sea Salt
- 3-4 Garlic Cloves, Grated
- 1/2 Cup of Green Onions, Sliced
- 4 Rounds Pita Bread, Cut in Halves

Instructions

Combine all ingredients in a large mixing basin.

Roll out the meatballs (about 26) and softly push down to flatten some for even griddle grilling.

Drizzle a little layer of olive oil on your Blackstone and set it over medium to medium-high heat.

Cook the turkey balls/patties for roughly 5 minutes on each side, using your dome halfway through to help them cook through.

Griddle Chili Dogs

8 Serv.   20 Min.

Ingredients

- All Beef Hotdogs
- 8 Hotdog Buns
- 1 Cup of Grated Cheddar Cheese (for topping)
- 1 Tablespoon of Olive Oil
- 1 Large White Onion, Diced (for topping)
- Chili Ingredients
- 1 1/2 Lb. of Ground Beef
- 2 Teaspoons of Ground Cumin
- 1 Tablespoon of Chili Powder
- 1/4 Cup of Ketchup
- 1 Can of Diced or Crushed Tomatoes
- 2 Tablespoons of Mustard
- 1/4 Cup of Water
- 1 Jalapeño (Diced)
- Salt and Pepper to Taste

Instructions

Heat the oil in a griddle over medium heat. Combine the onion, jalapeo, garlic powder, and cumin in a mixing bowl. Cook until it is transparent and tender.

Add the ground beef and use the metal spatula to break it up.

Cook until browned, seasoning with salt, pepper, and chili powder.

Combine the ketchup, tomatoes, and mustard in a mixing bowl.

Reduce the chili on the griddle top until it thickens. If the chili becomes too thick, thin it down with a couple tablespoons of water (you won't need the extra water if you're using chopped tomatoes because they have more moisture). When the chili is done, transfer it to a metal dish and keep it warm on the griddle top.

On two sides, crisscross slice the hotdogs. Coat the hotdogs with olive oil and roll them about on the griddle to coat them. Cook until the outside is crispy.

Toast the hotdog buns on the skillet with butter until golden brown.

Top the hotdog with hotdog chili, grated cheddar cheese, and sliced onions in the bun.

Mustard Dog With Sweet Ketchup Sauce

8 serv.   15 min.

Ingredients

- All Beef Hotdogs or Polish Dogs
- 8 Hotdog Buns
- Butter (to toast hotdog buns)
- 1 White Onion (diced)

- 1/2 Cup of Yellow or Spicy Brown Mustard
- Sweet Ketchup Sauce Ingredients
- 3/4 Cup of Ketchup
- 3/4 Cup of Brown Sugar
- 2 Tablespoons of BBQ Sauce
- 1/4 Cup of Honey
- 2 Teaspoons of Apple Cider Vinegar
- 2 Teaspoons of Worcestershire Sauce
- 1/2 Teaspoon of Onion Powder
- 1/4 Teaspoon of Black pepper

Instructions

In a microwave-safe bowl, combine ketchup, brown sugar, BBQ sauce, honey, cider vinegar, Worcestershire sauce, onion powder, and black pepper to make the sauce. Microwave on high for 1 minute intervals until the sugar is completely dissolved. Allow it cool before pouring into a squeeze container made of plastic.

Preheat your griddle to medium and coat it lightly with oil.

Make crisscross incisions in the hot dogs approximately a quarter of the way through with a sharp knife. This should be done on both sides of the hotdogs. This increases the hotdogs' surface area, ensuring that they are more mustard-covered.

Cook the hotdogs on each side for about 3 minutes. Squeeze roughly a spoonful of mustard onto each hotdog while it's still on the griddle. Allow them to fry for another minute or two on the griddle.

Butter the hotdog buns and cook them till golden brown on the griddle.

Top the hot dog with ketchup sauce and chopped white onions before putting it on the bun.

Patty Melt

1 serv.   10 min.

Ingredients

- 1 1/2 Lb. of Ground Beef
- 2 Large Yellow Onions
- 12 Slices Rye Bread
- 12 Slices Swiss Cheese (or use half Cheddar Cheese)
- 2 Tablespoons of Dijon Mustard
- 1 Tablespoon of Worcestershire Sauce
- Butter
- Olive Oil
- Salt & Pepper to taste

Instructions

Make 1/4 pound patties out of the meat. Smash the patties between parchment paper with a large object or the bottom of a saucepan to roughly 1/4" thick.

Preheat the griddle to medium-low heat.

Onions should be sliced. Place a spoonful of butter and a tablespoon of olive oil on the griddle. Season all of the onion slices with salt and pepper and place them on the griddle.

Sauté the onions until tender, then stir in the Dijon mustard and Worcestershire sauce and simmer for a few minutes more, until well blended.

Place the onions in a mixing dish.

Preheat the griddle to medium-high and place the burger patties on top. Season with salt and pepper to taste. Cook until done, then remove from heat and put aside while assembling the sandwiches.

Arrange all of the bread pieces on the table. Place a piece of cheese on top of the burger patty, then top with caramelized onions and another slice of cheese. Each sandwich should have butter on the top and bottom.

Reduce the heat to medium-low and place the sandwiches on the griddle. Cook until both sides are golden brown, then remove and serve.

Mango Tango Turkey Burger

1 serv.   10 min.

Ingredients

- Lb. of Ground Turkey or Chicken
- 2 Tablespoons of Minced Garlic
- 1 1/2 Tablespoons of Organic Great Value Mango Habanero Seasoning
- (Walmart brand) or Jamaican Jerk Seasoning
- Fresh Mango Salsa (Available in Grocery Produce Coolers)
- 1 Cup of Mayonnaise
- 1 Tablespoon of Chili Garlic Sauce (Found Next to Sriracha Sauce)
- 1/2 Red Onion, Sliced
- 6 Fresh JalapeÃ±o Peppers
- Monterrey Jack Cheese Slices
- 1 Bunch Fresh Cilantro
- 6-8 Torta Rolls

Instructions

Preheat the Blackstone griddle to its highest setting. Coat the griddle top with mild olive oil once it's hot.

2 tbsp. Mango Habanero Seasoning, pounded turkey, and 2 tbsp. Garlic, minced Form the burgers into medium-sized patties.

Jalapeos should be washed, seeded, and sliced.

Red onion should be peeled and sliced into big burger-sized pieces.

Combine 1 cup mayonnaise and 2 tablespoons chili garlic sauce in a mixing bowl.

Clean and cut the cilantro.

Place the turkey patties on the griddle while it is still hot. When the bottom side of the patties is seared, flip them. After you've turned your patties, use your spatula to smooth them out.

Place the jalapeos on the griddle. Drizzle the peppers with oil and season with salt.

As each burger patty nears completion, add a piece of Monterrey Jack cheese. Top the cheese with the jalapeos that have been sautéed. Melt the cheese into the jalapeos with a Blackstone 12" Round Basting Cover.

Meanwhile, lay the inside down cut Torta roll on the greased griddle top. Toast the buns till golden brown.

Put the burger together. In the bottom roll, spread the Chili Garlic Mayo. On top of the mayo, place 2 onion slices. Place the patties, cheese, and jalapeos on top of the onion. Serve with Mango Salsa and chopped cilantro on top. Serve with the top bun.

Pretzel Sliders

1 Serv. 10 Min.

Ingredients

- 1 Lb. of Ground Beef
- 1 Envelope Onion Soup Mix (Lipton or Comparable)
- 1 Package Bacon
- 6 Slices Cheddar Cheese
- 6 Slices Sliced Provolone Cheese
- 6 Slices Sliced Baby Swiss Cheese
- Granulated Garlic to taste
- Cracked Black Pepperto taste
- Sea Salt to taste
- Classic Yellow Mustard to taste

- 6 Pretzel Slider Rolls (Labriola brand can be found in Costco's bakery)

Instructions

Preheat the Blackstone griddle to high or medium heat. On the griddle, cook enough bacon strips to cover all of the sliders. To keep the bacon from curling up, use the Blackstone Bacon Press (included in the Blackstone Breakfast Kit). Turn one of the end burners off and transfer the bacon to the other side of the griddle to keep it heated.

1 pound ground beef + 1 packet onion soup mix = 1 pound ground beef + 1 packet onion soup mix = 1 pound ground beef + 1 packet onion soup mix = 1 pound Make mini slider patties with the same diameter as the pretzel slider rolls.

On the griddle, place slider patties. Add granulated garlic, cracked black pepper, and sea salt to taste.Once the patties have a decent blackened sear on one side, flip them. Season the patties on the other side.

It's time to add the cheese when the patties are almost done cooking. Cut huge sandwich-sized cheese slices down to slider-sized cheese slices using an upside-down drinking glass or a biscuit/cookie cutter. Add one slice of cheddar, one slice of provolone, one slice of baby Swiss, and one more slice of cheddar to each burger.

Add two bacon slices that are crossed. To quickly melt the cheese, use the Blackstone 12" Round Basting Cover.

Pretzel slider rolls should be cut in half.

Place the rolls (both crowns and heels) on the griddle top upside down. Check the rolls regularly to ensure that they are toasting to a golden brown color.

Serve with traditional yellow mustard on top of the burger and enjoy!

Country Western Burger

1 serv.   10 min.

Ingredients

- Lb. of Ground Beef
- 1/4 Cup of Liquid Smoke
- Granulated Garlic to taste
- Salt and Pepper to taste
- 1 Package Thick Sliced Black Pepper Bacon
- 1 Bag Breaded Onion Rings
- 10-12 Slices Monterrey Jack Cheese Slices
- Country Bob's All Purpose Sauce (Available at Walmart and other Grocery Stores)
- Texas Toast Bread

Instructions

Preheat the Blackstone griddle to its highest setting. When the griddle is hot, gently oil the top.

4 lbs. of mixture 1/4 cup liquid smoke, ground meat

On the griddle top, place frozen battered onion rings. When the first side of the onion rings is crispy and slightly browned, flip them.

On the griddle, place bacon strips. To keep bacon flat, use the Blackstone Bacon Press (included in the Blackstone Breakfast Kit).

Place burger patties on top of a heated griddle. Use your favorite burger or western-style seasoning, or season with garlic, salt, and pepper to taste.

Move the onion rings to one end of the griddle when they're done. Turn off the heat zone and keep the onion rings warm while the patties finish cooking.

When the first side is browned and somewhat blackened, flip the patties. Season the second side of the burger patty with salt and pepper.

As the burger patty nears completion, add a piece of Monterrey Jack cheese.

Top the burger patty with two slices of fried bacon and one or two onion rings. To quickly melt the cheese, use the Blackstone 12" Round Basting Cover.

Place pieces of Texas Toast on top of the griddle. Toast till golden brown on one side, then turn and toast the other.

Place the burger on a plate and cover it with Country Bob's all-purpose sauce.

Bacon Jalapeño Popper Burger

1 serv.   10 min.

Ingredients

- Lb. of 80/20 Ground Beef
- 1 Lb. of Bacon
- 8 Oz. of Cream Cheese
- 8 Oz. of Shredded Cheddar Cheese
- 2 Fresh JalapeÃ±os, Diced
- 1 TapatÃo Hot Sauce (Extra for Bacon)
- 2 Teaspoons of Horseradish
- 1 Red Onion, Sliced
- 2 Large Tomatoes, Sliced
- 6-8 Hamburger Buns

Instructions

Preheat griddle to medium-high heat.

Make 6-8 patties out of your hamburger.

Place the bacon on the griddle in its whole. Season the bacon lightly with pepper and sprinkle with Tapato Hot Sauce to taste.

Remove the bacon from the griddle when it's done and slice it into tiny pieces.

Jalapeos, diced, sauteed on griddle (use some of the bacon grease).

Cream together cream cheese, shredded cheddar, cooked jalapeos, diced bacon, 1 tablespoon Tapato, and 2 teaspoons horseradish in a large mixing basin.

Season your burgers with salt and pepper before placing them on the griddle.

When one side of your burger has browned, flip it. Then put the cheese mixture on top of each burger.

Using a basting cover, baste the burgers until the cheese mixture is melted.

On the griddle, toast hamburger buns.

Serve your burgers with slices of tomato and onion (lettuce optional).

Beer Braised Bratwurst

1 serv.   10 min.

Ingredients

- 10 Bratwursts
- 2 Bottles of Beer (any Lager or Ale will work)
- 2 Large Onions
- 2 Green Peppers
- 2 Red Peppers
- 1 Stick of Butter
- 10 Bratwurst Buns
- Stone Ground Mustard (or Spicy Brown)
- Kosher Salt
- Fresh Ground Black

- 1 Teaspoon of Garlic powder

Instructions

Preheat the griddle to medium-high temperature.

On the griddle top, place a tin tray or a 9x13â cake pan (make sure it is does not have a non-stick coating on it).

Pour the beer into the tray, then season it with Kosher salt, black pepper, and garlic powder.

Slice the onions and peppers, then toss them in with the beer.

For about 5 minutes, bring the braising liquid to a gentle simmer.

Add all of the bratwurst to the braising liquid and cook, rotating once, for about 5 minutes.

Transfer the bratwurst on the griddle top and cook until golden brown on both sides. Transfer the onions and peppers on the griddle with the bratwurst and heat until they begin to brown as well.

Serve the bratwurst with the onion, peppers, and stone ground mustard on a toasted bratwurst bun.

Philly Cheesesteak

1 serv. 10 min.

Ingredients

- Lb. of Thinly Sliced Beef (Rib-Eye Roast, Sirloin, Tri-Tip Roast, Rump Roast, or Flank Steak)
- 1 Onion, Sliced
- 1 Green Pepper, Sliced
- 1 Red Pepper, Sliced
- 1 Teaspoon of Garlic Powder
- 2 Tablespoons of Butter
- Salt & Fresh Ground Black Pepper to Taste
- 3 Tablespoons of Red Wine Vinegar (or apple cider vinegar)
- 12-18 Slices of Provolone Cheese
- 1 Jar of Cheese Whiz
- 6 Hoagie Rolls

Instructions

1. Preheat the griddle to high medium heat
2. 1 tablespoon butter and a little oil on the griddle
3. On the heated griddle, add the onions, green peppers, and red peppers.
4. Add salt, pepper, vinegar, and 12 teaspoon garlic powder to taste. Toss to mix and evenly coat.

5. On the other side of the griddle, add another tablespoon of butter and some oil.
6. On the griddle, place the thinly sliced meat. To help it cook evenly, chop it up with your metal spatulas. Salt, pepper, and another 12 teaspoon garlic powder to the meat.
7. When the meat is done, split it evenly into 6 heaps on the griddle.
8. Reduce the heat to medium.
9. Preheat the griddle to high medium heat.
10. 1 tablespoon butter and a little oil on the griddle
11. On the heated griddle, add the onions, green peppers, and red peppers.
12. Add salt, pepper, vinegar, and 12 teaspoon garlic powder to taste. Toss to mix and evenly coat.
13. On the other side of the griddle, add another tablespoon of butter and some oil.
14. On the griddle, place the thinly sliced meat. To help it cook evenly, chop it up with your metal spatulas. Salt, pepper, and another 12 teaspoon garlic powder to the meat.
15. When the meat is done, split it evenly into 6 heaps on the griddle.
16. Reduce the heat to medium.

Ramen Burger

1 serv.   10 min.

Ingredients

- Ramekins
- 5 Packages of Ramen
- 5 Hamburger Patties
- 5 Eggs
- 2 Pinches Sea Salt
- 2 Pinches - Black Pepper
- 2 Pinches Granulated Garlic
- 1 Cup of KC Masterpiece BBQ Sauce
- 1-2 Tablespoons of Mr. Yoshida's Teriyaki Sauce
- 1/4 Cup of Chopped Green Onion

Instructions

Ramen noodle packets should be boiled and strained.

In a bowl, crack eggs and season with a pinch of Sea Salt, Black Pepper, and Granulated Garlic. In a mixing dish, combine all of the ingredients.

In a bowl of boiling Ramen noodles, pour the egg mixture. Everything should be completely combined.

Fill 6 ramekins halfway with Ramen noodles and wrap with plastic wrap. Refrigerate the ramekins for 15 minutes.

In a mixing dish, pour the KC Masterpiece BBQ Sauce. Mr. Yoshida's Teriyaki Sauce and green onion, chopped Combine all of the ingredients in a large mixing bowl and put aside.

Preheat the griddle on high and drizzle with olive oil. On the griddle, place ramen patties and hamburger patties. Garlic granules can be used to season burger patties. Place turkey bacon strips on the griddle. When the Ramen patties are golden brown, flip them. Glaze each of the hamburger patties with the sauce when they're almost done. Place a hamburger patty, turkey bacon, and shredded lettuce between the two Ramen buns once everything is done. Enjoy! O

Griddle Cheesy Chicken Quesadilla Recipe

This flavorful Griddle Cheesy Chicken Quesadilla Recipe is a quick supper alternative that your entire family will enjoy!! Take it from Chef Sherry: this restaurant-quality quesadilla dish created with only a few fundamental ingredients will impress your family!

Total Time: 25 MINUTES

Ingredients

- Chicken, Small Diced 1 1/2 lbs (730 g)
- Mushrooms, White - Sliced 8 oz (225 g)
- Peppers, Small Diced 3/4 cup (3 oz) (80 g)
- Onion, White - Sliced 2 cups (5 oz) (140 g)
- Flour Tortillas, Soft Taco Shell - 8" 6 each
- Cheese, Shredded - Mexican Blend 2 cups (8 oz) (227 g)
- Salt, Seasoned - Lawry's 1/2 teaspoon (0.1 oz) (3 g)
- Pepper, Seasoned 1/4 teaspoon (0.05 oz) (1 g)
- Olive Oil 1 tablespoon (0.55 oz) (16 g)

Instructions

1. Quesadilla de Pollo de Pollo de Pollo de Pollo de Pollo de Pollo de Pollo
2. To create your chicken quesadilla, gather all of your ingredients.
3. Preheat the griddle to medium.
4. Place 12 tbsp of olive oil on an area of the griddle when it has been warmed up.
5. Arrange the veggies over the heated oil.
6. Add the remaining 12 tablespoon of olive oil on the griddle on the other side.
7. Season the diced chicken with seasoned salt and pepper and place it on top of the oil.
8. Cook until the veggies are tender and the chicken is cooked through.
9. On the griddle, combine the vegetables and cooked chicken.

10. 3 tortilla shells should be placed on the griddle.
11. 1/3 of the vegetable/meat combination should be placed on the shell.
12. Add 1/3 of the shredded cheese to each quesadilla, then the tortilla shell on top of the melted cheese.
13. To sauté the other side of the chicken quesadilla, flip it over.

Blackstone Pork Egg Rolls

4 Serv. 20 Min.

Ingredients

- 8 Egg Roll Wraps
- 1/2 Lb. of 80/20 Ground Pork
- 1 1/2 Tablespoons of Minced Garlic
- 1 Tablespoons of Minced Ginger
- 1 Tablespoon of Sesame Oil
- 1/3 Cup of Sliced Green Onion
- 2 Cups of Shredded Cabbage (pre-shredded Cole Slaw mix is a great substitute)
- 2 Tablespoons of Soy Sauce
- Olive Oil
- Spray Vegetable Oil

Instruction

Preheat your griddle to medium-high heat and your Blackstone to 400°.

Drizzle a little olive oil on the griddle before adding the ground pork. Cook, stirring often, for 4-5 minutes.

Cook for another 2-3 minutes after adding the garlic and ginger.

Cook for another 2 minutes, stirring often, after adding the sesame oil and cabbage.

Toss in the green onions and soy sauce until well combined.

Place a few teaspoons of the pork mixture in the middle of each egg roll wrapper. Wet the border edges of the egg roll wrapper with a little water and fold one corner to the center. Wrap each side of the wrapper into the centre and roll it to meet the other end. These should resemble little burritos. Continue with the remaining egg rolls.

Coat the egg rolls in spray oil and place them in th basket. Return the basket to the and cook for another 6-7 minutes. For a more even hue, flip the egg rolls halfway through.

Serve with a sweet Thai chili sauce on the side.

Griddle Girl Apple Fries

Ingredients:

- 2 large green apples
- 1 cup graham cracker crumbs

- ¼ cup sugar
- 2 eggs
- 1 cup flour
- Cooking spray
- Caramel Dip

Instructions:

Apples should be peeled and thinly sliced.

Combine graham cracker crumbs and sugar in a mixing basin. Scramble two eggs in a separate dish. Pour flour into the third basin.

Coat each apple slice with flour, then egg mixture, and finally graham crumbs, working in batches.

Cooking spray should be sprayed on the Air fryer tray. Reduce the heat to medium.

Cook for 5 minutes after adding apple slices to the tray.

Cook for 3 minutes more on the other side.

Remove the apples from the oven and serve with a caramel apple dip.

Enjoy!

Griddle Girl Toasted Ravioli Bruschetta

Ingredients:

- 2 large tomatoes diced
- 2 tbsp fresh basil
- 1 tbsp minced garlic
- ¼ cup shredded parmesan
- 1 tbsp olive oil
- Salt and pepper
- 2 eggs
- ¼ cup milk
- 1 cup bread crumbs
- ½ cup grated parmesan
- 1 tbsp Italian seasons
- 3 cheese ravioli
- Balsamic glaze
- Cooking spray

Instruction:

Chop the tomatoes and place them in a bowl. Toss in the fresh basil, garlic, olive oil, and grated parmesan cheese. Set aside after stirring until everything is well blended.

1 cup bread crumbs, Italian seasonings, and grated parmesan cheese in a mixing bowl Scramble two eggs with milk in a separate dish.

Cook ravioli for 5 minutes in salted water, then drain.

Repeat the procedure of dipping each ravioli into the egg mixture and then into the bread crumb mixture until all raviolis are covered.

Set the air fryer tray to medium and coat it with cooking spray. Cook for 5 minutes before flipping the raviolis and cooking for an additional 3 minutes.

Place the raviolis on a platter after removing them from the air fryer. Top with the bruschetta mixture, extra parmesan, and a balsamic glaze drizzle.

Ricotta Lemon Griddle Cakes

4 Serv. 20 Min.

Dry ingredients:

- 1 cup all purpose flour
- 1 tbsp baking powder
- 1 tbsp baking soda
- 2 tbsp sugar
- ¼ tsp salt
- Wet Ingredients:
- 1 ¼ cup whole milk ricotta
- 2 eggs
- ⅔ cup milk
- Juice from one large lemon
- 1 ½ tsp pure vanilla extract
- Butter for cooking

- Zest from one large lemon

Instructions:

Combine the wet ingredients in one mixing bowl and the dry ingredients in the other. Combine the wet ingredients in a mixing bowl.

To blend the dry and wet ingredients, add them slowly to the wet mixing bowl. Allow to sit for 10 minutes or until the Blackstone reaches medium heat.

Using a 14 cup measuring cup per pancake, swirl butter to melt where the pancakes will be cooked.

Cook for 2 minutes per side, turning once, or until bubbles emerge.

Enjoy!

Thai Kai Chicken Sliders

1 serv.   10 min.

Ingredients

- 3 Lb. of Ground Chicken
- 2 Cup of Shredded Carrots
- 1/2 Cup of Chopped Green Onion
- 4-5 Cloves of Minced Garlic
- 1 Cup of Chili Galic Sauce
- 1-1Â¼ Cups of Diced Red Cabbage
- 1/2 Cup of Mayonnaise

- 1/4 Cup of Sweet Thai Chili Sauce
- 1 Teaspoon of Granulated Garlic
- Chopped Cilantro
- Sea Salt or Pink Himalayan Salt
- Green Leaf Lettuce
- Sweet Hawaiian Rolls
- Ice-Cream Scoop with Lever

Instructions:

In a large mixing bowl, combine 3 pounds of ground chicken. Shredded carrots, sliced green onion, minced garlic, chile garlic sauce, and Himalayan Pink Salt are all good additions. Everything should be completely combined.

Start with a bowl of sliced red cabbage for the Southeast Asian slaw. 1 tsp granulated garlic, mayonnaise, Sweet Thai Chili Sauce, tiny handfuls of cilantro To make a thick coleslaw, combine all of the ingredients in a mixing bowl.

Preheat the griddle on high and drizzle with olive oil. Place scoops of chicken on the griddle using an ice cream scoop with a lever. Once the bottom is blackened, flip it. Once the outsides of the patties are seared, reduce the heat to medium-low to prevent the outsides from burning while the insides continue to cook. Place the burgers on Sweet Hawaiian Rolls after they're done. Add the South East Asian Slaw and some Green Leaf Lettuce. Enjoy!

Cheese Sausage Stuffing Balls

1 serv.   10 min.

Ingredients

- 1 Lb. of Sage Flavored Breakfast Sausage
- 2-3 Celery Stalks, Diced Small
- 1 Onion, Diced Small
- 3 Tablespoons of Salted Butter
- 2 Cloves Garlic, Grated
- 1 Teaspoon of Poultry Seasoning
- 1 14oz Bag Herb Seasoned Stuffing, like Pepperidge Farm Herb Seasoned Classic Stuffing
- 1 Cup of Chicken Stock
- 1 Cup of Cheddar Cheese
- 1/2 Cup of Parmesan Cheese
- 3 Eggs, Beaten
- 1/4 Cup of Curly Parsley, chopped
- Salt and Pepper to Taste
- Vegetable Oil and 1-2 TBSP butter for cooking

Instructions

Set aside the sausage once it has been cooked and crumbled in a skillet or on the Blackstone.

Cook onions and celery in 3 tbsp butter in the same pan or on the Blackstone until tender. Cook for a further minute after adding the garlic and poultry seasoning.

Allow 5 minutes for the mixture to cool before adding it to the sausage.

Add the dry stuffing mixture to the sausage mixture (you may use chopped up bread instead of shop purchased stuffing if you want), then add the chicken broth and gently stir to coat.

Season to taste with salt and/or pepper.

Gently fold in the cheese, eggs, and parsley. Refrigerate the dough for at least 20 minutes before making the balls; this will make the process simpler.

Form balls with your hands to your desired size. I recommend a small amount for an appetizer and a large size (about 14 cup) for dinner servings.

Preheat your Blackstone to 350 degrees Fahrenheit.

Mix together vegetable oil and 1-2 tbsp genuine butter on the griddle.

Place the sausage balls on top and cook for about 1-2 minutes on each side, flipping to ensure equal cooking.

For dipping, serve with gravy or cranberry sauce.

Cheese Steak Egg Rolls

1 serv.   10 min.

Ingredients

- 1 Lb. of Chopped Steak (Thin Sliced Sirloin or Ribeye or Ground Beef)
- 4-5 Slices White American Cheese
- 1/4 Cup of Green Pepper, Diced Small
- 1/4 Cup of White Onion, Diced Small
- 1 Tablespoon of Worcestershire Sauce
- 8 Wonton Wrappers
- Garlic Powder
- Salt and Pepper
- Vegetable Oil
- Sriracha Ketchup

Instructions

Drizzle a little vegetable oil on the Blackstone griddle and place it on medium heat. Cook the onions and peppers for 3 minutes, seasoning with salt and pepper. Set aside and preheat the griddle to high. Chopped steak or ground beef can be added.

Chop your meat into small pieces using your Blackstone spatula and scraper. Reduce the heat to low, add the worcestershire, season with salt, pepper, and garlic powder to taste, then stir in the peppers and onions.

To steam melt the cheese, place it on top of the meat and cover with a dome. Remove the meat from the griddle and place it in a large mixing bowl with the cheese to evenly coat it. Cover and let aside to cool somewhat so you can handle the meat mixture when making the eggrolls.

Place wrappers in a diamond form spoon on an oval shaped layer of meat in the middle, following the directions on the back of the wonton wrapper. Fold the bottom up and around the filling, then fold in the sides and roll upwards. Rub warm water along the seams to seal them. Put them on parchment paper until you're ready to cook them.

Return the Blackstone griddle to high heat and pour a liberal amount of vegetable oil onto the side of the griddle opposite the grease drain. It helps to slightly tilt the griddle so that the oil runs where you want it to by inserting a 14-inch wedge beneath both wheels so that the oil does not run to the wrong side and off the griddle, which is important since you need a lot of oil to cook the eggrolls. Place the eggrolls in the heated oil and flip to brown all sides of the wonton wrappers.

With Sriracha Ketchup on the side.

Salmon Tacos With Avocado & Corn Salsa

1 serv. 10 min.

Ingredients

- Avocado and Corn Salsa
- 3 Large Avocados, Peeled, Cored and Diced
- 1 Can Whole Kernel Corn (Drained)
- 1/3 Cup of Diced Red Onion
- 1 Bunch Cilantro, Chopped
- 1 Jalapeño (Diced)
- 2 Garlic Cloves, Minced
- 1 Lime, Juiced
- Teaspoons of Olive Oil
- 2 Tablespoons of Apple Cider Vinega
- Salmon Tacos
- 2 Lb. of Salmon, Skinned (Any Pin Bones Removed)
- 2 Tablespoons of Olive Oil
- 1 Lime
- 1 Teaspoon of Ground Cumin
- 1 Teaspoon of Chipotle Chili Powder
- 1 Teaspoon of Onion Powder
- 1 Teaspoon of Paprika
- 1 Teaspoon of Ground Coriander
- 1/2 Teaspoon of Salt
- 1/2 Teaspoon of Black Pepper
- 10 Corn Tortillas, Warmed
- 2 Cups of Red Cabbage, Thinly Sliced
- 1/2 Cup of Crumbled Cotija Cheese

Instructions:

To make the Avocado and Corn Salsa, combine all of the ingredients from the Avocado and Corn Salsa ingredient group in a mixing bowl. To taste, season with salt and pepper. Mix everything together gently, taking care not to over-mash the avocado.

To make the salmon, whisk together olive oil, 1 lime juice, chipotle chili powder, cumin, onion powder, paprika, coriander, salt, and freshly ground black pepper in a mixing bowl. Rub the mixture all over the fish.

Preheat the griddle to medium-high temperature. Cook the fish for 3 minutes on each side on a griddle. Take the fish from the griddle and cut it into bits.

Preheat the griddle to high. Warm the corn tortillas on the griddle for 30 seconds to 1 minute per side.

To make the tacos, start by layering the salmon in the tortilla. Toss in the cut cabbage and the avocado salsa. Cotija cheese is sprinkled on top, and fresh lime juice is squeezed over the top.

Bonzai Pipeline Tacos

1 serv.   10 min.

Ingredients

- 1 Lb. of Diced Boneless, Skinless, Chicken Breast
- 20 Oz. of Crushed Pineapple in Juice
- 1 Cup of Mr. Yoshida's Marinade & Cooking Sauce: Original Gourmet - Sweet & Savory
- Granulated Garlic to taste
- Salt & Pepper to Taste
- 2 Diced JalapeÃ±os with Seeds Removed
- 1 Diced Red Onion
- 1 Green Pepper, Sliced
- 12 Flour Street Taco-Sized Tortillas (approximately 5" in diameter)
- 1 Bunch Fresh Chopped Cilantro

Instructions:

Preheat the Blackstone griddle to its highest setting. Coat the griddle top with mild olive oil once it's hot.

Place chopped chicken on one of the heated griddle's top zones. Season with garlic granules, salt, and black pepper to taste.

Place the jalapeo, onions, and green pepper in a different zone of the heated griddle. Salt and pepper to taste.

Place the crushed pineapple in a different zone of the heated griddle top.

As the ingredients cook on the griddle top, mix and turn them with a spatula.

Peppers and onions should be slightly browned and onions should be largely transparent. Pineapple should be slightly charred after cooking. Cook the chicken until it is fully cooked and the exterior is slightly browned.

Reduce the heat to a low setting on the griddle.

Add Mr. Yoshida's Marinade and use spatulas to combine all ingredients on the griddle top.

Warm the tortillas on the griddle until they are golden brown. Don't let them become too hot.

Fill each Tortilla evenly with the hot combined ingredients. To taste, garnish with fresh chopped cilantro.

Bonzai Pipeline Tacos have a hot, sticky, sweet flavor.

Greek Gyros (Pork Or Chicken)

1 serv. 10 min.

Ingredients

- 2 Pork Tenderloins (or 4 Chicken Breasts)
- Onion (1/2 shredded, 1/2 thinly sliced)
- Garlic Cloves, finely minced
- 1 Tablespoon of Dried Marjoram
- 1 Tablespoon of Dried Ground Rosemary
- 2 tsp of Kosher Salt
- 3 Tablespoons of Extra Virgin Olive Oil
- 1/2 Teaspoon of Ground Black Pepper
- 1/4 Cup of White Wine
- 1 Tablespoon of Butter
- 2 Large Tomatoes, halved then sliced
- Tzatziki Sauce (Store bought or see recipe below)
- 8 Pieces Pita Bread

Instructions

The onion should be cut in half. 1/2 of the onion should be shredded in a large mixing basin. Set aside the remaining half of the onion to dice later.

Combine the shredded onion, garlic, marjoram, rosemary, salt, olive oil, black pepper, and white wine in a large mixing bowl.

Any white membrane on the tenderloins should be removed. Tenderloins should be cut lengthwise and then sliced into 1/4" pieces.

Place the pork in the marinade, cover, and marinate for up to 24 hours in the refrigerator.

Preheat the griddle to a medium-high temperature.

Cook the pork until it is half done on the griddle.

Toss the meat with 2 Tablespoons butter and a few more Tablespoons wine. Toss to melt the butter and mix until all of the ingredients are cooked. Make sure the meat isn't overcooked.

Remove from the fire and top with sliced tomatoes, chopped onions, and Tzatziki Sauce over Greek Pita Bread.

Sweet Spicy Bang Bang Shrimp

1 serv. 10 min.

Ingredients

- 1 Lb. of Peeled and De-veined Shrimp
- 1 Cup of Butter Milk
- 1 Cup of Corn Starch
- 1/2 Teaspoon of Garlic Powder
- 1/4 Cup of Sliced Green Onions
- 1-2 Tablespoon of Toasted Tuxedo Sesame Seeds
- 3/4 Cup of Mayo
- 1/2 Cup of Sweet Chili Sauce
- 1-2 Tablespoon of Sriracha Sauce

Instructions

Remove the tails and peel and devein the shrimp. Place the shrimp and buttermilk in a freezer bag and chill for 30 minutes to 2 hours.

Mix mayo, sweet chili sauce, and sriracha sauce together to make your Bang Bang sauce. Set aside after adjusting the ingredients to your satisfaction (more mayo and sweet chili for sweeter, more sriracha for spicy). Set aside your green onions after slicing them. If you haven't previously done so, roast your sesame seeds (toast a few minutes in a dry skillet)

Place shrimp in a colander to drain. In a fresh freezer bag, combine corn starch and garlic powder, then add shrimp and shake to coat evenly.

Preheat the Blackstone griddle to medium-high to high. Shake off any excess cornstarch before adding a fair quantity of vegetable oil and shrimp. Allow to fry for 3-5 minutes on one side until golden brown. Cook for another 3-5 minutes on the other side. Drizzle extra oil on the backs of the shrimp just before flipping, then add more oil as required beneath the shrimp to make them crispy!

Remove the pan from the heat and place it on a paper towel-lined plate to absorb any excess oil. Toss with 12-34% of the Bang Bang Sauce until uniformly coated, adding more as necessary. Sesame seeds, green onions, and additional sauce are sprinkled on top.

Serve as an appetizer or as a side dish with Bang Bang Tacos and Shrimp Rice Bowls!

Garlic Soy Pork Chops

1 serv. 10 min.

Ingredients

- 5-7 Thick Cut Pork Chops
- 3-4 Garlic Cloves
- 1/2 Cup of Extra Virgin Olive Oil
- 1/2 Cup of Low Sodium Soy Sauce
- 1/2 Teaspoon of Garlic Powder
- 1/2 Teaspoon of Sea Salt
- 1 Teaspoon of Fresh Cracked Black Pepper
- 1/2 Cup of Curly Parsley
- 1/2 Stick Real Butter
- Extra Virgin Olive Oil for griddle top

Instructions

I get a large pork loin from Sam's Club or BJ's and cut the chops myself. I normally get four freezer bags, each with five to seven 1-1/4" thick chops. Freezing the additional three bags of chops in an airtight container! Alternatively, you may buy ready-to-eat thick-cut chops or have your butcher cut them thick for you!

Mix fresh chopped garlic, olive oil, soy sauce, salt and pepper, parsley (reserving some for garnishing), and garlic powder in a small mixing dish. Fill a freezer bag halfway with the mixture and chops and seal it tightly, rubbing everything to blend. Refrigerate for 30 minutes to 6 hours after marinating.

Remove pork chops from freezer bag and place on counter for 20-25 minutes to reach room temperature.

Preheat the Blackstone Griddle to medium-high heat. Add a drizzle of olive oil (approximately 12 tbsp) and 1 12 tbsp butter, mixing it in with the oil. Place your chops on the grill one at a time, ensuring sure they get garlic and parsley on them but without spilling the entire bag of marinade onto the griddle. I also like to put little additional marinade on top of each chop). Allow to fry for 4-5 minutes before turning and seasoning with cracked black pepper. Cook for 3-4 minutes after flipping and spreading 1.5 tbsp butter beneath the chops.

Over and around the chops, drizzle a dash of low sodium soy sauce (approximately 2 tbsp). Cook for another 2-4 minutes, then reduce to medium to medium low heat and flip 1-2 more times until chops are fully done.

Place the chops on top of 1 tbsp melted butter (a little extra won't harm) on a serving dish (one that can hold some liquid). Allow 10 minutes to REST before cutting into them. Serve with chopped parsley on top. Your dish will be dripping with dipping juices after 10 minutes! Thinly slice the chops and dip them in the sauce.

Wild Caught Jumbo Scallops With Shredded Sprouts & Prosciutto

1 serv. 10 min.

Ingredients

- 1 1/2 Lb. of Brussels Sprouts
- 4 Oz. of Diced Prosciutto
- 3 Garlic Cloves
- 1 1/2 Tablespoons of Extra Virgin Olive Oil
- Sea Salt & Fresh Cracked Pepper to Taste
- Juice of Half Lemon
- Zest of Half a Lemon
- 1/4 Cup of Fresh Grated Locatelli Pecorino Romano Cheese

Instructions

Wash and rinse the Brussels Sprouts (don't worry if they don't drain completely; the additional water helps the grill steam). Season with sea salt, fresh cracked pepper, and garlic powder after cutting in half and slicing thinly. 1.5 tablespoons extra virgin olive oil Cover and set aside while you finish the rest of your preparations.

Prosciutto should be diced. 3 garlic cloves, crushed and diced Scallops should be rinsed and patted dry. Season with cracked black pepper and sea salt.

Sauté garlic and prosciutto in 12 tbsp butter for around one minute. On medium heat, add the sprouts and simmer for about 5 minutes, stirring everything around. (I like to season with oils and spices ahead of time, especially with vegetables, so that I don't have to use any more oil during cooking.)

Melt 2 tbsp butter on med-med/high heat on the opposite side of the griddle at the same time. Cook the scallops in the butter for 3-4 minutes, then turn and add the juice of half a lemon and 1 tablespoon butter, cooking for another 3-4 minutes.

Garnish with fresh grated Locatelli Pecorino Romano cheese and lemon zest (or whatever cheese you like).

Octopus

1 serv. 10 min.

Ingredients

- 1 Package of Frozen Cleaned Octopus (17.6 oz-3 octopus)
- 2 Lemons
- 4 Tablespoons of Chopped Italian Parsley
- 2 Large Garlic Cloves
- 1 Bay Leaf

- 1/2 Cup of Dry White Wine or White Wine Vinegar
- 1 Tablespoon of Red Wine Vinegar
- 10 Whole Black Peppercorns
- Extra Virgin Olive Oil
- Sea Salt & Fresh Cracked Pepper to Taste

Instructions:

Allow octopus to defrost overnight in the refrigerator. Rinse well and place in a stockpot with enough water to cover. Add the wine, 1 smashed garlic clove, bay leaf, peppercorns, and half a lemon to the pan. Cook for 45 minutes at a low temperature.

Remove the octopus and rinse it thoroughly. Carefully slice off the head, leaving the legs attached. Place in a bowl and chill for 30 minutes at room temperature, covered with plastic wrap. 1 garlic clove chopped, 2 12 tbsp chopped parsley, squeeze of lemon, salt, and pepper are added to a thick drizzle of extra virgin olive oil to coat evenly. Allow 30 minutes to marinate on the counter, covered, with lemon wedges.

Preheat your Blackstone to high and grill for 3-4 minutes on each side. Remove and dish whole or cut sections (1 to 1-2 leg pieces) with extra virgin olive oil, sea salt, freshly cracked pepper, the remaining chopped parsley, and a squeeze of lemon. Serve with lemon slices on the side.

Buffalo Blue Cheese Chicken Balls

1 serv.   10 min.

Ingredients

- Lb. of Ground Chicken
- 3 Eggs
- 2 Cups of Plain Panko Bread Crumb
- 1/3 Cup of Sliced Green Onions
- 1/3 Cup of Carrots, Sliced & Diced Small
- 1 Celery Stalk (the Center leafy stalks are best, use the leaves too!)
- 3 Oz. of Blue Cheese (crumble bigger pieces)
- 1/4 Cup of Sweet Baby Rays Buffalo Sauce
- 1 Teaspoon of Garlic powder
- Sea Salt & Fresh Cracked Pepper to Taste

Instructions

Green onions should be thinly sliced, carrots and celery should be diced, and blue cheese should be crumbled into little bits.

With a spoon, combine all ingredients in a large mixing basin. 30 meatballs, rolled out (10 meatballs per 1 pound of chicken).

Drizzle vegetable oil over Blackstone and fry meatballs over medium heat, rotating to cook each side. Use a dome halfway through and steam. Continually drizzle with vegetable oil as required. Cooking time varies based on the size of the meatballs and the temperature, but it took 15 minutes total for 30.

Ham Fried Rice

1 serv.   10 min.

Ingredients

- 4 Cups of Cooked Rice
- 1 Lb. of Diced Ham
- 1 Onion
- 4-6 Garlic cloves, Minced
- 1 Tablespoon of Minced Fresh Ginger (or 1 tsp Ground Ginger)
- 1/4 Teaspoon of Ground Black Pepper
- One 12 Oz. of Bag of Frozen Peas and Carrots
- 1 Tablespoon of Butter
- 3 Eggs
- 4 Green Onions, Diced
- 3 Tablespoons of Soy Sauce
- Juice from 1 Lemon

Instructions

Preheat the griddle to a medium-high setting.

Spritz the griddle with oil.

Begin sauteing the onion and cook until it begins to soften. Garlic, ginger, and black pepper are added. Cook until the mixture is aromatic.

Add a little more oil to the griddle next to the onions, then add the frozen peas and carrots, as well as the cubed ham.

On top of the onion, garlic, and ginger mixture, sprinkle the cooked rice. Toss everything together.

Combine the peas, carrots, and diced ham with the rice after the peas, carrots, and diced ham are cooked through. Everything should be completely combined.

On the griddle, melt the butter and add the three eggs. Scramble the eggs until they're thoroughly cooked, then fold them into the rice mixture.

Toss the rice with soy sauce, green onions, and lemon juice. Toss everything together. To taste, add extra soy sauce.

Remove off the griddle and serve immediately.

Mongolian Beef Lettuce Wraps

1 serv.   10 min.

Ingredients

- Lb. of Flank Steak (or other Available Beef Cut)
- 1/2 Cup of Corn Starch (more if needed to coat all of the beef)
- 1/4 Cup of Vegetable Oil
- 3/4 Cup of Soy Sauce
- 1/2 Cup of Brown Sugar
- 1 Teaspoon of Minced Fresh Ginger
- 2-4 Cloves Minced Garlic
- 1/2 Cup of Water
- 4 Green Onions, Sliced
- 2 Heads of Butter Lettuce

Instructions

Cut flank steak into thin 2 inch slices across the grain "length strips of fabric Various beef cuts, such as Beef Chuck or other types of steak, can be used. Just be careful to remove any excess fat before cutting into thin 2 slices "strips of paper

Combine the meat and corn starch in a large mixing basin. Toss until the beef is well covered. If necessary, add more corn starch to ensure that all of the steak is covered.

Combine the soy sauce, water, brown sugar, garlic, and ginger in a saucepan or microwave-safe bowl. Heat until the sugar is completely dissolved.

Preheat the griddle to a medium-high temperature.

Toss the griddle with the oil.

Cook the meat on the griddle until it becomes crispy on the outside.

Allow 1 minute for the sauce to thicken after adding the sauce and half of the sliced green onions to the meat.

Remove the steak from the heat and set it aside. Serve in individual lettuce leaves with chopped green onions as a garnish.

In the lettuce wraps, you can also offer cooked white rice as an option. Simply layer the rice, steak, and sauce on top.

Mongolian Chicken Lettuce Wraps

1 serv.   10 min.

Ingredients

- 1/2 Lb. of Boneless Skinless Chicken Thighs
- 1/2 Cup of Corn Starch (more if needed to coat all of the chicken)
- 1/4 Cup of Vegetable Oil
- 3/4 Cup of Soy Sauce
- 1/2 Cup of Brown Sugar
- 1 Tablespoon of Minced Fresh Ginger
- 2-4 Cloves Minced Garlic
- 1/2 Cup of Water
- 4 Green Onions, Sliced
- 2 Heads of Butter Lettuce

Instructions

Cut the chicken into 2" pieces after trimming it. Combine the chicken and corn starch in a large mixing basin. Toss until the chicken is completely covered. If necessary, add more corn starch to ensure that all of the chicken is covered.

Combine the soy sauce, water, brown sugar, garlic, and ginger in a saucepan or microwave-safe bowl. Heat until the sugar is completely dissolved.

Preheat the griddle to a medium-high temperature.

Toss the griddle with the oil.

Cook the chicken on the griddle until it becomes crispy on the outside.

Allow the sauce to thicken for about 1 minute after adding the sauce and half of the sliced green onions to the chicken.

Remove the chicken from the heat and set it aside. Serve in individual lettuce leaves with chopped green onions as a garnish.

Chicken Piccata Pasta

1 serv. 10 min.

Ingredients

- Large Boneless Skinless Chicken Breasts (or 1 lb. of Chicken Tenderloins)
- 1/2 Cup of Flour
- 2 Tablespoons of Extra Virgin Olive Oil
- 2 Tablespoons of Butter
- 2 Garlic Cloves, Minced
- 1/2 Cup of White Wine
- 1/2 Cup of Chicken Broth
- 1 or 2 Lemons (Juiced and Zested)
- 1/4 Cup of Capers (drained and rinsed)
- 1 Lb. of Cooked Spaghetti (Al Dente)
- 2 Tablespoons of Chopped Flat-Leaf Parsley
- Salt & Pepper to Taste

Instructions

Each chicken breast should be completely butterflyed, resulting in four equal pieces.

Season the chicken with salt and pepper before dredging it in flour. Remove any extra flour by shaking it off.

Preheat the griddle to medium. 2 tablespoons butter, 2 tablespoons olive oil, 2 tablespoons butter, 2 tablespoons olive oil, 2 tablespoons olive oil, 2 tablespoons olive oil, 2 tablespoons olive oil, 2 teaspoons

Combine the wine, chicken stock, lemon juice, lemon zest, and capers in a mixing bowl.

In a mixing bowl, combine the chicken, butter, and olive oil. Cook the chicken until both sides are golden brown.

Add 2 tablespoons of butter on the griddle next to the chicken while it's still cooking. Cook for 30 seconds after adding the minced garlic. Toss the cooked pasta with the garlic and butter. Toss to evenly coat.

Toss the pasta with the lemon wine sauce to coat it and decrease the sauce. To deglaze the griddle and coat the chicken, add approximately 14 cup of the sauce to the chicken.

Continue to mix and decrease the sauce by adding any excess sauce to the pasta. Remove it from the griddle after the sauce has thickened and covered all of the pasta. Serve with chopped parsley as a garnish.

Chicken Stir Fry Noodles

1 serv.   10 min.

Ingredients

- Lb. of Boneless Skinless Chicken Thighs (trimmed and cut into 1â�� pieces)
- 2 Packs of 6 Oz Chow Mein Noodles (could substitute spaghetti noodles)
- 4 Tablespoons of Vegetable oil
- 1 Tablespoon of Fresh Ginger (finely diced or grated)
- 2 Cloves Garlic (finely diced)

- 1 Head Broccoli (stems and florets chopped)
- 1-2 Tablespoons of Soy Sauce (more or less to taste)
- Fresh Ground Black Pepper
- Chicken Marinade
- 1 Teaspoon of Soy Sauce
- 1 Teaspoon of Sugar
- 1 Tablespoon of Corn Starch
- 1/2 Teaspoon of Backing Soda
- 1/2 Teaspoon of Salt
- 4 Tablespoons of Water
- 2 Cloves Garlic (finely diced)

Instructions

Place the compote in a basin. Combine the chicken and marinate ingredients in a mixing basin. Allow for at least 20 minutes of chilling time after covering.

Prepare the noodles as directed on the package, but shorten the cooking time by one minute because the noodles will continue to cook on the griddle. To avoid overcooking the noodles, drain them and rinse them in cold water.

Preheat the griddle to a medium-high setting. On the griddle, pour 2 teaspoons of oil. Allow the marinated chicken to brown in a single layer on the griddle. Cover the chicken with a basting dome and a couple tablespoons of water.

Cook the ginger and garlic in 2 tablespoons of oil on the opposite side of the griddle until fragrant (30-45 seconds). Toss in the broccoli with the ginger and garlic. Cover the broccoli with a couple tablespoons of water and the basting dome for about 1 minute.

As the sauce surrounding the chicken thickens, add a couple tablespoons of water to the chicken.

Reduce the griddle's temperature to medium low. Combine the chicken, noodles, and veggies in a large mixing bowl. Toss everything together until the seasonings are uniformly distributed and everything is heated. If the noodles are still too firm, toss them with a little water as you toss them.

To taste, season with soy sauce and black pepper. Toss everything together and serve.

Pepperoni Pizza

1 serv.10 min.

Ingredients

- 1 Crust of Pizza Dough
- 1/2 Cup of Pizza sauce (or vine ripened crushed tomatoes)
- 8 Oz. of Shredded Mozzarella Cheese
- 16-20 Slices Pepperoni
- 1/8 Cup of Shredded Parmesan Cheese

Instructions

Cook the bacon on the opposite side of the griddle with 2 tablespoons of oil. Preheat your pizza oven to medium-high.

Your pizza dough should be stretched out.

Toss in your sauce. Pizza sauce or a can of vine-ripened crushed tomatoes can be used. Most large box grocery stores carry the Cento brand of crushed tomatoes. San Marzano tomatoes are also excellent for pizza sauce.

Combine the mozzarella cheese and pepperoni pieces on a pizza pan.

Freshly grated parmesan cheese should be sprinkled on top.

Cook until the crust is golden brown, about 15 minutes.

Arugula And Prosciutto Pizza With Balsamic Reduction

1 serv.   10 min.

Ingredients

- 1 Crust of Pizza Dough

- 8 Oz. of Fresh Mozzarella Cheese (cut into 1/4" slices)
- 4 Slices Prosciutto (torn or cut into 1/2" pieces)
- 1 Cup of Baby Arugula
- 2-3 Tablespoons of Balsamic reduction
- 1/2 Cup of Fresh Crushed tomatoes (optional)
- 2 Tablespoons of Extra Virgin Olive Oil

Instructions

Preheat the pizza oven to medium-high heat.

Your dough should be stretched out.

Crushed tomatoes or extra virgin olive oil poured on top of your pizza might serve as the basis. For this pizza, any one will suffice.

Next, top with fresh mozzarella and bake in the Pizza Oven until the dough is golden brown.

Remove the pizza from the oven and cover it with prosciutto, arugula, and a balsamic reduction drizzle.

Flank Steak With Chimichurri Sauce

In Argentine cuisine, chimichurri sauce is a must-have. It's great on steak, but it goes well with virtually everything. It's delicious with chicken, pig, or fish. It's great on eggs, veggies, or just dipping bread slices in it.

Flank steak is a fantastic cut of meat because you get the most out of every bite. There isn't much garbage on the outside that has to be trimmed away and thrown away. Furthermore, when cut against the grain, it's as tender as any steak you'll ever eat.

1 serv. 10 min

Ingredients

- 1 Lb. of Flank Steak
- Kosher Salt
- Freshly Ground Pepper
- Canola Oil
- Chimichurri Sauce
- 2 Cups of Packed Fresh Italian Flat Leaf Parsley
- 4 Medium Garlic Cloves
- 1/4 Cup of Packed Fresh Oregano Leaves (or 4 tsp dried Oregano)
- 1/4 Cup of Red Wine Vinegar
- 1/2 Teaspoon of Red Pepper Flakes
- 1/2 Teaspoon of Kosher Salt
- Freshly Ground Black Pepper
- 1 Cup of Extra Virgin Olive Oil

Instructions

CHIMICHURRI SAUCE: In a food processor, combine parsley, garlic, oregano, vinegar, red pepper flakes, salt, and pepper. Pulse a few times to coarsely chop everything. Then start the food processor and drizzle in the olive oil gently. Place it in an airtight jar in the refrigerator for at least 2 hours to allow the flavors to meld.

If you don't have a food processor, finely chop the parsley, oregano, and garlic before mixing with the rest of the ingredients.

FLANK STEAK: Season steak with Kosher salt and freshly ground black pepper to taste. Coat each side with a little canola oil (we're using canola oil instead of olive oil since it can tolerate the griddle's high heat better).

Preheat your griddle to high. The steak could also be cooked on the Grill+Kabob using the provided grill grates.

Cook the steak for 4-5 minutes on each side. When the steak is done to your liking, remove it from the griddle and set it aside to rest for 5 minutes. Slice it against the grain and serve with Chimichurri sauce on the side.

Thai Chicken Quesadillas

1 serv.   10 min.

Ingredients

- 1 Lb. of Boneless Skinless Chicken Breast
- 4 Cups of Shredded Monterrey Jack Cheese
- 2 Cups of Sweet Chili Sauce
- 1/2 Cup of Green Onions, Sliced
- 1/4 Cup of Cilantro, Chopped
- Granulated Garlic to Taste
- Sea Salt to Taste
- Large 10-12" Flour Tortillas

Instructions

Preheat the Blackstone griddle to high heat and lightly oil the griddle surface.

Chicken breast should be diced into extremely tiny bits. Season chicken on the griddle with granulated garlic and sea salt to taste.

Reduce the heat on the burners to half-power (medium-low).

Make sure the top of the griddle is properly greased. Place two tortillas on top of the griddle. Cover one tortilla with 1 cup shredded Monterrey Jack, making sure the cheese is placed evenly and the tortilla is completely coated. Over the cheese, evenly distribute the required amount of chicken.

1/4 cup Sweet Chili Sauce, spooned or poured over cheese Cover with 1/4 cup chopped green onions and 2 TBSP cilantro right away. Then, using another cup of cheese, cover all of the items. On top of it, place another tortilla. Rep with the second tortilla.

As the cheese melts and the contents blend within the tortillas, flatten the quesadilla with the Blackstone Bacon Press (included in the Blackstone Breakfast Kit) or a spatula if required.

Use a spatula to check underneath the tortilla often to ensure it gets golden brown. Turn each quesadilla carefully and continue the cooking procedure on the other side. Quesadillas are done when both sides are golden brown and the cheese within the tortillas has completely melted.

Using a chef's knife, slice quesadillas in the same way you would a pizza. Depending on the chosen serving size, each quesadilla creates 4 or 8 individual pieces.

Thanksgiving Turkey Breast

1 serv.   10 min.

Ingredients

- Turkey Breast (Skin On)
- Parsley (About a Handful, Finely Chopped)
- 1 Tablespoon of Dried Sage
- 2-3 Tablespoons of Butter
- 1 Lemon
- Olive Oil
- 1/2 Cup of Chicken Stock
- Salt and Pepper

Instructions

In a tin tray pan, drizzle olive oil. Slice the lemon and place it in the pan.

Put turkey breast on top of lemon slices.

Combine butter, sage, and chopped parsley in a separate dish.

Pull the turkey's skin back and distribute a third of the butter mixture under it.

Replace the turkey skin and apply the remaining butter mixture on the turkey breast.

Drizzle extra olive oil on top and season with salt and pepper to taste.

In the bottom of the pan, pour chicken broth.

Using aluminum foil, cover the dish.

Preheat the Blackstone Patio Oven to 350°F and bake for 20-25 minutes.

Remove the foil for another 5 minutes to brown and crisp the turkey skin.

Allow 5-10 minutes for the turkey to rest before slicing.

Garlic Shrimp With Ponzu Rice

1 serv. 10 min.

Ingredients

- 1 Tablespoon of Olive Oil
- 2 Tablespoons of Butter
- 4 Garlic Cloves, Minced
- 12 Oz. of Shrimp
- 1 Pinch of Salt
- 1 Tablespoon of Freshly Squeezed Lemon Juice
- 3 Dashes Cayenne Pepper
- Chopped Parsley
- 2 Cups of Cooked rice
- 1 Teaspoon of Sesame Oil
- 2 Teaspoons of Soy Sauce
- 1 Tablespoon of Ponzu Sauce

Instructions

Heat the olive oil and butter in a griddle over medium heat.

Add the garlic and cook until fragrant.

Stir in the shrimp until everything is nicely combined.

After adding the salt and lemon juice, move the shrimp around to evenly cover them.

Sprinkle the cayenne pepper and parsley on top of the shrimp.

Place the shrimp to the side of the griddle and add the rice.

Toss the rice with the sesame oil, soy sauce, and ponzu. Toss the rice in the sauce to coat it. Mix in the chopped parsley and toss again.

Plate the rice first, then add the shrimp on top. Serve immediately with a bit additional fresh chopped parsley on top.

Chicken / Steak & Vegetable Hibachi

1 serv. 10 min.

Ingredients

- Boneless Skinless Chicken Breasts
- Two 16 oz Packages of Sirloin Steaks
- 2 Large White Onions
- 4 Large Green Zucchini
- 16 Oz. of Sliced Mushrooms
- 2 Tablespoons of Canola or Vegetable Oil
- 8 Tablespoons of Low Sodium Soy Sauce
- 4 Tablespoons of Butter or Garlic Butter
- 1 Dash Iodized Salt
- 1 Dash Ground Pepper
- 1 Dash Lemon Juice
- 1/2 Cup of Grated Carrot
- 1/2 Cup of Peas

- 2-3 Scrambled Eggs
- 1/2 Cup of Diced Onion
- 2 Tablespoons of Unsalted butter
- 3 Tablespoons of Low Sodium Soy Sauce
- 2 Cups of Uncooked Parboiled Rice
- 2 1/2 Cups of Cups Water

Instructions

Meat and vegetables should be cut into bite-sized pieces.

2 tablespoons butter, 2 tablespoons meat, 3 tablespoons soy sauce

Melt the remaining 2 tablespoons butter, then add the onions and zucchini, followed by the remaining 5 tablespoons soy sauce and a pinch of salt and pepper.

7–8 minutes, or until desired tenderness is reached, stir periodically.

Add lemon juice to the chicken for the last minute of cooking, and cook the steak to your preferred temperature.

Because mushrooms cook quickly, add them a few minutes before the meat is done.

2 12 cup water, brought to a roaring boil

Remove 2 cups rice from heat, cover, and cook for 20 minutes.

Remove the lid for 5 minutes to allow the rice to absorb any residual liquid. Melt the butter on a level surface.

Combine the scrambled eggs, carrots, peas, and onions on the griddle over medium heat after the rice has absorbed all of the water.

Cook for about 8 minutes, stirring often, after adding the soy sauce, salt, and pepper.

Orange Chicken

1 serv.   10 min.

Ingredients

- Lb. of Boneless Skinless Chicken Breasts (Cut into 1" Chunks)
- 1/2 Cup of Cornstarch
- Sauce
- 2 Teaspoons of Minced Garlic
- Teaspoons of Minced Ginger
- 1 Teaspoon of Red Pepper Flakes (Adjust to Taste)
- 3/4 Cup of Water
- 1/4 Cup of Soy Sauce
- 1/2 Cup of Brown Sugar
- 1/3 Cup of White Vinegar (or Rice Wine Vinegar)
- Zest of 1 Orange
- 2 Tablespoons of Orange Juice

General Tso's Chicken

2 serv.   10 min.

Ingredients

- Chicken
- 3 Lb. of Boneless Skinless Chicken Breasts Cut into 1" chunks
- 1/2 Cup of Corn Starch
- Sauce
- 1 1/2 Teaspoons of Fresh Minced Garlic
- 1 1/2 Teaspoons of Minced Ginger
- 3/4 Cup of Sugar
- 1/2 Cup of Soy Sauce
- 1/4 Cup of White Vinegar
- 1/4 Cup of Shaoxing Wine or Sherry cooking wine
- 14 1/2 Oz. of Chicken Broth (one can)
- 2-3 Teaspoons of Red Pepper Flakes, adjust to taste

Instructions

Set aside after combining all of the sauce ingredients.

Toss the chicken and cornstarch together in a large mixing basin until evenly coated.

Preheat the griddle to medium-high heat.

Cook your chicken on the griddle with a couple teaspoons of oil. Cook the chicken until it is golden brown on the exterior.

Pour half of the sauce mixture over the chicken when it's about 90% done, and toss the chicken around with a metal spatula to coat it completely. Continue to toss the chicken around and pour the remaining sauce and green onions on top.

Remove all of the chicken from the fire after the sauce has thickened (1-2 minutes).

Over white rice, serve.

Fajitas

4 serv.

25 min.

Ingredients

- 16 Oz. of Flank Steak, Thinly Sliced
- 1 Red Pepper, Thinly Sliced
- 1 Green Pepper, Thinly Sliced
- 1 Onion, Thinly Sliced
- Rice
- 4 Cups of Rice, Cooked
- 8 Oz. of Canned Green Chilles
- 8 Oz. of Canned Tomato Sauce
- Salt & Pepper to Taste
- 1/2 Teaspoon of Garlic Powder
- Marinade
- 1/3 Cup of Canola Oil
- 1/4 Cup of Lime Juice
- 1/2 Teaspoon of Cumin
- 1/2 Teaspoon of Garlic Powder
- Salt & Pepper to Tast
- Sauce Ingredients
- 1/2 Cup of Sour Cream
- 2 Teaspoons of Chili Powder
- Juice from 1 Lime
- Salt & Pepper to Taste

Instructions

To create the sauce, whisk together the sour cream, chili powder, lime juice, and salt and pepper in a mixing bowl.

To make the marinade, combine the canola oil, lime juice, cumin, garlic powder, and salt and pepper in a large resealable bag.

Refrigerate the flank steak for 1-2 hours after placing it in the marinade.

Preheat the griddle to medium high on the Blackstone. A small coating of oil should be applied on the griddle's surface.

Remove the meat from the marinade and lay it on the griddle to cook, turning regularly.

Sauté the peppers and onion with the meat for 3-5 minutes, or until desired softness is reached.

Add the rice ingredients to a different portion of the griddle and combine with a spatula. Cook for 4 minutes, or until somewhat reduced and well blended.

Serve with warm flour tortillas, rice, and your favorite toppings as soon as possible.

Buffalo Shrimp

6 serv.

20 min.

Ingredients

- 1 Lb. of Jumbo Shrimp
- Garlic Powder to Taste
- Pink Sea Salt to Taste
- Black Pepper to Taste
- 1 Cup of Flour
- 1 Cup of Buffalo Sauce
- Blue Cheese Crumbles
- Vegetable or Olive Oil

Instructions

Clean and peel the shrimp, then butterfly them slightly. Season with salt, pepper, and garlic powder to taste.

Place the shrimp in a freezer bag with the flour and shake to coat well.

Heat the Blackstone Griddle to medium-high and add the oil.

Shake off any extra flour from the shrimp before placing them in the oil. As required, squirt in more oil.

Crabby Melts

4 serv.

Ingredients

- Sauce
- 1/2 Cup of Mayonnaise
- 1/2 Teaspoon of Sugar

- 1/2 Teaspoon of Mustard Powder
- 1/2 Teaspoon of Lemon Juice
- 1 Teaspoon of Parsley, Dry
- 1 Teaspoon of Old Bay Seasoning
- 1 Teaspoon of Worcestershire Sauce
- 2 Tablespoons of Butter, Melted
- Crabby Melts
- 1 Lb. of Crabmeat
- 1 Green Pepper, Diced
- 1 Tablespoon of Extra Virgin Olive Oil
- 8 Rye Bread Slices
- Mayonnaise to Spread
- 8 Provolone Cheese Slices

Instructions

Combine all of the sauce ingredients in a mixing bowl, then fold in the crab meat without breaking up the lumps.

Cook peppers in olive oil on a Blackstone Griddle over medium-high heat until tender. To soften the peppers, use the Blackstone Basting Cover. Set peppers aside in a dish or on low heat.

Preheat the Blackstone to medium.

Place the bread on the griddle with a thin coating of mayonnaise on the exterior. Combine the provolone cheese, crab meat combination, and green peppers in a large mixing bowl.

Allow to simmer until golden brown and melted, stirring occasionally. With a splash of water around the sandwich, the Blackstone Basting Cover will help melt everything together!

Crispy Cod

2 serv.

23 min.

Ingredients

- Fresh Cod Loin pieces
- 3 Tablespoons of Mayonnaise
- Lemon Juice (1 lemon is enough)
- 1 â⸮‹1â⸮„2 Teaspoon of Old Bay Seasoning
- 1 Garlic Clove, minced
- 1 heaping Curly Parsley, chopped
- 1 â⸮‹1â⸮„2 Cup of Panko Breadcrumbs
- Salted Butter
- Vegetable Oil

Instructions

Clean the cod by rinsing it and patting it dry with paper towels. While cooking your sauce, set aside on paper towels to collect any excess liquid.

Set aside the panko breadcrumbs on a platter.

To make the sauce, combine the mayo, lemon, garlic, parsley, and old bay rub in a mixing bowl. (If using ordinary old bay, start with 1 tsp and taste; the rub is less salty and contains a hint of brown sugar.)

Brush a thick coating of sauce all over the fish using half of your sauce. Place the fish in the panko and carefully press the bread crumbs to cover both sides equally.

Place 1 tbsp each oil and butter on the Blackstone Griddle and melt together over medium to medium/low heat.

Place your fish on the grill for 4-5 minutes per side, depending on thickness, and turn once. To cook the opposite side, add extra butter and oil.

After the first flip, use the Blackstone basting dome for 3 minutes, then let the fish to finish cooking uncovered.

Serve the fish with the saved sauce, a lemon slice, and parsley on top. Serve on its own, over salad, tacos, or in a sandwich made with your favorite bread.

Salmon Potato And Brussel Sprout Boats

2 serv.

Ingredients

- 2-4 Oz. of Wild Caught Salmon Filets
- 1 Can Diced Potatoes, Drained and Rinsed
- 6 Oz. of Brussel Sprouts
- 2 Tablespoons of Salted Butter
- Sauce
- 1/4 Cup of Extra Virgin Olive Oil

- 2 Tablespoons of Dijon Mustard
- 2-3 Garlic Cloves, Chopped
- 1 Tablespoon of Lemon Juice, Freshly Squeezed
- 1/2 Tablespoon of Curly Parsley
- Pink Sea Salt to Taste
- Black Pepper, Fresh Cracked

Instructions

Set aside the sauce ingredients after whisking them together. Rinse and drain potatoes well. Brussel sprouts should be quartered.

Make two little circular tin foil boats to match your Blackstone. Basting Use two layers of tin foil to cover the dish.

Fill the foil with brussel sprouts and potatoes, equally distributed, leaving room in the middle for the fish.

Toss the veggies with half of the sauce (approximately two spoonfuls). Salmon should be well rinsed and dried. It's crucial to use dry fish.

12 tbsp butter in foil, salmon filet on top of butter Spread the remaining sauce over the fish, roughly 1 teaspoon per filet, then top with 12 tbsp butter.

Preheat your Blackstone to medium-high heat and cover the griddle with foil.

Cover with your Basting Cover, checking and mixing veggies every 2-3 minutes. Cooking time is around 10-12 minutes, with the final few minutes spent carefully turning the fish.

Serve with a slice of lemon and a sprig of parsley on top.

Shrimp Scampi

4 serv.

40 min.

Ingredients

- 1 Lb. of Shrimp, Cleaned and Slightly Butterflied
- 3 Tablespoons of Extra Virgin Olive Oil
- 3-4 Garlic Cloves, Chopped
- 2 Tablespoons of Curly Parsley
- Pink Sea Salt to Taste
- Fresh Cracked Black Pepper to Taste
- Crushed Red Pepper to Taste (optional)
- 2 Tablespoons of Unsalted Butter
- 1/4 Cup of Dry White Wine
  1 Lemon (Half for Cooking Half to Serve/Garnish)

Instructions

Leave the tails on the shrimp when peeling them. Clean out shrimp by butterflying them with a little knife.

In a dish or freezer bag, combine the shrimp, olive oil, salt & pepper, garlic, parsley, and crushed red pepper to marinate for 20 minutes.

Set the temperature on your Blackstone Griddle to medium-high.

Swirl in 1 tablespoon of butter. Toss the shrimp into the butter with tongs to ensure they are on all sides, and fry for 1-2 minutes.

Cook for 1 minute on the opposite side of the shrimp. 1 tbsp butter, and if necessary, raise shrimp onto butterflied tops.

Cook for a further minute after adding the white wine.

Plate with a drizzle of extra virgin olive oil. Serve with lemon wedges and parsley on top.

Shrimp Toast

4 serv.

55 min.

Ingredients

- 1 Lb. of Shrimp, Peeled
- 4 Tablespoons of Green Onion, Sliced
- 2 Garlic Cloves, Grated
- 1 Egg
- 1 Teaspoon of Sesame Oil
- 1/2 Teaspoon of Rice Wine Vinegar
- 1 Tablespoon of Low-Sodium Soy Sauce
- 2 Tablespoons of Cornstarch
- 1 Teaspoon of Ginger

- Pinch of Pink Sea Salt
- Pinch of White Sugar
- 8 White Bread Slices
- Black & White Sesame Seeds, Toasted
- Butter (For Frying)
- Vegetable Oil (For Frying)
- Yum Yum Sauce

Instructions

Smash the shrimp flat with a big chef's knife, then chop into small pieces and put on the cutting board. To prepare a paste, chop your shrimp for 1 minute, rotating your pile.

Place in a mixing dish with the rest of the ingredients and stir well to combine.

Refrigerate for 30 minutes after wrapping in plastic wrap.

Remove the crusts from all four sides of the bread and cut it into triangles. Spread the shrimp mixture on each piece of bread to a thickness of roughly the same as your bread. On the side with the shrimp mixture, sprinkle sesame seeds.

Heat your Blackstone Griddle to a medium-low setting.

In a mixing bowl, combine equal parts butter and vegetable oil. To ensure equal cooking, set the toast shrimp side down first, carefully pushing each corner flat into the griddle.

Allow it simmer for 2 minutes, or until a medium golden brown hue has developed.

Don't be in a hurry! To ensure that the shrimp are properly cooked, reduce the heat to a lower and slower setting.

Before switching to fry the second side for 1-2 minutes till the bread side is medium golden brown, add a bit extra butter and oil.

To absorb excess oil, place on paper towels. Serve with chopped green onions and yum yum sauce.

Zesty Chicken Caesar Sticks

20 serv.

25 min.

Ingredients

- Lb. of Ground Chicken
- 2 Cups of Panko
- 3 Garlic Cloves (grated or minced)
- 3 Tablespoons of Caesar Dressing
- 3 Tablespoons of Curly Parsley (chopped)
- 1 Cup of Pecorino Cheese (grated)
- 1 Tablespoon of Worcestershire Sauce
- 1 Tablespoon of Dijon Mustard\
- Lemon, Juiced and zested
- 1 Teaspoon of Black Pepper
- Salt to Taste
- Extra Virgin Olive Oil
- Kabob Sticks

Instructions

Set aside kabob sticks that have been soaked in water.

By hand, combine all ingredients, cover, and chill for 20 minutes.

Rinse the sticks and pat them dry.

Scoop out approximately a quarter cup of beef mixture, or as much as will fit in your hand, and shape into an oval shape to insert a kabob stick through.

Heat your Blackstone Griddle to medium and sprinkle with extra virgin olive oil before placing the kabobs on it.

Cook for 5 minutes on both sides or until golden brown.

Midway through, add a drop of water to the Basting Cover to assist the chicken cook through for about 1 minute.

Serve with shaved pecorino cheese, lemon wedges, and caesar dressing.

Honey Garlic Chicken Skewers

4 serv.

30 min.

Ingredients

- Marnade Ingredients
- 2 Tablespoons of Vegetable oil
- 2 Tablespoons of Sesame oil
- 3 Garlic Cloves, Minced
- 1/3 Cup of Soy Sauce
- 1/3 Cup of Honey
- Skewers Ingredients
- 4 Chicken Breasts, Chopped into Bite-Sized Pieces
- 2 Red Bell Peppers, Chopped into Chunks
- 1 Onion, Peeled and Sliced into Chunks
- 2 Tablespoons of Sesame Seeds
- 2 Tablespoons of Fresh Cilantro, Roughly Chopped

Instruction

In a gallon-size sealable plastic bag, combine all marinade ingredients.

Add the chicken to the marinade, close the bag, and knead the contents to completely coat the chicken. Refrigerate for 1 to 8 hours, rotating periodically.

To avoid burning, soak wooden skewers in water for 30 minutes before cooking; metal skewers don't need to be pre-soaked.

Preheat the griddle to medium-high.

Thread chicken, pepper, and onion onto your skewer in that order. Continue until the skewer is completely packed and you've used all of your skewers.

1 tbsp extra virgin olive oil on the griddle top

Place skewers on griddle and cook for 8-10 minutes, turning every 2-3 minutes until chicken is done (no longer pink in the middle or internal temperature reaches 165 degrees).

Serve your skewers on a dish with sesame seeds and cilantro on top.

Chicken Caesar Salad

2 serv.

35 min.

Ingredients

- Meat and salad
- 1 Romaine Lettuce Head (Large)
- 1 Lb. of Chicken Breasts (Boneless and Skinless)
- 4 Bacon Slices (Thickly Cut)
- Salt and Pepper or Rub (of your choice)
- Olive Oil
- 1 Cup of Croutons
- 1 Cup of Parm Reggiano (Shaved)
- caesar dressing
- Avocado (Ripe)
- 1/2 Lemon (Juiced)
- 2 Tablespoons of Olive Oil
- 2 Teaspoons of Anchovy Paste
- 2 Tablespoons of Parmesan Cheese (Finely Grated)
- 1/2 Teaspoon of Dijon Mustard
- 1 Garlic Clove

Instructions

In a food processor, mix all of the dressing ingredients. Blend for around 30 seconds on high speed. Scrape down the edges with a rubber spatula and pulse until the dressing is creamy. Remove from the equation.

Now it's time to fry the meats. Preheat the griddle to high heat and lightly oil it.

Season the chicken with salt and pepper or your favourite seasonings after coating it in olive oil.

Cook the chicken breasts on the griddle until done. Remove from the oven and set aside to cool.

Cook until thickly cut bacon is done on the griddle. Remove the item and place it away.

Reduce the heat on the burners to medium.

Season the head of romaine with salt and pepper after lightly oiling it. Place the romaine head on the griddle. Rotate it so that each side has a beautiful char.

Chop the bacon and slice or cube the chicken.

Place the cooked romaine head on a dish. Arrange the chicken on top of the romaine lettuce. Avocado caesar dressing, crumbled bacon, parmesan reggiano, and croutons are sprinkled on top.

Sweet And Spicy Mexican Chicken

8 serv.

25 min.

Ingredients

- Oz. of Achiote Paste]
- 1 Orange (Fresh)
- 1/2 Red Onion (Cut in Quarters)
- 2 Oz. of White Vinegar
- 2 Lb. of Chicken Legs
- 2 Lb. of Chicken Thighs
- 1/4 Stick of Butter

Instructions

In a medium-sized mixing bowl, place the achiote paste. Mix in the juice from a fresh orange and the vinegar until all of the components are thoroughly diluted, with no lumps. Place a plastic bag in a separate dish. Combine the chicken legs and half of the achiote mixture in a mixing bowl. Then spin the bag until the mix has completely coated the legs. Half of the onions should be added, then the bag should be closed and the air removed.

For the chicken thighs, repeat the plastic bag method.

Preheat the griddle for 5 minutes on medium heat. Spread the butter all over the surface. Cook the chicken legs and thighs, flipping them over every few minutes. At 176 degrees, it takes around 15 minutes to cook.

Bbq Chicken Stir-Fry

4 serv.

35 in.

Ingredients

- 4 Chicken Breasts (Deboned and Skinless)
- 1/2 Cup of BBQ Sauce
- Salt and Pepper or BBQ Rub
- 4 Eggs
- 3 Tablespoons of Soy Sauce (Chef Recommends Maggi Sauce)
- 3 Tablespoons of Ponzu Sauce
- 1 Garlic Clove (Minced)
- 1/4 Teaspoon of Ginger (Minced)
- 1/4 Teaspoon of Black Pepper
- 1 Large Sweet Onion (Sliced)
- 1 Medium Green Pepper (Medium, Cut into Strips)
- 1 Sweet Red Pepper (Medium, Cut into Strips)
- 12 Oz. of Peas and Carrots (Frozen)
- 1 Cup of Corn (Frozen)
- 4 Cups of Jasmine Rice (Pre-Cooked)

Instructions

Preheat your griddle to medium-high heat and coat the surface with cooking oil.

Season the chicken to taste with salt and pepper or a BBQ rub. Cook each side for a couple minutes. Continue to cook the chicken by dicing it into small pieces. Cook until desired doneness is reached, then add the BBQ sauce.

Start cooking the peppers and onions in a skillet until they soften. Garlic, ginger, and black pepper are added. Cook until the mixture is aromatic.

On the griddle, add extra oil next the onions. Separate the frozen peas, carrots, and corn from the garlic and ginger mixture on the griddle. Cooked chopped chicken can also be added.

On top of the onion, garlic, and ginger mixture, sprinkle the cooked rice. Toss everything together.

Incorporate the peas, carrots, corn, and chicken with the rice and stir to combine.

On the griddle, melt the butter and scramble the eggs. Scramble until the eggs are thoroughly cooked, then fold into the rice.

Toss the rice with the shoyu and ponzu sauces. Toss everything together.

Remove off the griddle and serve immediately.

California-Style Salmon Tacos

4 serv.

25 min.

Ingredients

- 1 1/2 - 2 Lb. of Salmon Fillet
- 5 Bacon Slices
- 1 Green, Red, or Yellow Peppers (Finely Chopped)
- 1/2 White Onion (Finely Chopped)
- 2 Pineapple Slices (Fresh, Finely Chopped)
- 2 Garlic Cloves (Finely Chopped)
- 2 Limes
- 1/4 Tablespoon of Celery Salt
- 1/4 Tablespoon of Paprika
- Cilantro (Bunch, Finely Chopped)
- 4 Corn Tortillas

Instructions

Preheat the griddle on medium heat using all of the burners.

Place the bacon strips on the griddle and fry until crispy. Remove the bacon strips and check to see if any fat is left on the griddle.

Spread the bacon grease all over the griddle's surface, then set the salmon skin side down on it. Cook for five to seven minutes after adding the paprika and celery salt.

While the salmon is cooking, use the bacon fat to start frying the green peppers, pineapple, onions, and garlic on one side of the griddle. Use the spatulas to properly distribute the veggies and sauté them. Sprinkle a pinch of celery salt over the vegetable mixture to season it (be careful; celery salt is strong and can overpower the flavors of the vegetable mix).

When the skin side of the salmon is done, turn it and cook for another four to seven minutes.

Remove the vegetable mixture from the griddle after it has finished cooking.

Place the cooked salmon fillet on a large chopping board, crumble the bacon into small pieces, and completely combine with the vegetable mixture. Garnish the salmon with the mixture and fresh cilantro.

Buffalo Chicken Fritters

4 serv.

20 min.

Ingredients

- 1 Lb. of Boneless and skinless chicken breast, diced small
- 1/3 Cup of Shredded mozzarella cheese
- 1/4 Cup of Blue cheese crumbles
- 2 Tablespoons of Mayonnaise
- 3 Tablespoons of Buffalo Sauce (and extra to drizzle on top)
- 1/3 Cup of All-purpose flour
- 1 Egg
- Salt & Pepper to taste
- Olive Oil for Cooking
- Ranch for Dipping

Instructions

Combine all of the ingredients in a large mixing bowl, except the olive oil and ranch dressing. Toss everything together until it's equally distributed. Make sure there aren't any flour lumps.

Preheat your Blackstone Griddle to medium-low heat and add 2 teaspoons of the chicken mixture to the pan. Make the chicken into a flat disc-like form by pressing it down. Rep with the rest of the chicken mixture.

Cook for 3-4 minutes per side, or until the chicken is cooked through. Serve with a little additional buffalo sauce and ranch dressing on the side.

Bacon Cheeseburger Quesadillas

4 serv.

15 min.

Ingredients

- 4-6 Strips Thick cut Bacon
- 1 Lb. of 80/20 Ground beef
- 2 Tablespoons of Blackstone All Purpose Seasoning
- 3 Tablespoons of Dill relish
- 2 Cups of Shredded cheddar cheese
- 4 Large Tortillas
- "Come Back" Sauce
- 1/4 Cup of Mayonnaise
- 1/4 Cup of Ketchup
- 2 Tablespoons of Worcestershire sauce]
- Tablespoons of Yellow mustard
- 1 Teaspoon of Garlic powder
- 1 Teaspoon of Blackstone All Purpose Seasoning

Instructions

Cook the bacon well done on your Blackstone Griddle over medium-high heat. Take the bacon from the pan and cut it finely.

Chop the ground beef with the Blackstone All Purpose spice on the griddle. As the meat cooks, make sure to include some of the residual bacon grease. Cook for a total of 3-4 minutes.

Toss in the chopped bacon and relish to combine everything. Cook for an additional 3 minutes.

Add your tortillas to the side of the griddle with the meat mixture. Spread a handful of cheddar equally across the tortillas, then set aside portion of the meat mixture. Cook

for another 2 minutes before folding in half. To keep the quesadilla in place, use a bacon press or a weight.Combine the mayonnaise, ketchup, Worcestershire sauce, mustard, garlic powder, and Blackstone All Purpose Seasoning in a small mixing basin. To include all of the ingredients, mix them together evenly.

Remove the quesadilla from the griddle once all of the cheese has melted and cut into quarters. Serve with the Comeback Sauce while it's still hot.

Chili-Mojo Steak Kebabs

4 serv.

10 min.

Ingredients

- Skewer Ingredients
- 2 Lb. of New York Strip Steak, cut into 2" cubes
- 2 Tablespoons of Blackstone All-Purpose Seasoning
- 1 Cup of Orange Juice
- 1/4 Cup of Tequila
- 2 Tablespoons of Garlic Powder
- 2 Teaspoons of Chili Powder
- 1/4 Cup of Lime Juice
- Wooden Skewers
- Mojo Ingredients
- 1/4 Cup of Orange Juice
- 3 Tablespoons of Lime Juice

- 1/4 Cup of Olive Oil
- 2 Tablespoons of Garlic Powder
- 2 Tablespoons of Fresh Oregano Leaves
- 2 Teaspoons of Chili Flakes
- Salt & Pepper

Instructions

Combine the steak, Blackstone All Purpose Seasoning, orange juice, lime juice, a little olive oil, garlic powder, and chili powder in a large mixing bowl. Refrigerate for 30-45 minutes after thoroughly mixing.

Skewer the meat with as many cubes as you like on the wooden skewers.

Blend all of the Mojo Ingredients in a small mixing dish and stir to combine evenly.

Get your Blackstone Griddle Charcoal Grill Combo's coals as hot as possible. Cook for 2 minutes on each side, then flip and sprinkle with Mojo. Repeat until the steak reaches the desired temperature.

To dish, arrange all of the skewers on a big tray and sprinkle with some of the Mojo.

Street Tacos With Pineapple Pickled Jalapeno Peppers

4 serv. 10 min.

Ingredients

- 1 Lb. of Thinly Sliced Steak (top round is a good cut for this)
- 2 Tablespoons of Blackstone Taco & Fajita Seasoning
- 2 Green Jalapeno Peppers, Sliced
- 2 Red Jalapeno Peppers, Sliced
- 1/4 Cup of Pineapple Juice
- 3 Tablespoons of Lime Juice
- 1 Teaspoon of Minced Garlic
- Fresh Cilantro
- Olive Oil
- Sauce Ingredients
- 1/3 Cup of Sour Cream
- 3 Tablespoons of Lime Juice
- 1 Tablespoon of Blackstone Taco & Fajita Seasoning

Instructions

Toss the sliced peppers with the pineapple juice, lime juice, olive oil, and minced garlic in a small bowl with a bit of salt and pepper. To coat evenly, mix everything together. Set aside for a later day.

Add a dab of olive oil to a large platter and season the steak with the Taco & Fajita

Seasoning. Allow for a 10-minute rest period to allow the meat to marinade.

On your Blackstone Griddle Charcoal Grill Combo, heat your charcoal as hot as you can. Cook for 2 minutes per side on thin steaks, then dice.

Lightly toast several corn tortillas on the griddle side of your Blackstone Griddle Charcoal Grill Combo.

To serve, place some steak on the bottom of each tortilla, followed by some sweet peppers, a drizzle of sauce, and fresh cilantro.

Pesto-Ranch Chicken Artichoke Flatbread

4 serv.

15 min.

Ingredients

- 4 Boneless & Skinless Chicken Cutlets
- 2-3 Tablespoons of Blackstone Chicken & Herb Seasoning
- 1/4 Cup of Ranch Dressing
- 3 Tablespoons of Mayonnaise
- 3 Tablespoons of Pesto
- 1 1/2 Cups of Artichoke Hearts
- 1/2 Cup of Sliced Black Olives
- 1/3 Cup of Capers
- 3 Cups of Mozzarella Cheese
- 4 Flat-Bread Rounds

Instructions

Season your chicken breasts on all sides with a little olive oil and some Blackstone Chicken & Herb Seasoning, then heat for 2-3 minutes each side on the griddle or until thoroughly done.

Remove the cooked chicken from the griddle, dice it, and place it in a large mixing bowl.

Stir in the ranch dressing, mayonnaise, and pesto until well combined.

14 of the chicken should be equally distributed across the surface of each flatbread. Evenly distribute artichoke hearts, olives, and capers on each flatbread, then top with mozzarella cheese.

Reduce the heat on the griddle to medium-low and lay each flatbread on it, covering it with a basting dome to melt the cheese and brown the bottom. 4-5 minutes for a lightly toasted crust, and a few minutes more for a crispier texture.

Slice and serve immediately.

Chicken & Sausage Gumbo Flatbread

4 serv.

15 min.

Ingredients

- 1 Lb. of Chicken Cutlets
- 2-3 Tablespoons of Blackstone Crazy Cajun Seasoning
- 1/3 Cup of Diced Red Bell Pepper
- 1/3 Cup of Diced Geen Bell Pepper
- 1/3 Cup of Diced Celery
- 1/3 Cup of Diced Yellow Onion
- 1/2 Cup of Sliced Okra
- 1/2 Lb. of Sliced Sausage
- 1/4 Cup of Beer (Lager is Best)
- 2 Tablespoons of Unsalted Butter
- 2 Cups of Shredded Mozzarella Cheese
- Olive Oil
- 4 Premade Flatbread

Instructions

Season each of the chicken cutlets with a little olive oil and some Blackstone Crazy Cajun Seasoning on a big platter.

Cook the chicken for 3-4 minutes each side on one side of the Griddle over medium-high heat, or until thoroughly done.

Over medium heat, add the butter to the opposite side of the griddle. Season with the Blackstone Crazy Cajun Seasoning and the veggies. Cook for 5-6 minutes, then top with the sausage and beer. Cook for another 4-5 minutes, stirring to blend.

Take the chicken off the griddle and cut it into little bite-size pieces.

Reduce one side of the griddle to low heat and toast the flatbread for 2-3 minutes.

To make your flatbread, spread part of the vegetables and sausage on each flatbread, then top with mozzarella cheese. Place part of the chicken on top of the cheese, then finish with a thin layer of cheese. For 4-5 minutes, cover with a basting dome. The crust will firm up and the cheese will melt.

Slice and serve immediately once the cheese has melted.

Chicken Enchiladas

2 serv.

18 min.

Ingredients

- 4 Corn Tortillas
- 1 Can of your favorite Enchilada Sauce
  - Oz. of Chunked Chicken Breast (In can)

- 4 Cheese Mexican Shredded Blend
- Shredded Iceberg Lettuce
- Freshly Chopped Cilantro
- Blackstone Taco & Fajita Seasoning
- Crema Mexicana

Instructions

Raise the temperature of your Blackstone Griddle to high. Drizzle olive oil over the griddle's top.

Heat enchilada sauce in a pan or small stock pot on a Range Top Combo range burner or griddle top.

Use tongs to dip corn tortillas in enchilada sauce after the griddle top has achieved high temperature. Make sure the sauce is evenly distributed on both sides. Place the enchiladas on top of the griddle. Allow at least a minute or two for the enchiladas to cook before moving on to the next step.

Place chicken in a line across the middle of each tortilla.

Fold both sides of the tortilla over the chicken using a spatula (one side at a time). Apply gentle pressure to the top of the tortilla with a spatula, forcing the enchilada to conform to the traditional enchilada shape.

To taste, sprinkle with cheese.

Immediately squirt water on the griddle top and cover the enchiladas with a Basting Cover or seal the griddle hood. The cheese will melt and the tortillas will effectively bake as a result.

Allow the tortillas to bake for 2.5-5 minutes, or until the cheese has melted and the texture is to your liking.

Remove the enchiladas from the griddle, season with Blackstone taco and fajita spice, and top with shredded iceberg lettuce, fresh chopped cilantro, and Crema Mexicana to taste.

Tequila Chicken Skewers

4 serv.   5 min.

Ingredients

- Boneless and Skinless Chicken Breast, cut into 1/2 inch cubes
- 1 Teaspoon of Garlic Powder
- 1 Teaspoon of Cumin
- 1 Teaspoon of Chili Powder
- 2 Tablespoons of Olive Oil
- The juice of 2 Limes
- 1/4 Cup of Orange Juice
- 1/4 Cup of Tequila
- 1/4 Cup of Fresh Cilantro
- 2 Red Chilies, Sliced Thin
- Salt and Pepper
- Wooden Skewers
- Sauce
- 3/4 Cup of Sour Cream
- The juice of 1 Lime
- 1 Teaspoon of Garlic Powder
- 1 Teaspoon of Chili Powder
- 1 Tablespoon of Tequila

Instructions

Combine the chicken, garlic powder, cumin, chili powder, olive oil, lime juice, orange juice, tequila, and a bit of salt and pepper in a large resealable plastic bag. Toss the ingredients in the bag to evenly coat them. To marinate the chicken, place it in the refrigerator for 1 hour.

Blend all of the sauce ingredients in a small mixing dish and stir to combine evenly. Refrigerate and save for later.

Remove the chicken from the marinade and start assembling the skewers. Use 2-3 cubes chicken per skewer for appetizer amounts, and more chicken per skewer for larger portions.

Add a little olive oil to your Blackstone and cook the skewers for 2-3 minutes per side over medium-high heat. Cook the skewers thoroughly by turning them often. Finish with a squeeze of lime juice for a delicious finish.

To dish, arrange the skewers on a serving tray and sprinkle with the sauce. Serve with fresh cilantro and chopped red chilies on the side.

Salmon With Honey Soy Glaze

4 serv.

13 min.

Ingredients

- 4 Salmon Fillets (6 oz. each, skin on)
- 1/4 Cup of Honey
- 1/4 Cup of Soy Sauce
- 2 Limes
- 2 Tablespoons of Dijon Mustard
- 2 Tablespoons of Water
- Salt & Pepper to taste
- Olive Oil

Instructions

Whisk together honey, soy sauce, lime juice from two limes, mustard, and water in a mixing bowl. Remove from the equation.

Preheat the griddle to medium-high temperature.

Remove any pin bones you discover from the salmon fillets.

Season the fillets with salt and pepper after coating them with a little oil.

Cook the fish for 3 minutes on each side (more or less depending on how thick your fillets are).

Pour the honey soy glaze over the fillets when they're approximately 90% done and let it decrease for a minute. To uniformly decrease the sauce, move it around with your spatula.

Serve with steamed asparagus after removing the fillets and sauce from the heat.

Steakhouse Classic

2 serv.

15 min.

Ingredients

- Ribeye or New York Strip Steaks
- 1 White or Yellow Onion
- 2 Garlic Cloves, minced
- Butter
- 2 Tablespoons of Balsamic Vinegar
- Chopped Parsley
- Kosher Salt
- Fresh Ground Black Pepper
- Canola Oil

Instructions

Allow the steaks to come to room temperature before serving.

Using a paper towel, pat the steaks dry.

Season each side of the steaks with Kosher salt and pepper, then drizzle each side with a little canola oil.

Preheat the griddle to a medium-high temperature.

Toss a tablespoon of butter and some oil on the griddle.

On the griddle, add the onion, garlic, and mushrooms.

Add the balsamic vinegar once the onions and mushrooms have started to soften. Reduce the heat to low on the far right burner and add the onions and mushrooms.

Place the steaks on the griddle. Cook for a few minutes until a beautiful sear develops. Flip the steaks over and top each one with a little pat of butter.

Continue to cook until the appropriate temperature is reached.

Remove the steaks from the fire and set them for 5 minutes, wrapped in tin foil (this step is very important).

Serve with the onions and mushrooms on top.

Steak, Arugula, Pear & Balsamic Flatbread

4 serv.

10 min.

Ingredients

- One 8-10 Oz. NY Strip Steak
- 2 Tablespoons of Blackstone Steakhouse Seasoning
- 1/3 Cup of Mayonnaise
- 2 Teaspoons of Fresh Rosemary, chopped

- 2 Teaspoons of Fresh Thyme, chopped
- 1 Lemon, juiced
- 1 Pear, sliced thin
- 2 Cups of Rocket Arugula
- 4 Pre-Made Flatbreads
- 1/2 Cup of Bleu Cheese Crumbles
- 1 Cup of Shredded Mozzarella Cheese
- 1/3 Cup of Balsamic Glaze
- Olive Oil

Instructions

Preheat the Blackstone Griddle to medium-high temperature.

Rub 1 tablespoon olive oil and 1 1/2 tablespoons Blackstone Steakhouse Seasoning all over the steaks to cover all sides. Cook the steaks for 4 minutes on each side or until done to your liking. Remove them off the griddle and set them aside to cool.

Combine the mayonnaise, chopped herbs, lemon juice, and 1/2 tsp Blackstone Steakhouse Seasoning in a small mixing basin. Toss everything together until it's equally distributed.

Preheat your griddle over medium-low heat and cook the flatbread for a few minutes on each sides.

Using a sharp knife, cut the steak into bite-size pieces.

Remove the flatbreads from the griddle and cover each with some of the sauce. Add some meat, followed by a tiny handful of arugula. Add a couple slices of pear and some crumbled blue cheese. Place the flatbread back on the low heat side of the griddle and top it with some shredded mozzarella cheese. To melt the cheese, cover with a basting dome.

To serve, cut each flatbread into four pieces and sprinkle with balsamic glaze.

Hawaiian Chicken Skewers

Ingredients

- 1 Package Chicken Tenders, around 2-2 1/2 LBS, Cut into Bite Size Pieces
- 1 Red Onion, Chopped into Bite Size Pieces
- 1 Handful Fresh Cilantro, chopped
- Kabob Stick
- Chicken Marinade
- 1 Tablespoon of Olive Oil
- 1/4 Cup of Low Sodium Soy Sauce
- 3/4 Cup of Pineapple Juice, from can of pineapple
- 1/4 Cup of Brown Sugar, packed
- 1/4 Cup of Ketchup
- 3 Garlic Cloves, grated
- 1/2 Teaspoon of Ground Ginger
- Sea Salt and Fresh Black Pepper, to taste
- Pineapple Marinade
- 20 Oz. of Can Pineapple Chunks in 100% Pineapple Juice (can substitute for fresh pineapple)

- 1/2 Cup of Brown Sugar

Instructions

Soak kabob sticks for at least 20 minutes in water. Marinate the chicken for at least 2 hours and up to overnight in a freezer bag. Marinate the pineapple for 30 to 2 hours.

In a deep container or plate, assemble your skewers with chicken, pineapple, and red onions. You'll want to save some, but not all, of the marinade from the assembly process to utilize when cooking!

Preheat your Blackstone to medium-high and arrange your skewers over the griddle.

Cook for 3 minutes before drizzling the remaining marinade over the skewers. The steam will aid in the cooking and moistening of the chicken.

Cook for another minute. Turn the griddle to medium-low heat and cook the skewers for another 3 minutes, or until the chicken is done.

Remove the skewers and let aside for 5 minutes to cool. Garnish with a pinch of salt and a sprig of cilantro.

Beer Battered Fish & Chips

2 serv.

Ingredients

- 4-5 Large Idaho Russet Potatoes, Peeled and Cut into Strips
- 3-5 Pieces of Meaty White Fish like Grouper, Cod, or Haddock
- 1 Cup of Flour
- 1 Beer (Heineken is used in this Recipe)
- 1 Tablespoon of Baking Powder
- 1/2 Tablespoon of Old Bay Seasoning\
- 1 Tablespoon of Corn Starch
- Vegetable Oil in a Squirt Bottle

Instructions

Cut fries should be soaked in cold salted water for 15 minutes before drying thoroughly with a clean dish towel.

Prepare your fish, chopping it if necessary; we're going to deep fry on a griddle, so don't make it too thick. Dry each fish fillet well with a paper towel.

Whisk together flour, baking powder, cornstarch, and old bay, then add beer. Add extra flour if the batter is too thin.

Preheat the griddle to medium and drizzle with vegetable oil before adding the fries. Cook until crispy, adding additional oil as required with your Blackstone spray bottle as needed to ensure even cooking.

During the first half of the cooking process, keep the heat low. Continue to fry, rotating and adding oil as required, on medium-high / high heat. Please don't hurry them! Move them to one side of your Blackstone when they're almost done.

On the other side, heat the vegetable oil over medium-high to high heat, then dip the fish in the batter before placing it in the heated oil.

Apply extra oil to the front of each piece of fish closest to you using your squirt bottle, allowing the oil to flow back and under the fish. Before turning, cook 3-4 minutes on each side with oil.

Season the fish and chips with salt and pepper. With tartar sauce and malt vinegar on the side!

Caribbean Jerk Chicken

6 serv.

20 min.

Ingredients

- 1 Yellow Onion, chopped into quarters
- 2 Green Onions, chopped
- 1 Habanero Chili Pepper, seeded and chopped
- 2 Garlic Cloves
- 1 Tablespoon of Five-Spice Powder
- 1 Teaspoon of Allspice
- 1 Teaspoon of Dried Thyme
- 1/2 Teaspoon of Ground Nutmeg
- 1 Teaspoon of Salt
- 1 Teaspoon of Ground Black Pepper
- 1/2 Cup of Soy Sauce
- 1 Tablespoon of Vegetable Oil
- 3 Lb. of Chicken Pieces (breasts, thighs, or drumsticks)

Instructions

In a food processor or blender, mix all ingredients except the chicken to prepare the marinade. Blend everything together until it's basically smooth (it will resemble a course and gritty paste).

Place the chicken pieces in a gallon-sized resealable bag and pour over the marinade. Seal the bag securely and knead it to fully cover the chicken.

Allow the chicken to marinade in the fridge for 6-8 hours.

Remove the chicken from the fridge, heat the griddle to medium-high, and brush the chicken with a thin layer of olive oil.

Place chicken on griddle and cook for 8-10 minutes, flipping every two minutes (until internal temperature reaches 165 degrees).

Seared Ahi Tuna

4 serv.

36 min.

Ingredients

- One 5-6 Oz. of Ahi Tuna Steak, sushi grade
- 3 Tablespoons of Ponzu Sauce
- 1/4 Cup of Toasted Sesame Seeds (or enough to coat filet completely)
- 2 1/2 Tablespoons of Sesame Oil

Instructions

Refrigerate ahi tuna for 30 minutes in ponzu sauce, flipping fish over every 5 minutes.

Preheat the Blackstone to a high temperature.

Fill a small dish with sesame seeds and use it to coat the tuna steak on all sides.

Place 1 tbsp sesame oil on a prepared griddle and rapidly sear tuna for 1-1.5 minutes, depending on how rare you want it.

1 tbsp sesame oil, 1 tbsp sesame oil, 1 tbsp sesame oil, 1 tbsp sesame oil, 1 tbsp sesame oil, 1 tbsp sesame oil

In the remaining 1/2 tbsp sesame oil, sear the edges of the steak for 20-30 seconds all over using tongs.

Remove the tuna from the can and set it on the Blackstone cutting board, where it will be sliced into thin strips.

Hawaiian Meat Marinade And Sauce For Chicken Or Pork

Ingredients

- 1-1.5 Lb. of Boneless Skinless Chicken Breast or Pork Shoulder Butt
- 5 Cup of Soy Sauce
- 1.5 Cup of Pineapple Juice
- 1 Cup of Brown Sugar, packed
- 1 Tablespoon of Brown Sugar, packed
- 8 Garlic Cloves, chopped
- 2 Tablespoons of Fresh Ginger, chopped

Instructions

Combine soy sauce, pineapple juice, garlic, and ginger in a large mixing basin.

Take one cup of the sauce mixture and set it in a separate bowl with 1 TBSP brown sugar to marinade your meat before adding the brown sugar. Mix 3/4 cup brown sugar into the original marinade bowl and combine the two bowls until the sugar is completely dissolved.

Place the meat in a freezer bag with the marinade. If using pork shoulder butt, chop the flesh into bite-sized bits that can be skewered, then skewer the meat after it has marinated overnight in the freezer bag.

Sauce should be refrigerated overnight.

In a small sauce pan, gradually simmer the sauce over low heat, stirring every few minutes. The sauce will thicken somewhat as it cooks. This may be done in a sauce pan right on your Blackstone Griddle!

Drizzle a light layer of vegetable oil over the chicken thighs or pork skewers on a Blackstone set to medium high heat. The amount of time it takes to cook depends on the thickness of the meat.

Chicken Bruschetta

7 serv.

10 min.

Ingredients

- 4 Chicken Cutlets
- 3-4 Tablespoons of Blackstone Chicken and Herb Seasoning
- 4 Large Tomatoes, diced
- 3/4 Cup of Small Diced Red Onion
- 3 Tablespoons of Minced Garlic
- 6-8 Basil Leaves, chiffonade
- Sixteen 1" Thick Slices of French Bread
- Balsamic Glaze
- Olive Oil
- Salt & Pepper

Instructions

Toss the tomatoes, red onion, garlic, and basil in a large mixing basin with a drizzle of olive oil and a pinch of salt and pepper. Mix everything together gently and evenly.

Toss the chicken cutlets with a drizzle of olive oil and Blackstone Chicken and Herb Seasoning to cover evenly.

Cook the chicken cutlets for 2-3 minutes each side or until thoroughly done on your Blackstone over medium-high heat. Remove the chicken from the griddle and cut it into small pieces.

Combine the chicken and tomatoes in a large mixing bowl.

Lightly toast the slices of French bread in your Blackstone with a little olive oil.

Add a few teaspoons of the chicken bruschetta to the toasted bread to serve. Serve chilled with a sprinkle of balsamic glaze on top.

Marinated Lamb Chops

Ingredients

- 1 Package Lamb Chops
- 1/2 Cup of Extra Virgin Olive Oil
- 1/2 Cup of Red Wine Vinegar
- 6-8 Fresh Garlic Cloves, one per lamb chop
- 2 Teaspoons of Dried Oregano
- Salt and Pepper to Taste
- Butter for the Griddle

Instructions

Garlic cloves should be peeled, pressed, and coarsely chopped.

Drizzle olive oil and balsamic vinegar over the lamb chops.

Garlic, oregano, salt, and pepper to taste. Rub evenly over the chops.

Allow meat to marinate on the counter for at least 15-20 minutes before cooking.

Preheat the griddle to medium-high/high. Spread a tablespoon or two of butter on the griddle and fry the lamb chops in it. Cooking time depends on griddle temperature, chop thickness, and preferred meat temperature. I prefer medium to medium-well cooked lamb.

Sear the opposite side of the chops, using more butter if necessary. To finish cooking, reduce the heat to medium-low. My one-inch chops take around 3-4 minutes per side to cook from room temperature.

Allow lamb chops to sit on a plate with a tablespoon or two of butter on top before serving. This will provide you with enough of tasty dipping fluids to enjoy with each slice!

CJ's Buffalo Wild Wings Chili Con Queso

20 inis 4 serv

Ingredients:

- Tortilla Chips
- 16 oz box Velveet Cheese
- 1 cup milk
- 2 tsp paprika
- 1/2 tsp Ground Cayenne Pepper
- 2 Cans Hormel Chili with Beans
- 1lb Ground Beef
- 3 tsp Chili Powder
- 2 tsp Garlic Powder
- Tequila Lime Seasoning
- Lime Juice
- 2 tsp Ground Cumin
- 1 Yellow onion
- Diced Tomato
- Diced Jalapeno
- Cilantro

Instructions

1. Your Blackstone should be preheated in two zones: medium and high. On your high zone, place a large aluminum tin pan.
2. While the oven is heating up, cube your Velveeta cheese and place it in the pan. This simply aids in the melting of the cheese. 1 or 2 cans of canned chili, I prefer two. 2 tsp Paprika, 1/2 tsp Ground Cayenne Pepper, 3 tsp Chili Powder, 2 tsp Garlic Powder, 2 tsp Ground Cumin, 1 cup Milk Reduce the heat to medium low as the cheese begins to melt, stirring regularly to avoid burning.
3. Add 1 pound of ground beef to the medium heat zone and season with salt, pepper, and Tequila lime Seasoning. Cook till golden brown.
4. Half a yellow onion, chopped, should be added to the beef while it is cooking.
5. 1 tomato, 1 jalapeo, 1 tomato, 1 jalapeo, 1 tomato, 1 jalapeo, 1 tomato, 1 jalapeo, 1 tomato, 1 jalapeo, 1 tomato, 1 jalap Squeeze half a lime over the top, season with salt, pepper, and tequila lime spice, and toss to combine. Set aside a little amount of cilantro to chop.
6. To plate, spoon your queso into a shallow bowl, or whichever bowl you want, and then scoop a few spoonfuls of your beef and onions into the center of the queso in the bowl, without mixing it up. Add a spoonful of seasoned tomatoes and jalapeos on the top of the beef.

Finish with a pinch of cilantro and a thin dusting of Blackstone Tequila Lime seasoning.Surround the bowl with tortilla chips on a plate or cutting board. ENJOY!

CJ's Mexican Pizza

20 mins 4 serv

Ingredients:

- 8" flour tortillas (10" can work)
- 80/20 beef
- Yellow onion
- Can of Refried beans
- Vegetable Oil (for frying tortillas)
- Red Enchilada Sauce

Garnish

- Fresh jalapeño (garnish)
- Shredded lettuce (garnish)
- Diced red tomato (garnish)

Sauce

- Sour cream
- Lime Juice
- Tequila

Seasonings

- Garlic powder
- Kosher Salt
- Coarse Black Pepper

- Tequila Lime seasoning

Instructions

1. Two zones of your Blackstone should be preheated. One is set to a low setting, while the other is set to a medium setting. Set a small sauce pan in the corner of the low zone and add a can of refried beans. Allow to warm for a few minutes, stirring occasionally.

2. Add 1 pound of 80/20 meat to the middle zone. Cook until browned, seasoning with garlic powder, kosher salt, and coarse black pepper. Half a yellow onion, chopped, should be added to the beef while it's cooking. Season the steak and onions with Blackstone Tequila Lime seasoning after they're done.

3. Prepare your garnish while the beef is cooking. Chop lettuce, dice a tomato, and dice a jalapeo pepper.

4. Add a little olive oil to the low heat zone, spread it around, and set four tortillas down to toast and crisp up. For the Mexican pizza, these will be our crunchy layers. Each side should take no more than 2-3 minutes.

5. Combine 2-3 tablespoons sour cream, 1 tablespoon chipotle sauce, 1 teaspoon Tequila lime seasoning, and the juice of one or two limes in a mixing dish. If you have a squirt bottle, you could put the sauce in it and apply it at the end. If you don't have a squirt bottle, you can skip this step.

6. When one side of the tortillas is toasted, flip them over and begin assembling. To make one Mexican pizza, layer refried beans, meat, and red enchilada sauce on one tortilla and shredded cheese on the other. Allow the cheese to melt on the tortillas before serving. Place a little amount of shredded cheddar on top of the steak and drizzle with your particular sauce. Place the tortilla on top of the steak and beens once the cheese has melted. Drizzle with your personal sauce and garnish with lettuce, tomatoes, and jalapeos. I like to finish it off by dusting it with Blackstone Tequila Lime Seasoning. ENJOY!

7.

Philly Cheesesteak Egg Rolls

45 mins 6 serv

Ingredients:

- 1 Lb of thin sliced New York strip
- Vidalia onion, finely chopped
- Red pepper, finely chopped
- Green pepper, finely chopped
  - Oz of shiitake mushrooms, chopped
- 1/2 Poblano pepper, cut into 1" strips
- 4 fresh cayenne peppers
- 2 Tbsp salted butter

- 1 Small package of Velveeta cheese, cut into 1" cubes
- 1 Pack of egg roll wrappers

Instructions

1. Preheat your Blackstone Griddle on two burners to low heat. Allow for a 5-minute warm-up period.
2. Use salt and pepper to season your meat. Cook on a griddle until you reach your desired level of wellness. Meanwhile, butter the griddle and add the onion, red and green peppers, and mushroom. Cook until the vegetables are transparent, then add the meat in the last few minutes. Remove from heat and set aside to cool in a bowl.
3. Poblano peppers and charred cayenne peppers
4. Place a Blackstone Cup Liner on top of the griddle. Cook, stirring frequently, until the Velveeta cheese has melted, a bit at a time.
5. Preheat the Blackstone Airfryers at 350 degrees Fahrenheit. Cayenne and poblano peppers, finely chopped, are added to the melted Velveeta mixture heated on the griddle. Stir frequently.
6. Place 2-3 tablespoons of meat in egg roll wrappers and roll according to package recommendations. Lightly coat egg rolls with cooking spray. Place in the Blackstone Airfryer in a single layer. Cook for 10 minutes before rotating and cooking for another 10 to 15 minutes, or until lightly browned. Allow 5 minutes for the steak and cheese

egg rolls to cool in the air fryer. Continue to mix the Velveeta cheese dip.
7. Enjoy your egg rolls with a warm cheese dip.

Apple Pie Egg Rolls

Ingredients:

- 6 Granny Smith apples, diced
- 1 Tbsp of lemon juice
- 3/4 Cup of brown sugar
- 1/4 Cup of white sugar
- 2 Tbsp of cinnamon
- 1 Tbsp of vanilla extract
- 1 Pack of egg roll wrappers
- 4 Tbsp of butter
- Powdered sugar
- Blackstone Sweet Maple Seasoning
- Caramel sauce for dipping and drizzle

Instruction

1. Preheat the Blackstone Griddle to high heat in two zones and medium heat in the other two. In a skillet or a clean grease trap liner, heat canola oil to 350°F.
2. In a mixing dish, coat chopped apples with brown sugar, white sugar, cinnamon, vanilla essence, and lemon juice.

3. Place the butter in the medium heat zone and cook the apple combination until soft.
4. Remove the apple mixture from the oven and set aside to cool for 5 minutes.
5. Place the apple mixture in the center of the egg roll wrapper and roll as directed on the package, making sure to wet the wrapper's edges with water to seal in the contents.
6. Fry the egg rolls in the oil until golden brown, then remove them to a paper towel-lined dish to drain.
7. Dust with powdered sugar, Blackstone Sweet Maple Seasoning, then drizzle with caramel sauce on the plate and publish.

Vampire Breakfast Tamale

90 mins 4 serv

Ingredients:

For Tamales:

- Mesa mix
- Chorizo
- Egg
- Cheese
- Corn husks
- Water for tamales

For Pico:

- Roma tomato
- Cilantro
- Garlic
- Jalapeño
- Lime juice
- Onion

Instructions

1. Soak the corn husks in boiling water for a few minutes.
2. Use a prepared tamale masa mix to make tamale masa.
3. Brown the chorizo on the Blackstone till it is fully cooked, then add the eggs and stir well.
4. Dry corn husks with pressed tamale mix up to the husk's edges Fold in the meat mixture and cheese.
5. Boil a big pot of water and, using a steam basket, arrange the tamales inside for 1 hour. Every 10-15 minutes, add a bit more water to the pot.
6. Chop the tomato, cilantro, garlic, jalapeno, and onion while the tamales are cooking, then combine with some lime juice.
7. After an hour of cooking, remove the tamales from the heat, remove the husk, and set aside to cool for 5 minutes.
8. To serve with the tamales, griddle a couple of entire jalapeos.
9. To make a vampire tamale, heat the griddle to medium high and spread a thin layer of cheese on top, seasoning with the Blackstone Breakfast Blend. Place your tamale

on top of the cheese once it has melted. Fold the cheese over the tamale when it becomes crispy, remove from fire, and top with Pico.

CJ's Game Day Pizza Dip

20 mins 5 serv

Ingredients:

- Sliced Pepperoni
- Ground Mild Italian Sausage
- 8oz Cream cheese (softened)
- 1/2 C Shredded mozzarella cheese
- 1/2 C Shredded cheddar cheese
- 1/4 C Shredded Parmesan
- Pizza sauce or marinara (RAO)
- Bag of Pita Chips
- 1 tsp Italian seasoning
- 1tsp Garlic powder
- Fresh Basil
- Crushed red pepper flakes
- Aluminum Tin Pan

Instructions

1. One of your Blackstone's zones should be preheated to Medium High.
2. When your Blackstone is ready, add 1/2 pound of ground mild Italian sausage to the warmed zone and finish cooking. Make sure to stir the vegetables every now and then to ensure that they are properly cooked.
3. While the sausage is cooking, chop up a desired amount of pepperoni pieces and place them in a mixing dish. 8 oz melted cream cheese, 1/4 cup shredded mozzarella, 1/4 cup shredded cheddar cheese, a touch of shredded parmesan, 1-2 tsp garlic powder, 1 tsp Italian seasonings, a dash of crushed red pepper, a teaspoon of salt, and coarse black pepper, combined in a round aluminum pan.
4. While you're waiting for the sausage to cook, chop or tear your fresh basil leaves into little pieces for a garnish.
5. At this time, the sausage should be done, and you can spread a thin layer of it over the cheese mixture, followed by a layer of mozzarella, cheddar cheese, and a hearty amount of marinara or pizza sauce. More mozzarella, a little more cheddar, and a sprinkling of parmesan cheese on top. Add a pepperoni topping and your fresh basil on top of that.
6. Spray some water under a dome or large aluminum container and cover to melt all the cheeses. This should take no more than four to five minutes.
7. Remove the cheese from the griddle top once it has completely melted and begun to bubble.To serve, I set the platter on a big cutting board or tray, surround it with pita chips, then coat the dip and pita chips with

Blackstone Parmesan Ranch Seasoning.

Griddled Parmesan Spaghetti Tacos

20 mins 3 serv

Ingredients

- Grated Parmesan 12oz at least (2 oz per shell)
- Cooked spaghetti
- RAO marinara
- Lean beef, 90/10
- Chopped Red Onion
- Chopped Tomato
- 2 Tbsp Unsalted butter
- Basil
- Garlic powder
- Dried Oregano seasoning
- Blackstone Parmesan Ranch Seasoning
- Salt
- Pepper
- Blackstone Taco Rack

Instructions

1. You'll need to precook your spaghetti noodles, drain them, and have them ready before you start on your Blackstone Griddle.

2. Two zones of your griddle should be preheated. One is set to medium high and the other to low.

3. Put your favorite jarred marinara in a medium sauce pan and set it on low in the front corner of the heat zone. You're just getting your marinara ready for the final assembly.

4. Add the 90/10 lean meat to your medium high heat zone. Using your spatulas, break up the meat and season with kosher salt, coarse black pepper, garlic powder, and dried oregano. Cook, tossing periodically, until completely browned.

5. You'll need to prepare your Blackstone Griddle before you start cooking. While the beef is cooking, chop half a red onion and one red tomato and combine them in a small bowl with salt, pepper, and a thin sprinkling of garlic powder. Save it for a later date.

6. Stack around 4 or 5 fresh basil leaves on top of one another, roll into a tight coil, and cut into ribbons. This will be used as a garnish in the future.

7. Slide the meat to a cool zone or remove it from the griddle top when it's done.

8. To make our taco shells, heat our griddle to medium low, then grab small handfuls of grated parmesan and spread them out on the griddle top. It's critical not to eat too little or too much cheese. Per shell, you'll use about 2 oz. Make a circle about the same size as a corn tortilla.

When it's cooking, you'll notice little bubbles on the borders at first, which will eventually spread to the middle. The edges of the cheese will begin to get golden brown after about 2-3 minutes. With your spatula, gently remove the cheese off the griddle, being careful not to tear it, and flip to cook the other side.When both sides are golden brown, remove the cheese crisp from the oven and lay it on top of the Blackstone Taco Rack. You're not going to use the rack like you normally would; instead, you're going to use the raw in reverse to hang the cheese to cool. Continue in this manner until you have the required number of shells. You can cool 5 shells at a time on your rack.

9. While your shells cool and crisp, combine your precooked spaghetti noodles, enough marinara to coat the pasta, and one or two tablespoons unsalted butter in a mixing bowl. Toss everything together until the butter has melted and is evenly distributed throughout the spaghetti.

10. To assemble your Spaghetti Tacos, place your shells in the taco rack, spoon a portion of your pasta into each shell, top with one of two spoonfuls of cooked and seasoned beef, a drizzle of marinara, and garnish with your tomato and red onions, fresh basil ribbons, and Blackstone Parmesan Ranch Seasoning. Serve and have fun!!

Griddled Peach Crostini with Balsamic Glaze

10 mins 4 serv

Ingredients:

- 1 Peach
- Baguette loaf
- Baby Arugula
- Prosciutto
- Basaltic glaze
- Goats cheese
- Kosher Salt
- Coarse Black Pepper
- Olive oil
- Unsalted Butter
- Blackstone Sweet Maple Seasoning

Instructions

1. One of your Blackstone's zones should be preheated to Medium High.
2. Slice one peach into small wedges while your griddle heats up. When done, drizzle a small bit of olive oil and 1 tbsp unsalted butter over the griddle top. Toss the peach wedges in the oil and butter until they are uniformly coated. Season with a pinch of Koser salt and coarse black pepper once coated. It doesn't take much; a small quantity goes a long way in this recipe. Toss one more,

then arrange your peach slices on the side to caramelize.

3. Slice your baguette loaf on the bias into 1/2" - 3/4" slices while your peaches are cooking. About 4-5 slices are required. Your peaches will be ready to flip at this stage.Each side should only take around 90 seconds to caramelize to a light brown color. Make sure not to overcook the potatoes or they will become mushy. Your peach should still have a touch of bite to it.

4. Place your bread next to the peaches on the skillet to toast on one side only. It shouldn't take more than two minutes to complete this task. Remove the bread and peaches off the griddle when they are golden brown on one side.

5. To plate, place the toasted side of the bread on a serving tray. Toss in some baby arugula, a slice of prosciutto, one or two peach wedges, a few crumbles of goat cheese, a drizzle of balsamic sauce, and a light dusting of Blackstone Sweet Maple Seasoning, and serve!

Tequila Lime Roasted Corn Guacamole

15 mins 4 serv

Ingredients:

- avocado
- Tomato
- Red onion
- Jalapeño
- Cilantro
- Limes
- Corn on the cob
- Queso fresco Cheese
- Garlic powder
- Salt
- Pepper
- Tortilla chips
- Sour cream,
- Tequila
- Blackstone Tequila Lime Seasoning

Instructions

1. Preheat your griddle and air fryer to medium high and low, respectively.
2. Let's get our ingredients ready for the griddle while it's heating up. From north to south, cut your avocado in half. Your knife will come to a halt at the seed inside and simply slice around it, pulling a section apart to reveal the seed. Remove the seed from the pod, leaving the skin on, and lay it on the

griddle. Add a little sprinkle of olive oil to each avocado before placing it on the grill to toast. It won't be long before a light brown toast appears on the avocado. Take two limes, cut them in half, and toast them in the same oil as the avocado.While that's going on, grab one ear of corn and slice off the top of the griddle, leaving the fresh corn on the griddle to roast/toast. Drizzle a little olive oil over the corn and toss to coat evenly with kosher salt and coarse black pepper. You don't need to toss the corn until one side is toasted to achieve the desired color. So make sure you don't have a corn pile; you want all of the corn to be touching the griddle top.

3. While your ingredients are cooking on the griddle, dice or mince your red onion into bite-size pieces. Small nibbles are my preference. Cut your tomato and jalapeo into roughly the same size bites by slicing and chopping them. In addition to rough cutting your cilantro

4. You now have the opportunity to open your bag of tortilla chips and reheat them in your air fryer. This isn't required, but WOW, such a nice touch.

5. Your avocado, limes, and corn should be ready at this point. Remove them from the griddle and mash your avocado in a mixing basin. I prefer little chunks in my avocado, but you can mash it to your desired consistency. Make sure you finish this step before adding the rest of your ingredients. Once mashed, add your tomato, jalapeo, red onion, and salt and pepper to taste. Corn that has been roasted (LEAVING SOME ASIDE FOR GARNISH),1 tsp garlic powder, two hefty pinches of kosher salt, and one pinch of coarse black pepper, combined with a desired amount of cilantro, two halves of lime juice, 1 tsp garlic powder, two hefty pinches of kosher salt, and one pinch of coarse black pepper, and gently mixed. After you've mixed everything together, taste it to make sure you've added enough salt. If necessary, add extra. It's great to keep adding as you go.

6. Now it's time to make our signature tequila lime drizzle. Add two table spoons of sour cream, one lime's juice, a drizzle of tequila, salt, pepper, and a teaspoon of Blackstone Tequila Lime Seasoning to a mixing bowl. To apply, I like to put mine in a little squeeze bottle.

7. To serve, place your guacamole in a bowl, top with some broken up queso fresco, a little extra roasted corn, cilantro, a drizzle of tequila lime sauce, and a dusting of Tequila Lime Seasoning. Place the dish on a big tray, remove the warmed chips from the air fryer and arrange them around the bowl, season with Blackstone Tequila Lime Seasoning, and serve!

White BBQ Sauce Chicken Party Platter

240 mins 5 serv

Ingredients:

- 3 lb chicken breast
- 1/4 c oil, avocado or extra light tasting olive oil
- 1 tbsp dried parsley
- White BBQ Sauce:
- 2 cups Mayo, Dukes preferred
- 4 fresh Garlic cloves, finely grated
- 3 tbsp fresh squeezed Lemon Juice (or one small lemon)
- 1 tbsp Black Pepper
- 1 tsp Salt
- 1 tsp Sugar
- 1 /3 cup White Wine Vinegar

Instructions

1. Combine all of the ingredients for the White BBQ Sauce and chill for at least 30 minutes before using.
2. Cut chicken into bite-size pieces and marinate in 1/2 cup white bbq sauce, 1/4 cup oil, and dried parsley for 30 minutes to 4 hours. (Or just enough to coat gently)
3. On medium high heat, cook the chicken until it is fully cooked.
4. Serve the chicken with a dipping sauce made from white barbecue sauce.

CJ's Chicken Flautas with Griddled Salsa Verde

30 mins 4 serv

Ingredients:

- Chicken cutlets
- Corn tortillas
- Pre shredded Mexican blend cheese
- Large aluminum tin
- Toothpicks
- Olive Oil
- 4-6 Tomatillos (depending on the size)
- 3 limes
- White or yellow onion
- 3 jalapeños
- Cilantro
- Garlic
- Salt
- Pepper
- Blackstone Taco Fajita Seasoning
- Blender

Instructions

1. Pre-heat one side of your griddle on high, then fry in a big shallow tin pan with olive oil or another oil replacement. The temperature of the oil should be around 375 degrees. Another zone should be preheated on medium high.

2. Our chicken cutlets must first be seasoned. Simply brush both sides with a small coating of oil and season with salt and pepper before placing on the Blackstone griddle to cook. This won't take long, so keep an eye on it and turn as needed to ensure even cooking.

3. Let's get started preparing our salsa ingredients. Remove the husk on the outside of the tomatillos as well as the stem before cutting into quarters.

4. Split the stem off your jalapeos and cut them in half lengthwise. You can leave the seeds out if you want a milder salsa. I prefer the warmth, so I keep them in. Take two limes and cut them in half, as well as one white or yellow onion, which should be cut into large chunks. As the onion cooks on the griddle, it will break up.

5. Your chicken should be done by now. Remove the chicken from the grill and toss the salsa ingredients on top with a little olive oil to coat. I also like to season with salt and pepper at this point. I add 3-4 garlic cloves, a bit extra oil, and some salt and pepper around 3 minutes into cooking these items. Allow the ingredients to caramelize as they cook.The limes will begin to turn color, and the jalapeos will begin to roast. When the ingredients have cooked down a little, toss them occasionally and remove them. You don't want the tomatillos to go mushy, so keep an eye on them. They can go straight into a blender once they've been removed from the griddle. DON'T MIX THE LIMES.

6. After you've added the remaining ingredients, set those aside to squeeze the juice. Squeeze the lime juice into your blender with tongs, season with a pinch of salt and pepper, and process until smooth and integrated. While you complete the rest of your meal, lay this aside to chill.

7. Your corn tortillas should now be steaming. I'll place the little Blackstone cutting board on on the griddle, spread out the tortillas on the board, grab the huge basting dome, and spray water beneath and around the cutting board, covering the process. This procedure ensures that the tortillas do not break when being rolled. Warm them in the microwave with a damp paper towel on top.

8. You can slice the chicken cutlets into small thin slices while the tortillas are heating. Once those are completed, your tortillas are nearly finished. They should feel warm when you touch them.

9. To make your flautas, lay one tortilla down, add a few pieces of chicken, and some shredded cheese, then gently roll the tortilla. Once it's rolled, insert a toothpick into the tortilla to keep all of your contents in place while deep frying. Rep until all of your chicken and tortillas have been used.

10. Your oil should be ready to use at this point. Cook your rolled flautas in tiny batches of 6-8 per round in

the oil. Because the chicken is already cooked, this won't take long. Cook for about 2-3 minutes, or until the shell is crisp. When they're done, drain them on paper towels and season with Blackstone Taco Fajita Seasoning immediately away.

11. You can start coating your flautas as they cool. Add some fresh salsa verde to a small bowl, stack your flautas with or without toothpicks, top with cilantro and a griddled lime, and enjoy!

Fried Oreos & Funnel Cake

20 mins 20 serv

Ingredients:

- Krusteaz Pancake Mix
- Water
- 1pk Oreos
- Vanilla
- Powdered Sugar

Instructions

1. In a mixing basin, combine 3 cups of pancake mix and enough water to make it the consistency of pancake batter. Mix with 2 tsp vanilla extract well.

2. To fry, heat a cast iron pan with oil to 300-325 degrees on the Blackstone.
3. Dip Oreos in batter and fry them.
4. Cook until golden brown on the bottoms, then flip (about 3minutes each side)
5. Enjoy with powdered sugar on top!

CJ's Chimichurri Steak Street Tacos

25 mins 5 serv

Ingredients

- 1 Skirt Steak
- Corn and/or Small Flour Tortillas
- Pre Shredded Mexican blend Cheese
- Cilantro
- Flat Leaf Parsley
- 2-3 cloves Garlic
- 1 Red Bell Pepper
- 1 Green Bell Pepper
- 1 Red Chile
- 1 Sweet Yellow Onion
- 1 Shallot
- Olive oil
- Salt
- Pepper
- 4 Limes
- Sour Cream
- 1 Bag of Microwave ready Uncle Bens Jazmine Rice

- Herdez Salsa Verde
- Blackstone Taco Fajita Seasoning
- Blackstone Tequila Lime Seasoning

Instructions

1. Warm up your Blackstone ahead of time. Turn the griddle to high.
2. It's time to start making your chimichurri. Chop cilantro and flat leaf parsley in equal amounts (leave just a pinch or two of cilantro for later). 2-3 garlic cloves, roughly minced 1-2 tablespoons fresh shallot, minced 1 red chili, minced Combine the ingredients in a mixing dish with 2-3 pinches of kosher salt. 1 tsp. black pepper, coarse 2 limes' juice and 1/4 cup extra virgin olive oil If it's too thick, thin it out with more olive oil and lime juice and set it aside.
3. Let's cut up our other veggies while your griddle is still heating up. This is a straightforward procedure.Simply cut your red and green bell peppers, as well as your sweet yellow onion, into juliennes and set them aside.
4. Place your skirt steak on a large platter, sprinkle with olive oil on both sides, then season generously with Blackstone Tequila Lime and Taco Fajita seasoning on both sides.At this point, your griddle should be blazing hot and ready to cook your skirt steak. Place your steak on the griddle top after adding another little sprinkle of olive oil. Because skirt steak is so thin, it will cook quickly. We're looking at a

time frame of 2-3 minutes each side. And you'll know it's ready to flip when the cooked side of the steak has a lovely sear and crust.
5. While your skirt steak is cooking, put a thin drizzle of olive oil next to your steak on the griddle and mix your onions, red and green bell peppers, and a pinch of salt and pepper in the olive oil to coat.You can now reduce the heat to medium on your griddle. Remember to inspect your steak and turn it when it's done.
6. Let's get our special sauce ready while that's cooking. Mix 1/2 cup sour cream, 2 tablespoons Herdez salsa verde, a splash of Blackstone tequila lime and taco fajita seasoning, and 2-3 tablespoons fresh chimichurri in a mixing bowl until thoroughly combined.
7. Now it's time to reheat our Uncle Bens Jazmine rice, which is microwave-ready. Empty the bag onto the griddle top and spritz with water to steam it up, along with a touch of salt, a pinch of pepper, the juice of one lime, and a pinch of the leftover cilantro. To heat up the ingredients, toss them together for about 2 minutes and then remove them.
8. When your steak is done, remove it from the grill and set it aside to rest for about 5 minutes. Also, toss your vegetables every now and then. You can now lower the heat on your griddle so that we can warm up our tortillas. The vegetables are done at this stage and can be removed or slid to the cool side of your

griddle.Cleaning the surface of your griddle with a scraper to the back grease trap before heating up your tortillas is a smart idea. After it's been cleaned, lay down your corn or flower tortillas to warm for around 2 minutes.

9. You can chop your skirt steak while your tortillas are cooking up. There is now a method for chopping up your skirt steak. Cutting against the grain is the way to go. Going along the grain means you'll see small lines on the steak. Cut your skirt steak against the grain by turning it 45 degrees. As a result, each mouthful is soft and easy to chew. To fit the steak in the tortilla, slice and chop it into little chunks. After then, it's time to remove your tortillas.

10. To assemble, I place one tortilla in my Blackstone Taco holder, add a piece of steak, a little cilantro lime rice, some sautéed bell peppers and onions, shredded cheese, a spoonful of fresh chimichurri, and a dab of your particular sauce. You're now ready to dine!

Upside Down Pizza

30 mins 6 serv

Ingredients:

- Stonefire thin artisan pizza crust, 2 pack
- ½ lb provolone, Boar's head
- Fresh mozzarella, ball, log or pearls
- Fresh Basil

Meat of choice:

- Boars Head sopressata, pepperoni cups, salami, Italian sausage

Sauce

- 1 can San Marzano tomatoes (San Marzano tomato of Agro Sarnese-Nocerino D.O.P. Preferred) or substitute good quality crushed tomatoes
- 2 tbsp Extra Virgin olive oil
- 3 garlic cloves, smashed & chopped
- 1 tsp oregano
- 4 basil leaves, torn
- Salt

Garlic oil

- 4 tbsp extra virgin olive oil
- 2-3 large cloves fresh garlic, minced
- ½ tsp dried basil
- ½ tsp dried oregano
- ½ tsp dried parsley
- 1 tsp crushed red pepper (optional)

Instructions

1. Toss tomatoes with a few spoonfuls of excess juice in a mixing dish. Slightly crush tomatoes with your hands. Combine the oil, torn basil, oregano, garlic, and salt to taste in a mixing bowl. The sauce is now ready to use. Because the pizza will be griddled, the sauce can be prepared in a small saucepan immediately on the Blackstone griddle for even heating a few minutes before the pizza is started. Because this is a griddle top pizza rather than a pizza oven baked pizza, heating the sauce will also help the cheeses melt.
2. Add the pizza crust upside down to heat and slightly crisp the top of the pizza crust on medium low heat. Depending on how crisp or soft you prefer your crust to be.To begin cooking and crisping up the bottom, flip and reduce heat to low, giving you time to add seasonings.
3. 1 tbsp garlic oil, drizzled around the pizza Provolone cheese should be uniformly distributed across the pie.
4. Add the pizza sauce and spread it out with a spoon.
5. Spread fresh mozzarella all over the pie. Raise the heat on the griddle to medium and cook until the desired crispness is achieved, checking the bottom regularly. If needed, a dome can be used to keep the mozzarella from melting too soon once it is placed on top of the warm pizza sauce.
6. Remove the pizza from the oven and top with fresh basil. Optional: drizzle with garlic oil.

Griddled banana bread with cream cheese glaze and candied bacon

15 mins 4 serv

Ingredients:

- 1 loaf Banana Bread
- ½ tbsp Butter per slice of bread for frying
- 6-8 slices Bacon
- 1 tbsp real Maple Syrup
- 1 tbsp Sriracha
- Blackstone sweet Maple seasoning
- Candied Walnuts, optional

Cream cheese glaze:

- 4 oz Whipped Cream Cheese
- 1 1/2 cups Powdered Sugar
- 1 teaspoon Vanilla Extract
- 2 tablespoons Milk (adjusted as needed)

Instructions

1. Preheat the Blackstone airfryer to 400 degrees. Cut bacon pieces in

half and spray both sides with maple syrup and sriracha. On both sides, season with Blackstone sweet maple seasoning. Place the bacon on parchment paper coated airfryer racks and cook for 8-10 minutes, checking frequently. Remove the bacon from the pan when it's done and set it aside to rest on a cooling rack; the bacon will stiffen as it cools.

2. Preheat the griddle to a medium-low heat setting. Banana bread should be cut into 1-2 inch slices. Swirl a little butter around the griddle before adding the bread pieces to cook for around 2-3 minutes per side. Removing when both sides have been roasted and warmed completely.

3. Cream together cream cheese, powdered sugar, and vanilla in a mixing dish using a fork or a whisk until smooth and thin enough to drizzle.

4. Serve banana bread with a cream cheese frosting on top and candied bacon slices or crumbled bacon on top.

Lamb Lollipops with Mint Chimichurri

15 mins 4 serv

Ingredients:

- 12 Lamb Lollipops
- 2 tablespoons spicy brown Mustard
- 1 bunch Italian flat leaf Parsley
- ½ bunch fresh Mint Leaves
- 1 tablespoon minced Garlic
- The juice of 1 Lemon
- The juice of 2 Limes
- 2 tablespoon Red Wine Vinegar
- 2 teaspoons Red Pepper Flakes
- Olive oil
- Salt and pepper

Instructions

Heat your griddle to a high setting.

Combine the parsley and mint in a mixing basin and finely chop. Combine the garlic, lemon and lime juices, red wine vinegar, red pepper flakes, and a pinch of salt and pepper in a mixing bowl. Mix in some olive oil to ensure that all of the ingredients are uniformly distributed. Set aside for a later date.

With a little olive oil, mustard, and salt and pepper, season the lamb lollipops. Cook for 1-2 minutes per side over high heat, or until caramelized and cooked to your preference.

To serve, lay the cooked lamb lollipops on a big family-style tray and drizzle with the mint chimichurri. Serve immediately.

Buffalo Cauliflower

15 mins 6serv

Ingredients:

- 1 head of Cauliflower
- 1 cup Frank's Hot Sauce
- ½ stick Butter
- 2 tbs Vinegar
- 1 tbsp Worcestershire Sauce
- 1 tsp Garlic Powder

Instructions

1. Cauliflower should be chopped into bite-size pieces.
2. Melt butter in a microwave-safe bowl. Combine the remaining ingredients in a mixing bowl. Remove from the equation.
3. Preheat to the highest
4. Cook for 5-7 minutes, or until cauliflower is slightly browned.
5. Remove the items from the oven and place them in an airtight container. 12 of the sauce should be poured over the cauliflower, then the lid should be sealed and shaken.
6. Continue to cook for 3 minutes.
7. Remove the cauliflower from the tray and place it on a serving platter. Pour the leftover sauce over the cauliflower and serve with celery and blue cheese dressing as dipping accompaniments.

Zucchini Pizza Bites

15 mins 6 serv

Ingredients:

- Zucchini
- Rao's Marinara Sauce
- Pepperonis
- Shredded Mozzarella

Instructions

1. Zucchini should be cut into 14-inch slices.
2. Finish with a drizzle of marinara sauce, pepperoni, and a sprinkling of cheese.
3. Preheat the Air Fryer on high and spray it with cooking spray.
4. Cook for 5-7 minutes, or until the tops of the zucchini bites are toasted, on an air fryer tray.
5. Remove from the oven and serve right away.

Betty's Ricotta Donuts

20 mins 4 serv

Ingredients:

- 1 C whole milk ricotta cheese
- 1 large egg
- 1 tbsp white rum
- Zest of ½ - 1 whole lemon
- 1 C all purpose flour
- 2 tbsp white sugar
- 2 tsp baking powder

Canola or Vegetable oil for frying

- Sturdy pan for deep frying
- Powdered Sugar

Instructions

1. Turn the Blackstone to high and heat a small robust pan with your preferred oil.
2. Combine the ricotta, egg, rum, and lemon zest in a large mixing basin.
3. Combine flour, sugar, and baking powder in a separate basin.
4. Slowly add the dry ingredients to the wet ingredients, a quarter cup at a time, and stir to blend. It's best if the dough is thick and sticky.
5. Carefully dip a wooden chopstick or toothpick into the oil; if bubbles emerge around the wooden stick, the oil is ready to fry (or use a thermometer oil should be perfect between 350-375 degrees)
6. Drop a dough ball into the oil slowly with two spoons. Allow to fry for 3-5 minutes, or until deep golden brown in color. If the donuts do not turn over on their own, gently flip them to ensure even cooking.
7. Drain on paper towels after removing from the oil.
8. Dust with powdered sugar before serving.

SweetBabyTots

20 mins 10 serv

Ingredients:

- 20 Frozen Tator-Tots
- 10 slices bacon, thin cut
- 20 slices pickled jalapeno
- 1/4 c Sweet Baby Rays BBQ Sauce
- 20 toothpick

Instructions

1. Preheat the Blackstone Airfryers to 425 degrees or high heat.
2. Place frozen tator-tots in a plate on the counter for 5 minutes to slightly defrost, just long enough for a toothpick to glide through them.
3. Bacon pieces should be cut in half.
4. Place a jalapeño slice on top of the bacon, then a tomato top, and wrap

in bacon. Using a toothpick, secure the bacon.

5. Brush bacon with Sweet Baby Rays BBQ sauce of your choice.

6. Place tator-tots equally spaced in the preheated Blackstone Airfryer drawer. Cook for 8 to 10 minutes. To ensure consistent cooking, check tots halfway through, lightly shake them, or flip them.

7. Serve with extra barbecue sauce on the side for dipping.

8. Enjoy!

Korean Fire Chicken Lettuce Wraps

30 min 4 serv

Ingredients:

- 2 LBS Chicken Thighs, boneless skinless
- 1 head Butter Lettuce
- 2 cups Mayonnaise
- 1 tbsp Rice Wine Vinegar
- 2 tbsp Sesame Oil
- 1/2+ c Blackstone Korean Fire Sear and Serve Sauce
- Green Onions, sliced and divided
- toasted Sesame Seeds
- 2 tbsp seasoned wok or stir-fry oil

Instructions

1. Whisk together mayonnaise, rice wine vinegar, sesame oil, and Blackstone Korean Fire Sear and Serve Sauce in a mixing bowl. Depending on how hot you like it, use more or less Korean Fire Sauce.

2. Green onions should be sliced with the white and green ends separated.

3. Raw chicken breast should be diced into little bite-size pieces.

4. Toss the chicken in 2 tbsp seasoned wok oil to evenly coat it.

5. Preheat the Blackstone to medium-high heat and place the chicken in a single layer on the grill to cook. Cook until the chicken is golden brown, tossing every couple of minutes.

6. Reduce the heat to medium-low and coat the chicken with about half of the sauce. Allow 2 minutes to cook after tossing. Toss in the white ends of the green onions for the last minute of cooking.

7. Remove the chicken and top with sesame seeds, green onions that have been set aside, and a dab of Korean Sweet Fire Sauce.

8. Fill lettuce leaves with chicken, more sauce, sesame seeds, and green onions.

9. Enjoy!

Bite Sized Chinese Meatballs

30 min 6 serv

Ingredients:

- 1 lb Ground Pork
- 1.5 tbsp Cornstarch
- 1 tsp fresh Ginger, grated
- 3-4 Garlic Cloves, grated
- 3 tsp Brown Sugar
- 3 tsp Soy Sauce
- 1 tsp Five Spice
- 5 Green Onions, sliced (3 for the mixture and 2 for a garnish)
- Stir Fry Oil or Olive oil for cooking
- Sesame Seeds for garnish

Instructions

1. Combine the first 8 ingredients in a mixing bowl with a spoon. Roll in little bite-size meatballs (leave around 2 stalks of green onion on the side for garnish). This recipe serves approximately 24 people.
2. Cook meatballs on each side until browned in olive oil on a Blackstone Griddle over medium heat. 5 minutes per side, adding extra oil as needed when rolling onto each side to fry.
3. To assist the meatballs finish cooking, use the Blackstone dome near the end.

4. Serve with dipping sauce and garnished with sliced green onions and sesame seeds!
5. Enjoy!

Parmesan Crisp Bruschetta

10 mins 4 serv

Ingredients:

- ½ cup Shredded Parmesan
- ½ cup Grana Padano
- 1 cup finely diced Tomato
- ¼ cup finely diced Red Onion
- 1 tablespoon minced Garlic
- 2 tablespoons chopped fresh Basil
- Balsamic Glaze
- Salt and Pepper
- Olive Oil

Instructions

1. Combine the tomatoes, onions, garlic, basil, and a pinch of parmesan in a large mixing basin. A drizzle of olive oil and a few pinches of salt and pepper complete the dish. Combine all ingredients in a large mixing bowl and set away for later.
2. Preheat the griddle to medium-low. Combine the cheeses and spread about a spoonful of the mixture on the griddle in a round 2-3 inch circle. Cook for 2-3 minutes, or until the bottom of the cheese begins to

crisp. Cook for another 2 minutes, or until the cheese is golden and crunchy on both sides. Remove the griddle from the heat and set aside to cool.

3. To serve, place the cheese chips on a serving platter and spoon a tablespoon of the tomato mixture on top. Add a drizzle of balsamic glace and a few basil leaves to finish.
4. Enjoy!

THYME Wings

30 min 3 serv

Ingredients:

- 2 lb fresh chicken wings (about 10)
- ¼ cup Extra light tasting olive oil
- 2 tbsp thyme, dried
- 2 tsp coarse salt
- 1 tsp black pepper
- 2 tsp garlic powder
- 2 tsp onion powder

Instructions

1. Wings, drums, and drumettes should all be cut into parts.
2. Pat wings dry using paper towels and place them between paper towels on a baking sheet. Refrigerate uncovered overnight.
3. Remove the wings from the fridge and coat them in extra light olive oil.

Toss the wings with salt, pepper, garlic, onion powder, and thyme to evenly cover them.

4. Allow 30-60 minutes for wings to sit at room temperature in a mixing dish on the kitchen counter before cooking.
5. Add wings to a Blackstone griddle that has been preheated to medium-low heat. To ensure that the wings are cooked through, turn them every few minutes. It should take about 15-20 minutes to cook the wings.
6. Increase the heat to high near the end to crisp the skin to your taste.
7. Enjoy

Griddle Girl Cinnamon Apple Pie Cups

Ingredients:

- 2 large green apples
- ¼ cup brown sugar
- 1 tbsp apple pie spice
- 2 tbsp melted butter
- 1/4 cup flour
- cooking spray
- vanilla ice cream
- caramel sauce

Instructions

1. Apples should be peeled and chopped into small bits.
2. Combine apples, brown sugar, apple pie spice, and 1 tablespoon butter in a mixing bowl. Remove from the equation.
3. Using a rolling pin, flatten the cinnamon rolls. Using cooking spray, coat silicone muffin cups. 1 roll should be placed in each cup.
4. Cook cinnamon rolls for 5 minutes and set to medium.
5. Melt 1 tbsp butter on the griddle top and cook apples on medium until mushy while the cinnamon rolls are baking.
6. Remove the cinnamon rolls and place the apples in each cup, cook for 3 more minutes.
7. Remove the silicone wrappers from the apple pie cups and top with ice cream and caramel drizzle.
8. Enjoy!

Griddle Girl Toasted Ravioli Bruschetta

Ingredients:

- 2 large tomatoes diced
- 2 tbsp fresh basil
- 1 tbsp minced garlic
- ¼ cup shredded parmesan
- 1 tbsp olive oil
- Salt and pepper
- 2 eggs
- ¼ cup milk
- 1 cup bread crumbs
- ½ cup grated parmesan
- 1 tbsp Italian seasons
- 3 cheese ravioli
- Balsamic glaze
- cooking spray

Instructions

1. Chop the tomatoes and place them in a bowl. Toss in the fresh basil, garlic, olive oil, and shredded parmesan cheese. Set aside after stirring until everything is well blended.
2. 1 cup bread crumbs, Italian seasonings, and grated parmesan cheese in a mixing bowl Scramble two eggs with milk in a separate bowl.
3. Cook ravioli for 5 minutes in salted water, then drain.
4. Repeat the process of dipping each ravioli into the egg mixture and then into the bread crumb mixture until all raviolis are coated.
5. Set the air fryer tray to medium and coat it with cooking spray. Cook for 5 minutes before flipping the raviolis and cooking for an additional 3 minutes.
6. Place the raviolis on a platter after removing them from the air fryer. Top with the bruschetta mixture,

extra parmesan, and a balsamic glaze drizzle.

7. Enjoy

7. Remove the apples from the oven and serve with a caramel apple dip.
8. Enjoy!

Griddle Apple Fries

Ingredients:

- 2 large green apples
- 1 cup graham cracker crumbs
- ¼ cup sugar
- 2 eggs
- 1 cup flour
- cooking spray
- caramel dip

Instructions

1. Apples should be peeled and thinly sliced.
2. Combine graham cracker crumbs and sugar in a mixing basin. Scramble two eggs in a separate bowl. Pour flour into the third basin.
3. Coat each apple slice with flour, then egg mixture, and finally graham crumbs, working in batches.
4. Cooking spray should be sprayed on the tray. Reduce the heat to medium.
5. Cook for 5 minutes after adding apple slices to the tray.
6. Cook for 3 minutes more on the other side.

Halloween Buffalo Chicken "Pumpkins"

20 mins 6 serv

Ingredients:

- 1 lb ground chicken
- 1 egg, beaten
- 1 cup panko bread crumb
- 1/4 c carrots, grated or diced small
- 1/2 c celery, center leafy stalks, diced small
- 1/4 cup crumbled blue cheese
- 1/4 c green onions, chopped small
- 1 tbsp Blackstone Parmesan Ranch Seasoning
- 1 tbsp buffalo sauce
- olive oil
- Sauce:
- 1/2 cup buffalo sauce
- 1 tbsp butter
- 1/4 c ranch dressing

Instructions

1. Except for the oil, combine the ground chicken with the remaining ingredients. Make about 16 meatballs.

2. Preheat the Blackstone to medium-low heat.
3. In a small pot, combine the sauce ingredients and cook on the Blackstone.
4. Drizzle some olive oil over the Blackstone and toss in the meatballs. Allow meatballs to cook fully, flipping them once to ensure even cooking. Allow for a golden brown on all sides, and cover if necessary. Cooking time for meatballs should be around 8-10 minutes.
5. Serve meatballs on a plate. Drizzle the sauce on top. Serve with green onions as a garnish. Turn meatballs into pumpkins with ripped celery leaves and green onions for a Halloween theme!
6. Enjoy!

Bacon Chicken Party Dip

Ingredients:

- 3 chicken breast , diced small
- 1 package bacon , diced small
- 1 heaping cup of mayo, Dukes preferred
- 2 blocks cream cheese, softened
- 1 bunch green onions, chopped
- 1 8 oz block cheddar cheese, grated
- 3 garlic cloves, grated
- 1-4 oz jar pimentos, drained

- Blackstone Parmesan Ranch Seasoning

Instructions

1. Chicken and bacon should be diced into little bite-size pieces. On the Blackstone, cook the chicken and bacon separately over medium low heat. Chicken should be seasoned with Blackstone Parmesan Ranch seasoning. When you're finished, set it away.
2. Combine cream cheese, mayonnaise, garlic, pimentos, half of the green onions, and about one tablespoon of Parmesan Ranch seasoning in a large mixing bowl.
3. Combine the chicken and half of the bacon in a mixing bowl.
4. Fill a casserole or baking dish halfway with the ingredients. Top with the leftover bacon and cheddar cheese. Dip can be reheated in the oven or served straight from the Blackstone. When ready to serve, add the leftover green onions!

Lamb Tacos

Ingredients

- 1 Lb. of Ground Lamb
- 1 Teaspoon of Dried Mint
- 1/4 Teaspoon of Garlic Powder
- 1/4 Teaspoon of Dried Parsley
- Salt and Pepper to taste

- 4 Large Tortilla Shells
- 1 Cucumber, diced
- 1 Tomato, diced
- 1/4 Cup of Red Onion, sliced thin
- 1 Cup of Feta Cheese, crumbled
- Tzatziki Sauce or Sour Cream

Instructions

Add the ground lamb to Blackstone and cook over medium heat.

Chop the ground beef with the Blackstone scraper or spatula and cook for 4-5 minutes, or until the flesh begins to brown.

Drain some, but not all, of the fat by pushing the ground beef to one side of the griddle and scraping the excess fat liquid off. Because lamb has a larger fat content than beef, be cautious of spatter.

Combine the dry ingredients and stir thoroughly.

Â

On the Blackstone Griddle, lightly toast the tortillas and serve with lettuce, tomato, cucumber, red onion, and tzatziki or sour cream.

Italian Sausage And Cheese

Ingredients

- 3 Long Italian Rolls or 4-6 flour toritillas
- 1 Lb. of Ground Italian Sausage, mild or hot
- 1 Green Bell Pepper, diced
- 1 Red Bell Pepper, diced
- 1 Onion, diced
- 1 Cup of Portobello Mushrooms, diced
- 2-3 Fresh Garlic Cloves, grated
- Italian Seasoning
- Garlic Powder
- Salt and Pepper
- 2 Tablespoons of Mayo (for toasting rolls)
- 1-2 Cups of Shredded Italian Blend Shredded Cheese
- 1-2 Cups of Marinara (Victoria marinara is a good choice)
- Extra Virgin Olive Oil

Instructions

Prepare all of your ingredients by chopping the red and green peppers, onions, and mushrooms, as well as grating the garlic.

Heat the Blackstone to medium and sprinkle with olive oil. Toss in the peppers and onions. Cook for 4 minutes, stirring occasionally. Salt & pepper to taste.

Cook for another 2-3 minutes after adding the mushrooms to the peppers and onions. On low to no heat, move the veggies to the side.

Place a small saucepan with a cup or two of marinara in the corner of your griddle to heat through before cooking your meat.

Cook the sausage thoroughly on the griddle, breaking it up like taco meat. Lightly season with garlic powder and Italian spice.

Heat tortillas for 30-60 seconds on low heat. Turn over and top with cheese and meat. Fold the tortilla in half and heat until golden brown on both sides, rotating halfway through. If you're using rolls instead of tortillas, apply a thin layer of mayonnaise on the interior of the rolls and toast them over low heat with the mayo side down while the meat cooks.

Reduce the heat to low in the Blackstone where the beef is, add the grated garlic, and well incorporate it into the flesh. Toss the cooked sausage with the veggies. Toss in half of the cheese and toss to combine.

Divide the meat into three parts and arrange them in three stacks.

Top each layer of meat with the remaining cheese. Top with a roll or tortilla and heat for another minute or two.

Flip the sandwiches over using your hand to hold the bread/tortilla and your spatula to slide beneath the sandwich. Serve with marinara on top or to dip on the side.

Tequila Lime Corn Salad

10 mins 4 serv

Ingredients

- 4 ears of Corn
- 15 oz can Black Beans, drained & rinsed
- 1 Red Bell Pepper, diced small
- ¼ cup Dukes Mayonnaise
- ¼ cup Sour Cream
- ¼ cup Parmesan Cheese
- ½ cup Cotija or Queso Fresco Cheese, plus some for garnish
- 1 Lime
- ½ cup Cilantro, chopped
- 2 Jalapeños, optional
- 3 fresh Garlic cloves, chopped
- 2 tbsp extra light tasting Olive Oil
- Blackstone Tequila Lime Seasoning

Instructions

1. Preheat the Blackstone griddle on low heat (e-series set to 325 degrees)
2. Remove the corn kernels from the cob.
3. Drizzle olive oil over the griddle and toss in the garlic to coat. Cook for 30-60 seconds before throwing in the corn. Allow 5 minutes for the corn to cook. Remove the corn and set it aside to cool for ten minutes.
4. Toss the corn with the black beans, bell pepper, cheeses, lime juice,

cilantro, sour cream, and mayonnaise, as well as the Blackstone Tequila Lime seasoning, to combine all of the ingredients.

5. Garnish with cilantro, cheeses, and jalapeos on a plate. Finish with a tequila lime coating and lime wedges, and enjoy!

S'mores Mini Pies

15 mins 6 serv

Ingredients:

- 6 mini Graham Cracker Pie Shells
- 1 cup Semi-Sweet Chocolate Chips
- 1 tbsp Butter
- 2 cups Mini Marshmallows

Instructions

1. Pour chocolate chips and butter into a microwave-safe bowl. Melt for 30 seconds at a time until completely melted.
2. Fill pie shells halfway with melted chocolate and a handful of marshmallows.
3. Preheat the Air Fryer to high.
4. Cook for 5-7 minutes, or until the tops of the S'mores pies are toasted, on an air fryer tray.
5. Remove from the oven and serve right away.

Betty's Burrata Sandwiches

5 mins 2 serv

Ingredients:

1. 4 slices Panini bread, Sourdough or Italian
2. 1 container Burrata, BelGioioso 4-2 oz "minis"
3. 4 slices Provolone Cheese
4. 4 slices Prosciutto
5. 4 slices Soppressata or Genoa Salami
6. 4 slices Capicola
7. roasted Red Peppers, Cento
8. Arugula
9. 2 tbsp Mayonnaise, Dukes preferred
10. Blackstone Parmesan Ranch seasoning

Instructions

1. Remove the burrata from the container and blot it dry with paper towels before storing it.
2. Preheat the Blackstone griddle on low.
3. Combine mayonnaise and 1 tablespoon Blackstone Parmesan Ranch seasoning in a small mixing bowl. Spread the mayo mixture on one side of each slice of bread and set it on the Blackstone with the mayo side down.
4. Top each slice of bread with provolone cheese. Between the

sandwiches, equally layer Italian meats. Add a handful of arugula and as much roasted peppers as you want.

5. Top each sandwich with two burrata minis and a little dusting of Blackstone Parmesan Ranch spice.
6. Sandwich the two pieces of bread together and place on a cutting board when the crust is golden brown. Cut the sandwish in half

The Lippy Spritz Cocktail

10 mins 4 serv

Ingredients:

- Bud Light Seltzer
- Malibu Rum 1.5 oz
- Pineapple Juice 1 oz
- Lime

Instructions

Fill a rocks glass halfway with ice. To begin, pour 1.5 oz. Malibu Coconut Rum into a cocktail glass. 1 oz pineapple juice (or more if you want it sweeter). Finish with a squeeze of lime juice and a splash of Bud Light Seltzer.

Spicy Griddle Pineapple Margarita

2 mins 1 serv

Ingredients:

- Silver Tequila
- Triple Sec
- 1 Fresh Pineapple
- 3 Limes
- Sugar
- Water
- 3 Jalapeños
- Blackstone Tequila Lime Seasoning

Instructions

1. Remove the pineapple's top and bottom. To use as a garnish, slice off one or two wheels.
2. Remove the rind and core from the pineapple, then slice the remaining pieces into slices to arrange on the griddle.
3. Before putting it on the griddle, blot it dry using paper towels to eliminate any excess moisture, which will aid in the caramelization process.
4. Blackstone should be preheated to a medium high temperature. Spray the flattop with Blackstone nonstick griddle spray.
5. Place pineapple on griddle and cook for 3-4 minutes on each side, or

until golden. Make certain you get all sides.

6. Limes should be cut in half and patted dry to remove any excess fluids. Place on the griddle and heat until golden and browned.

7. Combine equal parts sugar and water in a jar or container. After that, slice one fresh jalapeo and toss it in with the water and sugar. Shake the container with the cover on it until the sugar is completely dissolved.

8. Blend ice, half of the pineapple pieces, the lime juice from the griddle limes, 2-3 ounces spicy simple syrup, 2-3 ounces triple sec, and 3-4 ounces tequila in a blender until smooth.

9. Pineapple juice and Tequila lime seasoning are used to rim glasses. Fill glass halfway with blender contents, then top with a slice of griddled pineapple and a fresh jalapeo.

Griddled Grapefruit Shandy

15 mins 4 serv

Ingredients

- 2 Grapefruits, Cut in Half
- 4 Oz. of Simple Syrup
- 4 Oz. of Grapefruit-flavored Vodka
- Corona Beer

Instructions

1. Preheat the griddle to high. Both grapefruits should be cut in half and dried with a paper towel. To help with caramelization, put a very thin coating of vegetable oil on the griddle top using a paper towel. Cook until the grapefruit halves are caramelized on the griddle top.

2. To make our simple syrup, combine equal parts sugar and water in a plastic container with a lid and shake vigorously for 20-30 seconds, or until the sugar is completely dissolved.

3. 1 TBSP sugar, 1 tsp salt, and a pinch of cayenne pepper on a plate Season the glass rim with grapefruit juice and a pinch of salt.

4. One half of a grapefruit should be strained and squeezed in your glass. 1 oz simple syrup, 1 oz grapefruit flavored vodka, whisk well, and pour into an ice cold Corona. Garnish with a grapefruit slice.

Peach Bourbon Cocktail

15 mins 4 serv

Ingredients

- 2 Peaches, Sliced
- 8 Oz. of Thyme Simple Syrup
- 8 Oz. of Bourbon
- Ginger Ale

Instructions

1. Combine equal parts water and sugar in a plastic container, along with a sprig of fresh thyme. Close the jar and shake vigorously until the sugar is completely dissolved.
2. Preheat the griddle to high. Place two peaches on the griddle after slicing them into wedges and drying them with a paper towel. Cook for 90 seconds, or until they are brown and caramelized.
3. Add two peach wedges to a cocktail shaker. Push and flip the peach 5-6 times with a muddle to split it apart. Shake thoroughly with ice, 2 ounces thyme simple syrup, and 2 ounces bourbon.
4. Add some ice to a high ball glass and strain the drink. Garnish with a fresh peach wedge and fresh thyme and a splash of ginger ale.

Grilled Shrimp & Arugula Salad

Ingredients

- 1-2 Lb. of Raw Shrimp, tail on (amounts will vary depending on how many shrimp per salad)
- 1 Lemon
- Salt and Pepper
- Garlic
- Arugula (can add romaine as well, if desired)
- Boiled Egg
- Grape Tomatoes
- Avocado (cut into chunks)
- White Sharp Cheese, any kind (I used Beehive Seahive cheese)
- Lemon White Balsamic Vinegar
- Extra Virgin Olive Oil

Instructions

Thaw shrimp overnight in the refrigerator or in a colander under cold water until thawed.

In a basin large enough to marinate shrimp, zest and juice the lemon.

Garlic cloves (4-6) should be minced and added to the lemon juice.

Toss the thawed shrimp with the lemon juice. Season the shrimp with salt and pepper. Drizzle extra virgin olive oil on top. Toss once more.

Preheat the Blackstone griddle to medium, then reduce to low.

Pour the mixture over the Blackstone and equally distribute the shrimp on the griddle. If needed, season with more salt and pepper. Keep an eye on the shrimp since they cook rapidly. Turn them over as soon as they begin to turn pink. On either side, it could just take a minute or so. Remove them from the oven and cover with aluminum foil to keep them warm while you assemble the salads.

Assemble salads by placing the Arugula on the bottom and the lettuce on top (add some Romaine lettuce or other lighter lettuce if straight Arugula is too peppery for you

Cut the grape tomatoes in half and add them to the mix. If preferred, top with a boiled egg and some white sharp cheddar cheese ribbons. I used Beehive Seahive cheese (which is only available in Utah), but Parmesan would also be delicious! Add avocado chunks to the mix.

Drizzle the lemon balsamic vinegar and extra virgin olive oil over the cooked prawns. Enjoy!!

Ginger & Soy Glazed Salmon With Asian Green Beans

Ingredients

Glazed Salmon

- Wild Alaskan Salmon Filets with skin on
- Raw Shrimp (deveined)
- 6 Tablespoons of Extra Virgin Olive Oil
- 3 Tablespoons of Bragg's Liquid Aminos or Low Sodium Soy Sauce
- 2 Tablespoons of Dijon Mustard
- 1 Tablespoon of Ginger Paste (or grated fresh ginger)
- 1 Clove Fresh Garlic, pressed or finely diced
- Avocado Oil or Coconut Oil
- Toasted Sesame Seeds

Green Beans

- Green Beans
- 1 Red Pepper or Several Small Multi-Color Peppers
- 1/2 Onion
- 1-2 Garlic Cloves, pressed or finely diced
- 2 Tablespoons of Butter
- 1/2 Teaspoon of Salt
- 3 Tablespoons of Liquid Aminos or Low-Sodium Soy Sauce

- 1 Green Onion, finely sliced for garnish
- 1 Teaspoon of Toasted Sesame Seeds for garnish

Instructions

If your fish is frozen, defrost it overnight in the refrigerator or run it under cold water until it thaws.

Set the Blackstone to high heat and prepare the green beans in a pan of boiling water.

Combine olive oil, liquid aminos or soy sauce, dijon mustard, ginger paste, and garlic clove in a bowl to prepare the marinade. To blend, stir everything together thoroughly.

Season the shrimp and salmon to taste with salt and pepper.

Reduce the heat to medium and brush the griddle with avocado oil.

Place the salmon skin side down on the griddle. You may throw the shrimp on after a few minutes because they will cook in under 3-4 minutes. When the shrimp are done, remove them from the pan and cover them.

Drizzle the marinade over the shrimp and salmon. Toss the shrimp in the marinade to evenly coat them. Add water by the fish and cover with a basting dome to finish cooking.

Add the green beans to the boiling water with a teaspoon of salt while the salmon is cooking.

Slice the peppers and onion very thinly. Heat the oil on the griddle and cook the peppers and onions until they are soft.

Drain the green beans and add them to the peppers and onion after they have boiled for 1-2 minutes or until cooked. Cook for a minute or two more. Add a garlic clove, 2 tablespoons butter, a splash of aminos or soy sauce, and a pinch of salt. To avoid scorching the garlic, only cook for around 30 seconds. Remove from the heat and serve immediately.

By this time, your shrimp should be cooked and taken from the griddle. Keep an eye on the salmon and cook it until it's flaky in the centre and no raw spots remain. Give it a short spritz of aminos and turn it over to sear for 30 seconds to 1 minute after it's done. Turn off the heat. and serve with toasted sesame seeds as a garnish

Serve the salmon and shrimp over the green beans with sesame seeds on top. Enjoy!

Family-Style Mussels With Red Sauce

Ingredients

- 1-2 Lb. of Mussels, Cleaned and debarred
- 2 24 Oz. of Jars Marinara; Victoria or Rao are good quality sauces
- 1 Lb. of Ground Italian Sausage, hot or sweet
- 4-5 Garlic Cloves, smashed and chopped
- 1 Handful Roughly Chopped Flat Leaf Parsley, plus 1-2 tbsp chopped for garnish
- Extra Virgin Olive Oil
- Crushed Red Pepper Flakes, optional
- Loaf crusty bread, sliced
- *Recommended--disposable rectangular tin tray

Instructions

Heat the Blackstone to a medium-high temperature. Cook the sausage until it is totally cooked. Chop the beef like you would taco meat with your Blackstone scraper or spatula.

Place the tin tray on the Blackstone's clean side and sprinkle with extra virgin olive oil. Approximately 2 tablespoons

Toss in the garlic, crushed red pepper, and a few entire pieces of parsley, including the stems, to the oil. Cook garlic for 1-2 minutes, or until aromatic, shaking the pan or stirring it around. Make careful you don't burn the garlic.

Combine the cooked sausage and marinara sauce in the tin and stir to combine. Allow for a few minutes of cooking time, or until the sauce begins to boil.

Mix the mussels into the sauce well, making sure they are uniformly distributed. Cover with foil and cook for 3-4 minutes, gently shaking the pan a number of times to assist mussels open.

Remove the foil, stir the mussels, and cook for another 30 seconds. Any mussels that require extra space to open will benefit from this. Remove the tin dish from the fire, add fresh chopped parsley, and serve!

Blackstone Airfryer Pork Egg Rolls

4 serv 20 min.

Ingredients

- 8 Egg Roll Wraps
- 1/2 Lb. of 80/20 Ground Pork
- 1 1/2 Tablespoons of Minced Garlic
- 1 Tablespoons of Minced Ginger
- 1 Tablespoon of Sesame Oil
- 1/3 Cup of Sliced Green Onion

- 2 Cups of Shredded Cabbage (pre-shredded Cole Slaw mix is a great substitute)
- 2 Tablespoons of Soy Sauce
- Olive Oil
- Spray Vegetable Oil

Instructions

Preheat your griddle to medium-high heat and your Blackstone Airfryer to 400°.

Drizzle a little olive oil on the griddle before adding the ground pork. Cook, stirring often, for 4-5 minutes.

Cook for another 2-3 minutes after adding the garlic and ginger.

Cook for another 2 minutes, stirring often, after adding the sesame oil and cabbage.

Toss in the green onions and soy sauce until well combined.

Place a few teaspoons of the pork mixture in the middle of each egg roll wrapper. Wet the border edges of the egg roll wrapper with a little water and fold one corner to the center. Wrap each side of the wrapper into the centre and roll it to meet the other end. These should resemble little burritos. Continue with the remaining egg rolls.

Coat the egg rolls in spray oil and place them in the Airfryer basket. Return the basket to the Airfryer and cook for another 6-7 minutes. For a more even hue, flip the egg rolls halfway through.

Serve with a sweet Thai chili sauce on the side.

Crispy Salmon Belly Salad With Honey Soy Glazed Shiitakes And Arugula

4 serv 10 min.

Ingredients:

- 1 pound salmon belly
- 2 teaspoons sesame oil
- 3 cups sliced shiitake mushrooms
- 1 teaspoon garlic powder
- 1 tablespoon honey
- 2 tablespoons soy sauce
- The juice of 1 lemon
- 2 cups baby arugula
- Salt and pepper
- Olive oil

Instructions

One side of your griddle should be heated to medium-high and the other should be left off. Toss the mushrooms with a little olive oil on the heated side of the griddle. Toss and heat for 3-4 minutes, then transfer the mushrooms to the griddle's cold side.

Increase the heat on the griddle's hot side to High.

Season the salmon belly with salt and pepper, as well as garlic powder. Sear the salmon for 2 minutes per side, or until golden and crisp.

Combine the honey, soy sauce, and sesame oil in a small bowl. Toss the mushrooms in the sauce to thoroughly distribute it.

Combine the arugula, lemon juice, a sprinkle of pepper, and a drizzle of olive oil in a mixing bowl. Toss lightly to coat the arugula evenly.

Return the mushrooms to the high heat side of the griddle once the fish is 90% done, tossing to caramelize the honey and soy sauce (about 1 minute).

To plate, place some mushrooms in the middle of your dish, followed by a handful of arugula gently packed. Cut the fish into strips and scatter a few over the arugula. Garnish with sesame seeds or crushed black pepper.

Gochujang Sticky Steak Bites

4 serv 10 min.

Ingredients:

- 2, 1" thick NY strip steaks, cut into 1" cubes

- 3 tablespoons hoisin sauce
- 1/3 cup gochujang
- 2 tablespoon soy sauce
- The juice of 1 lime
- ¼ cup sliced green onion
- ¼ cup chopped cilantro
- 2 red chilis (or red jalapenos)
- ¼ cup beer (lager is best)
- 8 cloves fresh garlic, smashed
- 1 tablespoon sesame oil
- Salt and pepper
- Olive oil

Instructions

Preheat the griddle to medium-high heat.

Combine the steak, olive oil, and salt and pepper in a large mixing basin. Toss to combine evenly.

Preheat your griddle to high and place the steak slices on it. Cook for 3-4 minutes, tossing halfway during the cooking time.

Whisk together the gochujang, hoisin, soy sauce, sesame oil, lime juice, and beer in the same mixing bowl you used for the meat.

Add some green onions, cilantro, red chilis, and crushed garlic once the steak has caramelized on all sides. Toss in 12 tablespoons of the sauce. Cook for another 2 minutes before tossing in the remaining half of the sauce. Cook for another 2 minutes before transferring the steak to a serving plate.

Garnish with a sprinkling of sesame seeds and additional fresh cilantro and green onions.

Chef Nathan Lippy's recipe

Whiskey-Honey Salmon With Cajun Stir Fried Rice

4 serv 10 min.

Ingredients:

- 4, 6 ounce fillets of skinless salmon
- 3 cups cooked white rice
- ¼ cup diced yellow onion
- ¼ cup sliced okra
- ¼ cup diced bell pepper
- Blackstone Crazy Cajun Seasoning
- ¼ cup whiskey
- 3 tablespoons honey
- Olive oil

Instructions:

Preheat your griddle to medium-high heat on one side and low heat on the other. Drizzle a little olive oil on the heated side. Combine the onion, okra, and bell pepper in a large mixing bowl. Toss in a couple shakes of Blackstone Crazy Cajun Seasoning to combine. Cook for a total of 3-4 minutes.

On all sides, season each salmon fillet with Blackstone Crazy Cajun Seasoning.

Slide the vegetables to the griddle's colder side. Toss in a little extra olive oil and the salmon fillets on the heated side. Cook for 3 minutes per side or until desired doneness is reached.

Combine the whiskey and honey in a small mixing bowl and stir well.

Toss the rice with the vegetables to properly combine them.

Pour 75% of the whiskey honey mixture over the tops of each fillet after the salmon is 90% done. As the liquid starts to evaporate, flip them over. The fish should be completely covered in the sweet syrup. Toss the rice with the remaining whiskey.

To plate, first place the rice on a platter, then top with the salmon. Warm it up and serve.

Shrimp Lejon With Thousand Island Dressing

8 serv 15 min.

Ingredients:

- 1 lb shrimp, peeled tails on
- ½ pack bacon, thin
- Prepared horseradish

Thousand Island Dressing:

- ¾ c Dukes mayo
- ¼ c ketchup
- 1 tbsp white vinegar
- ⅓ c sweet pickle relish
- 2 tsp sugar
- 2 tsp onion powder
- Pinch pink sea salt and pepper

Instructions:

To butterfly the shrimp, run a knife along the top and remove any veins.

Horseradish should be stuffed into each shrimp.

Wrap half a slice of bacon around each packed shrimp in a single layer.

Pre-heat the Blackstone Airfryer to medium to medium-high and cook the shrimp for 3 minutes. Cook for another 3-5 minutes, flipping or moving any that require it.

For dipping, serve with a thousand island dressing.

Slammin' Cajun Salmon

4 serv.

Ingredients:

- 12-16 oz. salmon fillets
- Olive oil, to taste
- Blackstone Crazy Cajun Seasoning, to taste
- 1 lb linguine or fettuccine
- 1/2 c unsalted butter
- 4-6 garlic cloves
- 1 Jalapeno pepper, cored and diced
- 1 pint heavy whipping cream
- 2 cups fresh tomatoes, diced
- Fresh basil leaves, to taste
- 1-3 tbsp flour (enough to thicken)
- Louisiana (cayenne-based) hot sauce, to taste
- Fresh lemon juice, to taste
- Green onion, sprinkled for garnish

Instructions:

Preheat the griddle top to a medium-high temperature. The exact setting will be determined by the size of your griddle and the number of burners. Make sure the top of the griddle is hot enough to sear.

Salmon fillets should be cut into four serving-size chunks.

Olive oil should be rubbed on the salmon fillets.

Rub Blackstone's Crazy Cajun Seasoning on the flesh sides of salmon fillets (the pink meat side). The seasoning will remain adhered to the olive oil.

Meanwhile, fill the Deep Fryer Attachment halfway with water, turn the burner on high, and bring the water to a boil. To make the water taste better, season it with salt and olive oil.

On the heated griddle, place a cast iron or seasoned steel skillet.

In a skillet, melt the butter. Allow the butter to soften. To keep the butter from burning, stir it often.

Garlic, minced, should be added to the butter. To avoid the garlic from burning, stir it into the butter.

Toss in the diced jalapeo with the butter and garlic.

Stir in the heavy whipping cream as you pour it into the skillet. To maintain the sauce simmering without boiling or burning, you may need to adjust the flame beneath your skillet. Continue to stir as needed.

Submerge pasta in boiling water in a deep fryer basket, pushing pasta down as needed.

Place the salmon fillets on the heated griddle top, flesh side down.

Once the initial side of the salmon fillets has been seared, flip them over.

Make sure the spaghetti isn't sticking by checking it and stirring it as needed. Cooking times for pasta vary, but you should cook it until it's al dente.

Lift the fryer basket and drain the spaghetti over boiling water as you make the remainder of the preparation.

As desired, add chopped tomatoes and basil leaves to the sauce. Stir continuously.

Using flour, thicken the sauce. A few teaspoons of flour should be enough to thicken a pan full of sauce. Slowly mix in the flour until the sauce achieves the desired thickness.

Toss the spaghetti sauce with Louisiana spicy sauce. Add enough sauce to turn the white spaghetti sauce into a pinkish or peach hue. Sprinkle a few drops at a time until you have the proper amount of spicy sauce. Continue to stir.

Toss in some freshly squeezed lemon juice to the sauce.

Remove the salmon fillets when they are flaky and readily peel apart with a fork. Remove from the equation.

Place pasta in a pan with a creamy Cajun sauce using tongs. Gently toss the pasta in the sauce until it is totally coated.

As needed, plate portions. Begin with a bed of spaghetti with sauce, chopped green onion, and Blackstone Crazy Cajun Seasoning, followed by a salmon fillet. Freshly squeezed lemon juice should be sprinkled over the salmon fillet.

Seared Garlic Ribeye with Carrots, Asparagus, and Gremolata

4 serv 15 min.

Ingredients:

- 4, 8-10 oz. Ribeye steaks
- 5-6 carrots, cut in half lengthwise
- A handful of asparagus, cleaned and trimmed
- 6-8 large garlic cloves
- Olive oil
- Salt and Peppers

Gremolata ingredients:

- ½ cup chopped parsley
- 2 teaspoons lemon zest
- 1 teaspoon grated garlic
- 3 tablespoons lemon juice
- 3 tablespoons Olive oil
- Salt and pepper

Instructions:

Preheat the griddle to medium-high. Cook for 3-4 minutes with 1-2 tablespoons olive oil and the carrots cut side down.

Season the steaks with salt & pepper on both sides before placing them on the griddle. Depending on desired doneness, cook for 3-4 minutes per side. Add the garlic cloves and asparagus with a pinch of salt and pepper after the initial turn and cook for 4-5 minutes, flipping often.

In a mixing dish, equally combine all of the Gremolata ingredients and set aside for plating.

Remove the steaks from the griddle after they've reached the proper doneness and set aside to rest for 4-5 minutes.

To dish, arrange a few carrot and asparagus pieces on the platter before placing the steak on top. Finish with a few spoonfuls of Gremolata and a sprinkling of caramelized garlic.

Reversed Sear Ribeye with Smoked Garlic, Zucchini, and Squash

2 serv 45 min.

Ingredients:

- 1, 1 ½ pound boneless ribeye steak
- 6-10 large garlic cloves
- Blackstone Steakhouse Seasoning

- 2 tablespoon unsalted butter
- 2 zucchini, quartered lengthwise
- 2 squash, quartered lengthwise
- 1 cup applewood chips
- 2 sprigs rosemary
- Olive oil

Special Tools:

- Small Aluminum Tray
- Torch
- Blackstone Resting Rack
- Blackstone XL Dome

Instructions:

On the resting rack, place the steak, garlic, and aluminum tray. Light the flame and add the wood chips to the aluminum tray. Blow out the fire once the wood chips have started to burn to generate smoke. Close the hood or cover the entire resting rack with an XL Dome. Allow 20-30 minutes for the meat and garlic to smoke.

Add a little olive oil to your griddle and heat it to medium-high. Before adding the meat, wait for the oil to start smoking.

Place the steak in the smoking oil after liberally seasoning it with Blackstone Steakhouse Seasoning. Cook for another 2-3 minutes before flipping. Flip the steak as much as you wish, and don't forget to sear all surface regions by turning it on its side.

Add the garlic to the oil and softly caramelize it in the last few minutes of cooking.

To finish cooking, move the garlic to the colder side of the griddle, top with rosemary and a little water, and cover with a dome.

Remove the steak from the griddle when it's done to your liking and set it aside to rest for 5 minutes.

On the heated side of the griddle, melt the butter and then add the zucchini and squash. If desired, season with Blackstone Steakhouse seasoning. Cook for 2 minutes each side on each side.

To serve, slice the steak and dish it family style over the cut vegetables. Garnish the top with the garlic and rosemary.

Betty's Bigger Better Crab Bahms

8 serv 35 min.

Ingredients:

- 2 lbs jumbo lump crab meat
- 1 cup panko bread crumbs
- 1-1.5 sticks of salted butter
- 3/4 cup mayonnaise, Dukes preferred
- 1.5 tbsp white vinegar
- 1 tbsp old bay seasoning

Garnish:

- Flat leaf parsley for garnish
- Cocktail and or tartar sauce

Instructions:

Combine mayonnaise and old bay seasoning. Carefully combine the crab meat and panko, being careful not to split up the flesh.

Form 8 individual dinner size crab bahms (or little appetizer sized balls) using your hands and set on a baking pan in the refrigerated for 20 minutes.

To warm the airfryer, switch it between medium and high heat. Preheat the Airfryers and line them with parchment paper.

Melt the butter and vinegar together, then carefully arrange the crab bahms on the lined trays in the airfryer and drizzle with a teaspoon of the melted butter/vinegar mixture just before frying.

Cook for 10 minutes, checking midway during the cooking time. Increase the heat to high and cook for another 5 minutes, or until golden brown.

Remove airfryer drawers from trays and set aside to cool for a few minutes before carefully removing crab bahms.

Garnish with parsley, lemon, and an old bay sprig. With tartar sauce and cocktail sauce on the side. Enjoy!

Enchiladas

4-6 serv 20 min.

Ingredients:

- Flour or Corn tortillas (full size)
- 1 LB. Ground beef (80/20)
- Red sauce (Old El Paso)
- Cheese (block of sharp cheddar)
- Half Yellow onion
- Romaine lettuce
- Tomato (on the vine)
- Tortilla Chips (garnish)
- Blackstone taco seasoning
- Red Chile Sauce
- Green Chile Sauce
- Salsa

Instructions:

Preheat the griddle to medium-high temperature.

Season the meat with salt and pepper before placing it on the griddle.

Add approximately a chopped yellow onion when the meat is halfway cooked and continue to simmer until the onions are caramelized and the steak is browned.

Season lightly with Blackstone Taco Seasoning. And then switch to indirect heat.

Reduce the heat to a minimum or turn it off completely. Place your tortillas on the griddle to warm up after adding a small quantity of olive oil on the griddle.

Add a light layer of shredded cheddar cheese, meat and onions, and 2-3 teaspoons of red chile sauce to your warmed tortilla. To make the enchilada, fold both ends of the tortilla together with a spatula and tongs. To keep the tortilla rolled, the cheese inside should function as an adhesive. Remove the item from the table.

Next, we'll make our cheese enchiladas. Use only shredded cheddar cheese and green chilies within, and follow the same methods as the meat. Roll as many as you like and lay them aside.

Turn one of your griddle's burners to high. Place one cheese enchilada and one beef enchilada on your Blackstone cast iron serving dish. Both shredded cheddar and pre-shredded Mexican mix cheese should be used. More redchile sauce on the beef enchilada, and more green chiles on the cheese enchilada.

Place the cast iron serving tray on the griddle's hot side, sprinkle it with water, and cover it with the basting dome. Allow 2-3 minutes for the enchiladas to heat up and all of the cheese to melt. Remove the basting dome, remove the griddle's serving pan, garnish with shredded lettuce, tomato, and onions, and serve!

Chicken Cordon Bleu

Ingredients:

- 1 half boneless skinless chicken breast
- 1 slice deli ham (honey, maple, or Black Forest work best)
- 1 slice Swiss cheese
- 1 cup bread crumbs
- 1 cup oil
- Salt and Pepper
- Toothpicks

Instructions:

Preheat your air fryer to 400 degrees Fahrenheit.

Butterfly the chicken by slicing down the centre of the breast with your knife parallel to the cutting board. Make sure you don't cut the chicken all the way through. You should come as near to the edge as possible without cutting all the way through.

Season the interior of the chicken, as well as the sliced side, with salt and pepper.

Place the cheese on top of the ham and wrap the ham around it to fit the cheese into the chicken.

Using 2-3 toothpicks, fix the seams of the chicken over the ham.

Dredge the chicken bundle in the oil first, then in the breadcrumbs, ensuring that it is equally coated. If required, repeat on any sparsely covered areas.

Cook the chicken breast in the air fryer for 12-14 minutes, or until it reaches a temperature of 165 degrees Fahrenheit.

Remove the toothpicks and remove the food from the air fryer.

Serve immediately.

Potato Chip Crusted Halibut

4 serv

Ingredients:

- 4 4-oz Halibut filets, skin removed
- 1 cup potato chips
- 1 cup panko breadcrumbs
- 2 tablespoons lemon pepper divided
- 2 eggs
- 1/2 cup cornstarch
- 1/2 cup white wine
- Lemon wedges

Instructions:

To make the dredging, combine the cornstarch and eggs in a mixing bowl.

Add a spoonful of white wine at a time to the dredging until it resembles pancake batter.

Stir in the lemon pepper to mix the dredging.

Break down the potato chips in a food processor until they are the consistency of breadcrumbs.

In a mixing dish, add the potato chip crumbs and panko and whisk to incorporate.

Season the halibut filets with salt and lemon pepper on both sides.

Dredge the halibut in the egg mixture, then in the pecan breadcrumbs, ensuring sure the fish is thoroughly coated.

Rep with the rest of the fish.

Preheat your air fryer to 375 degrees Fahrenheit.

In the air fryer, cook the potato chip-crusted halibut for about 8 minutes, or until it reaches an internal temperature of 140F, turning once. Serve with a slice of lemon.

Thai Style Beef Souvlaki With Peanut Sauce

15 mins 4 serve

Souvlaki Ingredients:

- 1 lb. 80/20 Ground Beef
- 2 tablespoons Tamari or Soy Sauce
- 3 tablespoons chopped green onion
- 2 teaspoons ground ginger
- 2 teaspoons garlic powder
- Wooden Skewers

Sauce Ingredients:

- 1/3 cup creamy peanut butter
- 3 tablespoons Thai Chili Sauce
- 2 tablespoons Ponzu
- 1 tablespoon sesame oil
- 2 tablespoons Tamari

Garnish:

- 2 tablespoon, sliced green onion (for garnish)
- 1/4 cup chopped cashews (for garnish)

Instructions

1. Combine all of the souvlaki ingredients in a large mixing basin and stir to combine evenly. Pack the meat mixture onto the skewers loosely. They should be a touch softer than a meatball in terms of holding together.
2. Add a little olive oil to your Blackstone and heat it to medium-high heat. Cook the souvlaki for 2 minutes on each side, or until done.
3. Combine all of the sauce ingredients in a small mixing dish and stir to combine. If necessary, thin it out with a little water.

4. To serve, arrange the souvlaki on a tray and sprinkle the sauce over the tops. Serve garnished with sliced green onions and chopped cashews.

Pineapple and Prosciutto Shrimp Poppers

4 serv

Ingredients:

- 1 pound extra jumbo shrimp (16/20) peeled and deveined
- 1 can pineapple wedges
- 4 oz prosciutto

Instructions

1. Remove any shells, veins, or other debris from the shrimp and pat them dry with a paper towel.
2. Using a paring knife, slice 14 inch thick relief cu
3. ts along the inside curve of the shrimp, spaced about the paring knife's width apart, while holding the shrimp by the tail. This will help the shrimp to lay flat, making wrapping much easier.
4. Quarter the pineapple chunks lengthwise to create strips.

5. Prosciutto should be cut into strips that are about 2 inches wide and 4 inches long.
6. Place the shrimp on a prosciutto strip and top with 1-2 pineapple strips.
7. Roll the prosciutto around the shrimp and pineapple tightly, then fasten with a toothpick.
8. Preheat your air fryer to 400 degrees Fahrenheit.
9. Cook the poppers in the air fryer for 8 to 10 minutes, turning once, until the prosciutto is crispy and the shrimp is thoroughly cooked, working in batches.
10. Serve right away.

Sweet & Spicy Parmesan Pickle Chips

Ingredients:

- 16 oz jar sweet pickle chips
- 1 cup flour
- 2 eggs
- 1 tablespoon Sriracha
- 2/3 cup panko breadcrumbs
- 1/3 cup grated Parmesan cheese

Instructions

1. Drain the pickle chips and spread them out on a few sheets of paper towel in a single layer. Cover with more paper towel sheets and let them dry completely to remove any remaining liquid.
2. Mix the eggs with the Sriracha sauce to make a dredging station.
3. Combine the panko breadcrumbs and Parmesan cheese in a mixing bowl.
4. Dredge the pickle chips in flour to lightly coat them before dipping them in the egg wash and then into the Parmesan and breadcrumb mixture.
5. Preheat your air fryer to 400 degrees Fahrenheit.
6. Cook the Parmesan pickle chips in batches for 8-10 minutes, stirring once, until golden brown and crispy.
7. Serve right away with a side of ranch dressing for dipping.

Ultimate Breakfast Platter

20 mins 6 serv

Ingredients:

Griddled Items:

- Bacon
- Sausage Links
- Pancakes

Air Fryer Items:

- Eggs

Additional Items:

Fruit:

- Strawberries
- Raspberries
- Blackberries
- Oranges
- Juice

Lox and Bagels:

- Mini Bagels (toast on griddle top for a couple minutes)
- Salmon
- Cream Cheese
- Cucumbers
- Red Onions
- Sesame Seeds

Yogurt Parfait:

- Strawberry Yogurt
- Granola
- Fresh Raspberries

Instructions

1. Begin by browning your bacon and sausage in a skillet. Then cook your pancakes with your preferred pancake mix.
2. Place eggs on the tray of your Air Fryer and turn it to low. Set a timer for 15 minutes and prepare a large dish of ice water in advance.

3. Remove the eggs from the oven when the timer goes off and place them in the ice bath to cool.
4. Begin to arrange all of your components on a large platter in a pleasing manner. Your guests will be enthralled by its splendor and eager to dive in!

Mini Beef Wellingtons

Ingredients:

- 1 pound ground beef
- 1 packet onion soup mix
- 1 teaspoon Worcestershire sauce
- 1 tablespoon Dijon mustard
- 1 egg
- 1 packet puff pastry sheets
- 1 egg + 1 tablespoon water

Instructions

1. In a large mixing bowl, combine the ground beef, onion soup mix, Worcestershire sauce, Dijon mustard, and egg. Refrigerate for 1 hour or up to 24 hours, covered, to enable the flavors to come together.
2. Preheat the griddle to medium-high heat.
3. Divide the ground beef mixture into 8 parts, each weighing 2 oz.
4. Place the parts on the griddle after rolling them into balls. Lightly press

down on the meatballs with a spatula and parchment paper to flatten both the top and bottom into a disc that is almost as tall as it is wide.

5. Cook for 2 minutes on each side of the ground beef. Sear the sides of the meatballs slightly with tongs. You may also sear the sides of the meat by rotating it along the griddle's side.

6. Place them on a cooling rack in the refrigerator to chill.

7. Follow the guidelines on the puff pastry box to build it, allowing it to come to a malleable condition first. The dough is thawed just enough to cut and fold after 30 minutes at room temperature.

8. The secret to puff pastry's charm is keeping it very cold, so work quickly and store completed parts in the refrigerator if your kitchen is warm.

9. Puff pastry should be cut into 4-inch pieces, or at least twice the width of the meatball.

10. In the center of the puff pastry square, place the meatball. On the top of the meatball, join all four corners of the puff pastry together, sealing to shut and bind them to one another.

11. Any remaining puff pastry should be crimped tightly around the meatball with your fingers. Make a pastry crust around the meatball that is tightly sealed.

12. Preheat your air fryer to 400 degrees Fahrenheit or the temperature specified on the puff pastry box.

13. To make an egg wash, whisk together the egg and water. Brush the egg wash all over the pastry, including the top, bottom, and sides. In the air fryer, this will help to brown the food.

14. Keep the tiny Wellingtons chilled until ready to serve.

15. In the bottom of the air fryer basket, place a piece of parchment paper. Air fried the small beef Wellingtons in batches for 16-18 minutes, or until the internal temperature reaches at least 140°F and the pastry puffs up and turns golden brown, flipping once.

Black Bean Triangle Bites

4 serve

Ingredients:

- 1 package wonton wrappers
- 1 can black beans or 2 cups cooked black beans
- ¾ cup corn
- ½ cup minced onion
- 1 tablespoon minced garlic
- 1 tablespoon cumin
- 1 tablespoon chili powder
- Pinch of cinnamon
- 1 egg

Instructions

1. On the griddle, sauté the minced onion and garlic in roughly 2 tablespoons of oil until transparent over low heat.
2. To enable the flavors to bloom, add the cumin, chili powder, and cinnamon to the onion mixture and cook for 2 minutes. Cook for an additional 2 minutes, stirring often to ensure that the flavors are well blended.
3. In a medium mixing bowl, set aside to cool.
4. If you're using canned beans, rinse and drain them thoroughly to remove as much moisture as possible.
5. Combine the beans, corn, and onion mixture in a mixing bowl.
6. Whisk together the egg and 1 tablespoon cold water to make an egg wash.
7. Lay a wonton wrapper on a dry work area to assemble the bites.
8. Make a point at the top of the wrapper. Assembling will be easier as a result of this.
9. Apply a light application of egg wash to the left and right sides of the wrapper with a pastry brush or your finger. Begin at one of the corners and coat the top half of the wrapper with egg wash on the outer 12 inch. Rep with the opposite corner.
10. Place a heaping tablespoon of filling above the lower point on the bottom third of the wrapper.
11. Make a triangle by folding from the bottom up. Make sure no filling reaches the triangle's outside 12 inch.
12. To completely seal the top and bottom of the wrapper together, use your finger. You can optionally crimp the wrapper's edges for a stylish seal.
13. Preheat the air fryer to 400 degrees Fahrenheit.
14. To enhance browning, lightly cover both sides of the triangles in oil.
15. Air fried for 8-10 minutes, or until golden brown and heated all the way through, flipping once.
16. Warm the dish before serving.

Bacon Fried Corn 3.0

20 mins 4 serv

Ingredients:

- Diced Pancetta
- 2 bags of Frozen Corn
- 2 Tomatoes
- Red Onion
- Fresh Basil
- Fresh Parsley
- Parmesan Cheese
- Salt
- Pepper
- Garlic Powder
- Blackstone All Purpose Seasoning

Instructions

1. Preheat the griddle on low heat. Begin by adding diced pancetta and heating it slowly so that we may render the fat gently without overcooking it. Also, toss the pancetta every now and then to brown all sides.
2. 2 tomatoes, diced, and 1/2 a red onion, minced while that's cooking By the time you've finished, the pancetta should have started to brown. If required, increase the heat to medium.
3. Chop your fresh basil and parsley as it finishes simmering. It's entirely up to you how much you chop. At this point, your pancetta should be done cooking.
4. Add your frozen corn to the pancetta, leaving all of the grease on the griddle. Season the corn with salt, pepper, and garlic powder after tossing it in the pancetta fat. The Blackstone All-Purpose Seasoning is the final seasoning you'll need to use. Toss in all of your ingredients and mix well.
5. Add the diced tomatoes, minced red onion, fresh basil, and parsley as the penultimate step. Toss this with the corn and pancetta on the griddle top.
6. Serve in a big serving dish with grated parmesan cheese on top.

Bigger Better Crab Bahms

35 mins 8 serv

Ingredients:

- 2 lbs jumbo lump crab meat
- 1 cup panko bread crumbs
- 1-1.5 sticks of salted butter
- 3/4 cup mayonnaise, Dukes preferred
- 1.5 tbsp white vinegar
- 1 tbsp old bay seasoning

Garnish:

- Flat leaf parsley for garnish
- Cocktail and or tartar sauce

Instructions

1. Combine mayonnaise and old bay seasoning. Carefully combine the crab meat and panko, being careful not to split up the meat.
2. Form 8 individual dinner size crab bahms (or little appetizer sized balls) with your hands and set on a baking pan in the refrigerator for 20 minutes.
3. To preheat the airfryer, switch it between medium and high heat. Preheat the Airfryers and line them with parchment paper.
4. Melt the butter and vinegar together, then carefully arrange the crab bahms on the lined trays in the

airfryer and drizzle with a teaspoon of the melted butter/vinegar mixture just before frying.

5. Cook for 10 minutes, checking midway through the cooking time. Increase the heat to high and cook for another 5 minutes, or until golden brown.

6. Remove airfryer drawers from trays and set aside to cool for a few minutes before carefully removing crab bahms.

7. Garnish with parsley, lemon, and an old bay sprig. With tartar sauce and cocktail sauce on the side. Enjoy!

Pineapple Chicken Quesadillas

30 mins 4 serv

Ingredients:

- 1 lb chicken tenders
- 2 tbsp mayonnaise, Dukes preferred
- 1 tbsp Blackstone All Purpose Seasoning
- 2 cups BBQ sauce
- 20 oz can crushed pineapple, drained
- 1 red onion, sliced thin
- 1 bunch cilantro, chopped
- 8 10 inch flour tortillas
- 1 16 oz block of cheddar cheese, shredded
- 1 cup sour cream
- 1 lime
- 1 tbsp cumin
- zest of lime

Instructions

1. Tenders should be diced into bite-size pieces. Place chicken in a storage bag with mayonnaise and All Purpose seasoning (or your preferred dry barbecue seasoning), massage bag to evenly cover chicken, and chill 20 minutes to overnight.

2. 1 tbsp cumin, 1 tbsp sour cream, 1 tbsp lime zest, and 1 tbsp lime juice Keep it refrigerated until you're ready to use it.

3. Preheat the Blackstone to medium-high heat and add the chicken to the pan to cook. Total time: 4-6 minutes Remove the chicken and set it aside.

4. Turn the Blackstone to low heat and add a little spritz or sprinkle of oil, removing any leftovers from the chicken frying.

5. Layer cheese, chicken, pineapple, cilantro, red onion, and a splash of barbeque sauce on tortillas.

6. Fold tortillas in half and heat on medium. When both sides are golden brown and crunchy. Remove from the oven and top with the sour cream mixture. Enjoy!

Onchos

20 mins 2 serv

Ingredients:

- 2 Servings of Frozen Onion Rings
- 1 lb Ground Beef
- Blackstone Taco Fajita Seasoning
- 1/2 Cup Black Beans
- 1 Cup Cheddar Jack Cheese
- Romaine Lettuce
- Tomato
- Salsa Verde
- Jalapeños

Instructions

1. Preheat the air fryer to medium-low. In the Airfryer, place 2 servings of Onion Rings.
2. Cook 1 pound of 80/20 ground beef on a medium high griddle. Add Blackstone Fajita Taco Seasoning when the beef is almost done.
3. To make the toppings, chop and dice the lettuce and tomato.
4. Place onion rings in a Blackstone cast iron serving plate when they are crispy and done. Cooked meat, black beans, and shredded cheese are added to the pan.
5. Return to griddle top, spray griddle top with water to produce steam, and cover until cheese is melted. Remove the cheese once it has melted and top with lettuce, tomato, jalapeos, and salsa verde.

Tequila Party Cakes

4 serv

Ingredients:

- 8 slices pound cake
- 4 tbsp butter, unsalted
- 1 8oz can pineapple, crushed or chunks
- 1.5 tbsp dark brown sugar
- 2 tbsp cilantro, plus some for garnish
- Pink sea salt
- Zest of one lime
- ¼ cup tequila

Cream:

- 1 c heavy whipping cream
- ½ c powdered sugar
- Splash tequila
- 1 tsp fresh lime juice

Instructions

1. With electric beaters, combine the cream ingredients and beat until thickened. It takes about 5 minutes. Refrigerate until ready to use.
2. Cook the pineapple and brown sugar for 3 minutes over medium heat, stirring to evenly coat the pineapple. Add half of the cilantro during the last minute. Remove the item and place it away.

3. Half of the butter should be melted on a preheated Blackstone set to medium to medium low.
4. Working rapidly, dip the bottom end of each slice of pound cake (about 14 inch) into tequila and place it in the melted butter.
5. Cook for 2 minutes, or until golden brown.
6. Add the remaining butter and carefully flip the cake over to fry until golden brown on the other side.
7. Serve fried cake pieces with a sprinkle of pink sea salt, pineapple, cream, and cilantro and lime zest on a plate.

Bruschetta Crostini

75 mins 6 serv

Ingredients:

Bruschetta:

- 4 tomatoes on the vine
- 3 garlic cloves smashed and chopped
- ½ red onion diced small
- 10-12 large basil leaves
- ¼ - ½ cup pecorino romano cheese
- ½ cup extra virgin olive oil
- salt to taste
- balsamic glaze

Crostini:

- 1 loaf bread, french baguette
- 1 log sliced mozzarella
- 1 large garlic clove
- ¼ c extra virgin olive oil

Instructions

1. To make the bruschetta, dice the tomatoes and lay them in a basin. Season with salt and pepper. Chop the garlic and dice the onions.
2. Chiffonade the basil by stacking the leaves, rolling them lengthwise, then slicing the stack to make strips or ribbons. Toss them in with the tomatoes.
3. Drizzle extra virgin olive oil over tomatoes and toss lightly to incorporate. Add as much grated cheese as you want.
4. Cover the bowl with plastic wrap and set it on top of a bigger container filled with ice to chill for 30-60 minutes before making the crostini.
5. Crostini: Preheat the Blackstone to medium.
6. Using a sharp knife, cut the baguette into 1 inch pieces.
7. Cut the garlic clove in half and smear the clove's cut side on the bread.
8. Brush one side of the sliced bread with olive oil and set the greased side down on the Blackstone. After 2-3 minutes, or until toasted, remove from the oven.
9. On toasted bread slices, place one piece of fresh mozzarella. Drizzle the

Balsamic glaze on top of the Bruschetta.

10. Enjoy!

Shrimp Lejon with Thousand Island Dressing

15 min 8 serv

Ingredients:

- 1 lb shrimp, peeled tails on
- ½ pack bacon, thin
- Prepared horseradish

Thousand Island Dressing:

- ¾ c Dukes mayo
- ¼ c ketchup
- 1 tbsp white vinegar
- ⅓ c sweet pickle relish
- 2 tsp sugar
- 2 tsp onion powder
- Pinch pink sea salt and pepper

Instructions

To butterfly the shrimp, run a knife along the top and remove any veins.

Horseradish should be stuffed into each shrimp.

Wrap half a piece of bacon around each packed shrimp in a single layer.

Pre-heat the Blackstone Airfryer to medium to medium-high and cook the shrimp for 3 minutes. Cook for another 3-5 minutes, flipping or moving any that require it.

For dipping, serve with a thousand island dressing.

Crispy Smashed Potatoes with Bacon and Cilantro

15 min 4 serv

Ingredients:

- 1 pound yellow potatoes
- 4-6 strips thick cut bacon
- 1/3 cup sour cream
- 1 tablespoon Blackstone Tequila Lime Seasoning
- 1 tablespoon lime juice
- 1-2 tablespoons beer (lager is best)
- 2-3 tablespoons chopped cilantro
- 2 teaspoons garlic powder
- Salt and pepper
- Olive oil

Instructions

1. Preheat your Blackstone griddle on a medium-low heat setting. After that, add 1-2 teaspoons of olive and oil, followed by the potatoes. Cover

and cook for 2-3 minutes. Lift the dome and pour in a quarter-cup of water. Steam for 3-4 minutes, covered with a dome. 3-4 minutes or until tender, add another 14 cup of water and simmer for another 3-4 minutes.

2. Cook your bacon until it is crisp and well done, then drain on paper towels.
3. Cook the potatoes in the bacon fat for 2 to 3 minutes, tossing often.
4. Combine the sour cream, Tequila Lime Seasoning, lime juice, and beer in a mixing bowl. Evenly combine the ingredients
5. Smash the potatoes into the bacon fat with a hard spatula or burger press. Season with salt and pepper, as well as garlic powder. Fry for 2 minutes on one side before flipping to cook the other.
6. Chop the bacon into small pieces if desired.
7. To serve, arrange the fried potatoes on a serving tray and top with chopped cilantro and bacon. Serve immediately with a dab of the sauce.

Black Stone Beef Tacos

Ingredients:

- 1 pound ground beef
- 12 corn hard taco shells
- 1 taco-seasoning packet or 2TBSP of Blackstone Taco and Fajita seasoning
- 1 cup water
- 2 cups shredded taco cheese blend (Monterey jack and cheddar)

Instructions

1. Preheat the griddle to medium temperature.
2. While the meat is cooking, chop it with a spatula on the griddle top, breaking it up into very minute granular pieces.
3. Fats render and oil is frequently liberated from the beef as it is cooked. These oils aren't necessary for the tacos and can be scraped into the grease trap and finally thrown.
4. Taco spice should be evenly distributed over cooked ground beef. To integrate the seasoning and beef, use a spatula to mix them together. Toss the seasoned beef with some water. Using a squirt bottle filled with water makes it much easier to aim the water to the meat.
5. Allow the steak and spices to simmer in the water until the water has evaporated and the meat is thoroughly coated. Remove the griddle from the heat and set it aside.
6. Reduce the temperature of the griddle to the lowest setting.
7. Place the taco shells in a metal taco holder if you have one.

8. Remove the hard corn taco shells from the griddle after two minutes of partial cooking.
9. Stuff two pieces of seasoned taco meat into each taco shell, then top with another two tablespoons of shredded cheese.
10. Return the stuffed taco shells to the air fryer for 3-4 minutes to melt in the optional holder. Serve immediately with additional toppings of your choice

Homemade Sweet And Savory Tortilla Chips

Ingredients:

Cinnamon Tortillas:

- 5 small flour tortillas
- 1 stick of butter
- 1 cup of sugar
- 2 tablespoons of cinnamon
- Cooking spray

Spicy Tortillas:

- 5 small corn tortillas
- 1 stick of butter
- 1 teaspoon Chili Powder
- 1 teaspoon Garlic Powder
- 1 teaspoon Smoked Paprika
- 1 teaspoon Onion Powder
- Pinch of Salt/Pepper

- Cooking spray

Cinnamon Roll Cheesecake Dip:

- 4 oz cream cheese
- 1/4 cup powder sugar
- 1/2 teaspoon cinnamon

Instructions

Note: The sweet and savory tortillas must be made in separate batches.

1. Tortilla Chips with a Sweet Flavour
2. Flour tortillas should be cut into triangles.
3. Melt butter in a microwave-safe bowl for 45 seconds. Combine cinnamon and sugar in a separate bowl.
4. Lay out as many flour tortillas as you can fit on a cutting board and brush both sides with butter. Sprinkle with cinnamon and sugar with a spoon.
5. Preheat to medium-high heat
6. Place tortillas on the trays that have been sprayed with cooking spray.
7. Cook for 5-6 minutes, or until golden brown, on each side. Flip the tortillas carefully and cook for another 3 minutes.

Loaded Bloody Marys

Ingredients

- 1.75 Liters Zing Zang Boody Marry Mix
- Titio's Vodka (or your preferred Vodka)
- 2 Tablespoons of Prepared Horseradish
- 1 Tablespoon of Worcestershire Sauce
- 1 Tablespoon of Celery Seed
- 1 Tablespoon of Old Bay
- 1 Lemon
- Tabasco hot sauce (or similar hot sauce) to taste

Instructions

1. Combine all of the Bloody Mary ingredients in a big pitcher. This can be kept in the fridge for up to 3 days.
2. Leave the tails on the shrimp when peeling them. Remove the veins and waste by butterflying the shrimp by slicing along the top.
3. Toss the shrimp with the olive oil and old bay seasoning.
4. Cook for 2 minutes on each side, or until firm to the touch. Allow to cool before using in a Bloody Mary.
5. Use a lemon wedge to wet the rim of your glass. To garnish the lip of your glass, pour old bay or Blackstone Breakfast Blend

seasoning into a flat dish. In layers, add ice and lump crab meat.
6. To guarantee that any seasonings that fell to the bottom of your Bloody Mary pitcher are incorporated before pouring, mix it before pouring.
7. Fill your glass halfway.
8. Add celery stalks, olives, shrimp, and extra crab meat for garnish. Cheers!

Teppanyaki Steak and Shrimp Recipe

35 mins 20 serv

Ingredients

- 1 tbsp mirin (Japanese sweet rice wine)
- 1 tsp Japanese soy sauce
- 1/2 tsp liquid seasoning (maggi)
- 3 tbsp vegetable oil
- 2 1/2 tbsp butter
- 1 medium white onion sliced
- 1 tsp garlic minced
- 1 medium green bell pepper cored and sliced into thin strips
- 1 medium carrot peeled and sliced into thin strips
- 1 cup sugar snaps
- 12 large prawns (sugpo) shelled with tails left on

- 4 medium squid (pusit) cleaned, tentacles removed, and cut into rings
- salt to taste
- 5 cups Japanese rice steamed
- 400 gr steak cut into large strips

Instructions

To make the teppanyaki steak, combine all of the ingredients in a large mixing bowl.

1. On the teppanyaki plate, heat a tiny amount of oil (or in a small frying pan). 1 to 2 minutes until the bel pepper, carrots, and sugar snaps are soft. Place in a bowl and put aside.
2. Over medium-high heat, drizzle 1 1/2 tablespoons of oil onto the plate. 2 tablespoons butter, melted Cook onions until they are transparent. Sauté garlic until aromatic. Reduce the heat to medium and toss in the steak slices.
3. Grill the steak strips until they reach the desired color (rare, medium, or well done).

Make the teppanyaki with seafood.

While the bell pepper is grilling, combine the mirin, soy sauce, and liquid spice in a mixing dish and toss in the shrimp and squid rings.

Increase the heat to high. Fill the plate with the shrimp and squid mixture. Cook until the shrimp is pink and the squid is white. To taste, season with salt and pepper.

Chicken Teppanyak

16 mins 6 serv

Ingredients

- 2 tablespoons mirin
- 2 tablespoons sugar - caster sugar if you have it
- 3 tablespoons light soy sauce
- 1 tablespoon dark soy sauce
- 1 knob of ginger - peeled and very finely chopped (you only need ½ teaspoon)
- 1 clove garlic - peeled and very finely chopped - or use a garlic press
- 1 teaspoon sesame oil
- a pinch or two of red pepper flakes

Instructions

1. Remove the sauce from the heat and set it aside.
2. In a small bowl, add a splash of soy sauce and the sliced chicken, stirring to coat.
3. Prepare the spring onions, as well as the eggs, if you're using them.
4. Heat up your wok with the vegetable oil.
5. Add the chicken to the wok and stir-fry it over high heat until it's almost done.
6. Take the chicken out of the pan and set it aside.

7. Combine the vegetables, rice, and 3 tablespoons of the sauce in the same wok.
8. Stir-fry for a few minutes, then return the chicken to the pan and cook for another minute.
9. Stir in the half-cooked eggs and continue to stir-fry until the dish is thoroughly done, adding more or all of the sauce as necessary.
10. That's all there is to it!
11. Serve with the spring onions and, if desired, the peanuts.

CJ's Chicken Flautas with Griddled Salsa Verde

30 mins 4 serv

Ingredients:

- Chicken cutlets
- Corn tortillas
- Pre shredded Mexican blend cheese
- Large aluminum tin
- Toothpicks
- Olive Oil
- 4-6 Tomatillos (depending on the size)
- 3 limes
- White or yellow onion
- 3 jalapeños
- Cilantro
- Garlic
- Salt
- Pepper
- Blackstone Taco Fajita Seasoning
- Blender

Instructions

1. Pre-heat one side of your griddle on high, then fry in a big shallow tin pan with olive oil or another oil replacement. The temperature of the oil should be around 375 degrees. Another zone should be preheated on medium high.
2. Our chicken cutlets must first be seasoned. Simply brush both sides with a small coating of oil and season with salt and pepper before placing on the Blackstone griddle to cook. This won't take long, so keep an eye on it and turn as needed to ensure even cooking.
3. Take two limes and cut them in half, as well as one white or yellow onion, which should be cut into large chunks. As the onion cooks on the griddle, it will break up.
4. Your chicken should be done by now. Remove the chicken from the grill and toss the salsa ingredients on top with a little olive oil to coat. I add 3-4 garlic cloves, a bit extra oil, and some salt and pepper around 3 minutes into cooking these items. Allow the ingredients to caramelize as they cook. When the ingredients have cooked down a little, toss them occasionally and remove them. They can go straight into a blender once they've been removed

from the griddle. After you've added the remaining ingredients, set those aside to squeeze the juice. Squeeze the lime juice into your blender with tongs, season with a pinch of salt and pepper, and process until smooth and integrated.

5. Your corn tortillas should now be steaming. I'll place the little Blackstone cutting board on on the griddle, spread out the tortillas on the board, grab the huge basting dome, and spray water beneath and around the cutting board, covering the process. This procedure ensures that the tortillas do not break when being rolled. Warm them in the microwave with a damp paper towel on top.

6. You can slice the chicken cutlets into small thin slices while the tortillas are heating. Once those are completed, your tortillas are nearly finished. They should feel warm when you touch them.

7. To make your flautas, lay one tortilla down, add a few pieces of chicken, and some shredded cheese, then gently roll the tortilla. Once it's rolled, insert a toothpick into the tortilla to keep all of your contents in place while deep frying. Rep until all of your chicken and tortillas have been used.

8. Your oil should be ready to use at this point. Cook your rolled flautas in tiny batches of 6-8 per round in the oil. When they're done, drain them on paper towels and season with Blackstone Taco Fajita Seasoning immediately away.

9. You can start coating your flautas as they cool. Stack your flautas, toothed or not, in a small bowl with some of your fresh salsa verde.

Chicken Green Chile Empanadas

35 mins 4 serv

Ingredients

- Chicken Cutlets
- 1/2 Can of Black Beans (Rinsed)
- 1/2 Yellow Onion Diced
- Puff Pastry (1 Sheet)
- 1/2 Can of Rotel
- 1 small can diced Green Chile
- 1 Lime
- 1 Cup Shredded Cheese (Mexican Blend)
- Sliced Pepper Jack Cheese
- 1 Tbs Blackstone Hatch Chile Cheddar Seasoning
- 1 tsp Tequila Lime Blackstone Seasoning
- Salt
- Pepper
- 1 Egg
- Cilantro
- Salsa Verde
- All Purpose flower
- Blackstone Egg Ring
- Blackstone Griddle and Seasoning Spray

Instructions

1. Set your Blackstone Air-fryer to medium heat. Low, with two burners on low and the other two turned off, and your griddle on top.

2. Place the chicken cutlets on the griddle and drizzle with olive oil. Place the diced yellow onion next to the chicken.

3. Add a little all-purpose flower on a cutting board to keep the puff pastry from sticking, then place your puff pastry on top to cut out with your Blackstone egg ring. Toss together 1/2 can Rotel, 1 small can chopped green chiles, 1/2 can drained black beans, 1/2 cup shredded Mexican mix cheese, 1 tbsp Blackstone Hatch Chile and cheddar spice, 1 tsp Tequila lime Blackstone Seasoning, a sprinkling of salt and pepper

4. Let's get started with the empanadas. One egg should be beaten in a small basin. This will be the glue that holds our empanadas together in the air fryer. Place your pastry circles on the same cutting board as before and gently stretch and pull them out. It wasn't much, just enough to make them a little longer. Cut a slice of pepper jack cheese into small pieces with a knife. On top of the puff pastry, place one of the cheese slices and a little spoonful of the chicken filling (DO NOT OVERFILL) because you don't want the filling to get too close to the edge. Brush a light amount of egg around the edge of the puff pastry, fold the puff pastry over your ingredients, and push the pastry along the edge with your fingertips. Grab a fork and run it along the full edge of the pastry once you think it's sealed. This will ensure that all of your components are completely wrapped inside the empanada and make a magnificent display for the finished product.

5. Spray some Blackstone Griddle spray on each tray in your preheated air fryer basket. As well as both sides of your empanada after it's done. Place a couple of them in each basket, leaving enough space between them to cook. Cook for 3-4 minutes with the baskets in place, then remove the baskets and flip the empanadas. Cook for another 3-4 minutes or until golden brown.

6. Remove the empanadas from the air fryer baskets and serve with chopped cilantro and a light dusting of Hatch Chile and Cheddar and Tequila Lime Seasonings on top. Serve with a small cup of salsa verde.

Lamb Lollipops with Mint Chimichurri

15 mins 4 serv

Ingredients:

- 12 Lamb Lollipops
- 2 tablespoons spicy brown Mustard
- 1 bunch Italian flat leaf Parsley
- ½ bunch fresh Mint Leaves
- 1 tablespoon minced Garlic
- The juice of 1 Lemon
- The juice of 2 Limes
- 2 tablespoon Red Wine Vinegar
- 2 teaspoons Red Pepper Flakes
- Olive oil
- Salt and pepper

Instructions

Heat your griddle to a high setting.

Combine the parsley and mint in a mixing basin and finely chop. Combine the garlic, lemon and lime juices, red wine vinegar, red pepper flakes, and a pinch of salt and pepper in a mixing bowl. Mix in some olive oil to ensure that all of the ingredients are uniformly distributed. Set aside for a later date.

With a little olive oil, mustard, and salt and pepper, season the lamb lollipops. Cook for 1-2 minutes per side over high heat, or until caramelized and cooked to your preference.

To serve, lay the cooked lamb lollipops on a big family-style tray and drizzle with the mint chimichurri. Serve immediately.

Seared Scallop Caprese

15 mins 4 serv

Ingredients:

- 12 large Scallops
- 1 large Beef Steak or Heirloom Tomato
- 4 thick slices fresh Mozzarella
- A few tablespoons Balsamic glaze
- Olive oil
- Salt and pepper
- Tapenade:
- ¼ cup Kalamata Olives
- 2 tablespoons Capers
- 2 tablespoon minced Sun-dried Tomatoes
- 2 Garlic cloves
- 4-6 Basil leaves
- 1 teaspoon Lemon zest
- 1 tablespoon Lemon Juice
- Salt and pepper

Instructions

1. With a touch of salt and pepper, toss the olives, capers, sun-dried tomatoes, garlic, and basil onto your cutting board. Combine all of the components in a finely chopped state. Toss in the lemon zest and lemon juice until equally distributed.
2. Heat your griddle to a high setting.
3. Season the scallops with salt and pepper after patting them dry.
4. Cook the scallops for 1-2 minutes per side on a griddle with some olive oil.
5. To plate, place one tomato slice on each plate. Over the tomato, spread some tapenade, then a few tears of fresh mozzarella, lightly burn the cheese, and stack three scallops on top. Serve with an olive oil drizzle, balsamic glaze, and fresh basil on top.

Crab Cakes with Grapefruit Salad

15 mins 4 serv

Ingredients:

- ½ lb Jumbo Lump Crab Meat
- ½ lb Lump Crab Meat
- ½ cup Panko breadcrumbs
- 1/3 cup Mayonnaise
- 3 tablespoons Dijon Mustard
- 2 Eggs
- 1 tablespoon Worcestershire Sauce
- 1 tablespoon Hot Sauce
- 2 tablespoons Lemon Juice
- 4 cups Spring Greens
- The juice of half of a Grapefruit
- The juice of half of a Lemon
- 2-3 tablespoons finely chopped Flat Leaf Parsley
- Salt and Pepper
- Olive Oil

Instructions

1. Combine the mayonnaise, Dijon mustard, eggs, Worcestershire sauce, spicy sauce, panko, lemon juice, and a bit of salt and pepper in a large mixing bowl. To ensure that all of the ingredients are evenly distributed, whisk them together.
2. Lightly mix in the crab meat to ensure that it is evenly distributed.
3. Add a drizzle of olive oil to your griddle and heat it to medium.
4. Form the crab mixture into cakes and fry for 2-3 minutes per side in the oil, or until golden brown and fully cooked.
5. Combine the spring greens, grapefruit juice, lemon juice, a drizzle of olive oil, and a sprinkling of salt and pepper in a large mixing basin.

To dish, start with a small portion of the salad, then top with the crab cakes. Serve immediately, garnished with parsley and a sprinkle of spicy sauce

Buttermilk Bathed Rosemary Chicken Thighs

4 serv

Ingredients:

- 8 chicken thighs with bone and skin
- 2 tablespoons kosher salt
- 1 pint buttermilk
- 1 oz fresh rosemary or about 8 sprigs

Instructions:

1. Using paper towels, pat the chicken thighs dry. Place the thigh in a zipper top bag and season both sides with kosher salt.
2. Remove the rosemary stems and add them to the chicken.
3. Allow 2 hours for the chicken to rest in the refrigerator.
4. Allow the chicken to marinate in the brine overnight after adding the buttermilk.
5. Allow as much of the buttermilk mixture to drain away from the chicken as possible in a strainer.
6. Preheat the air fryer to 375 degrees Fahrenheit.
7. Cook the chicken thighs in batches, 4 in each fry basket. Cook for 35 minutes, turning every 10 minutes, or until the skin is crispy and the

flesh reaches a safe internal temperature of 165F.

Sausage and Sage Thanksgiving Stuffing

8 serv.

35 min.

Ingredients:

- About 2 loaves high quality sandwich bread or soft Italian or French bread, cut into 3/4-inch dice, about 5 quarts
- 4 TBLS butter
- 1 pound sage sausage
- 1 onion, finely chopped
- Celery, finely chopped
- 2 cloves garlic
- 2 teaspoons dried sage
- 2 cups chicken stock
- Finely chopped parsley leaves
- Salt and pepper to taste

Instructions

1. Brown the sausage and set it aside ahead of time.
2. Bread should be cut into 34-inch pieces. In a griddle, melt the butter

and add the onions, garlic, and celery.

3. Cook until they begin to soften. Combine all of the bread ingredients in a large mixing bowl.
4. Add approximately 12 cup of chicken stock at a time until it's completely absorbed. Cook until the bread begins to become golden brown.
5. Season with salt and pepper to taste and add the sausage and sage.
6. Finish with a dusting of fresh parsley.
Enjoy!

Butter Bathed Filet and Lobster Surf & Turf

Ingredients:

- 4, 6-8 oz. Filet Mignon
- 4 Lobster Tails
- 2 stick of Unsalted Butter
- A few sprigs of Fresh Rosemary
- A few sprigs of Fresh Thyme
- 2 cloves Fresh Garlic, rough chop
- 1 Lemon
- A handful of Asparagus
- 2 pints Mushrooms
- Blackstone Steakhouse Seasoning
- Olive Oil

Instructions

1. Heat the Blackstone Air Fryer to medium-high temperature.
2. Cut the top of the lobster's shell through the middle all the way to the tail with shears, leaving the final rib attached. Squeeze the bottom portion of the shell until it breaks and releases. Pull the lobster meat out and over the top of the cut shell while keeping the meat linked at the end of the tail. Make small slashes on the surface of the lobster meat with a sharp knife to form a "cross hatch" pattern.
3. Add a small sauce pot to one side of your griddle and heat to medium. Melt the butter with the herbs and garlic.
4. Add a dab of olive oil to the opposite side of your griddle and heat it to high.
5. Season your steaks well on both sides with Blackstone Steakhouse spice and grill for 2-3 minutes per side over high heat.
6. Season the tops of each lobster tail with Blackstone Steakhouse Seasoning and a little of the melted butter. Cook for around 6-7 minutes in the Air Fryer.
7. Submerge the steaks in the herb butter once they've been cooked on both sides. Return to the griddle for another minute each side after coating both sides. Remove the pancakes from the griddle and set them aside to cool for a few minutes.

8. Sprinkle a couple shakes of Blackstone Steakhouse seasoning over the asparagus and mushrooms on the griddle. Cook for 4-5 minutes after adding a little of the herb butter.
9. Place the steak on one side of the platter and the lobster tail on the other. Place the veggies in the centre and brush the steak and lobster with a little extra butter.
10. Enjoy!

Steak Frites 2-Ways

4 serv.

20 min.

Ingredients:

- 4 NY Strip steaks
- 1 bag frozen French fries
- Salt and pepper
- Olive oil

Chimi-Style Sauce:

- 1 bunch flat leaf parsley
- 1 bunch cilantro
- The juice of 2 limes
- 2 teaspoons minced garlic
- 1 teaspoon red pepper flakes
- Olive oil
- Salt and pepper

Mustard Cream Sauce:

6 serv.

20 min.

Ingredients:

- 1 shallot, minced
- 2 garlic cloves minced
- A few sprigs fresh thyme
- 3 tablespoons Dijon mustard
- 2 tablespoons capers
- ¼ cup heavy cream
- Olive oil
- Salt and pepper

Instructions:

1. Heat the griddle to a medium-high temperature.
2. Heat the Air Fryer to medium-high heat before adding the frozen fries and cooking for 7-10 minutes.
3. On both sides, season the steaks with salt and pepper. Using a sprinkle of olive oil, brown the steaks for 3-4 minutes per side on the griddle.
4. Add a drizzle of olive oil, shallots, garlic, and fresh thyme to a sauté pan on the griddle top. Cook for a couple of minutes, stirring often. With a touch of salt and pepper, combine the mustard, capers, and

cream. To incorporate everything, give it a good stir.

5. Blend all of the "Chimi-Style" ingredients in a mixing bowl and stir to combine evenly.

6. Add some of the fries to the serving platter once the steaks are cooked to your preferred doneness, and then top with the steak. Serve immediately, garnished with one or both sauces.
Enjoy!

Pomegranate Soy Glazed Lamb Chops

6 serv.

20 min.

Ingredients:

- 12 Lamb Chops
- 3 cups Pomegranate Juice
- 1 cup Soy Sauce
- 2 bunches of Green Onion, cleaned and trimmed
- ½ large Red Onion, thinly sliced
- 2 cups Arugula
- 2 cups Spring Mix Lettuce
- ¼ cup Pomegranate Arils
- 2 Oranges
- Salt & Pepper
- Olive Oil

Instructions:

1. Preheat the griddle to medium-high temperature.

2. Add the pomegranate juice and soy to a large sauté pan over an open flame. Bring to a boil over high heat for 8-10 minutes. Reduce by 75% or until it resembles maple syrup in consistency. Turn off the heat and set aside to cool somewhat. (when it cools, it will thicken a little more)

3. On all sides, season the lamb chops with olive oil and salt and pepper.

4. Cook the lamb chops for 2-3 minutes each side on the griddle with a little olive oil, then finish fat side down for an extra 2 minutes.

5. Add the green onions and softly caramelize for the last 4-5 minutes of cooking.

6. Add the arugula, spring mix, red onion, and pomegranate arils to a large mixing bowl with a touch of salt and pepper. Remove the skin and pith from the oranges before cutting them into supremes and adding them to the bowl. Remove the orange and squeeze the leftover orange juice over the greens. Toss the salad with a sprinkle of olive oil to evenly coat it.

7. To plate, place some of the salad on the platter, followed by a few green onions. Drizzle the pomegranate soy reduction sauce over 3 lamb chops.

8. Enjoy!

Tamari Ponzu Salmon with Sweet Chili Broccoli and Potato Crisps

4 serv.

25 min.

Ingredients:

- 4, 6-8 oz skinless Salmon Filets
- 2 Large Russet Potatoes, cut into ¼ inch chips
- 12 oz Broccoli florets
- ½ tablespoon Ground Ginger
- ½ tablespoon Garlic Powder
- ¼ cup Tamari
- 3 tablespoons Ponzu
- 3 tablespoons Honey
- 1 tablespoon Sesame Oil
- ¼ cup sweet Thai Chili Sauce
- ¼ cup thinly sliced Green Onion
- 1 tablespoon toasted Sesame Seeds
- Salt and pepper
- Olive oil

Instructions

1. Preheat the griddle to medium-high temperature.
2. Salt and pepper the cut potatoes, as well as a pinch of garlic powder.
3. Toss the sliced potatoes on the griddle with a sprinkle of olive oil. Cook for another 2-3 minutes before flipping.
4. Using a small drizzle of olive oil, ground ginger, garlic powder, and a pinch of salt and pepper, season the salmon on both sides. Then add the hot griddle to the mix. Cook for 3-4 minutes per side, or until done to your liking.
5. With a touch of salt and pepper, toss in a little oil and the broccoli. If preferred, steam the broccoli for 4-5 minutes with a splash of water and a dome.
6. Combine the tamari, ponzu, honey, and sesame oil in a small mixing dish. 12 of the liquid should be poured over the fish during the last minute of cooking. If additional glaze is wanted, repeat the process.
7. Toss the broccoli with the sweet Thai chili sauce to combine.
8. To serve, arrange the potatoes in a fan arrangement on the plate, then top with the broccoli. Place the salmon on top and sprinkle with sesame seeds and chopped green onion.
9. Mix a little of the sweet Thai chili sauce with the remaining tamari mix and sprinkle over the top of the fish for an extra sauce.

Betty's Shrimp Fried Rice

4 serv.

40 min.

Ingredients:

- 4 cup White Rice
- 1 lb Shrimp, wild caught
- 3-4 Eggs
- 1 cup fresh Snow Peas, cut into thirds
- 1 large Onion, chopped (white or yellow)
- 3 Garlic cloves, minced
- 1 bunch Green Onions, sliced separated green/whites
- Wok or stir fry oil
- 2 tbsp Butter, unsalted
- Low Sodium Soy Sauce
- 1 tbsp Rice Wine Vinegar (toasted sesame)
- Sesame Oil
- Toasted Sesame Seeds

Spicy Mayo Sauce:

- ½ cup Mayo, Kewpie preferred
- ¼-½ cup Sriracha (depending on level of heat)
- 1.5 tbsp Sesame Oil

Instructions:

1. 1 tsp each reduced sodium and normal soy sauce, cooked rice (preferably in a rice cooker). To cook the rice, spread it out on a baking sheet and set it in the fridge uncovered overnight or for at least 4 hours to dry out.
2. Add a drizzle of wok oil (approximately 1 tbsp) to a medium to medium high heat and spread evenly over the Blackstone before adding the eggs. Break the yolks and softly scramble the eggs for 1 minute, then set them aside on low to no heat.
3. Add another drop of wok oil and sauté the chopped onions, snow peas, garlic, and sliced white onions for 3-4 minutes, turning the veggies continually with two spatulas. Then, with the eggs, transfer the veggies to the low or off side.
4. Add 1 tbsp butter and a drizzle of wok oil to melt together before adding the prawns. Cooking by tossing. If the shrimp are large, chop them into bite-sized pieces as they cook, which should take around 3-4 minutes. They may also be slid to the side.
5. Add the rice to a pan with some wok oil and 1 tbsp butter. Toss rice with a scraper and spatula to coat with oil and butter, breaking up any clumps.

Sesame Seared Ahi Tuna

6 serv.

1 Hour min.

Ingredients:

- Sushi grade Ahi Tuna
- Sesame Seeds
- Sesame Oil

Tuna Marinade:

- ¼ cup Soy Sauce
- 2 tbs Rice Vinegar
- 1 tbsp minced Garlic
- 1 tsp Sesame Oil
- 1 tbsp Brown Sugar
- 1 tsp Ground Ginger
- 2 tbsp Green Onion
- Juice from 1 Lime

Dipping sauce:

- 1 tbsp Brown Sugar
- 1 tbsp minced Garlic
- 1 tbsp Soy Sauce
- 1 tbsp Rice Vinegar
- 1 tsp Sesame Oil
- 1 tbsp Green Onions

Cucumber/Carrot Slaw:

- Spiralize 2 Carrots and 1 Cucumber
- 1 tbsp Hoisin Sauce
- ¼ cup Orange Juice
- 1 tbsp Soy Sauce
- 1 tsp Sesame Oil
- 1 tsp Ground Ginger
- 1 tsp Sesame Seeds

Instructions

1. To make the marinade, combine all of the ingredients. Place the tuna steaks in the marinade, cover, and let aside for 1 hour.
2. Spiralize cucumbers and carrots, then drizzle with dressing. Refrigerate for at least an hour.
3. Set aside all of the ingredients for the dipping sauce.
4. Preheat the griddle to high. Allow to become extremely heated, then sprinkle with sesame oil.
5. On a dish, pour 12 cup sesame seeds. Dip the ahi tuna into the seeds, evenly covering it.
6. Cook for 4 minutes on each side on a blistering hot griddle.
7. Remove the griddle from the heat and slice thinly.
8. Arrange slaw on a platter, top with seared tuna, and serve with dipping sauce on the side.

Crab Cakes with Grapefruit Salad

4 serv.

15 min.

Ingredients:

- ½ lb Jumbo Lump Crab Meat
- ½ lb Lump Crab Meat
- ½ cup Panko breadcrumbs
- 1/3 cup Mayonnaise
- 3 tablespoons Dijon Mustard
- 2 Eggs
- 1 tablespoon Worcestershire Sauce
- 1 tablespoon Hot Sauce
- 2 tablespoons Lemon Juice
- 4 cups Spring Greens
- The juice of half of a Grapefruit
- The juice of half of a Lemon
- 2-3 tablespoons finely chopped Flat Leaf Parsley
- Salt and Pepper
- Olive Oil

Instructions:

1. Combine the mayonnaise, Dijon mustard, eggs, Worcestershire sauce, spicy sauce, panko, lemon juice, and a bit of salt and pepper in a large mixing bowl. To ensure that all of the ingredients are uniformly distributed, whisk them together.
2. Lightly mix in the crab meat to ensure that it is equally distributed.
3. Add a drizzle of olive oil to your griddle and heat it to medium.
4. Form the crab mixture into cakes and fry for 2-3 minutes each side in the oil, or until golden brown and thoroughly cooked.
5. Combine the spring greens, grapefruit juice, lemon juice, a drizzle of olive oil, and a sprinkling of salt and pepper in a large mixing basin. Toss the salad gently to coat it evenly.
6. To dish, start with a small portion of the salad, then top with the crab cakes. Serve immediately, garnished with parsley and a sprinkle of spicy sauce.

Betty's Italian Cutlets

5 serv.

30 min.

Ingredients:

- 2-3 large boneless skinless Chicken Breast
- 4 Eggs
- 1 ½ cup Parmesan Cheese
- 2 c plain Bread crumbs
- 1 bunch flat leaf Parsley, chopped
- 1 tsp Paprika
- 1 tsp Garlic Powder
- ½ tsp Onion Powder
- Salt & Pepper

- Oil for frying, extra light tasting Olive Oil preferred
- Coarse Sea Salt, optional

Instructions:

1. Slice each chicken breast into 4-6 pieces, then flatten each chunk with the flat side of a meat mallet, pushing the mallet towards the exterior. Repeat with the remaining chicken breasts. Per chicken breast, you should receive 4-6 cutlets. Place them in a safe place while you set up your dredging station.
2. Arrange two shallow dishes or containers in a line. Add the eggs, a large handful of Parmesan cheese (12 - 34 cup), and a handful of chopped parsley (14 cup) to one of the bowls. Combine the ingredients in a mixing bowl, then add the cutlets to the cheesy eggs. This step may be done ahead of time, and the cutlets in the egg mixture can be stored in the refrigerator for up to overnight or used right away.
3. Bread crumbs, paprika, garlic, and onion powder go into the second shallow bowl. Salt & pepper to taste. Add a handful of cheese and minced parsley to the mix.
4. Remove one cutlet from the egg mixture and set it in the bread crumbs, turning and spreading the bread crumbs onto the chicken until it is well covered. Carry on with each cutlet in the same manner.
5. Allow the BLACKSTONE to heat to a medium-low temperature. Place a cooling rack next to or on one side of the griddle.
6. Using a BLACKSTONE squirt bottle filled with oil, softly spritz a tiny quantity of oil onto the cooking area and insert cutlets into the oil a few at a time, adding a small amount of oil before each batch of cutlets. Allow for 3-4 minutes of cooking time, or until golden brown. Add a little spray of oil to the cutlets on the flip side to allow them to shallow fry evenly for another 3-4 minutes. Low and slow cooking to avoid scorching the breadcrumbs.
7. As each cutlet cooks, remove it to a cooling rack and quickly sprinkle it with cheese and/or coarse sea salt. Plate and serve after all of the cutlets have been fried.

Seared Scallop Caprese

4 serv.

15 min.

Ingredients:

- 12 large Scallops
- 1 large Beef Steak or Heirloom Tomato
- 4 thick slices fresh Mozzarella
- A few tablespoons Balsamic glaze
- Olive oil
- Salt and pepper

- ¼ cup Kalamata Olives
- 2 tablespoons Capers
- 2 tablespoon minced Sun-dried Tomatoes
- 2 Garlic cloves
- 4-6 Basil leaves
- 1 teaspoon Lemon zest
- 1 tablespoon Lemon Juice
- Salt and pepper

Instructions

1. With a touch of salt and pepper, toss the olives, capers, sun-dried tomatoes, garlic, and basil onto your cutting board. Combine all of the components in a finely chopped state. Toss in the lemon zest and lemon juice until equally distributed.
2. Heat your griddle to a high setting.
3. Season the scallops with salt and pepper after patting them dry.
4. Cook the scallops in a little olive oil on your griddle for 1-2 minutes per side, or until brown and caramelized.
5. To plate, place one tomato slice on each plate. Over the tomato, spread some tapenade and a few tears of fresh mozzarella. Lightly char the cheese with a hand torch before stacking three scallops on top. Serve with an olive oil drizzle, balsamic glaze, and fresh basil on top.

Salmon Street Taco

4 serv.

25 min.

Ingredients:

- 4-6 oz Salmon filets, diced large cubes
- 1 tbsp Wok oil
- 1 tbsp Sesame oil
- 1 tbsp Sesame seeds
- 12 Flour Tortillas, street taco size
- 2 Avocados
- Slaw
- 2 c Green Cabbage, sliced thin
- ½ cup Green Onions, sliced
- 1-2 c Cilantro, rough chopped
- 1 juice of Lime plus Zest
- 2 tsp Wok oil
- 2 tsp Sesame oil
- BLACKSTONE Tequila Lime seasoning to taste
- Spicy Mayo Sauce
- 1 c Mayo, Dukes or Kewpie preferred
- ½- ¾ c Sriracha
- 2 tbsp Sesame Oil
- 1.5 tbsp Ponzu sauce
- 2 Garlic cloves, grated

Instructions:

1. Toss the salmon with sesame oil, wok oil, and sesame seeds to coat. While you're making the slaw and

sauce, let the meat marinade.In a large mixing basin, combine the cabbage, cilantro, and green onions. Toss with the wok oil, sesame oil, lime juice, and lime zest. To taste, season with BLACKSTONE tequila lime seasoning. Remove from the equation.

2. To make the spicy mayo, combine all ingredients and adjust the amount of sriracha to taste. Remove from the equation.

3. Preheat a BLACKSTONE griddle to medium-high heat and sear the salmon for 1 minute on each side.

4. Warm the tortillas on medium heat for 1-2 minutes each side while the fish cooks. Place cooked tortillas in the BLACKSTONE taco rack, top with slaw, fish, an avocado slice, and a dab of spicy mayo.

Lamb Lollipops with Mint Chimichurri

4 serv.

15 min.

Ingredients:

- 12 Lamb Lollipops
- 2 tablespoons spicy brown Mustard
- 1 bunch Italian flat leaf Parsley
- ½ bunch fresh Mint Leaves
- 1 tablespoon minced Garlic
- The juice of 1 Lemon
- The juice of 2 Limes
- 2 tablespoon Red Wine Vinegar
- 2 teaspoons Red Pepper Flakes
- Olive oil
- Salt and pepper

INSTRUCTIONS:

1. Heat your griddle to a high setting.
2. Combine the parsley and mint in a mixing basin and finely chop. Combine the garlic, lemon and lime juices, red wine vinegar, red pepper flakes, and a sprinkle of salt and pepper in a mixing bowl. Mix in some olive oil to ensure that all of the ingredients are uniformly distributed. Set aside for a later day.
3. With a little olive oil, mustard, and salt and pepper, season the lamb lollipops. Cook for 1-2 minutes per side over high heat, or until caramelized and cooked to your preference.
4. To serve, lay the cooked lamb lollipops on a big family-style tray and drizzle with the mint chimichurri. Serve immediately.

Betty Springs Chicken

2 serv.

25 min.

Ingredients:

- 2 Chicken Breast
- ½ c Mayonnaise, Dukes preferred
- 4 slices Bacon
- 1-2 Portobello Mushrooms, sliced
- 4 oz Cheddar Cheese, shredded
- 4 tbsp Dijon Mustard
- 2 tbsp + 2 tsp Blackstone Seasoning, Whiskey Burger
- 2 tbsp Butter, unsalted
- dried Parsley, garnish

Instructions:

1. Trim the chicken breasts and softly pound the thicker end with the palm of your hand to thin it out and make it even all around. Cooking time will be reduced and even cooking will be achieved by using a thinner chicken breast.
2. Mix up mayo with 2 tbsp Blackstone Seasoning (Whiskey Burger or Chicken and Herb are faves for this meal), then coat chicken breasts in the mayo mixture using a bowl or a food storage bag to coat evenly.
3. Cook the bacon on one side of your Blackstone griddle over low heat. Place on paper towels to absorb excess liquid until ready to use.
4. Meanwhile, warm 2 tbsp butter on the other side over medium heat and stir mushrooms in butter. 2 tablespoons Blackstone seasoning Tossing the mushrooms to ensure consistent cooking. To add flavor, slide mushrooms into part of the bacon grease. Remove from heat when done, or set aside on low-off heat.
5. Cook the chicken breasts for 4-5 minutes over medium heat, or until golden brown.
6. Spread 1 tbsp Dijon mustard over each chicken breast before flipping. Cooked mushrooms, bacon, and a handful of freshly grated cheddar cheese are sprinkled on top.
7. Allow 4-5 minutes for the dome to cook through and melt the cheese.
8. Remove the chicken from the pan and place it on a platter with dried parsley. Enjoy with Air Fryer French Fries from Blackstone.

Cheesesteak Pasta

4-6 serv.

30 min.

Ingredients

- 1 lb pasta, cooked reserving 1 cup pasta water
- 1 lb ground beef, (sub shaved ribeye or sirloin)
- 2 green bell peppers, diced
- 1 large sweet onion, diced
- mushrooms, sliced
- ¼ lb provolone cheese, deli sliced or grated
- ¼ lb American cheese, deli sliced or grated

- ¼ c worcestershire sauce
- 4 fresh garlic cloves, chopped
- Blackstone Cheese Steak Seasoning
- 1 tbsp oil
- 1 tbsp butter

Instructions:

1. Boil 1 pound of pasta until al dente, then drain, reserving 1 cup of the pasta water.
2. While the pasta is cooking, use your Blackstone to sauté onions, mushrooms, and peppers in oil and butter over medium heat. Cook until the vegetables are soft.
3. Cook your meat until cooked through on a separate heat zone, cutting ground beef or separating shaved beef.
4. Combine the cooked beef and veggies in a mixing bowl. After combining everything together, add half of the cheese to melt.
5. Toss the noodles with the meat mixture to combine.
6. Season with Blackstone cheese steak seasoning and the leftover cheese and pasta water. Toss everything together and serve!

Feta Pasta with Shrimp

Ingredients

- 1 lb shrimp (substitute protein of choice)
- 8 oz pasta cooked, drained reserve ¾ c pasta water
- 8 oz feta cheese, block
- 2 pints cherry tomatoes
- ½ c extra virgin olive oil
- 4 garlic cloves, smashed and chopped
- Handful each fresh Italian parsley and basil

Italian blend seasoning

- 1 tsp fennel seed
- 1 tsp minced garlic
- 1 ½ tsp minced onion
- 1 tsp basil
- 1 tsp oregano
- 1 tsp parsley flakes
- 1 ½ crushed red pepper flakes
- ½ tsp salt
- ¼ tsp sugar
- ½ tsp pepper
- ½ tsp celery seed

Instructions:

1. To produce an Italian blend, combine the dry ingredients. To store, place in an airtight container.

2. Cook pasta until al dente, then drain and put aside, reserving 12 cup pasta water.

3. Leave the tails on while peeling and butterflying shrimp. Place shrimp on skewers (if desired), sprinkle with olive oil, and season with Italian seasoning.

4. Toss tomatoes with a splash of olive oil and season with Italian blend in a small roasting pan (or create a roasting boat out of tinfoil to fit in the Blackstone airfryer drawer). Place the feta block in the center of the tomatoes, drizzle with the remaining oil, and season the top of the cheese.

5. In a preheated air fryer drawer set to high heat, combine tomatoes and cheese. Allow for 10 minutes of cooking time.

6. Meanwhile, fry the shrimp for 2-3 minutes per side over medium high heat.

7. Examine the tomatoes and the cheese. The tomatoes should burst or split apart, and the cheese should melt. Cooking time may need to be increased by up to 10 minutes, so check every five minutes.

8. Remove the tomatoes and cheese, add the fresh garlic, and combine the cheese and tomatoes to make your spaghetti sauce. Pour sauce over cooked pasta and add as much or as little pasta water as needed.

9. Toss with some fresh parsley and basil. Serve with shrimp on the side.

Chicken Green Chile Empanadas

2-4 serv.

35 min.

Ingredients

- Chicken Cutlets
- 1/2 Can of Black Beans (Rinsed)
- 1/2 Yellow Onion Diced
- Puff Pastry (1 Sheet)
- 1/2 Can of Rotel
- 1 small can diced Green Chile
- 1 Lime
- 1 Cup Shredded Cheese (Mexican Blend)
- Sliced Pepper Jack Cheese
- 1 Tbs Blackstone Hatch Chile Cheddar Seasoning
- 1 tsp Tequila Lime Blackstone Seasoning
- Salt
- Pepper
- 1 Egg
- Cilantro
- Salsa Verde
- All Purpose flower
- Blackstone Egg Ring
- Blackstone Griddle and Seasoning Spray

Instructions:

1. Set your Blackstone Air-fryer to medium heat. Low, with two

burners on low and the other two turned off, and your griddle on top.

2. Place the chicken cutlets on the griddle and drizzle with olive oil. Place the chopped yellow onion next to the chicken. The onions will gently caramelize as you toss them now and again. In addition, your chicken was flipped. Cook the chicken for about 4-5 minutes per side, or until thoroughly done.

3. Add a little all-purpose flower on a cutting board to keep the puff pastry from sticking, then place your puff pastry on top to cut out with your Blackstone egg ring. For smaller empanadas, the egg ring is the appropriate size for cutting out puff pastry. You'll notice that it's you. Puff pastry may be sliced into four pieces as is. You may knead the remaining dough, roll it out, and cut one or two more once you've gotten four cut out.

4. Your cutlets de poulet de poulet de poulet de poulet de poulet de poulet de poulet de Turn off the griddle, remove the chicken, and dice it into tiny bite-size pieces. Return the diced chicken to the griddle and add the other ingredients. Toss together 1/2 can Rotel, 1 small can chopped green chiles, 1/2 can drained black beans, 1/2 cup shredded Mexican mix cheese, 1 tbsp Blackstone Hatch Chile and cheddar spice, 1 tsp Tequila lime Blackstone Seasoning, a sprinkling of salt and pepper The ingredients will be heated and the cheese will be melted by the remaining heat from your Blackstone. Once it's ready, combine all of the ingredients in a big mixing dish.

5. Let's get started with the empanadas. One egg should be beaten in a small basin. This will be the glue that holds our empanadas together in the air fryer. Place your pastry circles on the same cutting board as before and gently stretch and pull them out. It wasn't much, just enough to make them a little longer. Cut a slice of pepper jack cheese into tiny pieces using a knife. On top of the puff pastry, place one of those pieces of cheese and a little spoonful of the chicken filling (DO NOT OVERFILL) since you don't want the filling to come too close to the edge. Brush a little amount of egg over the edge of the puff pastry, fold the puff pastry over your ingredients, and push the dough along the edge with your fingertips.Grab a fork and run it along the full edge of the pastry once you think it's sealed. This will guarantee that all of your components are completely wrapped within the empanada and make a magnificent display for the finished product.

6. Spray some Blackstone Griddle spray on each tray in your preheated air fryer basket. As well as both sides of your empanada after it's done. Place a couple of them in each basket, leaving enough space between them to cook. Cook for 3-4 minutes with the baskets in

place, then remove the baskets and turn the empanadas. Cook for another 3-4 minutes or until golden brown.

7. Remove the empanadas from the air fryer baskets and serve with chopped cilantro and a little sprinkling of Hatch Chile and Cheddar and Tequila Lime Seasonings on top. Serve with a small cup of salsa verde.

Cashew Peppered Beef Lo Mein

3-4 serv.

20 min.

Ingredients

- 1 tbsp minced Garlic
- 1 tbsp minced Ginger
- Green, and Red Bell Peppers
- Green Onion
- 1 tsp Sesame oil
- 1/4 Cup Rice Vinegar
- 1/4 Cup Soy Sauce
- 1/4 Cup Chicken broth
- 1 tbsp Sriracha
- 2 tbsp Sugar
- 1 tbsp Corn starch
- 2 bags of Chow Mein Egg Noodles (pre cooked)
- Crispy Chow Mein Noodles
- Salted Cashews
- Thin Sliced Ribeye Beef

Instructions:

1. Preheat your Blackstone Griddle to high heat before you begin.
2. Mix the sauce ingredients in a mixing basin. 1 tsp Sesame Oil, 1 tbsp Minced Garlic, 1 tbsp Minced Ginger, 1 tbsp Corn Starch, 2 tbsp Sugar, 1/4 cup chicken stock, 1/4 cup rice vinegar, 1 tbsp Sriracha, 1/4 Soy Sauce, 2-3 tbsp Ponzu, 1 tsp Sesame Oil, 1 tbsp Minced Garlic, 1 tb Set this aside once you've combined all of your sauce components.
3. Let's get our Red and Green Bell Peppers chopped up. Make sure the pith and seeds are removed. You may cut them up to any size you like, but a big chop is recommended.
4. It's time to fry our thinly sliced Ribeye on the griddle, which should be smoking hot by now. You may now buy your steak already cut or slice it yourself. If you're going to slice it yourself, put it in the freezer for about 20 minutes. The beef will get firmer as a result, making it simpler to slice. Also, don't skip the fat; it'll provide a lot of flavor that you won't want to lose out on. Place the steak on the griddle top with 1-2 tablespoons of olive oil. Toss the meat in the olive oil to coat it. We want a rapid sear but don't want to overcook the steak by cooking it too long.

5. While the steak is cooking, place the bell peppers right next to it to finish cooking. Your steak should be moved about at this point to ensure even cooking on all sides. Turn your burners to low and add your bell peppers to the beef along with around 2 tbsp soy sauce after the meat is 90% done. Before we add the rest of the ingredients, this will reduce and coat the steak and bell peppers. It should take around 2 minutes to decrease this to the point where it is ready for the next step.

6. Now that the steak is done, add both bags of precooked chow mein noodles, as well as 1/3 of your sauce, to the meat and bell peppers. In a large mixing bowl, combine all of the ingredients for the sauce. This will loosen your noodles and cause them to reduce in size.

7. Chop the green onion and cashews while everything is decreasing. You'll want to trim off the top 1-2 inches of the green onion. Because it has a lot of texture, you may remove it, as well as the bottom of your green onion. Chop the green onion as finely as you prefer, then add a large pinch to the meat and noodles, along with another third of the sauce. Add approximately 1/4 cup of your chopped cashes, mix to coat, and simmer the sauce more. When the sauce begins to thicken, add the remainder of your sauce, mix, and plate.

8. To dish, I prefer to start with some crispy chow mien noodles on the bottom of the plate, then top with your low main, a sprinkle of green onion, cashews, sesame seeds, and a little spray of sriracha.

Mahi Mahi with Pineapple Pico and Rice

4 serv.

20 min.

Ingredients:

- 4, 6-8oz filets of Mahi Mahi
- 1 cup white Rice
- 1 ½ cups Chicken Stock
- The juice of 1 Lime
- 2 tablespoons Blackstone Chicken and Herb Seasoning
- 1 tablespoon chopped Cilantro

Pineapple Salsa:

- 3-4, ½ inch slices of Pineapple
- 1 Jalapeno, thinly sliced
- 1 Red Chile, thinly sliced
- ¼ cup minced Red Onion
- 2 teaspoons minced Garlic
- 2 teaspoons Blackstone Sriracha Pineapple Seasoning
- The juice of 1 Lime
- Pinch of Salt

Instructions:

1. Combine the rice, chicken stock, lime juice, Blackstone Chicken and Herb Seasoning, and cilantro in a small aluminum pan. Cover with tin foil after stirring to ensure a uniform blend.
2. Place the tin foil rice pack on the griddle over high heat. Cook for 10 minutes before transferring to the griddle's cooler side.
3. Caramelize the pineapple slices on the griddle with a little olive oil over medium-high heat.
4. When the pineapple is done, chop it up into small pieces and place it in a big mixing basin. Stir in the remaining pineapple salsa ingredients until they are uniformly distributed.
5. Season both sides of the Mahi Mahi with the Blackstone Sriracha Pineapple.
6. Cook the Mahi Mahi for 3-4 minutes per side on a griddle with a little olive oil over medium-high heat.
7. To dish, lay the rice in the center of the plate or platter and top with the cooked fish. Garnish with a dollop of pineapple salsa and a sprig of fresh cilantro.

Cajun Catfish with Brown Sugar Butter Sauce

2-4 serv.

30 min.

Ingredients

- 8 Small Red Potatoes
- Half and Half
- Pink Himalayan Salt
- Zatarain's Shrimp & Crab Boil
- Blackstone Cajun Seasoning
- 4 Catfish fillets
- 1 can of Sweet Corn
- 1 can of Green Beans
- ¾ c of Brown Sugar
- Crystal Hot Sauce

Instructions:

1. Place 8 tiny red potatoes in a big saucepan and cut them into large pieces.
2. 2 teaspoons salt, 1 cup half-and-half, 34 cup water, and 12 teaspoons Zatarain's Shrimp and Crab Boil Cover and bring to a boil.
3. Fill a 32oz mason jar 34% full of Half & Half and 12 tsp Pink Himalayan Salt to create butter. Start shaking once you've sealed the package firmly. It will take around 5 minutes for it to thicken. When it begins to thicken, shake it and it will "Clunk."

Remove the cover and pour the buttermilk out (this can be used later to make buttermilk pancakes). Close it up and shake it for a few minutes longer. (You can also do this in a blender.)

4. Put it in the fridge to chill when it's finished.

5. The potatoes should be done by now. Drain the potatoes and mash them with salt and Blackstone Cajun Seasoning to taste. Continue mixing in 34 cup of the butter you just prepared. Allow to cool before serving.

6. Preheat your griddle to medium. Don't combine 1 can of green beans and 1 can of sweet corn. 12 tablespoons fresh butter should be added to each.

7. In a large sauce pan, melt the remaining butter and add 34 cup of brown sugar. To taste, add Crystal Hot Sauce (optional). To heat the sauce, place the pan immediately on the griddle and stir well. Remove from the heat once the butter has completely melted and been well combined.

8. Get your fish fillets out and season one side with Cajun spice before placing it on the griddle. Repeat with the other side. Cook for 3-5 minutes before flipping.

9. Put your meal on a plate and savor it!

10. *These dimensions are based on the video and may not be 100% accurate.

Gator Wings

2-4 serv.

20 min.

Ingredients:

- 32 OZ package of Alligator Bone in Legs
- Flour
- 3 Tbsp Blackstone Bayou Blend seasoning

Sauce

- 1 stick of Butter
- ½ cup Brown Sugar
- 2 ½ Tbsp Blackstone Bayou Blend seasoning
- Hot Sauce, to taste.

Instructions:

1. In a metal mixing bowl, combine 1 cube of butter and 12 cup brown sugar to prepare the sauce. 3 tablespoons Blackstone Bayou Seasonings should be combined. To taste, add spicy sauce (1tsp).

2. Place the bowl on the Blackstone and cook over medium heat until everything is melted and combined. Remove the pan from the heat and set it aside.

3. 2 12 cup flour and 3 tbsp Bayou in a separate big mixing bowl Mix in the seasonings.

4. Cut each leg at the joint with an alligator leg on a cutting board.
5. Mix the flour and seasonings with the alligator legs.
6. To fry, heat oil in a cast iron pan to 340-350 degrees.
7. Cook the alligator legs for 3-4 minutes, or until golden brown, then flipping and cooking for another 3-4 minutes.

Bruce Mitchell Gumbo

12-15 serv.

120 min.

Ingredients:

- 4 cups Flour
- Oil
- 6lbs of Chicken, sliced
- 14oz of Smoked Sausage, sliced
- 1 1/3 Cups Onion
- 1 1/3 Cups Green Bell Pepper
- 1 1/3 Cups Celery
- 1lb Crawfish
- 3 quarts Chicken Stock (3 cartons)
- 28oz chopped Okra
- Gumbo Filé
- Cooked Rice

Instructions:

1. Set griddle to medium heat and clean properly (so there is no oil remaining on the griddle top) to prepare your own roux.
2. Place 4 cups white flour on the griddle over medium heat and spread evenly around the griddle. Fold and distribute the flour on the griddle until it turns a dark brown color.
3. Fold in a little amount of oil at a time into the flour until it reaches the consistency of brownie batter.
4. Place everything in a big saucepan and set it aside.
5. Re-oil the griddle after cleaning it.
6. Place 6 pounds of chicken on the griddle in medium-sized slices. Add a large amount of Bayou Blend Seasoning.
7. Slice 14 ounces of smoked sausage and cook alongside the chicken.
8. Cook for 4-6 minutes on the griddle with 1 1/3 cup each of onion, green pepper, and celery. By adding water to the veggies, they will steam.
9. Add 1 pound of crawfish on the griddle top, along with a splash of Bayou seasoning. Cook for another 3-5 minutes after adding the spice.
10. Place the Roux pot on the griddle top and slowly pour in 3 cartons of chicken stock, stirring constantly.
11. Combine all of the food off the griddle in a saucepan with the roux and chicken stock mix.
12. Add one 28oz bag of chopped Okra and bring to a boil. Cook for 2 hours on medium to low heat after mixing.

(You may put this on top of the burner to save propane.)

13. Serve over rice with a dash of Gumbo File flavor (optional).

CJ's Chicken Flautas with Griddled Salsa Verde

3-4 serv.

30 min.

Ingredients:

- Chicken cutlets
- Corn tortillas
- Pre shredded Mexican blend cheese
- Large aluminum tin
- Toothpicks
- Olive Oil
- 4-6 Tomatillos (depending on the size)
- 3 limes
- White or yellow onion
- 3 jalapeños
- Cilantro
- Garlic
- Salt
- Pepper
- Blackstone Taco Fajita Seasoning
- Blender

Instructions:

1. Pre-heat one side of your griddle on high, then cook in a big shallow tin pan with olive oil or another oil replacement. The temperature of the oil should be approximately 375 degrees. Another zone should be preheated on medium high.

2. Our chicken cutlets must first be seasoned. Simply brush both sides with a small coating of oil and season with salt and pepper before placing on the Blackstone griddle to cook. This won't take long, so keep an eye on it and turn as needed to ensure even cooking.

3. Let's get started preparing our salsa ingredients. Remove the husk on the outside of the tomatillos as well as the stem before cutting into quarters. Split the stem off your jalapeos and cut them in half lengthwise. You may leave the seeds out if you want a milder salsa. I prefer the warmth, so I keep them in. Take two limes and cut them in half, as well as one white or yellow onion, which should be cut into large bits. As the onion cooks on the griddle, it will split apart.

4. Your chicken should be done by now. Remove the chicken from the grill and toss the salsa ingredients on top with a little olive oil to coat. I also like to season with salt and pepper at this point. I add 3-4 garlic cloves, a bit extra oil, and some salt and pepper around 3 minutes into cooking these items. Allow the ingredients to caramelize while they

cook. The limes will begin to turn color, and the jalapeos will begin to roast. When the ingredients have cooked down a little, toss them occasionally and remove them. You don't want the tomatillos to go mushy, so keep an eye on them. They can go straight into a blender once they've been removed from the griddle.DON'T MIX THE LIMES. After you've added the remaining ingredients, set those aside to squeeze the juice. Squeeze the lime juice into your blender using tongs, season with a pinch of salt and pepper, and process until smooth and integrated. While you complete the remainder of your meal, lay this aside to chill.

5. Your corn tortillas should now be steaming. I'll place the little Blackstone cutting board on on the griddle, lay the tortillas out on the board, take the large basting dome, and spray water under and around the cutting board and cover to step.Warm them in the microwave with a moist paper towel on top.

6. You may slice the chicken cutlets into little thin pieces while the tortillas are heating. Once those are completed, your tortillas are nearly finished. They should feel warm when you touch them.

7. To make your flautas, lay one tortilla down, add a few pieces of chicken, and some shredded cheese, then gently wrap the tortilla. Once it's rolled, insert a toothpick into the tortilla to keep all of your contents in place while deep frying. Rep until all of your chicken and tortillas have been utilized.Your oil should be ready to use at this point. Cook your rolled flautas in tiny batches of 6-8 each round in the oil. Because the chicken is already cooked, this won't take long. Cook for about 2-3 minutes, or until the shell is crisp. When they're done, drain them on paper towels and season with Blackstone Taco Fajita Seasoning immediately away.

8. You may start coating your flautas as they cool. Add some fresh salsa verde to a small bowl, stack your flautas with or without toothpicks, top with cilantro and a griddled lime, and enjoy!

Frog Legs 3 Ways

5-6 serv.

20 min.

Ingredients:

- 24 Frog Legs
- 2 Eggs
- ½ cup Half and Half
- Bayou Blend Seasoning
- 3 cups Zatarain's Frying Mix (any bread crumb mixture will work)
- Oil
- 3 tsp Sesame Oil
- ½ cup Soy Sauce
- 1 cube Butter
- Hot Sauce, to taste

Instructions:

1ST EDITION

1. To prepare the egg wash, whisk together 2 eggs and 12 cup half-and-half in a small bowl. Season to taste with Bayou Blend spices.
2. 8 legs should be soaked in the mixture.
3. In a larger mixing bowl, combine 3 cups Zatarain's Frying Mix (or any breading mix) and some Bayou Blend spice to produce the breading mixture.
4. Remove the legs from the egg wash and dip them one at a time in the breading mixture, placing them on a separate dish. Dip them in the egg wash again and then in the breading mixture to double coat.
5. Heat the oil to 320 degrees in a pan, then add the breaded frog legs and fry until golden brown.
6. Place on a plate and enjoy!

2ND EDITION

1. Place 8 frog legs in a small dish and season with salt and pepper. Bayou Combine spices and 3 tsp. sesame oil in a mixing bowl. Hand-mix the ingredients.
2. Allow the frog legs to marinate in 12 cup soy sauce for 2 minutes.
3. Cover the entire dish with a basting dome and place it on the griddle.
4. Cook for a total of 3-5 minutes.
5. Place on a plate and enjoy!

3rd edition

1. 1 cube of butter is melted on the griddle, and 8 frog legs are placed on the butter.
2. Toss in the spicy sauce and Bayou Season to taste and cover with a basting dome.
3. Cook for a total of 3-5 minutes.
4. Place on a plate and enjoy!
5. *Chicken is wonderful in these dishes!

Bayou Sous Vide Steak

3-4 serv.

120 min.

Ingredients:

- 1 Large Tomahawk Steak
- 1 cup Dale Seasoning
- 10 small Red Potatoes
- Water
- 24oz package of Bacon
- 3 Tbsp of Butter
- ½ cup Half and half
- ½ cup Green Onions
- ½ tsp of Garlic Powder
- 1 Tbsp of Chives
- ½ tsp Zatarain's Shimp and Crab Boil
- Steak seasoning

Instructions:

1. To marinate the steak, place it in a sealable bag with 1 cup of Dale seasoning.
2. Boil 2 quarts of water and pour into an ice chest with 2 quarts of warm water already in it.
3. Close the ice chest and place the bag with the meat inside. Allow it to sit for 2 hours.
4. 10 little red potatoes, sliced, should be placed in a big saucepan to prepare Mashed Bacon Potatoes. 1 quart water and 12 tablespoons Zatarain's Shimp and Crab Boil
5. Bring to a boil in a saucepan on the stove and simmer for 10-15 minutes.
6. Preheat the griddle to high and fry one 24-ounce package of thick-cut bacon.
7. Strain the potatoes and mash them with 3 tablespoons butter and 12 cup half-and-half.
8. Cut the bacon into tiny slices and incorporate it into the mashed potatoes.
9. Mix 12 cup green onion, 12 teaspoon garlic powder, and 1 tablespoon chives into mashed potatoes.
10. Remove the steak from the ice chest and set it on a chopping board with your favorite steak seasoning. Season the opposite side of the griddle after placing the seasoning side down. Cook each side for 3-5 minutes.
11. Remove the steak from the pan and set it aside for 10 minutes.

12. Slice, dish, and savor!

Jambalaya for 3

3 serv.

30 min.

Ingredients:

- 2 boneless Chicken thighs
- 6oz of Mandarin Sausage
- 8oz of cooked Crawfish
- ¼ of a large onion
- Bayou Blend Seasoning
- 3 cup Rice
- 6 cup Water
- 3 tsp Kitchen Bouquet Browning and Seasoning Sauce

Instructions:

1. Preheat the griddle to medium. Cook 2 boneless chicken thighs till browned in cubes.
2. Place 6 oz. cooked mandarin sausage and 8 oz. cooked crawfish on the griddle. Cook until warmed through, then add to chicken with a dab of Bayou Blend flavor.
3. Cook for 3-5 minutes after dicing 14 of a big onion. (To steam the onions, simply add a little water.) Once the meat is done, mix it with the onions and reduce the heat to low.
4. Reduce the heat to low on the rest of the griddle.

5. 1 cup rice, 2 cups chicken stock, 1 teaspoon Kitchen Bouquet Browning and Spice Sauce, and a sprinkle of Bayou Blend seasoning in each of the three Blackstone Grease Cup liners

6. Place on the griddle and equally distribute the meat into each one, stirring occasionally.

7. Make a tiny hole on the top of each one using aluminum foil.

8. Cook for around 20 minutes.

9. Take it off the fire and enjoy it!

CJ's Copy Cat Bourbon Chicken

2-3 serv.

20-25 min.

Ingredients:

- 4 Boneless Skinless Chicken Thighs
- 1 Green bell pepper
- 1 Yellow onion
- Green onion
- 2 bags of White or jasmine rice (Ben's microwave pre cooked)
- Olive oil
- 2 tsp Ground ginger
- Crushed Red Pepper
- 1 tsp Garlic powder
- 1/4 tsp Course black pepper
- 1/3 cup Soy sauce
- 1/3 cup Bourbon
- 1/2 cup Water
- 2 tbsp White Rice Vinegar

- 1/2 cup Brown sugar
- 1 tbsp Cornstarch dissolved in 3 tbsp cold water

Instructions:

1. Preheat one of your Blackstone's zones to medium high heat. While your griddle warms up, season your boneless skinless chicken thighs with kosher salt and coarse black pepper and a light coating of olive oil. Place your chicken on the griddle to fry after it has warmed up. When the cooked side is golden crispy, flip it over. You may turn the chicken many times to ensure that it is properly cooked.

2. Let's get started with our Bourbon Sauce. 1/3 cup soy sauce, 2 tbsp rice vinegar, and 2 tsp ground pepper in a large mixing bowl1/2 cup brown sugar, 1 tbsp Cornstarch dissolved in 3 tbsp cold water, 1/3 cup Bourbon, 1/4 tsp coarse black pepper, ginger, 1 tsp garlic powder, 1/2 tsp crushed red pepper flakes, 1/2 cup brown sugar, 1 tbsp Cornstarch dissolved in 3 tbsp cold water Set aside after stirring to incorporate all of the ingredients.

3. After that, remove the pith and seeds from 1 green bell pepper and slice it into a big chop (about 1/2 inch squares). One yellow onion, sliced into the same size as the yellow onion.

4. At this point, your chicken should be done. Remove the check from the griddle and cut it to about the same

size as your vegetables before returning it to the griddle.

5. Once the chicken is back on the griddle, toss in your vegetables, reduce the heat to low, and drizzle in the sauce in tiny batches. The sauce will thicken and cover your chicken and vegetables as a result of this. Do this in three to four small batches. As you can see, the sauce decreases and thickens into a thick glaze.

6. After you've finished glazing, place your precooked rice in one of your cooking zones, season gently with salt and pepper, and steam with a little water. You may dome your rice if you like, but toss it lightly to enable the water to steam and cook it up.

7. Remove the stem tips and base of one or two green onions before chopping them up for the platter. Place a bed of steamed rice on a platter, top with a piece of the bourbon chicken and veggies, garnish with chopped green onion, and a little sprinkling of sesame seeds, and serve!

Cheesesteak Pasta

cooking time: 30 minutes

Servings: 6

Ingredients

- 1 lb pasta, cooked reserving 1 cup pasta water
- 1 lb ground beef, (sub shaved ribeye or sirloin)
- 2 green bell peppers, diced
- 1 large sweet onion, diced
- mushrooms, sliced
- ¼ lb provolone cheese, deli sliced or grated
- ¼ lb American cheese, deli sliced or grated
- ¼ c worcestershire sauce
- 4 fresh garlic cloves, chopped
- Blackstone Cheese Steak Seasoning
- 1 tbsp oil
- 1 tbsp butter

Instruction

1. Boil 1 pound of pasta until al dente, then drain, reserving 1 cup of the pasta water.

2. While the pasta is cooking, use your Blackstone to sauté onions, mushrooms, and peppers in oil and butter over medium heat. Cook until the vegetables are soft.

3. Cook your meat until cooked through on a separate heat zone, cutting ground beef or separating shaved beef.

4. Combine the cooked beef and vegetables in a mixing bowl. After combining everything together, add half of the cheese to melt.

5. Toss the noodles with the meat mixture to combine.

6. Season with Blackstone cheese steak seasoning and the leftover cheese and pasta water. Toss everything together and serve!

Betty's Upside Down Pizza

cooking time: 30 minutes

Servings: 6

Ingredients

- Stonefire thin artisan pizza crust, 2 pack
- ½ lb provolone, Boar's head
- Fresh mozzarella, ball, log or pearls
- Fresh Basil
- Meat of choice:
- Boars Head sopressata, pepperoni cups, salami, Italian sausage

Sauce

- 1 can San Marzano tomatoes (San Marzano tomato of Agro Sarnese-Nocerino D.O.P. Preferred) or substitute good quality crushed tomatoes
- 2 tbsp Extra Virgin olive oil
- 3 garlic cloves, smashed & chopped
- 1 tsp oregano
- 4 basil leaves, torn
- Salt

Garlic oil

- 4 tbsp extra virgin olive oil
- 2-3 large cloves fresh garlic, minced
- ½ tsp dried basil
- ½ tsp dried oregano
- ½ tsp dried parsley
- 1 tsp crushed red pepper (optional)

Instruction

- Toss tomatoes with a few spoonfuls of excess juice in a mixing dish. Slightly crush tomatoes with your hands. Combine the oil, torn basil, oregano, garlic, and salt to taste in a mixing bowl. The sauce is now ready to use. Because the pizza will be griddled, the sauce can be prepared in a small saucepan immediately on the Blackstone griddle for even heating a few minutes before the pizza is started. Because this is a griddle top pizza rather than a pizza oven baked pizza, heating the sauce will also help the cheeses melt.
- Add the pizza crust upside down to heat and slightly crisp the top of the pizza crust on medium low heat. Depending on how crisp or soft you prefer your crust to be.To begin cooking and crisping up the bottom, flip and reduce heat to low, giving you time to add seasonings.
- 1 tbsp garlic oil, drizzled around the pizza Provolone cheese should be uniformly distributed across the pie.
- Add the pizza sauce and spread it out with a spoon.

- Spread fresh mozzarella all over the pie. Raise the heat on the griddle to medium and cook until the desired crispness is achieved, checking the bottom regularly. If needed, a dome can be used to keep the mozzarella from melting too soon once it is placed on top of the warm pizza sauce.
- Remove the pizza from the oven and top with fresh basil. Optional: drizzle with garlic oil.

Note: If using meat toppings, place them on the heated griddle surface during step 2 to cook. On the griddle, pepperoni cups, sopressata, and other deli meats will crisp up to perfection. If you're using sausage or vegetables as toppings, fry them first on the griddle before moving on to step 2.

On the Blackstone griddle, the stonefire crust holds up nicely and produces for a superb crispy real Italian pizza.

Betty Springs Chicken

cooking time: 25 minutes

Servings: 2

Ingredients

- 2 Chicken Breast
- ½ c Mayonnaise, Dukes preferred
- 4 slices Bacon
- 1-2 Portobello Mushrooms, sliced
- 4 oz Cheddar Cheese, shredded
- 4 tbsp Dijon Mustard
- 2 tbsp + 2 tsp Blackstone Seasoning, Whiskey Burger
- 2 tbsp Butter, unsalted
- dried Parsley, garnish

Instruction

1. Trim the chicken breasts and lightly pound the thicker end with the palm of your hand to thin it out and make it even all around. Cooking time will be reduced and even cooking will be achieved by using a thinner chicken breast.
2. Mix up mayo with 2 tbsp Blackstone Seasoning (Whiskey Burger or Chicken and Herb are faves for this meal), then coat chicken breasts in the mayo mixture using a bowl or a food storage bag to coat evenly.
3. Cook the bacon on one side of your Blackstone griddle over low heat. Place on paper towels to absorb excess liquid until ready to use.
4. Meanwhile, warm 2 tbsp butter on the other side over medium heat and stir mushrooms in butter. 2 tablespoons Blackstone seasoning Tossing the mushrooms to ensure consistent cooking. To add flavor, slide mushrooms into part of the bacon fat. Remove from heat when done, or set aside on low-off heat.
5. Cook the chicken breasts for 4-5 minutes over medium heat, or until golden brown.

6. Spread 1 tbsp Dijon mustard over each chicken breast before flipping. Cooked mushrooms, bacon, and a handful of freshly grated cheddar cheese are sprinkled on top.
7. Allow 4-5 minutes for the dome to cook through and melt the cheese.
8. Remove the chicken from the pan and place it on a platter with dried parsley. Enjoy with Air Fryer French Fries from Blackstone.

Notes: When chicken is coated in mayonnaise, no oil or butter is required, resulting in juicy, moist chicken with a gorgeous golden brown hue.

When trimming chicken breasts for presentation, preserve the trimmings and dip them in mayo and spice to make chicken "nuggets" for picky youngsters or to toss in a salad for lunch the next day.

Salmon Street Taco

cooking time: 25 minutes

Servings: 4

Ingredients

- 4-6 oz Salmon filets, diced large cubes
- 1 tbsp Wok oil
- 1 tbsp Sesame oil
- 1 tbsp Sesame seeds
- 12 Flour Tortillas, street taco size
- 2 Avocados
- Slaw
- 2 c Green Cabbage, sliced thin
- ½ cup Green Onions, sliced
- 1-2 c Cilantro, rough chopped
- 1 juice of Lime plus Zest
- 2 tsp Wok oil
- 2 tsp Sesame oil
- BLACKSTONE Tequila Lime seasoning to taste
- Spicy Mayo Sauce
- 1 c Mayo, Dukes or Kewpie preferred
- ½- ¾ c Sriracha
- 2 tbsp Sesame Oil
- 1.5 tbsp Ponzu sauce
- 2 Garlic cloves, grated

Instruction

Toss the salmon with sesame oil, wok oil, and sesame seeds to coat. While you're making the slaw and sauce, let the meat marinate.

In a large mixing basin, combine the cabbage, cilantro, and green onions. Toss with the wok oil, sesame oil, lime juice, and lime zest. To taste, season with **BLACKSTONE** tequila lime seasoning. Remove from the equation.

To make the spicy mayo, combine all ingredients and adjust the amount of sriracha to taste. Remove from the equation.

Preheat a **BLACKSTONE** griddle to medium-high heat and sear the salmon for 1 minute on each side.Warm the tortillas on medium heat for 1-2 minutes per side while the fish cooks.Place cooked tortillas in the BLACKSTONE taco rack, top with slaw, fish, an avocado slice, and a drizzle of spicy mayo.

Note: If you can't find wok or stir fry oil, gently heat oil of choice (extra light tasting olive oil preferred) in a small saucepan with crushed garlic cloves, spring onions or white onions, and ginger. Remove the garlic, ginger, and onions after cooling and straining. Oil should be kept refrigerated in an airtight container.

Betty's Italian Cutlets

cooking time: 30 minutes

Servings: 5

Ingredients

- 2-3 large boneless skinless Chicken Breast
- 4 Eggs
- 1 ½ cup Parmesan Cheese
- 2 c plain Bread crumbs
- 1 bunch flat leaf Parsley, chopped
- 1 tsp Paprika
- 1 tsp Garlic Powder
- ½ tsp Onion Powder
- Salt & Pepper
- Oil for frying, extra light tasting Olive Oil preferred

- Coarse Sea Salt, optional

Instruction

1. Slice each chicken breast into 4-6 pieces, then flatten each chunk with the flat side of a meat mallet, pulling the mallet towards the outside. Repeat with the remaining chicken breasts. Per chicken breast, you should receive 4-6 cutlets. Place them in a safe place while you set up your dredging station.
2. Arrange two shallow dishes or containers in a line. Add the eggs, a large handful of Parmesan cheese (12 - 34 cup), and a handful of chopped parsley (14 cup) to one of the bowls. Combine the ingredients in a mixing bowl, then add the cutlets to the cheesy eggs. This step can be done ahead of time, and the cutlets in the egg mixture can be stored in the refrigerator for up to overnight or used right away.
3. Add bread crumbs, paprika, garlic, and onion powder to the second shallow bowl. Salt & pepper to taste. Add a handful of cheese and minced parsley to the mix.
4. Remove one cutlet from the egg mixture and set it in the bread crumbs, flipping and spreading the bread crumbs onto the chicken until it is well covered. Carry on with each cutlet in the same manner.
5. Allow the BLACKSTONE to heat to a medium-low temperature. Place a cooling rack next to or on one side of the griddle.

6. Using a BLACKSTONE squirt bottle filled with oil, lightly squirt a tiny quantity of oil onto the cooking area and insert cutlets into the oil a few at a time, adding a small amount of oil before each batch of cutlets. Allow for 3-4 minutes of cooking time, or until golden brown. Add a little spray of oil to the cutlets on the flip side to allow them to shallow fry evenly for another 3-4 minutes. Low and slow cooking to avoid scorching the breadcrumbs.

7. As each cutlet cooks, remove it to a cooling rack and quickly sprinkle it with cheese and/or coarse sea salt. Plate and serve once all of the cutlets have been fried.

Note that :the shape of these old school cutlets will be completely imperfect and the appropriate size to serve alone or in sandwiches. Serve alone or with sandwich fixings on a family-style plate. One of our favorites is Italian rolls with fresh mozzarella, vodka sauce, fresh basil, and roasted peppers.

Betty's Shrimp Fried Rice

cooking time: 40 minutes

Servings: 4

Ingredients

- 4 cup White Rice
- 1 lb Shrimp, wild caught
- 3-4 Eggs
- 1 cup fresh Snow Peas, cut into thirds
- 1 large Onion, chopped (white or yellow)
- 3 Garlic cloves, minced
- 1 bunch Green Onions, sliced separated green/whites
- Wok or stir fry oil
- 2 tbsp Butter, unsalted
- Low Sodium Soy Sauce
- 1 tbsp Rice Wine Vinegar (toasted sesame)
- Sesame Oil
- Toasted Sesame Seeds
- Spicy Mayo Sauce:
- ½ cup Mayo, Kewpie preferred
- ¼-½ cup Sriracha (depending on level of heat)
- 1.5 tbsp Sesame Oil

Instruction

1 tsp each low sodium and regular soy sauce, cooked rice (preferably in a rice cooker). To cook the rice, spread it out on a baking sheet and set it in the fridge uncovered overnight or for at least 4 hours to dry out.

Add a drizzle of wok oil (approximately 1 tbsp) to a medium to medium high heat and spread evenly over the Blackstone before adding the eggs. Break the yolks and lightly scramble the eggs for 1 minute, then set them aside on low to no heat.

Add another drop of wok oil and sauté the chopped onions, snow peas, garlic, and sliced white onions for 3-4 minutes, turning the veggies continually with two spatulas.Then, with the eggs, transfer the vegetables to the low or off side.

Add 1 tbsp butter and a drizzle of wok oil to melt together before adding the prawns. Cooking by tossing. If the shrimp are large, cut them into bite-sized pieces while they cook, which should take around 3-4 minutes. They can also be slid to the side.

Add the rice to a wok with some wok oil and 1 tbsp butter. Toss rice with a scraper and spatula to coat in oil and butter, breaking up any clumps.

Betty's Ricotta Donuts

cooking time: 20 minutes

Servings: 4

Ingredients

- 1 C whole milk ricotta cheese
- 1 large egg
- 1 tbsp white rum
- Zest of ½ - 1 whole lemon
- 1 C all purpose flour
- 2 tbsp white sugar

- 2 tsp baking powder
- Canola or Vegetable oil for frying
- Sturdy pan for deep frying
- Powdered Sugar

Instruction

Turn the Blackstone to high and heat a small robust pan with your preferred oil.

Combine the ricotta, egg, rum, and lemon zest in a large mixing basin.

Combine flour, sugar, and baking powder in a separate basin.

Slowly add the dry ingredients to the wet ingredients, a quarter cup at a time, and stir to blend. It's best if the dough is thick and sticky.

Carefully dip a wooden chopstick or toothpick into the oil; if bubbles emerge around the wooden stick, the oil is ready to fry (or use a thermometer oil should be perfect between 350-375 degrees)

Drop a dough ball into the oil slowly with two spoons. Allow to fry for 3-5 minutes, or until deep golden brown in color. If the donuts do not turn over on their own, gently flip them to ensure even cooking.

Drain on paper towels after removing from the oil.

Dust with powdered sugar before serving.

The size of the donuts should be comparable to that of a ping pong ball. The number of donuts (servings) will be determined by the doughnut size.

SweetBabyTots

cooking time: 20 minutes

Servings: 10

Ingredients

- 20 Frozen Tator-Tots
- 10 slices bacon, thin cut
- 20 slices pickled jalapeno
- 1/4 c Sweet Baby Rays BBQ Sauce
- 20 toothpick

Instruction

1. Preheat the Blackstone Airfryers to 425 degrees or high heat.
2. Place frozen tator-tots in a plate on the counter for 5 minutes to slightly defrost, just long enough for a toothpick to glide through them.
3. Bacon pieces should be cut in half.
4. Place a jalapeño slice on top of the bacon, then a tomato top, and wrap in bacon. Using a toothpick, secure the bacon.
5. Brush bacon with Sweet Baby Rays BBQ sauce of your choice.
6. Place tator-tots equally spaced in the preheated Blackstone Airfryer drawer. Cook for 8 to 10 minutes. To ensure consistent cooking, check tots halfway through, lightly shake them, or flip them.
7. Serve with extra barbecue sauce on the side for dipping.
8. Enjoy!

Bettys Buffalo Chicken Cheesesteaks

cooking time: 20 minutes

Servings: 2

Ingredients

- 2 large Chicken Breast
- 1/2 c Wing Sauce, Sweet Baby Rays Mild preferred
- 1/4 cup Ranch Dressing
- 1 tsp Garlic Powder
- 1 tsp Dried Parsley
- Salt and Pepper to taste
- 1 tbsp Oil
- 1/4 lb good quality deli thin sliced American Cheese, Cooper sharp preferred
- 2 foot long Italian Hoagie rolls

Instruction

1. Prepare raw chicken by chopping it into small pieces. This can be prepared ahead of time and kept refrigerated until ready to use.
2. Preheat the Blackstone griddle to a medium-high temperature. Drizzle some oil on top. Cook for 3-4 minutes, or until chicken is cooked through, tossing occasionally.
3. Reduce the heat to medium. Add salt, pepper, garlic, and parsley to taste.
4. Stir in the hot sauce and toss to evenly coat, adding more if necessary.
5. In a mixing bowl, combine the ranch and blue cheese dressings.
6. About 6 slices of cheese should be added, and the cheese should be melted throughout the chicken.
7. Reduce the heat to a medium low setting. Divide the chicken into two heaps, add a few more pieces of cheese to each pile, and bake the rolls for 30-60 seconds on top of the cheese.
8. Place one hand on top of the roll and use the other to turn the sandwich with a long Blackstone spatula.
9. Place on a plate and enjoy!

Korean Fire Chicken Lettuce Wraps

cooking time: 30 minutes

Servings: 4

Ingredients

- 2 LBS Chicken Thighs, boneless skinless
- 1 head Butter Lettuce
- 2 cups Mayonnaise
- 1 tbsp Rice Wine Vinegar
- 2 tbsp Sesame Oil
- 1/2+ c Blackstone Korean Fire Sear and Serve Sauce
- Green Onions, sliced and divided
- toasted Sesame Seeds
- 2 tbsp seasoned wok or stir-fry oil

Instruction

1. Whisk together mayonnaise, rice wine vinegar, sesame oil, and Blackstone Korean Fire Sear and Serve Sauce in a mixing bowl. Depending on how hot you like it, use more or less Korean Fire Sauce.
2. Green onions should be sliced with the white and green ends separated.
3. Raw chicken breast should be diced into little bite-size pieces.
4. Toss the chicken in 2 tbsp seasoned wok oil to evenly coat it.

5. Preheat the Blackstone to medium-high heat and place the chicken in a single layer on the grill to cook. Cook until the chicken is golden brown, tossing every couple of minutes.
6. Reduce the heat to medium-low and coat the chicken with about half of the sauce. Allow 2 minutes to cook after tossing. Toss in the white ends of the green onions for the last minute of cooking.
7. Remove the chicken and top with sesame seeds, green onions that have been set aside, and a dab of Korean Sweet Fire Sauce.
8. Fill lettuce leaves with chicken, more sauce, sesame seeds, and green onions.

Enjoy!

Notes:

Wok oil, also known as stir-fry oil, is flavored with ginger, garlic, onion, and herbs and used for high-heat cooking. You can use whichever oil you choose and season lightly with dried or fresh ginger, as well as garlic and onion powder.

Betty's Bite Sized Chinese Meatballs

cooking time: 30 minutes

Servings: 6

Ingredients

- 1 lb Ground Pork
- 1.5 tbsp Cornstarch
- 1 tsp fresh Ginger, grated
- 3-4 Garlic Cloves, grated
- 3 tsp Brown Sugar
- 3 tsp Soy Sauce
- 1 tsp Five Spice
- 5 Green Onions, sliced (3 for the mixture and 2 for a garnish)
- Stir Fry Oil or Olive oil for cooking
- Sesame Seeds for garnish

Dipping Sauce

- 1/4 c Honey
- 1/2 c low sodium Soy Sauce

Instruction

1. Combine the first 8 ingredients in a mixing bowl with a spoon. Roll in little bite-size meatballs (leave around 2 stalks of green onion on the side for garnish). This recipe serves approximately 24 people.
2. Cook meatballs on each side until browned in olive oil on a Blackstone

Griddle over medium heat. 5 minutes per side, adding extra oil as needed when rolling onto each side to fry.

3. To assist the meatballs finish cooking, use the Blackstone dome near the end.
4. Serve with dipping sauce and garnished with sliced green onions and sesame seeds!

Enjoy!

Garlicky Sesame Teriyaki Yaki Soba Noodles

cooking time: 20 minutes

Servings: 4

Ingredients

- 1 lb Ground Beef
- 1 17.75 oz pack refrigerated Yaki Soba Noodles
- ½-1 c Blackstone Sesame Teriyaki Sear & Serve
- 1 bunch or 1 c Green Onions, sliced and divided
- 5 Garlic Cloves, chopped
- 2 tbsp + 1 tsp seasoned Wok Oil or Stir Fry Oil
- 2 tbsp Sesame Seeds

Instruction

Green onions should be sliced into quarters, with the whites and some green reserved for frying and the rest for garnishing.

Prepare yaki soba noodles according to package directions by either microwaving to warm and separate them or running them under warm water and tossing them with a light drizzle of 1 tsp wok oil, then setting them aside.

1 tbsp wok oil, drizzled over medium-high to high heat, then ground beef to cook. Chop the meat with a spatula or scraper until it is cooked through.

Form an open space in the center of the ground beef pile and pour in 1 tbsp wok oil, followed by the garlic and green onions, including the whites of the onions, and cook for 30-60 seconds.In a large mixing bowl, combine the garlic and onions with the ground meat.

Toss together the prepared yaki soba noodles with two spatulas.

Reduce heat to medium to medium low and stir in the Blackstone Sesame Teriyaki Sear and Serve sauce to coat evenly.

Remove from the pan, place on a platter, and top with sesame seeds and green onions.

Enjoy!

Notes:

Use any vegetables you choose and/or substitute pork, chicken, or seafood for the beef!

Seasoned wok oil or stir fry oil is flavored with sesame, ginger, garlic, and onion, and is designed for high-heat cooking. Look for Tsang or Sun Luck brands.

Betty's Burrata Sandwiches

cooking time: 30 minutes

Servings: 6

Ingredients

- 4 slices Panini bread, Sourdough or Italian
- 1 container Burrata, BelGioioso 4-2 oz "minis"
- 4 slices Provolone Cheese
- 4 slices Prosciutto
- 4 slices Soppressata or Genoa Salami
- 4 slices Capicola
- roasted Red Peppers, Cento
- Arugula
- 2 tbsp Mayonnaise, Dukes preferred
- Blackstone Parmesan Ranch seasoning

Instruction

1. Remove the burrata from the container and blot it dry with paper towels before storing it.
2. Preheat the Blackstone griddle on low.
3. Combine mayonnaise and 1 tablespoon Blackstone Parmesan Ranch seasoning in a small mixing bowl. Spread the mayo mixture on one side of each slice of bread and place it on the Blackstone with the mayo side down.
4. Top each slice of bread with provolone cheese. Between the sandwiches, evenly layer Italian meats. Add a handful of arugula and as much roasted peppers as you want.
5. Top each sandwich with two burrata minis and a little dusting of Blackstone Parmesan Ranch spice.
6. Sandwich the two pieces of bread together and place on a cutting board when the crust is golden brown. The sandwich should be cut in half.
   Enjoy!

Notes: Make sure to put the provolone on each slice of bread first; the melted cheese will keep your sandwich together.

Burrata cheese is a popular topping for pizza, salads, and pasta meals.

Betty's THYME Wings

cooking time: 30 minutes

Servings: 3

Ingredients

- 2 lb fresh chicken wings (about 10)
- ¼ cup Extra light tasting olive oil
- 2 tbsp thyme, dried
- 2 tsp coarse salt
- 1 tsp black pepper
- 2 tsp garlic powder
- 2 tsp onion powder

Instruction

- Wings, drums, and drumettes should all be cut into parts.
- Pat wings dry using paper towels and place them between paper towels on a baking sheet. Refrigerate uncovered overnight.
- Remove the wings from the fridge and coat them in extra light olive oil. Toss the wings with salt, pepper, garlic, onion powder, and thyme to evenly cover them.
- Allow 30-60 minutes for wings to sit at room temperature in a mixing dish on the kitchen counter before cooking.
- Add wings to a Blackstone griddle that has been preheated to medium-low heat. To ensure that the wings are cooked through, turn them every few minutes. It should take about 15-20 minutes to cook the wings.
- Increase the heat to high near the end to crisp the skin to your taste. **Enjoy**

If you have a Blackstone Airfryer, you may cook them in the air fryer for about 15 minutes on high, split between the two airfryer drawers. Toss the baskets a few times while they're cooking. In the Airfryer, reheat leftover wings!

Savory Candied Sweet Potatoes

cooking time: 10 minutes

Servings: 6

Ingredients

- 3-4 large sweet potatoes, diced small
- 1 lb savory sage ground sausage, bob evans
- 2 tbsp oil
- 4-5 tbsp butter, unsalted
- 1-1.5 c brown sugar
- Salt & pepper
- Dried parsley

Instruction

1. Place sweet potatoes in a large mixing basin and dice them into small pieces. Season with salt and pepper and toss to lightly coat with oil.
2. Preheat the Blackstone to medium-low heat. Simmer the sausage and crumble on one side while the potatoes cook on the other. Cooking time is faster if the dice are smaller. When the potatoes are soft, combine them with the cooked sausage.
3. Reduce the heat on Blackstone to the lowest level. In the center of the sausage and potato mixture, make a well. Melt the butter in the center, then add the brown sugar and mix it in somewhat with the butter before tossing everything together to coat evenly. Add a little sprinkle of parsley and cook for another 1-2 minutes.
4. If wanted, top with extra parsley on the plate.Depending on the amount of potatoes used, butter and brown sugar measurements may vary.

Jambalaya

cooking time: 35 minutes

Servings: 8

Ingredients

- 4 8.8 oz packages Ready Rice
- 13-16 oz andouille sausage, diced
- 1-1.5 lb boneless chicken thighs, diced
- 1 lb shrimp, optional
- 1 large yellow onion, diced
- 1 c each red, green, yellow, poblano peppers, diced
- 2-3 celery stalks, diced
- 3 garlic cloves, chopped
- 1-2 tbsp creole seasoning or Blackstone cajun seasoning
- 1 bunch green onions, chopped divided in half
- 24 oz tomato sauce
- Olive oil
- Sour cream, optional

Instruction

If using prepackaged rice packages, knead packaging to loosen rice and place in a bowl if using leftover cold white rice. Remove from the equation.

Preheat the Blackstone on one side to medium heat. Drizzle 1-2 tbsp olive oil, then add the celery and yellow onions and sauté for 3-4 minutes before adding the peppers and cooking for another 2-3 minutes. Preheat the Blackstone to medium high on the opposite side, drizzle with 1 tbsp olive oil, and add the chicken to fry for 4 minutes. Cook for 3 minutes after adding the sausage and shrimp. Lightly season everything with creole or cajun seasoning.!

Turn all of the burners to medium or medium low and combine the vegetables and meat in a large mixing bowl. Toss in the rice and mix well.

Toss in the tomato sauce.

Toss in the garlic and half of the green onions. Combine the remainder of your seasonings and season to taste. If desired, season with salt and pepper.

Place on a plate and serve! The leftovers are much better!

Ricotta Lemon Griddle Cakes

cooking time: 20 minutes

Servings: 4

Ingredients

Dry Ingredients:

- 1 cup all purpose flour
- 1 tbsp baking powder
- 1 tbsp baking soda
- 2 tbsp sugar
- ¼ tsp salt

Wet Ingredients:

- 1 ¼ cup whole milk ricotta
- 2 eggs
- ⅔ cup milk
- Juice from one large lemon

- 1 ½ tsp pure vanilla extract
- Butter for cooking
- Zest from one large lemon

Instruction

Combine the wet ingredients in one mixing bowl and the dry ingredients in the other. Combine the wet ingredients in a mixing bowl.

To blend the dry and wet ingredients, add them slowly to the wet mixing bowl. Allow to sit for 10 minutes or until the Blackstone reaches medium heat.

Using a 14 cup measuring cup per pancake, swirl butter to melt where the pancakes will be cooked.

Cook for 2 minutes per side, flipping once, or until bubbles emerge.

Enjoy!

Buttermilk Bathed Rosemary Chicken Thighs

4 serv

Ingredients:

- 8 chicken thighs with bone and skin
- 2 tablespoons kosher salt
- 1 pint buttermilk

- 1 oz fresh rosemary or about 8 sprigs

Instructions:

1. Using paper towels, pat the chicken thighs dry. Place the thigh in a zipper top bag and season both sides with kosher salt.
2. Remove the rosemary stems and add them to the chicken.
3. Allow 2 hours for the chicken to rest in the refrigerator.
4. Allow the chicken to marinate in the brine overnight after adding the buttermilk.
5. Allow as much of the buttermilk mixture to drain away from the chicken as possible in a strainer.
6. Preheat the air fryer to 375 degrees Fahrenheit.
7. Cook the chicken thighs in batches, 4 in each fry basket. Cook for 35 minutes, turning every 10 minutes, or until the skin is crispy and the flesh reaches a safe internal temperature of 165F.

Sausage and Sage Thanksgiving Stuffing

8 serv.

35 min.

Ingredients:

- About 2 loaves high quality sandwich bread or soft Italian or French bread, cut into 3/4-inch dice, about 5 quarts
- 4 TBLS butter
- 1 pound sage sausage
- 1 onion, finely chopped
- Celery, finely chopped
- 2 cloves garlic
- 2 teaspoons dried sage
- 2 cups chicken stock
- Finely chopped parsley leaves
- Salt and pepper to taste

Instructions:

1. Brown the sausage and set it aside ahead of time.
2. Bread should be cut into 34-inch pieces. In a griddle, melt the butter and add the onions, garlic, and celery.
3. Cook until they begin to soften. Combine all of the bread ingredients in a large mixing bowl.

4. Add approximately 12 cup of chicken stock at a time until it's completely absorbed. Cook until the bread begins to become golden brown.
5. Season with salt and pepper to taste and add the sausage and sage.
6. Finish with a dusting of fresh parsley.
7. Enjoy!

Butter Bathed Filet and Lobster Surf & Turf

Ingredients:

- 4, 6-8 oz. Filet Mignon
- 4 Lobster Tails
- 2 stick of Unsalted Butter
- A few sprigs of Fresh Rosemary
- A few sprigs of Fresh Thyme
- 2 cloves Fresh Garlic, rough chop
- 1 Lemon
- A handful of Asparagus
- 2 pints Mushrooms
- Blackstone Steakhouse Seasoning
- Olive Oil

Instructions:

1. Heat the Blackstone Air Fryer to medium-high temperature.
2. Cut the top of the lobster's shell through the middle all the way to the tail with shears, leaving the final rib attached. Squeeze the bottom portion of the shell until it breaks and releases. Pull the lobster meat out and over the top of the cut shell while keeping the meat linked at the end of the tail. Make small slashes on the surface of the lobster meat with a sharp knife to form a "cross hatch" pattern.
3. Add a small sauce pot to one side of your griddle and heat to medium. Melt the butter with the herbs and garlic.
4. Add a dab of olive oil to the opposite side of your griddle and heat it to high.
5. Season your steaks well on both sides with Blackstone Steakhouse spice and grill for 2-3 minutes per side over high heat.
6. Season the tops of each lobster tail with Blackstone Steakhouse Seasoning and a little of the melted butter. Cook for around 6-7 minutes in the Air Fryer.
7. Submerge the steaks in the herb butter once they've been cooked on both sides. Return to the griddle for another minute each side after coating both sides. Remove the pancakes from the griddle and set them aside to cool for a few minutes.
8. Sprinkle a couple shakes of Blackstone Steakhouse seasoning over the asparagus and mushrooms on the griddle. Cook for 4-5 minutes after adding a little of the herb butter.

9. Place the steak on one side of the platter and the lobster tail on the other. Place the veggies in the centre and brush the steak and lobster with a little extra butter.
10. Enjoy!

Steak Frites 2-Ways

4 serv.

20 min.

Ingredients:

- 4 NY Strip steaks
- 1 bag frozen French fries
- Salt and pepper
- Olive oil

CHIMI-STYLE SAUCE:

- 1 bunch flat leaf parsley
- 1 bunch cilantro
- The juice of 2 limes
- 2 teaspoons minced garlic
- 1 teaspoon red pepper flakes
- Olive oil
- Salt and pepper

MUSTARD CREAM SAUCE:

- 1 shallot, minced
- 2 garlic cloves minced
- A few sprigs fresh thyme
- 3 tablespoons Dijon mustard

- 2 tablespoons capers
- ¼ cup heavy cream
- Olive oil
- Salt and pepper

Instructions:

1. Heat the griddle to a medium-high temperature.
2. Heat the Air Fryer to medium-high heat before adding the frozen fries and cooking for 7-10 minutes.
3. On both sides, season the steaks with salt and pepper. Using a sprinkle of olive oil, brown the steaks for 3-4 minutes per side on the griddle.
4. Add a drizzle of olive oil, shallots, garlic, and fresh thyme to a sauté pan on the griddle top. Cook for a couple of minutes, stirring often. With a touch of salt and pepper, combine the mustard, capers, and cream. To incorporate everything, give it a good stir.
5. Blend all of the "Chimi-Style" ingredients in a mixing bowl and stir to combine evenly.
6. Add some of the fries to the serving platter once the steaks are cooked to your preferred doneness, and then top with the steak. Serve immediately, garnished with one or both sauces.
7. Enjoy!

Pomegranate Soy Glazed Lamb Chops

6 serv.

20 min.

Ingredients:

- 12 Lamb Chops
- 3 cups Pomegranate Juice
- 1 cup Soy Sauce
- 2 bunches of Green Onion, cleaned and trimmed
- ½ large Red Onion, thinly sliced
- 2 cups Arugula
- 2 cups Spring Mix Lettuce
- ¼ cup Pomegranate Arils
- 2 Oranges
- Salt & Pepper
- Olive Oil

Instructions:

1. Preheat the griddle to medium-high temperature.
2. Add the pomegranate juice and soy to a large sauté pan over an open flame. Bring to a boil over high heat for 8-10 minutes. Reduce by 75% or until it resembles maple syrup in consistency. Turn off the heat and set aside to cool somewhat. (when it cools, it will thicken a little more)
3. On all sides, season the lamb chops with olive oil and salt and pepper.
4. Cook the lamb chops for 2-3 minutes each side on the griddle with a little olive oil, then finish fat side down for an extra 2 minutes.
5. Add the green onions and softly caramelize for the last 4-5 minutes of cooking.
6. Add the arugula, spring mix, red onion, and pomegranate arils to a large mixing bowl with a touch of salt and pepper. Remove the skin and pith from the oranges before cutting them into supremes and adding them to the bowl. Remove the orange and squeeze the leftover orange juice over the greens. Toss the salad with a sprinkle of olive oil to evenly coat it.
7. To plate, place some of the salad on the platter, followed by a few green onions. Drizzle the pomegranate soy reduction sauce over 3 lamb chops.
8. Enjoy!

Tamari Ponzu Salmon with Sweet Chili Broccoli and Potato Crisps

4 serv.

25 min.

Ingredients:

- 4, 6-8 oz skinless Salmon Filets
- 2 Large Russet Potatoes, cut into ¼ inch chips
- 12 oz Broccoli florets
- ½ tablespoon Ground Ginger
- ½ tablespoon Garlic Powder
- ¼ cup Tamari
- 3 tablespoons Ponzu
- 3 tablespoons Honey
- 1 tablespoon Sesame Oil
- ¼ cup sweet Thai Chili Sauce
- ¼ cup thinly sliced Green Onion
- 1 tablespoon toasted Sesame Seeds
- Salt and pepper
- Olive oil

Instructions:

1. Preheat the griddle to medium-high temperature.
2. Salt and pepper the cut potatoes, as well as a pinch of garlic powder.
3. Toss the sliced potatoes on the griddle with a sprinkle of olive oil. Cook for another 2-3 minutes before flipping.
4. Using a small drizzle of olive oil, ground ginger, garlic powder, and a pinch of salt and pepper, season the salmon on both sides. Then add the hot griddle to the mix. Cook for 3-4 minutes per side, or until done to your liking.
5. With a touch of salt and pepper, toss in a little oil and the broccoli. If preferred, steam the broccoli for 4-5 minutes with a splash of water and a dome.
6. Combine the tamari, ponzu, honey, and sesame oil in a small mixing dish. 12 of the liquid should be poured over the fish during the last minute of cooking. If additional glaze is wanted, repeat the process.
7. Toss the broccoli with the sweet Thai chili sauce to combine.
8. To serve, arrange the potatoes in a fan arrangement on the plate, then top with the broccoli. Place the salmon on top and sprinkle with sesame seeds and chopped green onion.
9. Mix a little of the sweet Thai chili sauce with the remaining tamari mix and sprinkle over the top of the fish for an extra sauce.

Betty's Shrimp Fried Rice

4 serv.

40 min.

Ingredients:

- 4 cup White Rice
- 1 lb Shrimp, wild caught
- 3-4 Eggs
- 1 cup fresh Snow Peas, cut into thirds
- 1 large Onion, chopped (white or yellow)

- 3 Garlic cloves, minced
- 1 bunch Green Onions, sliced separated green/whites
- Wok or stir fry oil
- 2 tbsp Butter, unsalted
- Low Sodium Soy Sauce
- 1 tbsp Rice Wine Vinegar (toasted sesame)
- Sesame Oil
- Toasted Sesame Seeds

SPICY MAYO SAUCE:

- ½ cup Mayo, Kewpie preferred
- ¼-½ cup Sriracha (depending on level of heat)
- 1.5 tbsp Sesame Oil

Instructions:

1. 1 tsp each reduced sodium and normal soy sauce, cooked rice (preferably in a rice cooker). To cook the rice, spread it out on a baking sheet and set it in the fridge uncovered overnight or for at least 4 hours to dry out.
2. Add a drizzle of wok oil (approximately 1 tbsp) to a medium to medium high heat and spread evenly over the Blackstone before adding the eggs. Break the yolks and softly scramble the eggs for 1 minute, then set them aside on low to no heat.
3. Add another drop of wok oil and sauté the chopped onions, snow peas, garlic, and sliced white onions for 3-4 minutes, turning the veggies continually with two spatulas. Then,

with the eggs, transfer the veggies to the low or off side.
4. Add 1 tbsp butter and a drizzle of wok oil to melt together before adding the prawns. Cooking by tossing. If the shrimp are large, chop them into bite-sized pieces as they cook, which should take around 3-4 minutes. They may also be slid to the side.
5. Add the rice to a pan with some wok oil and 1 tbsp butter. Toss rice with a scraper and spatula to coat with oil and butter, breaking up any clumps.

Sesame Seared Ahi Tuna

6 serv.

1 Hour min.

Ingredients:

- Sushi grade Ahi Tuna
- Sesame Seeds
- Sesame Oil

TUNA MARINADE:

- ¼ cup Soy Sauce
- 2 tbs Rice Vinegar
- 1 tbsp minced Garlic
- 1 tsp Sesame Oil
- 1 tbsp Brown Sugar
- 1 tsp Ground Ginger

- 2 tbsp Green Onion
- Juice from 1 Lime

DIPPING SAUCE:

- 1 tbsp Brown Sugar
- 1 tbsp minced Garlic
- 1 tbsp Soy Sauce
- 1 tbsp Rice Vinegar
- 1 tsp Sesame Oil
- 1 tbsp Green Onions

CUCUMBER/CARROT SLAW:

- Spiralize 2 Carrots and 1 Cucumber
- 1 tbsp Hoisin Sauce
- ¼ cup Orange Juice
- 1 tbsp Soy Sauce
- 1 tsp Sesame Oil
- 1 tsp Ground Ginger
- 1 tsp Sesame Seeds

Instructions:

1. To make the marinade, combine all of the ingredients. Place the tuna steaks in the marinade, cover, and let aside for 1 hour.
2. Spiralize cucumbers and carrots, then drizzle with dressing. Refrigerate for at least an hour.
3. Set aside all of the ingredients for the dipping sauce.
4. Preheat the griddle to high. Allow to become extremely heated, then sprinkle with sesame oil.
5. On a dish, pour 12 cup sesame seeds. Dip the ahi tuna into the seeds, evenly covering it.
6. Cook for 4 minutes on each side on a blistering hot griddle.

7. Remove the griddle from the heat and slice thinly.
8. Arrange slaw on a platter, top with seared tuna, and serve with dipping sauce on the side.

Crab Cakes with Grapefruit Salad

4 serv.

15 min.

Ingredients:

- ½ lb Jumbo Lump Crab Meat
- ½ lb Lump Crab Meat
- ½ cup Panko breadcrumbs
- 1/3 cup Mayonnaise
- 3 tablespoons Dijon Mustard
- 2 Eggs
- 1 tablespoon Worcestershire Sauce
- 1 tablespoon Hot Sauce
- 2 tablespoons Lemon Juice
- 4 cups Spring Greens
- The juice of half of a Grapefruit
- The juice of half of a Lemon
- 2-3 tablespoons finely chopped Flat Leaf Parsley
- Salt and Pepper
- Olive Oil

Instructions:

1. Combine the mayonnaise, Dijon mustard, eggs, Worcestershire

sauce, spicy sauce, panko, lemon juice, and a bit of salt and pepper in a large mixing bowl. To ensure that all of the ingredients are uniformly distributed, whisk them together.

2. Lightly mix in the crab meat to ensure that it is equally distributed.

3. Add a drizzle of olive oil to your griddle and heat it to medium.

4. Form the crab mixture into cakes and fry for 2-3 minutes each side in the oil, or until golden brown and thoroughly cooked.

5. Combine the spring greens, grapefruit juice, lemon juice, a drizzle of olive oil, and a sprinkling of salt and pepper in a large mixing basin. Toss the salad gently to coat it evenly.

6. To dish, start with a small portion of the salad, then top with the crab cakes. Serve immediately, garnished with parsley and a sprinkle of spicy sauce.

Betty's Italian Cutlets

5 serv.

30 min.

Ingredients:

- 2-3 large boneless skinless Chicken Breast
- 4 Eggs
- 1 ½ cup Parmesan Cheese
- 2 c plain Bread crumbs
- 1 bunch flat leaf Parsley, chopped
- 1 tsp Paprika
- 1 tsp Garlic Powder
- ½ tsp Onion Powder
- Salt & Pepper
- Oil for frying, extra light tasting Olive Oil preferred
- Coarse Sea Salt, optional

Instructions:

1. Slice each chicken breast into 4-6 pieces, then flatten each chunk with the flat side of a meat mallet, pushing the mallet towards the exterior. Repeat with the remaining chicken breasts. Per chicken breast, you should receive 4-6 cutlets. Place them in a safe place while you set up your dredging station.

2. Arrange two shallow dishes or containers in a line. Add the eggs, a large handful of Parmesan cheese (12 - 34 cup), and a handful of chopped parsley (14 cup) to one of the bowls. Combine the ingredients in a mixing bowl, then add the cutlets to the cheesy eggs. This step may be done ahead of time, and the cutlets in the egg mixture can be stored in the refrigerator for up to overnight or used right away.

3. Bread crumbs, paprika, garlic, and onion powder go into the second shallow bowl. Salt & pepper to taste. Add a handful of cheese and minced parsley to the mix.

4. Remove one cutlet from the egg mixture and set it in the bread crumbs, turning and spreading the bread crumbs onto the chicken until it is well covered. Carry on with each cutlet in the same manner.

5. Allow the BLACKSTONE to heat to a medium-low temperature. Place a cooling rack next to or on one side of the griddle.

6. Using a BLACKSTONE squirt bottle filled with oil, softly spritz a tiny quantity of oil onto the cooking area and insert cutlets into the oil a few at a time, adding a small amount of oil before each batch of cutlets. Allow for 3-4 minutes of cooking time, or until golden brown. Add a little spray of oil to the cutlets on the flip side to allow them to shallow fry evenly for another 3-4 minutes. Low and slow cooking to avoid scorching the breadcrumbs.

7. As each cutlet cooks, remove it to a cooling rack and quickly sprinkle it with cheese and/or coarse sea salt. Plate and serve after all of the cutlets have been fried.

Seared Scallop Caprese

4 serv.

15 min.

Ingredients:

- 12 large Scallops
- 1 large Beef Steak or Heirloom Tomato
- 4 thick slices fresh Mozzarella
- A few tablespoons Balsamic glaze
- Olive oil
- Salt and pepper

TAPENADE:

- ¼ cup Kalamata Olives
- 2 tablespoons Capers
- 2 tablespoon minced Sun-dried Tomatoes
- 2 Garlic cloves
- 4-6 Basil leaves
- 1 teaspoon Lemon zest
- 1 tablespoon Lemon Juice
- Salt and pepper

Instructions:

1. With a touch of salt and pepper, toss the olives, capers, sun-dried tomatoes, garlic, and basil onto your cutting board. Combine all of the components in a finely chopped state. Toss in the lemon zest and lemon juice until equally distributed.
2. Heat your griddle to a high setting.
3. Season the scallops with salt and pepper after patting them dry.
4. Cook the scallops in a little olive oil on your griddle for 1-2 minutes per side, or until brown and caramelized.
5. To plate, place one tomato slice on each plate. Over the tomato, spread

some tapenade and a few tears of fresh mozzarella. Lightly char the cheese with a hand torch before stacking three scallops on top. Serve with an olive oil drizzle, balsamic glaze, and fresh basil on top.

Salmon Street Taco

4 serv.

25 min.

Ingredients:

- 4-6 oz Salmon filets, diced large cubes
- 1 tbsp Wok oil
- 1 tbsp Sesame oil
- 1 tbsp Sesame seeds
- 12 Flour Tortillas, street taco size
- 2 Avocados

SLAW

- 2 c Green Cabbage, sliced thin
- ½ cup Green Onions, sliced
- 1-2 c Cilantro, rough chopped
- 1 juice of Lime plus Zest
- 2 tsp Wok oil
- 2 tsp Sesame oil
- BLACKSTONE Tequila Lime seasoning to taste
- Spicy Mayo Sauce
- 1 c Mayo, Dukes or Kewpie preferred

- ½- ¾ c Sriracha
- 2 tbsp Sesame Oil
- 1.5 tbsp Ponzu sauce
- 2 Garlic cloves, grated

Instructions:

1. Toss the salmon with sesame oil, wok oil, and sesame seeds to coat. While you're making the slaw and sauce, let the meat marinade.
2. In a large mixing basin, combine the cabbage, cilantro, and green onions. Toss with the wok oil, sesame oil, lime juice, and lime zest. To taste, season with BLACKSTONE tequila lime seasoning. Remove from the equation.
3. To make the spicy mayo, combine all ingredients and adjust the amount of sriracha to taste. Remove from the equation.
4. Preheat a BLACKSTONE griddle to medium-high heat and sear the salmon for 1 minute on each side.
5. Warm the tortillas on medium heat for 1-2 minutes each side while the fish cooks. Place cooked tortillas in the BLACKSTONE taco rack, top with slaw, fish, an avocado slice, and a dab of spicy mayo.

Lamb Lollipops with Mint Chimichurri

4 serv.

15 min.

Ingredients:

- 12 Lamb Lollipops
- 2 tablespoons spicy brown Mustard
- 1 bunch Italian flat leaf Parsley
- ½ bunch fresh Mint Leaves
- 1 tablespoon minced Garlic
- The juice of 1 Lemon
- The juice of 2 Limes
- 2 tablespoon Red Wine Vinegar
- 2 teaspoons Red Pepper Flakes
- Olive oil
- Salt and pepper

INSTRUCTIONS:

1. Heat your griddle to a high setting.
2. Combine the parsley and mint in a mixing basin and finely chop. Combine the garlic, lemon and lime juices, red wine vinegar, red pepper flakes, and a sprinkle of salt and pepper in a mixing bowl. Mix in some olive oil to ensure that all of the ingredients are uniformly distributed. Set aside for a later day.
3. With a little olive oil, mustard, and salt and pepper, season the lamb lollipops. Cook for 1-2 minutes per side over high heat, or until caramelized and cooked to your preference.
4. To serve, lay the cooked lamb lollipops on a big family-style tray and drizzle with the mint chimichurri. Serve immediately.

Betty Springs Chicken

2 serv.

25 min.

Ingredients:

- 2 Chicken Breast
- ½ c Mayonnaise, Dukes preferred
- 4 slices Bacon
- 1-2 Portobello Mushrooms, sliced
- 4 oz Cheddar Cheese, shredded
- 4 tbsp Dijon Mustard
- 2 tbsp + 2 tsp Blackstone Seasoning, Whiskey Burger
- 2 tbsp Butter, unsalted
- dried Parsley, garnish

Instructions:

1. Trim the chicken breasts and softly pound the thicker end with the palm of your hand to thin it out and make it even all around. Cooking time will be reduced and even cooking will be

achieved by using a thinner chicken breast.

2. Mix up mayo with 2 tbsp Blackstone Seasoning (Whiskey Burger or Chicken and Herb are faves for this meal), then coat chicken breasts in the mayo mixture using a bowl or a food storage bag to coat evenly.

3. Cook the bacon on one side of your Blackstone griddle over low heat. Place on paper towels to absorb excess liquid until ready to use.

4. Meanwhile, warm 2 tbsp butter on the other side over medium heat and stir mushrooms in butter. 2 tablespoons Blackstone seasoning Tossing the mushrooms to ensure consistent cooking. To add flavor, slide mushrooms into part of the bacon grease. Remove from heat when done, or set aside on low-off heat.

5. Cook the chicken breasts for 4-5 minutes over medium heat, or until golden brown.

6. Spread 1 tbsp Dijon mustard over each chicken breast before flipping. Cooked mushrooms, bacon, and a handful of freshly grated cheddar cheese are sprinkled on top.

7. Allow 4-5 minutes for the dome to cook through and melt the cheese.

8. Remove the chicken from the pan and place it on a platter with dried parsley. Enjoy with Air Fryer French Fries from Blackstone.

Cheesesteak Pasta

4-6 serv.

30 min.

Ingredients

- 1 lb pasta, cooked reserving 1 cup pasta water
- 1 lb ground beef, (sub shaved ribeye or sirloin)
- 2 green bell peppers, diced
- 1 large sweet onion, diced
- mushrooms, sliced
- ¼ lb provolone cheese, deli sliced or grated
- ¼ lb American cheese, deli sliced or grated
- ¼ c worcestershire sauce
- 4 fresh garlic cloves, chopped
- Blackstone Cheese Steak Seasoning
- 1 tbsp oil
- 1 tbsp butter

Instructions:

1. Boil 1 pound of pasta until al dente, then drain, reserving 1 cup of the pasta water.
2. While the pasta is cooking, use your Blackstone to sauté onions, mushrooms, and peppers in oil and butter over medium heat. Cook until the vegetables are soft.
3. Cook your meat until cooked through on a separate heat zone,

cutting ground beef or separating shaved beef.

4. Combine the cooked beef and veggies in a mixing bowl. After combining everything together, add half of the cheese to melt.

5. Toss the noodles with the meat mixture to combine.

6. Season with Blackstone cheese steak seasoning and the leftover cheese and pasta water. Toss everything together and serve!

Feta Pasta with Shrimp

Ingredients

- 1 lb shrimp (substitute protein of choice)
- 8 oz pasta cooked, drained reserve ¾ c pasta water
- 8 oz feta cheese, block
- 2 pints cherry tomatoes
- ½ c extra virgin olive oil
- 4 garlic cloves, smashed and chopped
- Handful each fresh Italian parsley and basil

ITALIAN BLEND SEASONING

- 1 tsp fennel seed
- 1 tsp minced garlic
- 1 ½ tsp minced onion
- 1 tsp basil

- 1 tsp oregano
- 1 tsp parsley flakes
- 1 ½ crushed red pepper flakes
- ½ tsp salt
- ¼ tsp sugar
- ½ tsp pepper
- ½ tsp celery seed

Instructions:

1. To produce an Italian blend, combine the dry ingredients. To store, place in an airtight container.

2. Cook pasta until al dente, then drain and put aside, reserving 12 cup pasta water.

3. Leave the tails on while peeling and butterflying shrimp. Place shrimp on skewers (if desired), sprinkle with olive oil, and season with Italian seasoning.

4. Toss tomatoes with a splash of olive oil and season with Italian blend in a small roasting pan (or create a roasting boat out of tinfoil to fit in the Blackstone airfryer drawer). Place the feta block in the center of the tomatoes, drizzle with the remaining oil, and season the top of the cheese.

5. In a preheated air fryer drawer set to high heat, combine tomatoes and cheese. Allow for 10 minutes of cooking time.

6. Meanwhile, fry the shrimp for 2-3 minutes per side over medium high heat.

7. Examine the tomatoes and the cheese. The tomatoes should burst or split apart, and the cheese should

melt. Cooking time may need to be increased by up to 10 minutes, so check every five minutes.

8. Remove the tomatoes and cheese, add the fresh garlic, and combine the cheese and tomatoes to make your spaghetti sauce. Pour sauce over cooked pasta and add as much or as little pasta water as needed.

9. Toss with some fresh parsley and basil. Serve with shrimp on the side.

Chicken Green Chile Empanadas

2-4 serv.

35 min.

Ingredients

- Chicken Cutlets
- 1/2 Can of Black Beans (Rinsed)
- 1/2 Yellow Onion Diced
- Puff Pastry (1 Sheet)
- 1/2 Can of Rotel
- 1 small can diced Green Chile
- 1 Lime
- 1 Cup Shredded Cheese (Mexican Blend)
- Sliced Pepper Jack Cheese
- 1 Tbs Blackstone Hatch Chile Cheddar Seasoning
- 1 tsp Tequila Lime Blackstone Seasoning
- Salt
- Pepper

- 1 Egg
- Cilantro
- Salsa Verde
- All Purpose flower
- Blackstone Egg Ring
- Blackstone Griddle and Seasoning Spray

Instructions:

1. Set your Blackstone Air-fryer to medium heat. Low, with two burners on low and the other two turned off, and your griddle on top.

2. Place the chicken cutlets on the griddle and drizzle with olive oil. Place the chopped yellow onion next to the chicken. The onions will gently caramelize as you toss them now and again. In addition, your chicken was flipped. Cook the chicken for about 4-5 minutes per side, or until thoroughly done.

3. Add a little all-purpose flower on a cutting board to keep the puff pastry from sticking, then place your puff pastry on top to cut out with your Blackstone egg ring. For smaller empanadas, the egg ring is the appropriate size for cutting out puff pastry. You'll notice that it's you. Puff pastry may be sliced into four pieces as is. You may knead the remaining dough, roll it out, and cut one or two more once you've gotten four cut out.

4. Your cutlets de poulet de poulet de poulet de poulet de poulet de poulet de poulet de Turn off the griddle, remove the chicken, and dice it into tiny bite-size pieces.

Return the diced chicken to the griddle and add the other ingredients. Toss together 1/2 can Rotel, 1 small can chopped green chiles, 1/2 can drained black beans, 1/2 cup shredded Mexican mix cheese, 1 tbsp Blackstone Hatch Chile and cheddar spice, 1 tsp Tequila lime Blackstone Seasoning, a sprinkling of salt and pepper The ingredients will be heated and the cheese will be melted by the remaining heat from your Blackstone. Once it's ready, combine all of the ingredients in a big mixing dish.

5. Let's get started with the empanadas. One egg should be beaten in a small basin. This will be the glue that holds our empanadas together in the air fryer. Place your pastry circles on the same cutting board as before and gently stretch and pull them out. It wasn't much, just enough to make them a little longer. Cut a slice of pepper jack cheese into tiny pieces using a knife. On top of the puff pastry, place one of those pieces of cheese and a little spoonful of the chicken filling (DO NOT OVERFILL) since you don't want the filling to come too close to the edge. Brush a little amount of egg over the edge of the puff pastry, fold the puff pastry over your ingredients, and push the dough along the edge with your fingertips.Grab a fork and run it along the full edge of the pastry once you think it's sealed. This will guarantee that all of your components are completely wrapped within the empanada and make a magnificent display for the finished product.

6. Spray some Blackstone Griddle spray on each tray in your preheated air fryer basket. As well as both sides of your empanada after it's done. Place a couple of them in each basket, leaving enough space between them to cook. Cook for 3-4 minutes with the baskets in place, then remove the baskets and turn the empanadas. Cook for another 3-4 minutes or until golden brown.

7. Remove the empanadas from the air fryer baskets and serve with chopped cilantro and a little sprinkling of Hatch Chile and Cheddar and Tequila Lime Seasonings on top. Serve with a small cup of salsa verde.

Cashew Peppered Beef Lo Mein

3-4 serv.

20 min.

Ingredients

- 1 tbsp minced Garlic
- 1 tbsp minced Ginger

- Green, and Red Bell Peppers
- Green Onion
- 1 tsp Sesame oil
- 1/4 Cup Rice Vinegar
- 1/4 Cup Soy Sauce
- 1/4 Cup Chicken broth
- 1 tbsp Sriracha
- 2 tbsp Sugar
- 1 tbsp Corn starch
- 2 bags of Chow Mein Egg Noodles (pre cooked)
- Crispy Chow Mein Noodles
- Salted Cashews
- Thin Sliced Ribeye Beef

Instructions:

1. Preheat your Blackstone Griddle to high heat before you begin.
2. Mix the sauce ingredients in a mixing basin. 1 tsp Sesame Oil, 1 tbsp Minced Garlic, 1 tbsp Minced Ginger, 1 tbsp Corn Starch, 2 tbsp Sugar, 1/4 cup chicken stock, 1/4 cup rice vinegar, 1 tbsp Sriracha, 1/4 Soy Sauce, 2-3 tbsp Ponzu, 1 tsp Sesame Oil, 1 tbsp Minced Garlic, 1 tb Set this aside once you've combined all of your sauce components.
3. Let's get our Red and Green Bell Peppers chopped up. Make sure the pith and seeds are removed. You may cut them up to any size you like, but a big chop is recommended.
4. It's time to fry our thinly sliced Ribeye on the griddle, which should be smoking hot by now. You may now buy your steak already cut or slice it yourself. If you're going to

slice it yourself, put it in the freezer for about 20 minutes. The beef will get firmer as a result, making it simpler to slice. Also, don't skip the fat; it'll provide a lot of flavor that you won't want to lose out on. Place the steak on the griddle top with 1-2 tablespoons of olive oil. Toss the meat in the olive oil to coat it. We want a rapid sear but don't want to overcook the steak by cooking it too long.

5. While the steak is cooking, place the bell peppers right next to it to finish cooking. Your steak should be moved about at this point to ensure even cooking on all sides. Turn your burners to low and add your bell peppers to the beef along with around 2 tbsp soy sauce after the meat is 90% done. Before we add the rest of the ingredients, this will reduce and coat the steak and bell peppers. It should take around 2 minutes to decrease this to the point where it is ready for the next step.

6. Now that the steak is done, add both bags of precooked chow mein noodles, as well as 1/3 of your sauce, to the meat and bell peppers. In a large mixing bowl, combine all of the ingredients for the sauce. This will loosen your noodles and cause them to reduce in size.

7. Chop the green onion and cashews while everything is decreasing. You'll want to trim off the top 1-2 inches of the green onion. Because it has a lot of texture, you may remove it, as well as the bottom of

your green onion. Chop the green onion as finely as you prefer, then add a large pinch to the meat and noodles, along with another third of the sauce. Add approximately 1/4 cup of your chopped cashes, mix to coat, and simmer the sauce more. When the sauce begins to thicken, add the remainder of your sauce, mix, and plate.

8. To dish, I prefer to start with some crispy chow mien noodles on the bottom of the plate, then top with your low main, a sprinkle of green onion, cashews, sesame seeds, and a little spray of sriracha.

Mahi Mahi with Pineapple Pico and Rice

4 serv.

20 min.

Ingredients:

- 4, 6-8oz filets of Mahi Mahi
- 1 cup white Rice
- 1 ½ cups Chicken Stock
- The juice of 1 Lime
- 2 tablespoons Blackstone Chicken and Herb Seasoning
- 1 tablespoon chopped Cilantro

PINEAPPLE SALSA:

- 3-4, ½ inch slices of Pineapple
- 1 Jalapeno, thinly sliced
- 1 Red Chile, thinly sliced
- ¼ cup minced Red Onion
- 2 teaspoons minced Garlic
- 2 teaspoons Blackstone Sriracha Pineapple Seasoning
- The juice of 1 Lime
- Pinch of Salt

Instructions:

1. Combine the rice, chicken stock, lime juice, Blackstone Chicken and Herb Seasoning, and cilantro in a small aluminum pan. Cover with tin foil after stirring to ensure a uniform blend.
2. Place the tin foil rice pack on the griddle over high heat. Cook for 10 minutes before transferring to the griddle's cooler side.
3. Caramelize the pineapple slices on the griddle with a little olive oil over medium-high heat.
4. When the pineapple is done, chop it up into small pieces and place it in a big mixing basin. Stir in the remaining pineapple salsa ingredients until they are uniformly distributed.
5. Season both sides of the Mahi Mahi with the Blackstone Sriracha Pineapple.
6. Cook the Mahi Mahi for 3-4 minutes per side on a griddle with a little olive oil over medium-high heat.
7. To dish, lay the rice in the center of the plate or platter and top with the

cooked fish. Garnish with a dollop of pineapple salsa and a sprig of fresh cilantro.

Cajun Catfish with Brown Sugar Butter Sauce

2-4 serv.

30 min.

Ingredients

- 8 Small Red Potatoes
- Half and Half
- Pink Himalayan Salt
- Zatarain's Shrimp & Crab Boil
- Blackstone Cajun Seasoning
- 4 Catfish fillets
- 1 can of Sweet Corn
- 1 can of Green Beans
- ¾ c of Brown Sugar
- Crystal Hot Sauce

Instructions:

1. Place 8 tiny red potatoes in a big saucepan and cut them into large pieces.
2. 2 teaspoons salt, 1 cup half-and-half, 34 cup water, and 12 teaspoons Zatarain's Shrimp and Crab Boil Cover and bring to a boil.
3. Fill a 32oz mason jar 34% full of Half & Half and 12 tsp Pink Himalayan Salt to create butter. Start shaking once you've sealed the package firmly. It will take around 5 minutes for it to thicken. When it begins to thicken, shake it and it will "Clunk." Remove the cover and pour the buttermilk out (this can be used later to make buttermilk pancakes). Close it up and shake it for a few minutes longer. (You can also do this in a blender.)
4. Put it in the fridge to chill when it's finished.
5. The potatoes should be done by now. Drain the potatoes and mash them with salt and Blackstone Cajun Seasoning to taste. Continue mixing in 34 cup of the butter you just prepared. Allow to cool before serving.
6. Preheat your griddle to medium. Don't combine 1 can of green beans and 1 can of sweet corn. 12 tablespoons fresh butter should be added to each.
7. In a large sauce pan, melt the remaining butter and add 34 cup of brown sugar. To taste, add Crystal Hot Sauce (optional). To heat the sauce, place the pan immediately on the griddle and stir well. Remove from the heat once the butter has completely melted and been well combined.
8. Get your fish fillets out and season one side with Cajun spice before placing it on the griddle. Repeat with the other side. Cook for 3-5 minutes before flipping.
9. Put your meal on a plate and savor it!

10. *These dimensions are based on the video and may not be 100% accurate.

Gator Wings

2-4 serv.

20 min.

Ingredients:

- 32 OZ package of Alligator Bone in Legs
- Flour
- 3 Tbsp Blackstone Bayou Blend seasoning

SAUCE

- 1 stick of Butter
- ½ cup Brown Sugar
- 2 ½ Tbsp Blackstone Bayou Blend seasoning
- Hot Sauce, to taste.

Instructions:

1. In a metal mixing bowl, combine 1 cube of butter and 12 cup brown sugar to prepare the sauce. 3 tablespoons Blackstone Bayou Seasonings should be combined. To taste, add spicy sauce (1tsp).
2. Place the bowl on the Blackstone and cook over medium heat until everything is melted and combined.

Remove the pan from the heat and set it aside.

3. 2 12 cup flour and 3 tbsp Bayou in a separate big mixing bowl Mix in the seasonings.
4. Cut each leg at the joint with an alligator leg on a cutting board.
5. Mix the flour and seasonings with the alligator legs.
6. To fry, heat oil in a cast iron pan to 340-350 degrees.
7. Cook the alligator legs for 3-4 minutes, or until golden brown, then flipping and cooking for another 3-4 minutes.

Bruce Mitchell Gumbo

12-15 serv.

120 min.

Ingredients:

- 4 cups Flour
- Oil
- 6lbs of Chicken, sliced
- 14oz of Smoked Sausage, sliced
- 1 1/3 Cups Onion
- 1 1/3 Cups Green Bell Pepper
- 1 1/3 Cups Celery
- 1lb Crawfish
- 3 quarts Chicken Stock (3 cartons)
- 28oz chopped Okra
- Gumbo Filé
- Cooked Rice

Instructions:

1. Set griddle to medium heat and clean properly (so there is no oil remaining on the griddle top) to prepare your own roux.
2. Place 4 cups white flour on the griddle over medium heat and spread evenly around the griddle. Fold and distribute the flour on the griddle until it turns a dark brown color.
3. Fold in a little amount of oil at a time into the flour until it reaches the consistency of brownie batter.
4. Place everything in a big saucepan and set it aside.
5. Re-oil the griddle after cleaning it.
6. Place 6 pounds of chicken on the griddle in medium-sized slices. Add a large amount of Bayou Blend Seasoning.
7. Slice 14 ounces of smoked sausage and cook alongside the chicken.
8. Cook for 4-6 minutes on the griddle with 1 1/3 cup each of onion, green pepper, and celery. By adding water to the veggies, they will steam.
9. Add 1 pound of crawfish on the griddle top, along with a splash of Bayou seasoning. Cook for another 3-5 minutes after adding the spice.
10. Place the Roux pot on the griddle top and slowly pour in 3 cartons of chicken stock, stirring constantly.
11. Combine all of the food off the griddle in a saucepan with the roux and chicken stock mix.
12. Add one 28oz bag of chopped Okra and bring to a boil. Cook for 2 hours on medium to low heat after mixing.

(You may put this on top of the burner to save propane.)
13. Serve over rice with a dash of Gumbo File flavor (optional).

CJ's Chicken Flautas with Griddled Salsa Verde

3-4 serv.

30 min.

Ingredients:

- Chicken cutlets
- Corn tortillas
- Pre shredded Mexican blend cheese
- Large aluminum tin
- Toothpicks
- Olive Oil
- 4-6 Tomatillos (depending on the size)
- 3 limes
- White or yellow onion
- 3 jalapeños
- Cilantro
- Garlic
- Salt
- Pepper
- Blackstone Taco Fajita Seasoning
- Blender

Instructions:

1. Pre-heat one side of your griddle on high, then cook in a big shallow tin pan with olive oil or another oil replacement. The temperature of the oil should be approximately 375 degrees. Another zone should be preheated on medium high.

2. Our chicken cutlets must first be seasoned. Simply brush both sides with a small coating of oil and season with salt and pepper before placing on the Blackstone griddle to cook. This won't take long, so keep an eye on it and turn as needed to ensure even cooking.

3. Let's get started preparing our salsa ingredients. Remove the husk on the outside of the tomatillos as well as the stem before cutting into quarters. Split the stem off your jalapeos and cut them in half lengthwise. You may leave the seeds out if you want a milder salsa. I prefer the warmth, so I keep them in. Take two limes and cut them in half, as well as one white or yellow onion, which should be cut into large bits. As the onion cooks on the griddle, it will split apart.

4. Your chicken should be done by now. Remove the chicken from the grill and toss the salsa ingredients on top with a little olive oil to coat. I also like to season with salt and pepper at this point. I add 3-4 garlic cloves, a bit extra oil, and some salt and pepper around 3 minutes into cooking these items. Allow the ingredients to caramelize while they cook. The limes will begin to turn color, and the jalapeos will begin to roast. When the ingredients have cooked down a little, toss them occasionally and remove them. You don't want the tomatillos to go mushy, so keep an eye on them. They can go straight into a blender once they've been removed from the griddle.DON'T MIX THE LIMES. After you've added the remaining ingredients, set those aside to squeeze the juice. Squeeze the lime juice into your blender using tongs, season with a pinch of salt and pepper, and process until smooth and integrated. While you complete the remainder of your meal, lay this aside to chill.

5. Your corn tortillas should now be steaming. I'll place the little Blackstone cutting board on on the griddle, lay the tortillas out on the board, take the large basting dome, and spray water under and around the cutting board and cover to step.Warm them in the microwave with a moist paper towel on top.

6. You may slice the chicken cutlets into little thin pieces while the tortillas are heating. Once those are completed, your tortillas are nearly finished. They should feel warm when you touch them.

7. To make your flautas, lay one tortilla down, add a few pieces of chicken, and some shredded cheese, then gently wrap the tortilla. Once it's rolled, insert a toothpick into the tortilla to keep all of your contents in place while deep frying. Rep until

all of your chicken and tortillas have been utilized.Your oil should be ready to use at this point. Cook your rolled flautas in tiny batches of 6-8 each round in the oil. Because the chicken is already cooked, this won't take long. Cook for about 2-3 minutes, or until the shell is crisp. When they're done, drain them on paper towels and season with Blackstone Taco Fajita Seasoning immediately away.

8. You may start coating your flautas as they cool. Add some fresh salsa verde to a small bowl, stack your flautas with or without toothpicks, top with cilantro and a griddled lime, and enjoy!

Frog Legs 3 Ways

5-6 serv.

20 min.

Ingredients:

- 24 Frog Legs
- 2 Eggs
- ½ cup Half and Half
- Bayou Blend Seasoning
- 3 cups Zatarain's Frying Mix (any bread crumb mixture will work)
- Oil
- 3 tsp Sesame Oil
- ½ cup Soy Sauce
- 1 cube Butter
- Hot Sauce, to taste

Instructions:

1ST EDITION

1. To prepare the egg wash, whisk together 2 eggs and 12 cup half-and-half in a small bowl. Season to taste with Bayou Blend spices.
2. 8 legs should be soaked in the mixture.
3. In a larger mixing bowl, combine 3 cups Zatarain's Frying Mix (or any breading mix) and some Bayou Blend spice to produce the breading mixture.
4. Remove the legs from the egg wash and dip them one at a time in the breading mixture, placing them on a separate dish. Dip them in the egg wash again and then in the breading mixture to double coat.
5. Heat the oil to 320 degrees in a pan, then add the breaded frog legs and fry until golden brown.
6. Place on a plate and enjoy!

2ND EDITION

1. Place 8 frog legs in a small dish and season with salt and pepper. Bayou Combine spices and 3 tsp. sesame oil in a mixing bowl. Hand-mix the ingredients.
2. Allow the frog legs to marinate in 12 cup soy sauce for 2 minutes.
3. Cover the entire dish with a basting dome and place it on the griddle.
4. Cook for a total of 3-5 minutes.
5. Place on a plate and enjoy!

1. 1 cube of butter is melted on the griddle, and 8 frog legs are placed on the butter.
2. Toss in the spicy sauce and Bayou Season to taste and cover with a basting dome.
3. Cook for a total of 3-5 minutes.
4. Place on a plate and enjoy!
5. *Chicken is wonderful in these dishes!

Bayou Sous Vide Steak

3-4 serv.

120 min.

Ingredients:

- 1 Large Tomahawk Steak
- 1 cup Dale Seasoning
- 10 small Red Potatoes
- Water
- 24oz package of Bacon
- 3 Tbsp of Butter
- ½ cup Half and half
- ½ cup Green Onions
- ½ tsp of Garlic Powder
- 1 Tbsp of Chives
- ½ tsp Zatarain's Shimp and Crab Boil
- Steak seasoning

Instructions:

1. To marinate the steak, place it in a sealable bag with 1 cup of Dale seasoning.
2. Boil 2 quarts of water and pour into an ice chest with 2 quarts of warm water already in it.
3. Close the ice chest and place the bag with the meat inside. Allow it to sit for 2 hours.
4. 10 little red potatoes, sliced, should be placed in a big saucepan to prepare Mashed Bacon Potatoes. 1 quart water and 12 tablespoons Zatarain's Shimp and Crab Boil
5. Bring to a boil in a saucepan on the stove and simmer for 10-15 minutes.
6. Preheat the griddle to high and fry one 24-ounce package of thick-cut bacon.
7. Strain the potatoes and mash them with 3 tablespoons butter and 12 cup half-and-half.
8. Cut the bacon into tiny slices and incorporate it into the mashed potatoes.
9. Mix 12 cup green onion, 12 teaspoon garlic powder, and 1 tablespoon chives into mashed potatoes.
10. Remove the steak from the ice chest and set it on a chopping board with your favorite steak seasoning. Season the opposite side of the griddle after placing the seasoning side down. Cook each side for 3-5 minutes.
11. Remove the steak from the pan and set it aside for 10 minutes.

12. Slice, dish, and savor!

Jambalaya for 3

3 serv.

30 min.

Ingredients:

- 2 boneless Chicken thighs
- 6oz of Mandarin Sausage
- 8oz of cooked Crawfish
- ¼ of a large onion
- Bayou Blend Seasoning
- 3 cup Rice
- 6 cup Water
- 3 tsp Kitchen Bouquet Browning and Seasoning Sauce

Instructions:

1. Preheat the griddle to medium. Cook 2 boneless chicken thighs till browned in cubes.
2. Place 6 oz. cooked mandarin sausage and 8 oz. cooked crawfish on the griddle. Cook until warmed through, then add to chicken with a dab of Bayou Blend flavor.
3. Cook for 3-5 minutes after dicing 14 of a big onion. (To steam the onions, simply add a little water.) Once the meat is done, mix it with the onions and reduce the heat to low.
4. Reduce the heat to low on the rest of the griddle.

5. 1 cup rice, 2 cups chicken stock, 1 teaspoon Kitchen Bouquet Browning and Spice Sauce, and a sprinkle of Bayou Blend seasoning in each of the three Blackstone Grease Cup liners
6. Place on the griddle and equally distribute the meat into each one, stirring occasionally.
7. Make a tiny hole on the top of each one using aluminum foil.
8. Cook for around 20 minutes.
9. Take it off the fire and enjoy it!

CJ's Copy Cat Bourbon Chicken

2-3 serv.

20-25 min.

Ingredients:

- 4 Boneless Skinless Chicken Thighs
- 1 Green bell pepper
- 1 Yellow onion
- Green onion
- 2 bags of White or jasmine rice (Ben's microwave pre cooked)
- Olive oil
- 2 tsp Ground ginger
- Crushed Red Pepper
- 1 tsp Garlic powder
- 1/4 tsp Course black pepper
- 1/3 cup Soy sauce
- 1/3 cup Bourbon
- 1/2 cup Water

- 2 tbsp White Rice Vinegar
- 1/2 cup Brown sugar
- 1 tbsp Cornstarch dissolved in 3 tbsp cold water

Instructions:

1. Preheat one of your Blackstone's zones to medium high heat. While your griddle warms up, season your boneless skinless chicken thighs with kosher salt and coarse black pepper and a light coating of olive oil. Place your chicken on the griddle to fry after it has warmed up. When the cooked side is golden crispy, flip it over. You may turn the chicken many times to ensure that it is properly cooked.
2. Let's get started with our Bourbon Sauce. 1/3 cup soy sauce, 2 tbsp rice vinegar, and 2 tsp ground pepper in a large mixing bowl1/2 cup brown sugar, 1 tbsp Cornstarch dissolved in 3 tbsp cold water, 1/3 cup Bourbon, 1/4 tsp coarse black pepper, ginger, 1 tsp garlic powder, 1/2 tsp crushed red pepper flakes, 1/2 cup brown sugar, 1 tbsp Cornstarch dissolved in 3 tbsp cold water Set aside after stirring to incorporate all of the ingredients.
3. After that, remove the pith and seeds from 1 green bell pepper and slice it into a big chop (about 1/2 inch squares). One yellow onion, sliced into the same size as the yellow onion.
4. At this point, your chicken should be done. Remove the check from the griddle and cut it to about the same size as your vegetables before returning it to the griddle.
5. Once the chicken is back on the griddle, toss in your vegetables, reduce the heat to low, and drizzle in the sauce in tiny batches. The sauce will thicken and cover your chicken and vegetables as a result of this. Do this in three to four small batches. As you can see, the sauce decreases and thickens into a thick glaze.
6. After you've finished glazing, place your precooked rice in one of your cooking zones, season gently with salt and pepper, and steam with a little water. You may dome your rice if you like, but toss it lightly to enable the water to steam and cook it up.
7. Remove the stem tips and base of one or two green onions before chopping them up for the platter. Place a bed of steamed rice on a platter, top with a piece of the bourbon chicken and veggies, garnish with chopped green onion, and a little sprinkling of sesame seeds, and serve!

Crawfish and Grits

3-4 serv.

30 min.

Ingredients:

- 25-30 fresh Crawfish, or 1lb of frozen Crawfish meat
- 2 cups Quaker Grits
- 1 cube butter
- 1 cup Half and Half
- Cajun Seasoning
- Hot sauce
- Salt and Pepper

Instructions:

1. Cook 25-30 fresh crawfish for 5 minutes in boiling water (seasoned with salt or any other flavour you choose). Remove the saucepan from the heat and soak for 30 minutes in the hot water. Set aside after straining.
2. In a large sauce pan, combine 2 cups Quaker Grits and season with Cajun Seasoning to taste. 12 cubes of butter and 4 cups of water are added.
3. Place on a hot griddle and cook for about 20 minutes, covered.
4. Break open the crawfish and remove the flesh from the claws and tail into a separate bowl while the grits are cooking.Returning to the grits, they should be thickening at this point. Stir in the remaining 12 cubes of butter until they are melted and well mixed with the grits.
5. Mix in roughly a cup of half-and-half, then carefully fold in all of the crawfish meat.

6. Turn off the heat, cover, and set aside for 15 minutes.
7. Dust with Cajun Seasoning and spicy sauce to taste before plating and serving.

Salmon Cakes

2-3 serv.

20 min.

Ingredients:

- Stovetop stuffing (1 box)
- Chicken Stock
- 2 eggs
- 2 6oz cans of Salmon
- Flour

Instructions:

1. 1 Stovetop box should be emptied Filling a medium saucepan with the ingredients. Mix with a little amount of Chicken Stock (approximately 1 cup) until the stuffing is moistened and soft (no surplus liquid should remain).
2. Place the saucepan on top of the griddle over medium heat and cook for 5 minutes while stirring.
3. Fill a large mixing bowl halfway with the ingredients and mash it with a spoon. Gently fold in two eggs. Meanwhile, preheat the Blackstone to high and fill a cast iron pan halfway with oil to use for frying.

4. In the Stovetop mixture, gently fold in two 6oz cans of salmon. 2 tblsp flour, or until mixture thickens

5. When the oil reaches a temperature of 330-360 degrees. Place a generous dollop of the mixture in a flower dish and evenly coat it. With your hands, form a patty and lay it in oil. Repeat

6. Cook for 3 minutes or until the bottoms are golden brown before flipping. Cook for a another 2 to 3 minutes.

7. Remove the lid and squirt Blackstone Bayou on top. Blend Season to taste and enjoy!

Sausage Gravy and Biscuits

4-5 serv.

15 min.

Ingredients:

- 1 lb Ground Breakfast Sausage
- 1 cube Butter
- 1 ½ cup Flour
- 1 cup Milk
- Salt and Pepper
- 1 package frozen biscuits

Instructions:

1. Preheat the air fryer to medium-high and drop 10 biscuits inside.

2. Preheat the griddle on high and set a pan on the Blackstone to melt 1 cube of butter.

3. Cook the ground beef on the Blackstone, adjacent to the skillet.

4. 12 cup flour, melted butter, and 12 cup flour, melted butter, 12 cup flour, 12 cup flour, 12 cup flour, 12 cup flour, 12 cup flour, 12 cup Mix in a little amount of flour until the mixture resembles thick mashed potatoes.

5. Stir in 12 cup milk to the flour mixture (do not stop stirring or the mixture will burn). Stir with a bit more milk until the desired consistency is reached; add more milk for a thinner gravy.

6. Season to taste with salt and pepper.

7. Mix in the sausage with the gravy. Take it off the heat and let it aside for 5 minutes.

8. When the biscuits are done, remove them from the oven and place them on a dish with gravy on top.

Griddled Parmesan Spaghetti Tacos

2-3 serv.

20 min.

Ingredients

- Grated Parmesan 12oz at least (2 oz per shell)
- Cooked spaghetti
- RAO marinara
- Lean beef, 90/10
- Chopped Red Onion
- Chopped Tomato
- 2 Tbsp Unsalted butter
- Basil
- Garlic powder
- Dried Oregano seasoning
- Blackstone Parmesan Ranch Seasoning
- Salt
- Pepper
- Blackstone Taco Rack

Instructions:

1. You'll need to precook your spaghetti noodles, drain them, and have them ready before you start on your Blackstone Griddle.
2. Two zones of your griddle should be preheated. One is set to medium high and the other to low.
3. Put your favorite canned marinara in a medium sauce pan and set it on low in the front corner of the heat zone. You're just getting your marinara ready for the final assembly.
4. Add the 90/10 lean meat to your medium high heat zone. Using your spatulas, break up the meat and season with kosher salt, coarse black pepper, garlic powder, and dried oregano. Cook, tossing periodically, until completely browned.
5. While the beef is cooking, cut half a red onion and one red tomato and combine them in a small bowl with salt, pepper, and a thin sprinkling of garlic powder. Save it for a later date.
6. Stack around 4 or 5 fresh basil leaves on top of one another, roll into a tight coil, and cut into ribbons. This will be used as a garnish in the future.
7. Slide the meat to a cool zone or remove it from the griddle top when it's done.
8. To make our taco shells, heat our griddle to medium low, then grab small handfuls of grated parmesan and spread them out on the griddle top. It's critical not to eat too little or too much cheese. Per shell, you'll use around 2 oz. Make a circle about the same size as a corn tortilla. When it's cooking, you'll see little bubbles on the borders at first, which will eventually spread to the middle. The edges of the cheese will begin to get golden brown after approximately 2-3 minutes. With your spatula, carefully remove the cheese off the griddle, being careful not to tear it, and flip to cook the other side. When both sides are golden brown, remove the cheese crisp from the oven and lay it on top of the Blackstone Taco Rack. You're not going to use the rack like you normally would; instead, you're going to use the raw in reverse to hang the cheese to cool. Continue in

this manner until you have the required number of shells. You can chill 5 shells at a time on your rack.While your shells cool and crisp, combine your precooked spaghetti noodles, enough marinara to coat the pasta, and one or two tablespoons unsalted butter in a mixing dish. Toss everything together until the butter has melted and is evenly distributed throughout the spaghetti.

9. To assemble your Spaghetti Tacos, place your shells in the taco rack, spoon a portion of your pasta into each shell, top with one of two spoonfuls of cooked and seasoned beef, a drizzle of marinara, and garnish with your tomato and red onions, fresh basil ribbons, and Blackstone Parmesan Ranch Seasoning. Serve and have fun!!

The LaChanga

1 serv.

5 min.

Ingredients:

- Large Tortilla
- Shredded Mexican blend cheese
- TD's Brew & BBQ Zesty Taco Seasoning
- Leftover lasagna
- Butter

Instructions:

1. Preheat the Blackstone griddle over medium-high heat.
2. Apply a thin layer of shredded Mexican Blend cheese on a tortilla and season with TD's Brew & BBQ Zesty Taco Seasoning. Place a tortilla on the Blackstone and spread a thin layer of shredded Mexican Blend cheese on a tortilla.
3. In the center of the tortilla, place a slice of leftover lasagna. Fold the tortilla in half, then roll it up tightly.
4. Place the LaChanga seam side down on the melted butter on the griddle. Remove the LaChanga from the fire after flipping it and cooking it on all sides until golden brown.
5. On the griddle, melt some shredded Mexican Blend cheese (added with TD's Brew & BBQ Zesty Taco Seasoning) with a racklette, then pour on the LaChanga.
6. ¡Salud! Down with the ciao!

Surf and Turf Blackstone Style

2-4 serv.

15 min.

Ingredients

- Fresh baked rolls

- Roast beef (rare) sliced
- American cheese
- Meat from two lobsters
- Chives
- Shrimp
- French fries
- A couple kabob sticks
- Tony's creole seasoning
- Lemon
- Worcester sauce
- Garlic
- Butter
- Salt
- Pepper

Instructions:

1. 1 pound shrimp, peeled and cleaned Using oil and Tony's Creole Seasoning, coat the chicken. Using a skewer, attach the shrimp to the skewer. Cook until done on the Blackstone. Set out to the side.
2. Butter the sides of the rolls after cutting them. Toast the bread on the Blackstone till golden brown. Toss the toasted rolls off to the side.
3. With a little Worcester sauce, garlic, butter, salt, and pepper, cook the roast beef pieces. Reduce the heat on one side of the griddle and transfer to the cold side.
4. On the Blackstone, brown some butter with garlic and chives, then add the lobster flesh and cook until done.
5. Cook French fries according to package guidelines.
6. Plate and savor your meal.

Wisconsin Cheesesteak

3 serv.

25 min.

Ingredients:

- ¼ Cup of butter, melted
- ¼ Cup of flour
- ½ Tsp of garlic powder
- ½ Tsp of onion powder
- 1 Cup of milk
- ⅔ Cup beer of choice
- 1 Cup sharp cheddar, shredded
- ½ Cup mozzarella cheese, shredded
- ½ Cup Swiss cheese, shredded
- Blackstone Cheesesteak Seasoning
- Shaved beef
- Onions
- Peppers
- Sauerkraut
- Hoagie roll
- Bratwurst

Instructions:

1. Melt butter in a medium skillet over medium heat, then stir in flour, garlic powder, cayenne pepper, and onion powder. 1 minute of cooking
2. Pour in a little amount of beer and milk at a time, stirring after each addition. Cook over medium heat until the sauce is thick and bubbling.

3. Reduce the heat to low and stir in the cheeses until smooth.
4. Cheesesteak
5. Preheat the Blackstone Griddle to medium-high heat.
6. Butterfly your bratwurst by cutting it down the center. Place on a griddle with the open side down. Allow for roughly 8 minutes of cooking time. Oil the griddle and add the onions and peppers. Toss the onions and peppers with Blackstone Cheese Steak Seasoning. Check the beer cheese sauce and flip the bratwurst.
7. Add the shaved beef to the griddle after your onions and peppers are about 80 percent done. Add the Blackstone Cheesesteak Seasoning and spread it evenly. Toast your hoagie bun and reheat your sauerkraut on the griddle at this time.
8. Combine the meat, pepper, and onions in a mixing bowl with a splash of beer. Combine the meat, peppers, and onions in a mixing bowl. Assemble the sandwich once all of the ingredients have been incorporated. Place your bratwurst on the bottom of the hoagie. After that, add the sauerkraut and the meat pepper onion mixture.
9. Pour the beer cheese over the top. Serve and have fun.

Mexican Street Corn Shrimp Tacos

4-6 serv.

20 min.

Ingredients:

- 1 Cup of Mexican Crema
- 1/4 Duke's Mayonnaise
- 3 Limes
- 1/2 Tbsp garlic powder
- 2 Lbs of shrimp
- 1 Can of chipotle peppers in adobo sauce
- Bag of tricolor slaw mix
- 2 Packs of frozen corn
- 2 Limes
- 2 Avocados Corn tortillas
- Olive oil Cotija cheese
- Blackstone Taco and Fajita Seasoning
- Blackstone Tequila Lime Seasoning

Instructions:

1. Preheat all zones of the Blackstone Griddle to medium-high.
2. To taste, combine the Mexican crema, mayonnaise, lime juice, garlic powder, and Blackstone Tequila Lime Seasoning.
3. In a mixing bowl, toss the shrimp with olive oil, chipotle adobo sauce, Blackstone Taco and Fajita

Seasoning, and Blackstone Tequila Lime Seasoning until thoroughly covered.

4. Apply some olive oil to all of the griddle's zones before adding the shrimp and frozen corn.

5. Season the frozen corn with Blackstone Tequila Lime Seasoning, then add the juice of 1/2 a lime when it has done cooking.

6. Place corn tortillas on the griddle once the shrimp has finished cooking and heat until warm on both sides.

7. Place a corn tortilla on the bottom, top with tricolor slaw mix, roasted corn, and shrimp, then top with cotija cheese and tequila lime crema.

8. After all tacos are built and plated, finish with a dusting of Blackstone Tequila Lime Seasoning and serve.

Philly Cheesesteak Egg Rolls

4-6 serv.

45 min.

Ingredients:

- 1 Lb of thin sliced New York strip
- Vidalia onion, finely chopped
- Red pepper, finely chopped
- Green pepper, finely chopped
- Oz of shiitake mushrooms, chopped
- 1/2 Poblano pepper, cut into 1" strips
- 4 fresh cayenne peppers
- 2 Tbsp salted butter
- 1 Small package of Velveeta cheese, cut into 1" cubes
- 1 Pack of egg roll wrappers

Instructions:

1. Preheat your Blackstone Griddle on two burners to low heat. Allow for a 5-minute warm-up period.

2. Use salt and pepper to season your meat. Cook on a griddle until you reach your desired level of health. Meanwhile, grease the griddle and add the onion, red and green peppers, and mushroom. Cook until the vegetables are transparent, then add the meat in the last few minutes. Remove from heat and set aside to cool in a bowl.

3. Poblano peppers and charred cayenne peppers

4. Place a Blackstone Cup Liner on top of the griddle. Cook, stirring often, until the Velveeta cheese has melted, a bit at a time.

5. Preheat the Blackstone Airfryers at 350 degrees Fahrenheit. Cayenne and poblano peppers, finely chopped, are added to the melted Velveeta mixture heated on the griddle. Stir often.

6. Place 2-3 tablespoons of meat in egg roll wrappers and roll according per package recommendations. Lightly coat egg rolls with cooking

spray. Place in the Blackstone Airfryer in a single layer. Cook for 10 minutes before rotating and cooking for another 10 to 15 minutes, or until lightly browned. Allow 5 minutes for the steak and cheese egg rolls to cool in the air fryer. Continue to mix the Velveeta cheese dip.

7. Enjoy your egg rolls with a warm cheese dip.

CJ's Garlic Toast Steak Sandwich

3 serv.

20 min.

Ingredients:

- 1 Ribeye Steak
- Texas Garlic Toast (Frozen)
- Olive oil
- Worcestershire
- 1 Lime
- Garlic powder
- Mayo
- Hoarse sauce
- Soy sauce
- Kosher salt
- Course ground pepper
- Blackstone Steak House Seasoning
- Baby Arugula
- 1 Yellow onion
- Sharp White cheddar, sliced
- Pepper Jack Cheese, sliced

- Blackstone Steak House Seasoning

Instructions:

On your Blackstone, pre-heat one zone to high.

Apply a little quantity of Olive Oil on both sides of the ribeye steak, then season generously with Kosher Salt, Course Black Pepper, and Blackstone Steak House Seasoning before placing it immediately on your high heat zone. Cook to desired internal temperature after a beautiful sear on either side. I prefer a medium steak, so cook it for 2-3 minutes on each side. When the steak and onions are done, set them aside to rest.

Half a yellow onion, sliced, and a little olive oil next to your steak. Place your yellow onions in the oil and season with kosher salt, coarse black pepper, and a dash of garlic powder.

2-3 tbsp Dukes mayo, 1 tbsp horseradish, 1 tbsp soy sauce, 1 tbsp Worcestershire sauce, 1 tsp garlic powder and onion powder, and 1 tsp Blackstone Steak House Seasoning in a mixing basin, mix well, and put away.

Place your Texas toast Garlic Toast in the steak fat and onion oil once the meat and onions have been removed. Set the heat to medium low and brown each side before moving on to the next step.

Slice the steak into short pieces and construct little heaps on the griddle top on low or medium low once it has rested for 5

320

minutes. Melt one piece of sharp cheddar and one slice of pepper jack cheese on top of the stacks.

You may start building once the cheese has melted. Place a little quantity of baby arugula, a mound of your steak with melted cheese, some caramelized onions, and additional special sauce on the bottom bun, then top with the second slice of Texas toast. Serve with a small bowl of the special sauce on the side for dipping. ENJOY!

CJ's Game Day Ham and Cheese Sliders

3-4 serv.

15 mins

Ingredients:

- 12 Count package of Hawaiian rolls
- 3/4 lb of cooked deli ham (thin sliced)
- 3/4 lb Swiss cheese Slices
- 1 Stick unsalted Butter
- Jarred Jalapeños
- 1-2 TBSP Dijon Mustard
- 1 TBSP Poppy Seeds
- 2 tsp dried minced onion
- 2 tsp Worcestershire
- 1 tsp Blackstone Steak House Seasoning

Instructions:

In two zones, pre-heat your Blackstone griddle. One is set to Medium Low while the other is set to Low.

Place a sauce pan in the corner of the Medium Low zone and add one stick of unsalted butter. 1 TBSP Poppy Seeds, 1 tbsp Jalapeo juice from the jar, 1 tsp Blackstone Steak House Seasoning, 1-2 TBSP Dijon Mustard, 2 tsp Worcesteshire, 2 tsp dry minced onion, 1 TBSP Poppy Seeds, 1 tbsp Jalapeo juice from the jar, 1 tsp Blackstone Steak House Seasoning Allow to melt for a few minutes, stirring periodically.

Open the Hawaiian Rolls packaging and keep all of the rolls together. They should not be separated. Place the whole loaf on the cutting board and cut it in half horizontally to make a big top and bottom. Your special sauce should be melted by now. Place a spoonful or two on the griddle top and spread them out. The buttery sauce will be used to toast the buns. Both sides of the bun should be facing down.

Start slicing the deli ham and placing it on the griddle next to the bread. Place them in a square that is the same size as your bun. Don't simply put one piece down at a time. I like to fold them and lay them flat.Place a layer of sliced mozzarella on top of the ham and let to melt. This should take no more than two or three minutes.

Your bread should be toasted on the inside at this point. Turn the pan over and toast the other side. Place a small bit of sauce on the inside bottom bun after it has been turned. Transfer the ham and cheese on the huge bottom bread with two large spatulas. Place a couple jalapeos on the bottom bun and top with the top bun. Remove off the griddle top, slice into slider-size sandwiches, brush or drizzle with sauce, and serve. On a side note, I like to keep a small dish of sauce on the table for dipping. Enjoy!

Alaskan Salmon

30 mins

3 serv

Ingredients

- 3 4-oz salmon filets
- 1.5 teaspoon kosher salt
- 3 tablespoons Soy Vay teriyaki
- 1.5 tablespoon cooking oil

Instructions

1. Place the salmon on a chopping board or work surface, skin side down, and run your fingertips down the flesh side.
2. If you notice any pin bones in the salmon, remove them with kitchen pliers or tweezers and discard.
3. Turn the fish over to the flesh side.
4. Score the skin side with diagonal hashes in 2-3 areas using a sharp knife. This will make it easier for it to stay flat during cooking.

5. Half of the salt should be evenly distributed on each of the two filets, covering all exposed flesh (not skin)
6. Preheat your griddle for 15 minutes on medium-high heat (375-400F).
7. Spread the frying oil out over a 10-inch surface on the griddle.
8. Place the fish on the griddle skin-side down and cook for about 4 minutes.
9. Cook for 2 minutes with the skin up on the fish.
10. Cook for one further minute on each side if your fish can be flipped. If not, cook skin side up for a total of 4 minutes.
11. Turn the griddle off and evenly pour the teriyaki sauce over the filet.
12. Cover the sauced fish with a basting dome and let it stay on the griddle for another 2 minutes if preferred.
13. Serve right away.

Grill Scallops & Shrimp

5 mins

4 Serv

Ingredients

- 1 pound scallops
- 1 pound jumbo shrimp peeled and deveined
- 1 pat butter
- 1 tablespoon lemon pepper

- 1 tablespoon all-purpose bbq rub

Instructions

1. Preheat your Blackstone Griddle to 400 degrees Fahrenheit on medium-high heat.
2. Pat the scallops and shrimp dry with several layers of paper towels.
3. Melt the butter on the griddle.
4. Cook for a few minutes with the shrimp in the butter.
5. Cook the scallops until they are golden brown on the griddle.
6. Season the scallops with the BBQ seasoning.
7. Season the shrimp with the lemon pepper.
8. Turn the shrimp and scallops after 2 minutes on each side.
9. Cook for an additional 2 minutes.
10. Remove the scallops from the pan.
11. Check to determine if the shrimp have lost their gray hue and opaqueness. Cook for an extra minute if the shrimp are still slightly opaque.
12. Serve right away.

French Toast Sandwich

13 mins

4 Serv

Ingredients

- 2 Eggs
- ¼ cup Half and half or milk
- 1 tablespoon Ground cinnamon
- 1 loaf French bread
- 8 strips bacon

Instructions

1. Preheat your griddle to 350 degrees Fahrenheit.
2. Start frying the bacon strips on the griddle.
3. Prepare the other ingredients while the bacon cooks.
4. Thinly slice the bread into 2 inch thick pieces.
5. Whisk together the eggs and half-and-half in a large mixing basin.
6. Whisk together the eggs and cinnamon.
7. Switch to the opposite side of the skillet to flip the bacon.
8. Dip both sides of French bread slices into the egg mixture for a few seconds.
9. Place the egg-coated bread on the griddle in the bacon grease that has been rendered.
10. Continue with the remaining bread slices.
11. Cook the bacon until it's done to your liking, then remove it and pat it dry with paper towels.
12. Cook for 3 minutes or until golden brown, then flip.
13. Cook the second side of the bread for 3 minutes more, or until golden brown.

14. Remove two pieces of French toast from the pan and sandwich them between two slices of bacon.
15. Serve right away.

Potato Pancakes

30 mins

7 Serv

Ingredients

- 1.31 cups shredded potato
- 0.22 cup flour
- 1.75 eggs
- 0.22 cup milk
- 0.22 cup finely diced onion
- 0.22 cup finely diced green onions
- 0.88 teaspoon baking powder
- 0.88 teaspoon salt
- 0.88 teaspoon pepper

Instructions

1. Whisk together the eggs and milk until foamy.
2. Stir in the remaining ingredients to incorporate them with the egg mixture.
3. Allow 20 minutes for the mixture to rest.
4. Heat the griddle to medium-high.
5. Apply a thin layer of oil to the cooking surface.
6. Add approximately 14 cup of potato pancake batter on the griddle when the oil begins to shimmer.

7. Continue with the remaining batter.
8. Flatten the batter and fry for 3-4 minutes on each side until golden brown, rotating once.

Delicious Smash Burgers

10 mins

4 Serv

Ingredients

- 16 oz Ground beef 80:20
- 4 Burger buns
- 4 slices American cheese
- 2 tablespoons butter

Seasoning

- 2 teaspoons garlic salt
- 1 teaspoon pepper

Burger toppings

- 1 leaf Lettuce
- 2 slices tomato
- 1 slice sweet onion
- 1 tablespoon ketchup
- 1 teaspoon mayonnaise
- 1 teaspoon mustard
- 1 teaspoon relish

Instructions

1. Preheat your griddle for around 10 minutes on high.
2. While the griddle warms up, gently shape the ground beef into four equal-sized balls, each weighing approximately 4 ounces.
3. On the griddle, melt the butter and toast the cut side of the burger buns until golden brown.
4. Keep the buns warm by putting them to the side.
5. Allow the ground beef balls to cook for 2 minutes on the griddle, spacing them out approximately 8 inches apart.
6. Place a sheet of parchment paper over one of the burger balls and press the meat flat onto the griddle with a bacon press or a firm spatula to approximately 14-inch thickness.
7. Repeat with the remaining burgers.
8. Using the garlic salt and pepper combination, season the burgers.
9. Scrape beneath the burgers with a strong spatula when they start sweating or leaking juices on the pushed side.
10. Cook for a further 2 minutes, or until the American cheese has melted, on the cooked side of each of the burgers.
11. Top the grilled burger with your chosen toppings and serve.

Spicy-Sweet Street Corn

30 mins

6 serv

Ingredients

- 4 ears fresh corn
- 4 slices thick-cut bacon
- 1 medium sweet onion diced
- ½ cup pickled jalapeno
- Optional toppings:
- Juice of ½ lime
- ½ cup Cojtilla cheese
- 1 tablespoon Tajín Clásico Seasoning

Instructions

1. Corn should be shucked. Make sure all of the silk has been removed.
2. Remove the corn kernels off the cob with a sharp knife and the two-bowl technique.
3. Place the bacon pieces on top of one another in a stack.
4. To dice the bacon, make a cut through the middle and then across the bacon. The chopped bacon should be approximately half an inch long and no broader than a pencil's width.
5. Cut your sweet onion into dice.
6. To gently split up the jalapeño rings, coarsely chop them.

7. Set your Blackstone Griddle for two-zone cooking and preheat it to medium-high.
8. Render the bacon first, heating it until it's approximately 80% done.
9. Place the bacon on the griddle's cool side.
10. In the bacon fat, sauté the onion for three minutes.
11. Cook for three minutes more after adding the jalapenos to the onion.
12. Slide the jalapeño and onion to the griddle's cold side.

Shrimp Burger On The Blackstone Griddle With Jasmine Rice Bun

35 mins

4 Serv

Ingredients

- Shrimp
- 1 pound raw shrimp peeled and deveined
- 2 tablespoons minced garlic
- 2 tablespoons oil
- 1 tablespoon smoked paprika
- Jasmine Rice Bun
- 4 cups cooked Jasmine rice
- 1 egg
- ½ cup mayonnaise
- Other ingredients
- 8 slices bacon
- 1 avocado sliced
- 1 Roma tomato sliced
- Salt and Pepper
- Oil

Instructions

1. Prepare the buns using cooked and cooled Jasmine rice. Mix the egg and mayonnaise together until smooth, then fold in the rice until everything is completely incorporated.
2. Wrap 1 cup of rice in plastic wrap and press into a large ramekin to form. Remove the rice bun with care and set it on a platter lined with parchment paper. To create four buns, repeat with the remaining rice.
3. To firm the rice buns, place them in the freezer for one hour.
4. Combine the shrimp, minced garlic, oil, and paprika in a large mixing basin. Set aside to marinate for a few minutes in the refrigerator.
5. Start frying the bacon on the griddle over medium-high heat.
6. Oil the free space on the griddle and lay the mostly frozen rice buns on the griddle when the bacon is approximately halfway cooked. The rice buns should have a crispy crust and be heated all the way through. Cook for around five minutes before gently turning the rice bun, since it is prone to breaking apart.

7. Cook for three to five minutes on the second side, or until the bread has warmed through with a good golden outside. Remove from the equation.
8. Cook the bacon until it is fully cooked and then set it aside.
9. Spread any oils or bacon grease on the griddle in a thin layer using a spatula before starting to fry the shrimp.
10. Cook the shrimp for 5–7 minutes, or until they are no longer translucent and cooked through.
11. Place the jasmine rice bun on a plate to build the Shrimp Burger on the Blackstone Griddle dish.
12. Place the bacon, avocado slices, and Roma tomato on top. Divide the shrimp into thirds and place them on top.
13. Open-faced is the best way to serve this dish.

Wagyu Smash Burger

10 mins

4 Serv

Ingredients

- 1 pound ground beef
- 4 Burger buns
- 1 cup Beef Chili
- 4 oz sharp cheddar cheese finely grated

Instructions

1. Preheat your griddle to 500 degrees Fahrenheit.
2. Cut the meat into four chunks of similar size.
3. Place the pork balls on the griddle.
4. Allow 90 seconds for the meat ball to cook.
5. Cover the beef ball with a square of parchment paper.
6. The meat should be pressed or smashed into the griddle.
7. Scrape beneath the burger with a strong spatula and flip.
8. Allow another 90 seconds for the burger to cook.
9. If desired, season with more salt and pepper.
10. Using a burger press, bacon press, or firm spatula, grate 1 oz cheddar cheese onto each burger.
11. Allow 90 seconds for the crushed beef to cook, or until fluids begin to pool on the meat.
12. 14 cup chili on top of each burger
13. Serve right away.

Griddle Steak Recipe

1 hr 15 mins

1 Serv

Ingredients

- 1 boneless ribeye steak 10 oz
- 1 teaspoon kosher salt
- 1 tablespoon cooking oil

Instructions

1. Take the steak out of the fridge.
2. On all sides, pat the steak dry with paper towels.
3. Season the meat on both sides with salt.
4. Allow steak to rest for 1 hour at room temperature on a wire rack with a plate below.
5. Preheat your griddle to medium-high heat, 400-425F, 15 minutes before cooking.
6. Begin cooking by patting the steak dry a second time on both sides with paper towels.
7. Half of the oil should be poured onto your griddle and distributed around with a spatula.
8. Place your steak on the greased griddle surface when the oil begins to sheen, just before smoking.
9. Cook the meat for 2 minutes without moving it.
10. Fill the griddle with the remaining oil. Allow 30 seconds to warm after spreading evenly.
11. Cook for a further 2 minutes after flipping the steak into the fresh oil.
12. Allow the steak to rest for 5-10 minutes on the griddle, covered loosely with foil.
13. Serve right away.

Fresh Corn on the Cob

25 mins

2 Serv

Ingredients

- Blackstone Air Fryer or Indoor Air Fryer
- ears corn
- Protective gloves for handling hot food

Instructions

1. Check to see if the corn will fit in the air fryer basket. Break the stem off the corn if required to put it in the air fryer basket.
2. Preheat the air fryer to 450 degrees Fahrenheit.
3. Fill the air fryer basket with corn.
4. Cook for 20 minutes, or until done, turning every 5 minutes.

Homemade Smash Burger Recipe

10 mins

4 Serv

Ingredients

- 16 oz Ground beef 80:20
- Burger buns
- 4 slices American cheese
- 2 tablespoons butter

SEASONING

- 2 teaspoons garlic salt
- 1 teaspoon pepper

BURGER TOPPINGS

- 1 leaf Lettuce
- 2 slices tomato
- 1 slice sweet onion
- 1 tablespoon ketchup
- 1 teaspoon mayonnaise
- 1 teaspoon mustard
- 1 teaspoon relish

Instructions

1. Preheat your griddle for around 10 minutes on high.
2. While the griddle warms up, gently shape the ground beef into four equal-sized balls, each weighing approximately 4 ounces.
3. On the griddle, melt the butter and toast the cut side of the burger buns until golden brown.
4. Keep the buns warm by putting them to the side.
5. Allow the ground beef balls to cook for 2 minutes on the griddle, spacing them out approximately 8 inches apart.
6. Place a sheet of parchment paper over one of the burger balls and press the meat flat onto the griddle with a bacon press or a firm spatula to approximately 14-inch thickness.
7. Repeat with the remaining burgers.
8. Using the garlic salt and pepper combination, season the burgers.
9. Scrape beneath the burgers with a strong spatula when they start sweating or leaking juices on the pushed side.
10. Cook for a further 2 minutes, or until the American cheese has melted, on the cooked side of each of the burgers.
11. Top the grilled burger with your chosen toppings and serve.

Grilled Shrimp & Scallops Recipe

5 mins

4 Serv

Ingredients

- 1 pound scallops
- 1 pound jumbo shrimp peeled and deveined
- 1 pat butter
- 1 tablespoon lemon pepper
- 1 tablespoon all-purpose bbq ru

Instructions

1. Preheat your Blackstone Griddle to medium-high heat, at 400 degrees Fahrenheit.
2. Using numerous layers of paper towels, pat the scallops and shrimp dry.
3. On the griddle, melt the butter.
4. Place the shrimp in the butter and cook for a few minutes.
5. Place the scallops on the griddle and cook until they are golden brown.
6. Using the BBQ seasoning, season the scallops.
7. Using the lemon pepper, season the shrimp.
8. Cook for 2 minutes on each side, then turn the shrimp and scallops.
9. Cook for another 2 minutes.
10. Remove the scallops from the pan.
11. Check to determine if the shrimp have lost their gray hue and opaqueness. Cook for an extra minute if the shrimp are still slightly opaque.
12. Serve right away.

Grilled Salmon Recipe

30 mins

2 Serv

Ingredients

- 2 4-oz salmon filets
- 1 teaspoon kosher salt
- 2 tablespoons Soy Vay teriyaki
- 1 tablespoon cooking oil

Instructions

1. Place the salmon on a chopping board or work surface, skin side down, and run your fingertips down the flesh side.
2. If you notice any pin bones in the salmon, remove them with kitchen pliers or tweezers and discard.
3. Turn the fish over to the flesh side.
4. Score the skin side with diagonal hashes in 2-3 areas using a sharp knife. This will make it easier for it to stay flat during cooking.

5. Half of the salt should be evenly distributed on each of the two filets, covering all exposed flesh (not skin)
6. Preheat your griddle for 15 minutes on medium-high heat (375-400F).
7. Spread the frying oil out over a 10-inch surface on the griddle.
8. Place the fish on the griddle skin-side down and cook for about 4 minutes.
9. Cook for 2 minutes with the skin up on the fish.
10. Cook for one further minute on each side if your fish can be flipped. If not, cook skin side up for a total of 4 minutes.
11. Turn the griddle off and evenly pour the teriyaki sauce over the filet.
12. Cover the sauced fish with a basting dome and let it stay on the griddle for another 2 minutes if preferred.
13. Serve right away.

Made in the USA
Monee, IL
15 March 2022